# Praise for
## *Brian Moore: The Ch...*

"Sampson establishes a wholly plausible, multi-faceted sense of the writer at large. More importantly, he has fathomed his subject's life. Moore is incarnate in his novels, but with Sampson by one's elbow, reading that current of dark, swirling dreams becomes at once a questing adventure and an enlightenment."
Tom Adair, *The Irish Times*

"Denis Sampson is an exemplary literary biographer, clearly separating the life from the work, but also highlighting the ways in which they are imaginatively linked. This is a fine tribute to Moore's work."
Alannah Hopkin, *Magill Magazine*

"A uniquely interesting portrait."
David Staines, *The Ottawa Citizen*

"A superb biography . . . maintains a good balance between sympathy and distance."
Joan Givner, author of *Katherine Anne Porter: A Life* and *Mazo de la Roche: The Hidden Life*

# BRIAN MOORE

## The Chameleon Novelist

*Denis Sampson*

Doubleday Canada Limited

**Canadian Cataloguing in Publication Data**

Sampson, Denis
  Brian Moore: the chameleon novelist
ISBN 0-385-25799-6 (hardcover); ISBN 0-385-25824-0 (paperback)

1. Moore, Brian, 1921–1999. — Biography. 2. Novelists, Canadian (English) — 20th century — Biography.* I. Title.

PS8526.062Z86   1998      C813'.54      C98-931189-9
PR9199.3.M617Z86   1998

Cover photograph by Gary Campbell Photography
Cover design by Gordon Robertson
Text and insert design by Heidy Lawrance Associates
Printed and bound in the USA

Published in Canada by
Doubleday Canada Limited
105 Bond Street
Toronto, Ontario
M5B 1Y3

BVG   10   9   8   7   6   5   4   3   2   1

*For my son Bobby*

## The Novels of Brian Moore

1951    *Wreath for a Redhead*, rpt. *Sailor's Leave*

1951    *The Executioners*

1954    Bernard Mara, pseud., *French for Murder*

1955    Bernard Mara, pseud., *A Bullet for My Lady*

1955    *Judith Hearne*, rpt. *The Lonely Passion of Judith Hearne*

1956    Bernard Mara, pseud., *This Gun for Gloria*

1956    Michael Bryan, pseud., *Intent to Kill*

1957    *The Feast of Lupercal*, rpt. *A Moment of Love*

1957    Michael Bryan, pseud., *Murder in Majorca*

1960    *The Luck of Ginger Coffey*

1962    *An Answer from Limbo*

1965    *The Emperor of Ice Cream*

1968    *I Am Mary Dunne*

1970    *Fergus*

1971    *The Revolution Script*

1972    *Catholics*

1975    *The Great Victorian Collection*

1976    *The Doctor's Wife*

1979    *The Mangan Inheritance*

1981    *The Temptation of Eileen Hughes*

1983    *Cold Heaven*

1985    *Black Robe*

1987    *The Colour of Blood*

1990    *Lies of Silence*

1993    *No Other Life*

1995    *The Statement*

1997    *The Magician's Wife*

# CONTENTS

*Opening Scene*

# THE DISAPPEARANCE
# OF BRIAN MOORE

The idea of writing a critical biography of Brian Moore as a professional novelist came to me in 1993 when I read "Imagination and Experience," his short essay on why he has spent his lifetime writing novels. Two decades earlier, I had become fascinated by novels like *Judith Hearne*, *I Am Mary Dunne*, and *The Great Victorian Collection*. I read all the novels, reread many of them, and kept up as new novels appeared, usually every two or so years. I taught some of them, wrote notes on them, and became obsessed with this fictional magician — partly because I found myself mirrored in these books: Moore and I, both Irish Catholics by birth and formation, both immigrants in Montreal, and both in the grip of the mesmerising power of fiction.

"Imagination and Experience" awakened me to the possibilities of tracing the process by which Brian Moore has given his life to making these fictional worlds — a mysterious transformation he has reflected on over the length of his long career, as this essay and the interviews I began to read quickly revealed. Noticing how often he found aspects of his writing self mirrored in Joyce, Flaubert, Graham Greene, or others, and how often he spoke of techniques learned from them, I thought this biography of Moore would open the door on a celebrated novelist at work. And then I came upon a sentence he had quoted from Tolstoy, "There is no point in visiting a great writer for he is incarnate in his works," and I paused and wondered how wise it was to set off in search of Brian Moore.

I arranged to meet him in Toronto, where almost fifty years earlier, an unemployed young man with few prospects had arrived from London on the decisive step of his emigration from Belfast. A dozen years later he would win Canada's highest literary honour, the Governor General's Award, for *The Luck of Ginger Coffey*, his third novel; he would receive the prize a second time, in 1976, for *The Great Victorian Collection*. On this weekend in October 1994, the novelist had travelled from his home in California to receive tributes from a panel of British, Irish, and Canadian writers at the Harbourfront International Festival of Authors.

I sat in a crowded auditorium as the recipient of constant critical accolades and literary prizes over four decades heard his peers explain what his work meant to them. British novelist Julian Barnes called his brief talk "Elusive Author, Elusive Text" and spoke of his great pleasure in reading books that have escaped the awkward shadow of the author's own moral or ideological presence and that leave no trace of the techniques by which the fictional world is created. Echoing Graham Greene's remark that Moore "treats the novel as a tamer treats a wild beast," the British novelist praised him above all for his self-effacement as a practitioner of the craft of fiction.

Although for three decades Moore has lived a settled domestic routine by the ocean in California, he is not reclusive. An experienced newspaperman with a highly developed sense of the power of the mass media, he has made himself available to journalists and academics, but he has always guarded against the temptation to become a media "personality." In four decades of interviews, however, he has provided an eloquent commentary on the composition of different novels, a kind of autobiography of the novelist at work. What Barnes calls his "elusive" quality refers to that aspect of his talent that has allowed him to become an extraordinary creator of a multiplicity of other selves — of women and priests especially — and to reinvent himself over and over again as a novelist.

Since the early fifties, Brian Moore's gift as a storyteller has allowed him to be always and never himself. Constantly surprising in what he attempts to do, he is capable of keeping his reader engaged in many different fictional worlds. From the moving portrait of Judith Hearne's loneliness to a tense para-psychological thriller like *Cold Heaven*; from novels of repression and violence in Belfast to the marital dramas set in affluent New York, *An Answer from Limbo* and *I Am Mary Dunne*; from the fantasy mode of *Fergus* to historical settings in New France in *Black Robe*, or postwar France in *The Statement*; from realism to allegory to fable, Moore works out of his own core obsessions and yet is always seeing them and dramatizing them anew. His twenty novels are the performances of a restless author determined never to repeat himself.

Later in the weekend, as we sat looking across Lake Ontario, I tried to do what many others have tried since *Judith Hearne*, his first novel, was published in London in 1955. I attempted to uncover some small secret of his talent, that unique marriage of technique and temperament that has renewed his inspiration for four decades.

Our conversation began with Brian Moore describing the "perfect opening scene" of a novel: "The reader instantly forgets the author and is plunged into a scene as in the theatre. On a proscenium arch stage, we watch the characters moving as in real life; we don't think of the playwright; we enter their lives." The creator of these lives is invisible. I remembered the epigraph Moore had chosen from Argentinian writer Jorge Luis Borges for his then most recent novel, *No Other Life*: "God moves the player, he, in turn, the piece. But what god beyond God begins the round of dust and time and dream and agonies?" Are Moore's novels designed to be mirrors of a world from which God has disappeared?

I did not pose this question to Moore, for in spite of the fact that his conversation and his novels are full of echoes of other writers, Moore has always presented himself as a craftsman with little interest in literary history or theory. And then I remembered something he had recalled from the twenties:

> Once upon a time, before Disney cartoons ruled the morning television hours, children like myself used to visit public parks, sit on wooden seats, and stare at a small open-air theatre, where, on a tiny proscenium stage, Mr. Punch popped up regularly, club in hand, to hammer his wife Judy into insensibility. At the age of five, I became aware that those mysterious puppets were, in effect, gloves fitted over the hands of an unseen human being hidden behind that wooden stage. And from that moment on, my childish delight in the antics of Mr. Punch evaporated and was replaced by an overwhelming and unrequited curiosity as to the identity of that unknown creator.

Puppetmaster and God, director and actor, craftsman and artist: that "childish delight" in the theatrical performance, in the enchantment of storytelling, is rooted in the childhood years. Rooted there also is that endless fascination with "the identity of the unknown creator," for whatever metaphor we use to describe the creative personality in performance, it is evident that Moore's invisibility is both a point of honour as a novelist and a way of gaining distance for the surrender of his life to his characters. That surrender is both exciting and inspiring, for the ways in which Moore becomes "incarnate" in his characters and in his fictional world is a secret both to his readers and to himself. And that is the way he wishes it to be.

My reason for wanting to draw aside the puppetmaster's screen, to attend rehearsals as well as a polished performance, to indulge my own curiosity about "the identity of the unknown creator" arose indirectly after I had turned off my recorder. As we walked across the lakeside park in the unseasonably warm sunshine, the novelist remarked: "I'm always surprised when someone comes up to me at a book-signing and says, 'Mr. Moore, I've read all your books.' Each one is so different in my mind that I can't imagine someone being interested in all the different kinds of books I've written."

"Yes," I offered, "but you are preoccupied with the technical challenge which each book offers you, and so for you it is entirely new. Yet your readers are unaware of that; for them, it's your unmistakeable personality that they want to encounter again and again in each new book."

That is what this portrait of the novelist at work tries to capture: the life of an artist who, many years before, had characterized his alter ego, the novelist Brendan Tierney of *An Answer from Limbo*, as a man "beyond all self-recognition." It is a measure of art and of technical skill for Moore that he should disappear from his fictional creation in the opening scene of a novel; the expertise and grace of that performance and its constancy in such a great variety of novels are what compel me to search for the chameleon novelist.

*Part One*

# THE GRAMMARS
# OF EMOTION

# 1

# THE VICTORIAN
# INHERITANCE

Brian Moore was born in Belfast on 25 August 1921 in the house of his parents, Doctor James Bernard Moore and Eileen McFadden. It was a tall, red-brick Victorian house, built for the professional class of solicitors and doctors, close to the centre of the city. Long before he married at the age of forty-nine in 1917, Dr. Moore had already had an illustrious medical career, its foundations set in the Victorian age. Eileen McFadden had been his operating theatre nurse at the Mater Infirmorum Hospital and was more than twenty years younger than her husband. Within a few years of the marriage, she had already given birth to two girls and a boy and had suffered two miscarriages. At age thirty, she gave birth to Brian, the boy who would become her favourite child, and went on to have five more children, four girls and another boy.

Brian came to be known in the family as "Bomb" because of the circumstances of his birth. "English soldiers, brought over to keep Protestant Irish workingmen from Catholic Irish workingmen's throats, fired a sudden volley of rifle shot down Clifton Street. My mother, abed, thought a bomb had dropped. She dropped me." These domestic and political intersections that characterize the moment of Moore's birth mark his imaginative world also, recurring in realistic and allegorical patterns throughout his lifetime, but if the nickname is blunt and playful, a grim historical destiny is concealed in his official names. The novelist has commented on the ambiguous sectarian code, *Moore* being by tradition a Protestant name and *Brian* a sign of Catholic ancestry — especially when it is pronounced in the Gaelic style, Bree-an, as it was by his family. In adulthood, neither Catholic nor Protestant, Nationalist nor Unionist, Gaelic nor anglophile, the novelist seems, nevertheless, to have absorbed the ambivalent identity and the fearful anticipation of dissolution imprinted in his own names.

He was born some weeks after "The Treaty" was signed in London dividing Ireland into separate political jurisdictions: the Free State to the south, and Northern Ireland, which remained part of the United Kingdom.

Belfast, with its population of under half a million people, was a divided city with a history of racial and sectarian conflict. Moore was born into a state of conquest and colonial settlement in which racial origin and religion had been matters of life and death for centuries; the faiths of the fathers were at once absolutely true and, at every turn, under siege.

The faiths of his own family he has described as "moderate in politics" (nationalist) and "extreme in religion" (Catholic), yet such qualifications seem to count for little in the more polarized political circumstances in Ireland and Europe in the twenties and thirties. While nationalist, imperialist, and totalitarian politics, in extreme and violent forms, alienated the novelist as a young man, the significant paradigm that he absorbed was the security of such absolute conviction in counterpoint with the residual anxieties of lost belief. The situation of siege he was born into in that Catholic family in Belfast prepared his sensibility for absorbing the lessons of history he would learn first-hand in the war zones of Africa and Europe, in Poland as the Iron Curtain fell between East and West, and as an immigrant in North America.

Shifting boundaries and eroding identities determined by political and religious history are a backdrop to many novels of Brian Moore, from the early Belfast novels to *Catholics*, to the political fables of the eighties and nineties such as *The Colour of Blood* and *No Other Life*. But more central are the psychological pressures endured by his characters owing to the erosions of belief and certainty in more intimate and personal circumstances. Marital discord or the loss of religious faith are often filters for the bewildering cultural changes of this century. Moore's experience of exile in North America, of the upheavals within the Catholic Church, of being a literary artist in a time characterized by audio-visual media and commercial imperatives all focus and colour his sense of individual isolation and the burden of personal conscience.

Belfast struck the young Moore, who already aspired to be an artist at the age of twenty, as a claustrophobic provincial backwater, trapped in "the nightmare of history" and hence to be left behind as early as possible. In the fifty years of his writing career, his imagination has returned obsessively to probe the nature of commitment — of faith, love, trust, and identity, and their uprooting. He has often quoted the words of the French writer François Mauriac, "For the novelist, the door closes at twenty," and his imaginative return behind that door undoubtedly fuels his dramatic fictions of the darker fears and aggressions of twentieth-century life, be they set in Ireland, Canada, California, France, London, Poland, Haiti, or even in zones beyond the present or the natural.

The house of the O'Neills, which Judith Hearne visits on Sunday afternoons, as well as the home of Gavin Burke in *The Emperor of Ice Cream* are versions of Brian Moore's own childhood home on Clifton Street, just off Carlisle Circus, a little to the north of Royal Avenue, the main shopping street of central Belfast. It was a four-storey, semi-detached house on the street side, in which his father had his surgery on the ground floor, while the children had their domain on the top floor. "Our life was very strictly subdivided in that house: the upstairs belonged to the children, and we were brought downstairs only at teatime and when people came in to visit." This decidedly middle-class Catholic home provided a secure view of the Central Orange Hall of Belfast, crowned with a statue of King Billy on his white charger, across the street.

"Once it was one of six houses in a row," Moore recalled after a visit there in the early seventies,

Victorian town houses, occupied by doctors, dentists and a private nursing home. Now only my house and its adjacent twin remain standing on that block — the front door and windows are bricked up to prevent snipers using it as a shooting box, its rooms empty and evil-smelling, its roof askew, its brass and mahogany fittings long pilfered and gone. All around the house is rubble and the rest of the street is fenced off by corrugated iron hoardings on which the Provisional IRA have scrawled their sad defiant lies. Provo Country — British OUT. And as I stood there on a rainy afternoon seeing my home in its new isolation, it seemed to me that this house was a monument to a time, and a life, which is gone forever.

This shell of his first home was eventually demolished in the mid-nineties.

Just a few hundred yards up Crumlin Road is the Mater Hospital, where Dr. Moore worked for fifty years, and on the Antrim Road, another spoke from the Circus, again a few hundred yards away, is St. Malachy's Diocesan College, the secondary school of both father and son. These institutions were the foundations of Dr. Moore's world, and it did not seem to matter towards the end of Victoria's reign, when he settled on Clifton Street with his widowed mother, that the Central Orange Hall was directly opposite, and that there were many other Protestant institutions and churches in this neighbourhood. It may be that only an outsider to the Catholic community in Belfast would choose to live in such a spot — and James Moore was an outsider — but his scholastic and professional status connected him securely to a Catholic establishment that, during the novelist's childhood, continued, in spite of the political partition of the island, to consolidate its power through, for instance, large-scale expansion of the Mater Hospital.

In this house and community, Dr. James Moore — known, oddly, as Brian — established himself before the turn of the century. Over the decades, as he devoted himself to his practice at home and in the hospital, he created a secure and comfortable haven upstairs, first for his mother and two sisters and then, after his fiftieth year, for his wife and the nine children born to them. "Anyone who had that kind of background," the novelist has said, referring to his middle-class home, "can only say they had a happy childhood." Presiding over this order and security were two "very straight . . . admirable" parents, whose moral authority was uncomplicated and whose characters were honest and loving. While the novelist became an exile and adopted an oblique stance towards his many places of residence, his bonds to his siblings remained. Although he would renew his adult relationships with some more intimately than with others, this large family provided him with a lasting sense of connection to what he called, after James Joyce, "the commonplace."

The novelist has said that his home was a house of women, and the truth of that remark goes beyond the number of his sisters. The first two sisters, Eibhlis and Gráinne, had been followed by Séamus and Brian, who shared a bedroom all through their childhood and adolescence. Two other sisters, Marie-Therese and Una, followed, and then came Seán, five years younger than Brian. Seán would eventually follow Brian to Montreal in the early fifties, live with him for a time, and make his permanent home in Canada. Two other girls were born after Seán: Mairéad and Eilís. Brian was especially attached to Eilís, who became a nun in a convent in England.

In addition to those six sisters, there was the children's nurse. "I was brought up by a nurse called Nellie Ritchie. Nellie was with us until I was eight or nine, when she went off and got married. I don't really remember her face or anything about her, but I do remember that I was very much my nurse's creature. There was a joke told in the family that if I was sitting in Nellie's room waiting to go out, and my mother came in and said, 'Come along, Brian, we're going now,' I would say, 'No, I can't go yet, Nellie isn't here and Nellie won't let me go.'" And there were also two or three maids, "girls hired by my mother up from the country, and we used to lose them regularly: they would get pregnant by soldiers from the barracks and disappear." The barracks behind the house accommodated Irish soldiers, for "those were the days when people took the king's shilling and went to India, and the Irish were the backbone of the British army in India." Housemaids and young soldiers lived in a different world from that of the Moores, yet young Brian did take note, as he did of other marks of class, gender, and generational difference.

More memorable than Nellie or the nameless maids are two paternal aunts, Maggie and May, known to the children as Maximus and Minimus. After being educated at a French convent in Normandy with her sisters Taddie and May, Maximus — Maggie — had become a governess with aristocratic families in France. She had travelled to distant places around the world with some of these families, and had then retired to live with her mother and unmarried brother James. She was of the opinion that Irish children were much less well behaved than her French charges. Minimus — May — was a less authoritarian presence. She had married in Glasgow, but soon after the ceremony, her husband had suffered a severe mental breakdown and was confined to a hospital for the rest of his life. Brian Moore has included a portrait of this aunt in *Fergus* in the character of Aunt Mary, one of the ghosts who visits Fergus Fadden in his Californian home.

The aunts, the maids, his mother, and his six sisters made the reaches of the house above his father's surgery a female world, and by that the novelist means that it was a place in which animated conversation was endlessly revealing of personal truths. The conversation of women has always interested the novelist more than that of men: "In a curious way they are more honest when they talk to you." In contrast, his father's world was primarily a public and professional one, and even though James Moore is remembered by the novelist as a gentle and tolerant man, he was more like a distant and grandfatherly presence.

It has been said that imaginative children of small communities with a strong oral tradition "have the power of incorporating into their own lives a significant span of time before their individual births," and this is true not only of cultural attitudes but of the emotional history of parents and family members. Brian Moore was born into a large family, and the eloquence and wit of both of his parents being frequently noted, it is easy to see that the ancestral culture of his city and country were available to him in vivid forms in his own home. But if the future novelist absorbed a sympathy for the beliefs of his community and then lost that sympathy in adolescence, it was partly because he grew up in the enigmatic presence of a father whose formative decades had been lived before the turn of the century. James Bernard Moore was the past incarnate. In the seventies, when the novelist's interests became more historical in orientation, the titles of two novels, *The Great Victorian Collection* and *The Mangan Inheritance*, suggest how deeply Moore absorbed in childhood the Victorian world of his father and how that inheritance overshadowed his imagination.

The novelist's father was born in 1867 in the town of Ballymena, County Antrim, about twenty miles north of Belfast, in a part of Ireland with strong Scottish and Presbyterian traditions. On his father's maternal side were "the O'Rawes, an old Catholic family who fought in the 1798 Rising and lost their lands because they would not change their religion," and so it is somewhat unusual that his paternal grandfather, a solicitor in the town, came from a Presbyterian background. The novelist has expressed his surprise a number of times at the fact that his grandfather converted to Catholicism. Such a conversion in mid-nineteenth-century Ireland, at a time of intensifying sectarianism in Ulster, would have carried complex political as well as personal meanings, and although the reason for the conversion is not known, it is evident that his son, the novelist's father, absorbed the single-minded commitment of a convert and a fierce determination to succeed in the place of a father who, Moore suggests, James thought of as a failure.

This paternal grandfather died in 1879 when James Moore was only twelve, but the figure of that grandfather, associated so dramatically with ambiguous faith and early death, lived on as an ambivalent presence in the red-brick Victorian house off Carlisle Circus. The Moore children believed that he was a stern and bad-tempered man, and that his early death was due to over-indulgence in alcohol. It may be that James Moore's kindly disposition was in reaction to his father's patriarchal image; the novelist and his brother Seán have expressed admiration for their father's scholastic abilities but have mixed feelings about the effects of his gentleness. The issue of alcohol may be equally significant, for Dr. Moore's brother John, known to the children as Uncle Johnny, was characterized to them as a "wastrel," and a "bookies' tout" — the contrast of the two brothers evidently designed as a moral lesson.

Moral fibre, scholastic and professional accomplishment, and loyalty to one's sect were paramount; the dapper Uncle Johnny, pleasure-seeker and risk-taker, was displaced in the children's world by the figure of their aunt's husband, Eoin MacNeill, who was known to them as Uncle John. That contrast is vitally important in Moore's formation, for the figure of a "black sheep" uncle remained as a type in many of Moore's fictions, and in his unsettled youth he appears to have believed that he had inherited this destiny. In an odd way, that outsider grandfather, whatever the actual truth of his accomplishments or weaknesses, appears to have haunted the house fifty years after his death as the ghost of middle-class failure, a central image of the novelist's sense of himself and of his uncertain destiny as an irresponsible inventor of fantasies.

James Moore left Ballymena to become a boarder at St. Malachy's College in Belfast in 1879, and not only did he have a brilliant scholastic career at that school, but he maintained a close association with it all his life. It was the region's premier Catholic secondary school, a flagship of the emerging Catholic middle class, and James Moore was a star pupil. He became a leading figure for fifty years in that establishment, which was always conscious of its subservient place within the larger Protestant hierarchy of Belfast, although, to counteract this, it was proud of its links with the wider Catholic community throughout Ireland. Academic accomplishment was, then, a matter of personal and community pride, and James Moore was a dedicated proponent of this view all his life.

He was a scholarship boy, although the novelist describes him as a brilliant "exam-passer" rather than as an original mind. He had a talent for writing and won a gold medal for an English essay, placing first in all Ireland at his graduating examination in 1884. Moore thinks of his father's old-fashioned "flowery style" as a sign of his limitation as a writer, yet he recognizes the vital importance to his own formation of his father's lifelong love of reading and writing. It also seems that the father's professional success depended to a considerable extent on his oratorical skills, and his wit and eloquence were undoubtedly part of his son's inheritance.

At university, James Moore did not follow a course of study in Arts. Instead, he travelled south to Queen's College in Cork, where he studied medicine and, as his obituary notice in the *Irish News* said, "gained numerous scholastic distinctions before winning his degree in 1890 with honours." After some further study at the Royal Infirmary, Glasgow, he established a surgical practice in Belfast, which lasted until his death, fifty years later. James Moore embarked on a medical career with what appears to have been unstinting energy and commitment. His rewards came in the form of public promotions and honours and, equally, it seems clear, in the high regard in which he was held by his patients and colleagues. Just as he attached himself for life to St. Malachy's College, he also became a pillar of another Catholic institution, the Mater Hospital. After some years as an assistant surgeon, he was appointed to the senior surgical staff in 1900, and he studied for a fellowship at the Royal College of Surgeons of Ireland. He moved upwards through the ranks at the hospital, ending as honorary secretary of the Board of Management and chairman of the Staff Association.

A noteworthy aspect of James Moore's career is his role in the sensitive sectarian and political contexts of medical practice in Belfast. Hospitals and medical training were organized denominationally, and Catholics were forbidden from receiving medical training at Queen's University, Belfast. That is why James Moore studied in Cork, but when an arrangement was finally negotiated for the affiliation of the Mater Hospital as a teaching centre to Queen's, he became a Clinical Lecturer and Examiner at the University. He remained in those positions, became an Examiner to the Royal College of Surgeons in Dublin later, and was nominated a member of the Senate of Queen's University in 1927, the first Catholic to occupy such a position. James Moore's ability to move beyond the confines of dogmatic Catholic and nationalist thinking can be seen also in his wartime experiences. During the First World War, he was a surgical specialist to Victoria Barracks and during the Second World War, he was a member of the Northern Ireland Medical War Committee, as well as other intrainstitutional committees.

Dr. Moore was an outsider in Belfast, and he married an outsider, a farmer's daughter from the Gweedore area of County Donegal. A generation younger than her husband, Eileen McFadden was one of a family of nineteen children born in impoverished circumstances. Many of the children were "farmed-out" to relatives who could care for them, and Eileen grew up away from her family, in the care of an uncle who was a priest. In effect, then, the novelist's mother had a priest as her father, a curious circumstance given a strange permanence in a studio photograph of her adoptive "family." The isolated and economically undeveloped area at the northwestern extremity of Ireland remained Irish-speaking into the twentieth century, and the novelist has said that his mother grew up speaking her ancestral language. Other family members doubt this, but the truth may be that her parents and the siblings who remained at home in Gweedore spoke Irish, while her adoptive family spoke English, and English became her language through education and her movement to Belfast to study nursing. At any rate, the novelist thinks of her as "a real countrywoman," and that statement has far-reaching linguistic, cultural, and mythological associations in the formation of Moore's imagination.

Eileen McFadden contrasted sharply with her husband's distinctively urban identity and cultural context, although it is likely that their novelist son exaggerated and dramatized their differences. "I have these two Irish strains in me: my mother was the most Irish of Irish people, and my father was from some sort of Ulster Protestant background." In Moore's experience of family life, and, later, of school, the Catholic and nationalist strain was pervasive, but his sense of his mother as "the most Irish of Irish people" has less to do with sect than with her origins in the country, and, especially, with the West of Ireland. Images of poverty and uninhibited traditional styles of expression are associated with his mother's background: "she had a sense of humour, and she had a wicked tongue, like a lot of country people." Moore has also associated an unrepressed sexual ease with this country background, presumably from his observation of the maids and the young soldiers. If his father was formal, reserved, and controlled, his mother was direct, spontaneous, and did not hesitate to express her opinions.

Eileen McFadden was associated with the native culture of Ireland, rural and Gaelic-speaking, that survived in pockets in the west, although it had been severely eroded in other parts of the country since the beginning of the nineteenth century. Her roots lie in that increasingly mythologized West of Ireland celebrated by Irish writers and intellectuals around the turn of the century as a place in which the spirituality of the pre-Christian Celts still informed the peasant way of life. Nationalist movements for "the de-anglicization of Ireland," European scholars of the Irish language, folklorists, and "last Romantics" such as Yeats all looked to the west as a haven from the materialism and corruption of modern urban life. While his mother's impoverished rural background did not lend itself easily to romanticization, nevertheless it is evident that the novelist associated her background with the cultural and political nationalism that had burgeoned at the end of the nineteenth century.

This mythology of the authentic Ireland of the west was a significant part of the formation of James Moore through his association with Eoin MacNeill, his closest friend at St. Malachy's. Their friendship became even closer in 1898, when MacNeill married Agnes Moore, the novelist's Aunt Taddie. MacNeill had studied Law in Dublin and had settled there, but in the early 1890s, he had become prominent as a founder of the Gaelic League. He was one of those who consciously set about recovering the lost cultural identity, and he went on an annual visit to the Aran Islands from 1891 to 1908 to learn the Irish language. He gradually emerged as an academic historian of that older culture and became politically involved with those nationalists who wanted to organize a revolution and remove Ireland from British jurisdiction. By 1913, he had become the leader of the Irish Volunteers, but in countermanding the order for the Volunteers to join the Easter Rising in 1916, he came to be contrasted with the heroic martyrs of the Rising: Patrick Pearse, Thomas MacDonogh, James Connolly, and the other signatories of the 1916 Proclamation of the Irish Republic. This moderate nationalist with a deep love of Gaelic culture was a central figure in the life of James Moore, and at a later stage of his life, when he became "Uncle John" to the Moore children, he would leave a lasting impression on the novelist also.

It is not inappropriate to situate the match made between the aging doctor and the young nurse in this personal and cultural context, for long after the deaths of his parents, the novelist would explore his own subliminal associations of landscape and culture with the figures of his parents.

In middle age, Moore discovered the Atlantic coastline of Connemara, Cork, and Kerry, and he has associated it with his childhood memories.

> If I left Ireland because I feared it would not change, now I am drawn to return because it has not changed. I come back every year. Not to the North and its hatreds, but here, to the West of Ireland. Towns like Clifden, which still look much the way they did in the days of my childhood. . . . The faces, the people, the faith: perhaps it hasn't really changed since my father's day. . . . Perhaps it is some link with my father, a feeling of stepping back into the past, that brings me here year after year. . . . There is something about this place, some sense of the past thrusting itself forward, something eerie — ghostly — something almost metaphysical, which can change our normal way of seeing things. . . . The West is a place where I feel, suddenly that anything might happen, perhaps even a miracle.

The novelist speaks here in one breath of the West of Ireland, his father, the past, and a premonition of a metaphysical revelation, all elements of the imaginative worlds of *Catholics* and *The Mangan Inheritance* which, Moore has said, were inspired by such feelings. But if his father represents the unchanging past, his mother is also connected to the ocean coastline and to the miraculous, as becomes evident in the Californian novels. From *Fergus* to *The Great Victorian Collection* to *Cold Heaven*, notions of the miraculous are associated with Carmel-by-the-Sea and the Pacific coast on which his own home in Malibu is situated. These rugged landscapes and otherworldliness may be associated with his mother's first home in Donegal, and this in turn will be identified with the miraculous aspect of his own artistic talent.

In 1980, speaking of this phase of his career — what might be thought of as a Yeatsian or "Celtic Twilight" phase — he associated his spiritual and ghostly preoccupations with this landscape of his mother: "It is, perhaps, this feeling of being outside normal life which has, in recent years, turned my novels away from the truths of real life to another life. That life seems often to be present here, amid these still, lakelike sea bays, these bogs with turf piled up like funerary monuments to some lost tribe."

Apart from this tension between the "real" life of the present and landscapes associated with the beliefs of his dead parents, which the literary artist has felt and recreated, Moore's childhood in the house in Belfast absorbed other kinds of tensions from the contrasting backgrounds of his father and mother. Eileen McFadden was considered by many to be her husband's social inferior, and it is evident from references in interviews and novels that Moore's imagination has played with the significance of that perception. It seems that Dr. Moore's first family cast a strong shadow over his new domestic arrangements. It may be that Moore felt — even before he knew the facts — an identification with his mother as one who, in spite of public appearances as the doctor's wife, had experienced a sense of being judged second best. Such notions appear in his first novel in the thoughts of the protagonist, Judith Hearne, and at some level, the much later novel *The Doctor's Wife* probes a deep-seated dissatisfaction with marriage. At any rate, he has said that he always felt much closer to his mother than to his father, and differences of age and class have heightened that sense of essential difference.

Eileen McFadden was a traditional wife and mother throughout the novelist's childhood. Her competence as a manager of a large household and her role as the disciplinarian set her apart, in her children's perception, from the more gentle and grandfatherly character of the father. In public, and in educational matters, the father was the dominant figure, however, and this image of a subservient middle-class housewife is the figure who appears as Moira O'Neill in *Judith Hearne*, as Mrs. Burke in *The Emperor of Ice Cream*, and as Mrs. Fadden in *Fergus* — all portraits of the mother as echo of the father's opinions and protector of his peace of mind in the home. While Eileen McFadden may have had some doubts about her role as the doctor's wife, and was held to be his social inferior, she was in her own way a person who transmitted to the novelist a sense of independence and confidence.

His mother may, even more than his father, represent an image of genuineness central to Moore's personal mythology. While the father instilled in him a love of reading and writing, and a professional discipline and commitment to technical mastery, it may have been his mother who gave him a more rooted sense of artistic perception and integrity. "My mother seemed to be more in sync with me," Moore has said. "I was very fond of my mother. I think the fact that I had six sisters and that I was one of my mother's favourite sons, if not her favourite son, had an effect on me." The characterization of women is a skill of the novelist that has been much praised, and he comments, "perhaps there's something feminine in my character in that I find women more interesting than men." Women and old people, he says, interest him because "the fact of the history of a life stuns me and makes me want to find out its secret."

In the case of *An Answer from Limbo*, Moore says, "One of the things I tried to show is that it is much easier to live, as the mother does, with a fixed set of beliefs, even if they are the wrong ones, than to make up the rules as one goes along. Unfortunately, it is more difficult to live without a faith than with one." Yet while Mrs. Tierney has an unquestioned faith, in contrast to the characters about her who are desperately searching for new "rules" for living, the identification of Moore with most of his women characters is grounded on feelings of defeat and failure and on the more authentic self that can be felt in such states. From Judith Hearne to Mary Dunne to Sheila Redden and Maria Davenport, this portrait gallery of women created over a thirty-year period is unified by disorientation and loss rather than by "a fixed set of beliefs."

Yet perhaps more important for the novelist is not the matter of faith itself but the ability to enter into such characters, and Moore has connected this ability to the experience of growing up in "a house of women":

> Women live in a personal world, a very, very personal world. Men, I find, are always, as they say in America, "rolling their credits" at each other. They come on telling you what they've done, and who they are, and all the rest of it. Quite often, women don't do that, because life hasn't worked out that way for some of them. But when a woman tells me a story about something that happens to her, [I] often get a sudden flash of frankness which is really novelistic. It is as if a woman knows when she tells a story that it must be personal, that it must be interesting.

In this late observation, the novelist allows us to glimpse the connections between the contrasting images of his mother and father and his own talent for probing the crises of faith of his characters, especially of women and priests, both of whom are, in his conception of them, living a life that is focused on more intimately personal matters than the power and social success men associate with identity.

Brian Moore began his writing career by attempting to capture the city of his birth, concerning which he had, from adolescence on, deep feelings of "anger and bitterness which made me want to write it out of my system and look for a new world in which I and my characters could live." *Judith Hearne* and *The Feast of Lupercal* are high points of his achievement in novel-writing, and they do appear to shed the "sickness" of Belfast, yet after he had made the transition to a new world — in his life and in his fiction — his childhood came back to haunt his imagination, and, in particular, the imprints left by James Moore and Eileen McFadden:

> Parents form the grammar of our emotions. They have an influence on us which in my case was much stronger than anything I could have guessed. Writers feed on their families and . . . unlike normal healthy children who forget about their fathers and mothers when they reach the age of thirty . . . the writer has to go back. He's really reexamining his past and in the course of reexamining his past he's reexamining his parents all the time, so that they become a source of endless fascination to him. But they're no longer his parents, they're characters in this particular novel he's writing in his mind.

# 2

# VOCATIONS
# AND ROLES

The lasting impressions of Moore's crowded home that were absorbed below the range of conscious recall seem not to have aroused his deliberate interest. He did not read Proust until he settled in California in his mid-forties, and even a decade earlier, when he had close friends who were practising psychoanalysts, he devoted little time to the resonances of involuntary memory. Yet he did quote Baudelaire's comment that "Genius is the power to recover childhood," and glossed it: "I think he meant that, as children, we see the world around us with the clarity of ignorance. Everything is strange and new to us. As children, we see without judging, without knowledge, without preconception, that trinity of faults which so often clouds our adult vision." In spite of this apparent desire to write without the prejudices of "adult vision," he has said that he cannot remember his early childhood: "I'm sorry that I can't, but I've very blurred memories — just bits and pieces of scenes." His regret seems superficial, for in his large population of fictional characters, the marginal place of children is remarkable, and he has rarely recreated scenes of his own childhood. What he does remember, especially about adolescence, offers some clues to this partial amnesia, to his considerable difficulties in writing self-portraits in the 1950s, and to his often-stated desire to disappear into his fictional characters.

One of these recollections is a set piece in "Bloody Ulster," an essay on the revived "Troubles" written in 1970:

REMEMBER 1690. It is the one date in history I will not forget. When I looked out my bedroom window on the top floor of our house, across the street I could see, graven into a stone plinth on top of a building, the figures 1690. On the plinth, a cavalier stood in stirrups, brandishing his sword over his head as he stared in stone-eyed triumph at the chimneys of the York Street Flax Spinning Mills. He was William III of the Dutch House of Orange, atop the Kremlin of the Orange Order, the Central

Orange Hall, world headquarters of the Orangemen's movement. . . . REMEMBER 1690? Yes, I do.

The Glorious Twelfth. It came during school holidays, but we weren't allowed out. Unlike other Catholic children, we didn't mind being kept in on that day. For we had the rare distinction of being the only Papishes in the world with a grandstand viewing position, right across from the balcony where Sir Joseph Davidson, grand panjandrum of the Orange Order, watched the men set out on their march to Finaghy Field. A thrilling day for me, and I mean it, for what better excitement for a schoolboy than to have all those wild men, thousands strong, parading under your window and to know that you and yours were the very enemy they seek to destroy?

The child looked down on the pageantry of terror, excited in secret by this threat to his identity, and such fears and the ambiguous dangers implicit in such covert observation undoubtedly entered his psyche. That apocalyptic public world was an inescapable context of his childhood and youth; after the killing of about three hundred people in pogroms and assassinations in 1921–22, Belfast remained under curfew until Christmas 1924, and sporadic rioting continued until the next major outbreak of sectarian killings in 1935. Yet if tribal politics, sectarian prejudice, and incipient violence were the overall background of Moore's childhood in Belfast, he tends to concentrate his attention on Catholic, nationalist Belfast, and on the ways in which home and school imprinted its ethos on his character, so that, in adolescence, he came to consciously reject it.

My father, in an infrequent traverse through the kitchen, stops and asks the maid: "Where did we get this?" There is a loaf of wrapped bread on the kitchen table. Ormeau Bakery is printed on the wrapping paper. My father is puzzled. My mother is summoned. "Hughes and Kennedy are the Catholic bakers," my father says, holding up the offending loaf. "But Ormeau is cheaper, and they say their bread is very good," my mother tells him. "Hughes's bread is very good," my father says. "I don't care if it's a few pennies more. We shouldn't buy from Ormeau. They're Protestant bakers."

That his educated and successful father should have such vigilant sectarian antennae is an emblem of what lay below the most tolerant surfaces. Moore may have remained unaware until his late adolescence of the depression that gripped the city, where, in the 1920s and 1930s, unemployment was 20 per cent, on average. Brian Moore would become a radical socialist then, but the bloody manifestations of sectarian strife do not appear to have unduly over-shadowed the security of his middle-class home during the childhood years. If the comic vignette of his mother's delivery of her fourth child distances the author from the Protestant and Catholic workingmen on the street, his house and family seem to have preserved an unchallenged sense of order and pur-pose and a secure vantage point on the troubling world outside.

In the early years, the routines of home, church, and school fell into an unremarkable pattern presided over by his mother, remembered as a strict disciplinarian, aided by Maximus at the dinner table, and more selectively by his father. There was reading and storytelling. "My father was an omnivorous reader. He was the sort of man who sent one of us to the pub-lic library twice a week with a suitcase and said, 'Bring it back full of books.' He read everything; we all read a great deal. The house was absolutely full of books — books were my television." At an early age, Brian became a storyteller, for his brother Seán remembers him entertain-ing the younger siblings with his own stories. None of the adults are remembered as inspiring storytellers, and so it may be that his early apprenticeship to the arts of performance was his enthralled attendance at puppet-shows at Alexandra Park.

In these performances he discovered the joy of being enchanted, that would lead to his later interest in the theatre. Equally important was his discovery at age five of the trick, the "unseen human being hidden behind that wooden stage." More enchanting from this point on than watching "the antics of Mr Punch" was the "overwhelming and unrequited curiosi-ty as to the identity of the unknown creator." But more enchanting still was the realization that he too could be a performer; he could be the "unknown creator" who created the effect that captivated an audience. Soon he would begin to savour that power in writing his first school essays.

The routines of Dr. Moore's medical practice were made interesting by his home visits, on which he was often accompanied in the Morris Cowley by Séamus and Brian. The novelist has recalled the fun of such outings and has shown no morbid consciousness that his father was actually minister-ing to the sick and dying. In fact, this routine of following their father con-tributed to a lasting rivalry between the brothers. While competition between brothers only a year apart in age might be predictable, it became evident at some stage that Séamus would be his father's true heir and would go on to study medicine. That rivalry between the brothers would grow bitter in adolescence, and the novelist's rebellion was partially due to his realization that, unlike Séamus, he would fail to matriculate.

The social status of the role of doctor, as well as the selfless vocation of care-giving, left lasting impressions on Brian Moore that surface in his anxiety about success and failure. His own failure to become a doctor is only a part of that larger preoccupation. While his father worked at the Mater Hospital, he also had a private surgery downstairs. In addition to the many old people in his immediate family, the proximity of human suffering and mortality, although not commented on, must have contributed to the novelist's remarkable preoccupation in his fiction with doctors and human frailty. Doctors and priests are revealed to be singularly powerless in the face of the spiritual and mental conundrums that plague his characters. And yet to be a novelist is to take on an equally impotent role, for in spite of its concern with the truth of the human condition, Brian Moore has called the novelist's task a "surrogate life."

His father was an enigmatic presence who transcended petty rivalries and whose character and authority seem to have remained unquestioned until Moore's adolescence. In a vignette of the single-minded confidence and the puzzling contradictions in the character of this scientist, Moore has recalled that in 1927 a group of pilgrims to the Catholic shrine at Lourdes was accompanied by his father. The novelist remembers that on his father's return he told the family that his belief in miracle cures had been reaffirmed. Such was the power of his belief in medicine and in his Catholic faith that he could believe in both and accommodate the idea of a miraculous cure. The novel *Cold Heaven*, in which medicine and miracle are juxtaposed in a psychological thriller about a doctor who seems to return from the dead, might be an oblique recollection of the disturbing contradictions of this Victorian man's belief. The novelist has revealed an awareness of a parallel between this belief in prayer and miracles and his own power to create fictions.

With time, and with the novelist's questioning of his own belief, such associations became more overt. It is not unusual that the most vivid memories of childhood are of the unexpected or the exceptional rather than the routine. For this reason, summer holidays and travelling away from home often leave the most lasting trace, and in Moore's case, the most indelible trace of all was left by family holidays at the seaside. Each summer his father rented a house by the beach, most often at Portstewart on the Antrim coast. Those weeks stirred such profound feelings that the novelist's later life has been marked by a search for seaside places — on the Côte d'Azur or in the West of Ireland but, most lastingly, beside the Atlantic on Long Island and in Nova Scotia, and on the Pacific coast north of Los Angeles. In his life and in his writing, the sea would come to exert a ritualistic and primal force, and he has explained that force by reference to these holidays in Portstewart.

There were also summer holidays at the farm of his mother's brother in Gweedore:

Donegal is an extremely wild and rocky-looking place in the west of Ireland. I used to go there when I was a boy, to a farm owned by a poor Irish subsistence farmer. I would move from our middle-class world to an absolutely peasant environment. They ate different food. They didn't eat meat every day like we did; they ate eggs, milk, potatoes, home-baked bread, and I loved it. I could get up early and shoot rabbits, which we then ate. They treated me like a local boy. They were quite rough with me. This used to worry my mother a bit. And the financial differences did have some effect on me. I remember wearing sandals and short pants, and the third day out I fell into the mire and lost my sandals. We couldn't find them in the morass. My aunt gave me a terrible beating, not in anger at my falling, I later realized, but because the poor woman had to go out and buy me a new pair of sandals. My mother came down later and insisted on reimbursing the aunt, who wouldn't hear of it.

Finally, the novelist has referred on many occasions to his summer holidays in Dublin with his MacNeill cousins. Contact between James Moore and his sister Taddie and brother-in-law Eoin was regular and sustained throughout their lifetimes. They used holiday times to get together, and, as early as 1898, James and Eoin had gone on a cycling holiday in Normandy. As Eoin and Taddie began to have children, the unmarried James Moore spent time in their house in Dublin, but by the time he had children of his own, the MacNeill children were old enough to be like aunts and uncles to their cousins. In spite of large age differences, however, the Moore and MacNeill cousins remained in close contact. In his twenties Brian would benefit from his cousin's marriage to the prominent Dublin academic and politician Michael Tierney, and, after he settled in Montreal, he renewed a close friendship with his cousin Máire, a prominent Irish folklorist, married to the Harvard professor and art collector John L. Sweeney.

Later still, in the 1980s, when Moore reviewed Michael Tierney's biography of Eoin MacNeill, his lasting memories of his summer visits to Dublin were movingly recalled and their significance articulated. When the young Brian Moore spent his summer holidays in Dublin, MacNeill had retired from politics and had begun his final career as a Professor of Irish History at University College, Dublin. After the Treaty of 1921 and the establishment of the Free State government, he had become a minister and took on the difficult task of sitting on the Boundary Commission, which would draw the frontier of the partitioned island. His resignation from the deadlocked commission in 1926 had been characterized by more radical Republicans as betrayal and an acceptance of *de facto* partition. It is the nuanced and paradoxical aspects of MacNeill's character and career that Moore absorbed, his personal contact with his Uncle John providing him with a deeply influential lesson in the treacherous arena of interpreting history and politics.

Apart from MacNeill's kindness to his young nephew, in retrospect the aspect of his character that impressed Moore was the absence of pretensions to heroism. He refers to MacNeill as "the most unassuming of men and the physical opposite of the trench-coated revolutionary of popular fancy." For a novelist who would learn his trade as a writer of thrillers that exploited the male heroics of popular fancy and then write of the unheroic life of the obscure and lonely spinster Judith Hearne, this distinction has significance. The scholar-revolutionary MacNeill was a "cold and realistic thinker," Moore observes, who was not intoxicated by "the vanity and folly of useless bloodshed." Moore is writing at the most theatrical phase of the bloody Troubles in Northern Ireland, in the summer of 1981, when ten IRA hunger strikers died in prison. In the earlier Troubles, his uncle had refused to join those whose revolutionary zeal embraced the war as, in MacNeill's own words, "a stage upon which they might expect to play a part in the drama of heroism."

In Moore's review, he quotes with approval Emerson's remark that there is "properly no history, only biography," a remark which neatly allows the novelist of character to distinguish his kind of particular truths from broader historical generalizations about the destiny of the nation. A moderate political outlook, in opposition to militant Republicanism, was an inheritance of the Moore family, and in novels like *Catholics*, *The Colour of Blood* and *No Other Life*, the novelist dramatizes the dilemma of the moderate in the face of dogmatic political activists.

The years of his childhood are also marked by the influence of church, family, and school in ways which enforced a secret life of guilt and deception. The major theme of Moore's adolescence is sexual precociousness and the complications that enveloped it because of the ritual of confession, which became a public affirmation and reaffirmation of his religious faith from about the age of seven.

In the traditional Irish Catholic rite of passage, children made their First Communion, preceded by their First Confession, at the age of seven, and from that age onwards they were expected — an expectation enforced as a matter of communal routine in pious families such as this one — to confess their sins and receive communion regularly, sometimes as often as every week, certainly not less frequently than every month. In this way, religious belief became a matter not simply of anonymous attendance at church on Sunday, but of an intimate recounting of one's sins to a priest, followed by the public gesture of receiving communion, something that reassured one's family and the parish clergy that one was restored to a state of grace.

I started going to Confession as a child and I now date a lot of my troubles to that. I was a child who was incapable of confessing things to a stranger in a box; particularly sexual peccadillos like masturbation. I was a very highly sexed child and, to be perfectly frank about it, when people say my work is erotic it's because sex has played a big part in my life. I thought about it a great deal when I was growing up and often read books which opened up new worlds to me because I was looking for the 'hot' bits. . . . So I had trouble with Confession and I started telling lies, and that was a mortal sin, so automatically I thought there was something wrong with me — I think it affected my schooling.

As Moore has recounted his experience — with increasing frankness as the years pass — his situation was far from innocent or simple in the way it was designed to be. The traumatic emergence of his individual selfhood is related by him not only to the conflicting matters of sex and religious faith, but through them to a crisis at home and in school, and eventually to his decision to leave Belfast. Inevitably these traumatic developmental years left their mark on his fictional world and on his commitment to his role as writer.

In the Beginning was the Word. And the Word was 'No.' All things came from that beginning. . . . Then there was God. Who is God? . . . You must learn your catechism by heart. The big words will be explained later, when you go to school. *God is everywhere and he judges our most secret thoughts and actions*, the catechism said. . . . Q: *Who made the world?* A: *God.* The world was sweetie shops, Alexandra Park, the Antrim Road, Royal Avenue, Newington School, Miss Carey's garden, and the big pond in the waterworks. All these things were part of Belfast and Belfast was in Ireland. Dublin was in Ireland too. It was a whole day in the car to go to Dublin and come back. Then there was England.

England was across the Irish Sea. And America. . . . Then there was the Next World. It was the only one that counted, Mama said. The next world was heaven and hell and purgatory.

This is the opening of a short story written in 1956. "I wrote that little story — 'A Vocation' — and it's about the only thing I can consciously remember writing about my early childhood." The brief story is a Joycean exercise in dramatizing the stream of consciousness of a twelve-year-old boy, Joe, who is on retreat at school and, overcome by the weight of his sinfulness, is persuaded that only by becoming a priest does he have any chance of getting to heaven. It is unlikely that Moore entertained at any length such thoughts of a vocation for the priesthood, yet his joining the Joycean "priesthood of art" appears to have originated in similarly intense feelings of the cosmic and absolute meaning of one's actions.

There was Sin. It was an awful thing in the sight of God. Lies were sins. Losing your temper was a sin. Calling Mary a Dirty Pig was a sin. It was a sin to tell a lie. There was a song about that. It was a sin to steal Rory O'Hare's bike. That was a sin you got beaten for. . . . There was impurity. That was the worst sin. That was what you did. Impurity. Sins like murder and idolatry were only in books. . . . It was the only sin the priests asked about in confession. How many times? You must promise me never to do that again, will you promise me that? You will put those thoughts away, my child, won't you? Yes, Father. I will not sin, I am heartily sorry, I will not do it. No. That was impurity. There was your Immortal Soul. If you committed that sin again, you endangered your Immortal Soul. That is the only thing that counts. What doth it profit a man if he gain the whole world and suffer the loss of his soul?

This is the actual world of the young Brian Moore, not simply a literary exercise in imitation of James Joyce, the master artist of Irish Catholic life a generation earlier. The places named are his world; Newington School was his school from age six to age twelve, the place he learned his catechism by heart and prepared for his First Confession. The sensitivity of the adolescent to the years of training and to the religious ethos of home and school may seem artificially heightened in the story, just as later in *Fergus*, the confession/kangaroo court to which the middle-aged novelist is subjected may seem melodramatic, yet Moore's preoccupation with the impact on the growth of the individual psyche of the ritual of confession has been a lasting one for his own sense of self and for his sense of character in fiction.

The effect on his schooling did not become evident until much later, for the first phase of his academic career is marked by the early discovery of his talent as a writer. As Moore recalls it, at the end of his first year at Newington Elementary School, "the headmaster called me in and told me I could have a week off if I would write a sample essay on a number of assigned subjects. You know, things like 'my summer holiday' and all that jazz. I would write these essays, and then another boy with better hand-writing would copy them over. The headmaster put them into a little book and showed them as composition models to each year's succeeding classes. This gave me a feeling of great power." Elsewhere, the novelist has also spoken of his earliest thoughts of becoming a writer and mentioned the age of six as the first stage.

To be a writer was, then, a desirable and satisfying role, for it seems that the talent discovered in his first years of school was formed and encouraged at home by his father through the importance given to books and reading. And it is evident that the young Moore was a boy who happily escaped into books. His reading ability was far ahead of his age, and his choice of reading material, he has said, was largely an imitation of his father's taste and interests.

Moore's talent as a writer and his general knack for learning was remarked on when he moved to St. Malachy's Diocesan College, the *alma mater* of his father and his Uncle John, at the age of twelve. Yet now, his writing won a less official and public esteem: "I discovered that most boys' greatest problem was writing their English essay over the weekend; and I could knock these essays out in half an hour. So I would write about five essays over the weekend and get paid sixpence by each of five boys. In a way I was a professional writer from the word go." The casual diction here suggests that his career as a "professional writer" was an easy source of cash and self-esteem, yet it appears that in other ways, as he grew older, the sense of himself as a failure grew: socially, he thought of himself as "a misfit" and physically unattractive to girls. "I had nightmares about that after I left school and when I grew up." His misery there was unalleviated by his literary talent, and it seems that even it was blighted by the crude male posturing of his peers and by the priests' close monitoring of his scholastic progress.

I used to say that my secondary school was a priests' factory. It was quite a hard school, it still exists. We were beaten all the time. We were caned if we failed to recite our French irregular verbs properly in the morning. You were caned for every mistake you made. So that you go through the entire day being beaten on the hands, day in, day out, everything was taught by rote. It was a totally inferior method of teaching people, and I am still very angry when I think about it. This was a Catholic school in a predominantly Protestant milieu; therefore we had to get better marks than the Protestant schools. We were then beaten and coerced into achievement, and we weren't really taught anything. I remember when I first went to France, no one could understand the French I was speaking, not one word of it. Yet I knew all my irregular verbs.

That the years in St. Malachy's were unhappy ones is evident in how frequently Moore returns to speak of the caning and the repressive Catholic atmosphere. The bullying of the other boys in this all-male, status-conscious school is recalled in the Old Boys' Dance chapter in *The Emperor of Ice Cream*, and its conditions are recreated in the setting of his second novel, *The Feast of Lupercal*.

The evidence of the story "Preliminary Pages for a Work of Revenge" and the repetition of a similar scene in *An Answer from Limbo* suggest that an experience of humiliation and shame overshadowed his saving dream of becoming a writer, although the evidence of the fiction cannot be taken as confirmation of the details. The portrait of the writer in the story begins by emphasizing that, in contrast to Moore's own case, feelings of weakness and of being a failure dogged him from childhood. The picture of the talented young boy in a middle-class household, in which formal education was the passport to security and honour, appears to have other disturbing aspects also, for in this unusual story, written in imitation of Dostoievski's *Notes from Underground*, the self-hatred of the failed writer is imagined as having its origin in the double standards of which he became an early victim.

As a child I did not believe that I was clever. I feared myself to be stupid and cowardly and believed that I would be a disappointment to all who knew me. I read a great deal and like many unsure children I had a taste for tragic endings. But in my reading I discovered that, to fall from the heights of tragedy, heroes must first scale the peaks of achievement. In books, I searched for a suitable daydream. When I was fourteen we were asked to write an essay about our ambitions in life. I wrote all night. I was, for the first time in my life, inspired. I wrote that I would become a great poet. . . . This essay I submitted to my English master who, the following day, came to my desk, took my ear between his nicotined thumb and forefinger and led me before the class to read my essay aloud.

... What a perfect victim with which to win amusement from a class of captive boys!

But he is dead now, my master. I can no longer hate him for his use of me as a hunchback for his sallies. Nor can I hate you my classmates for the larger diversion you staged after school.

You may remember how a much larger audience assembled as I was dragged to the school drinking fountain, ducked under it and held until water ran down my spine, dripped into my trousers trickled down my skinny legs to fill my socks and shoes. You may remember that, after my ducking, I was forced to read my essay once more. Your motives were just, I suppose. You wanted to knock the pretensions from under me, to teach me the lesson I have been too long in learning. But I learned nothing. Soaking wet, my clothes torn, I read my essay, but with pride now, screaming out that I would do everything I had promised in it. And all of you, watching my pale face and trembling shoulders, hearing the true fanatic in my thin defiant scream, all of you turned away, uneasy of me. Because conviction — even a wrong conviction — makes the rest of us uneasy. For the first time in my life I had won. My own unsurety died and for the remainder of my years at school I grew in the wind of your disapproval. Your doubts that day made me a victim — the victim I still remain — of my own uncertain boast.

For I did not become great. I had no vocation for greatness.

In 1959, when that story was written, Moore was already the honoured author of two novels, was completing a third, and was living on Long Island, on a Guggenheim Fellowship. And yet his sense of himself as a failure, as a failed artist, remained, and from these images of early adolescence, it seems that those feelings were deeply implanted. The bitter style of self-loathing suggests that, although the public humiliations the story narrates may not have actually happened, there is an element of truth in the profound ambivalence, amounting to feelings of shame, that envelop the role of writer from adolescence on.

In part those feelings are due to the disappointment and anxiety of his parents, a situation he would dramatize in *The Emperor of Ice Cream*. Moore would outline in an autobiographical essay in 1974:

A six-year-old boy says he will be a fireman when he grows up. His parents smile. It's a stage some children go through. At seventeen he says he wants to be a writer. He is shaving once a week. His suits are too small for him. He reads a lot and has won an essay prize in school. He says he wants to be a writer. An adolescent phase, no doubt, but still it's a hint that perhaps he's not cut out to be a doctor or an engineer. So he's allowed to study for an arts degree. There are always openings for teachers. At eighteen, he is writing poems. He says he wants to be a writer. It's now a family joke. Good evening Shakespeare, his brother says. Don't disturb the Muse, says Sister to her Boy Friend as they come into a room where letters are being written. You can't be serious, his mother says. He says he *is* serious. But you *can't* be serious, his Father says. How many people do you know who make their living writing books and articles? Not one.

But the feelings of shame and guilt associated with becoming a writer seem to include and focus more than anxiety about his future career. He continued to be a reader. "I would always read ahead of my years. I was reading Mencken when I was fourteen and didn't know what it was all about, but liked that sort of thing. Because I was good at essays I think I read non-fiction all the time, which is strange. Most of the fiction I read was the kind of thing my father liked — A. E. W. Mason and the like." Soon he would no longer be reading what his father liked, and their diverging tastes in reading would mirror their diverging views on a wide range of issues. It is also evident that the other major theme bridging child-hood and adolescence — Confession and sexual guilt — had begun to assume a troubling prominence for him, and that it may be inextricable from his feelings about becoming a writer.

The moment at which his real life became overwhelmingly one of sinful-ness and shame, while his sense of his public role as a schoolboy was one of deception, varies in different retellings of this critical development. Yet the outline of the heightened emergence of conflicted self-consciousness remains the same. The young Brian felt perverted and hypocritical, and in Moore's judgement of the results, he underwent a crisis of self-confidence that led directly to his failure to matriculate, barring him from attending university. At the same time, he also began to feel more comfortable with his secret life through his discovery that literature offered in some sense the sexual identity his home and school and community denied him. A painful irony of his dif-ficulty in these years may be felt in his recollection of his father speaking to his mother, "You must trust the children, never tell them they have lied."

The claustrophobic secrecy, the exaggerated importance attached to minor transgressions of public codes of behaviour, the feelings of shame and failure that arise from the enforced practice of deception were ele-ments of Moore's own experience before he found the means to distance himself from them or the literary means to dramatize them. The deception and the fear of discovery that are integral elements of the drama in those novels might be seen also as elements of all of Moore's later novels — not simply the secret life and the fear of its unveiling, as in Judith Hearne's tippling, but his reliance on suspense and tight plotting, on a moment of crisis, and on variations of the thriller formula.

Yet if Moore's sense of his own adolescence was of a secret life concealed from his family — and his alienation from the world of St. Malachy's and Catholic Belfast was increasingly radical — his family still provided a secure vantage point on the world outside. When a teacher in Moore's history class at St. Malachy's slighted Eoin MacNeill for his less than exemplary role in the Republican drive to end partition, the novelist reports that his "father went to the school and demanded an apology. He got it." This episode is an indication of how intensely the interpretation of Irish nationalist history was argued in Belfast in the decades after the Treaty. The novelist remembers that his nationalist father placed loyalty to his friend and the nuances of the historical record before the "popular fancy" which had come to dominate the history class. Whether it was due to his father's action or to MacNeill's own behaviour, Moore writes that his Uncle John "in some ineluctable way, communicated an impression of complete integrity and truthfulness."

The image of the man of conscience, the gentle scholar with moderate political convictions, at odds with the more abrasive Republican views that dominated through bloodshed and hunger strikes, complemented the image of professional and social success of Moore's father, and both of these figures seem to have enhanced also the lasting impression of his mother's character rooted in her West of Ireland landscape. The fact that these qualities were his family's legacy and that they are "out of date" today, in the world in which Moore has moved in North America and, more generally, in the western world, is a matter of both wonder and despair to him. "While I disliked Catholicism," he has written, "and disliked my parents' religiosity, I think they were both very honest people, and were people who, if they hadn't had their faith, would have been more dishonest and less admirable." Moore's own experience of exile and of the radical historical changes of the twentieth century separated him forever from such certainty and integrity.

# 3

# A YOUTH OF
# THE THIRTIES

St. Malachy's Diocesan College was the world of Brian Moore's adolescence, and if he later had difficulty recalling his early childhood, this schoolboy world imprinted itself so indelibly on his consciousness and on his nascent sense of independence that it coloured his deepest feelings about the formation — and deformation — of selfhood. He recalls the deadening routine and its insidious undertow in his second novel, *The Feast of Lupercal.* In telling the story of Diarmuid Devine, a teacher at St. Michan's School, he exposes with considerable bitterness the sadism behind the hierarchical structure and Catholic self-righteousness of his father's *alma mater.*

> Sweating green walls, snuffling radiators, window sills which blew cold drafts into the back of the neck awaited him. . . . His pupils would show no respect: of that he was sure. Masters were tyrants and, like tyrants everywhere, their coin of fear was repaid in secret mockery. Every one of us, lay or clerical, is watched for weakness, Mr. Devine told himself. We are not loved, we have three hundred mouths to mock us. . . . It was a frightening prospect. But he was still the master: the cane lay in front of him, he could flog them, every blessed one of them. That was how the Dean would act: double the dose, hand out the medicine. What use was the medicine though? It was the Dean's medicine, the school medicine, which made this kind of boy.

The physical and emotional dreariness of the place and its vicious circle of fear, loneliness, and sadism are the quintessential qualities of Belfast itself in this novel and in *Judith Hearne,* but they are the realities which underlay the all-male, Catholic regime which Dr. Moore endorsed.

Throughout the novelist's childhood and youth, his father was St. Malachy's doctor and, more significantly, he was a founder and president of the Past Pupils' Union. He was a custodian of the prestige and tradition of the school, and so his expectations of his sons' behaviour and academic achievement carried this burden in addition to the common expectations of an academically successful parent. Dr. Moore was also a Lecturer and Examiner at Queen's University and a member of the University Senate, so that when the father in *The Emperor of Ice Cream* pronounces his son "a failure in life" because he failed his matriculation examination, the father seems to Gavin Burke to be "echoing the mysterious judgement of all authority." Even though Moore saw his father as an honest man, a man of considerable integrity, and later came to admire his character, at this time he saw him as an upholder of the public structures of authority and power.

The first irreversible sign that Brian was not going to follow in his father's footsteps in any conventional way was his comparative academic failure at the end of his years at St. Malachy's. "I was very good at some subjects and very bad at others. I was good at English, I was good at languages. I got high marks generally all round, but I couldn't pass Maths. You couldn't get your School Leaving Certificate without passing Maths, so I failed my School Leaving Certificate, at which point my father, who couldn't understand failure, completely wiped me off as a possibility to go to university."

The lasting education Brian Moore received during these years turned less on scholarship than on duplicity and hypocrisy, on intimidation and conformity, on the fierce gaps between the assertive public roles and the inner turmoil of feeling and conscience. It turned out to be an invaluable education for a novelist. While a constant pattern of Moore's imaginative world is the alienation of his protagonists from the public world, and their crises of eroding purpose and self-esteem, he seems to have discovered at this time that he, unlike many of his Belfast protagonists, did not have to remain a victim of his alienated fears and fantasies. A lasting opposition to abusive authority, expressed in his socialist commitment and in his belief in literature, was rooted in this first education in the personal cost of the clerical hegemony at St. Malachy's.

Moore began to discover that the contrary life of his own thoughts and desires was not unique and did not have to remain secret. That discovery grew slowly, supported by his increasing intellectual independence, especially in political and literary matters, and by the cultivation of friends and interests outside the Catholic ethos of home and school. While his new public roles from sixteen onwards were necessary rites of passage, it is uncertain if they actually alleviated the shame and sense of failure or contributed to a deepening of such feelings. The change was gradual over many years, and major stages of his personal liberation from St. Malachy's would not be possible until he left Belfast in his twenty-second year, nor indeed, would he ever fully "write it out of my system."

The undoubtedly gifted Brian Moore, younger brother of Séamus, who would excel at scientific subjects and go on to become a doctor, has explained how his difficulty with mathematics shaped his adolescent outlook:

> I was good at most subjects but bad at mathematics which was a subject you needed to pass the exams. So I began to think of myself as a failure at an early age and I also began to think of myself as someone who was concealing something. And that unhappiness — you can't blame poor old Belfast for that — that unhappiness is the thing which starts the unhappiness with Belfast and led me to criticize the Church itself and also my parents' political and religious ideals.

On more than one occasion the novelist has described *The Emperor of Ice Cream* as his most autobiographical novel, meaning that in it he drew in a more literal way on actual experiences. One can assume, then, that the family life of Gavin Burke, as well as his adventures in the Air Raid Precautions Unit, dramatize many of the feelings and situations of his own life in the years 1939–1941.

The separation from the worlds of home and St. Malachy's was facilitated by his growing political awareness and commitments and his sharp differences of opinion with his father on the course of European political events, as well as on the more local issue of Irish nationalism. The first event to polarize father and son was the Spanish Civil War and the partisan attitudes sharply expressed in the newspapers and in daily life. The Catholic newspaper of Belfast, the *Irish News*, owned by a friend of James Moore who was a fellow member of the Knights of Columbus, wrote enthusiastically in support of Franco and his campaign against "the Reds." Irish nationalists, for the most part, were ardent supporters of the "Catholic" Axis powers, and their political viewpoints were largely coloured by their primarily anti-British outlook. A well-known nationalist stance had been summed up long before as "England's difficulty is Ireland's opportunity."

Moore declared himself a socialist and an opponent of Franco, Mussolini, and Hitler, and, in the process, of Irish nationalism. His political commitment alienated him from his family, but was a sign of his new-found comfort with people and writers whose attitudes were more in tune with the times.

The left-wing thing was in the air at that time. I remember getting *The Faber Book of Modern Verse* and trying to find out more about people like Auden and Isherwood. At the end of the thirties political discontent was popular . . . and I latched on to this at once. I thought, we will change the world, we will blow Belfast up. It's always been a recurring dream of mine to blow Belfast up. So that led me, while I was still at school, to the Belfast Theatre Guild — people like Bernard Barnett and Harold Goldblatt who were Jews. It was great for me. It was very liberating. I remember selling *Socialist Appeal* on the street corners — about three copies sold in a whole afternoon! And I remember sitting in Campbell's Teashop just across from the Linen Hall Library here; that was our great hangout. All the teenage lefties used to go there and sit and drink tea and eat cream buns.

Gavin Burke's fantasies of liberation from his past, his "shameful secret excitement, a vision of the grownups' world in ruins," were shared then, to a degree, by Moore himself. It is difficult to know to what extent his later analysis of the political alignments reflects a conscious awareness of that time, but what is certain is that he did develop a strong political commitment in the late thirties and that it set him apart from his father and his home environment:

The Irish question, of course, had an effect on me because of my uncle and my father. But it was their revolution, not mine. I reacted against all that nationalistic fervour because I saw that their dislike of Britain extended to approval of Britain's enemies — such as Mussolini. I grew up, moreover, at the time of the Spanish Civil War. I was about seventeen at the time, and I thought my father was wrong very much as Gavin thought his father was wrong. I thought all my uncles and relatives were wrong because, the thing is they were idealists, but they were idealists of their generation — narrow, parochial idealists. Not that I pretend to have had any foresight about Hitler, but I realized that Franco and Mussolini were not the great Christian gentlemen we were told they were.

Perhaps more important than the political analysis and commitment was the atmosphere which surrounded his new social milieu. "My early friends in Belfast were not Catholics but were Jews and Protestants who were politically oriented the way I was, so I moved in a circle as a boy very much outside my own world. And so I've always thought that I was unusual in that I feel uneasy with allegiance to either group." The novelist is speaking here of his character as a non-partisan Belfast writer, of his distance from both sectarian orientations, and of his discovery of a free-thinking Theatre Guild that provided him with an imaginative space. He has spoken on a number of occasions of the pleasure and the surprise he experienced on discovering the Jewish Institute Dramatic Society, and, in fact, in these years there was an upsurge of interest in creating a lively semi-professional theatre in Belfast.

Three amateur groups joined forces, and there appears to have been considerable optimism, talent, and creative energy focused on giving Belfast an imaginative centre in theatre, which the city had never had. The two men Moore mentions, actor Bernard Barnett and producer Harold Goldblatt, became leading figures in maintaining a professional theatre that ran seasons of classical and popular plays for many years. These affiliations may have been important for the future novelist in that he participated, as Gavin Burke does, in the production of the plays, sitting in on rehearsals and observing technical challenges close up. The left-wing orientation of this group is reflected in the choice of plays, and Moore acted in a play by Clifford Odets. This apprenticeship may have left him with particular skills for his later career as scriptwriter or dramatist, or for the conception of the scene in fiction, but it would seem that the emotional comfort they offered the adolescent in his transition from school to the adult world was of primary importance.

He was ready, then, when he joined the Air Raid Precautions Unit in summer 1939, to take further strides away from home, and this seems to have happened in at least two ways: the experience of meeting a cross-section of Belfast society and the formation of a significant friendship with an older man who was very different from his own father and from the Fathers he had encountered at school.

At seventeen I met a much older man, who actually is the prototype for Ted Ormsby in *An Answer from Limbo* and Freddie Pilkington in *The Emperor of Ice Cream*. When I joined the ARP I met this man, who was about thirty and a sort of dilettante; he introduced me to Joyce, Yeats, the whole canon. Yet he wasn't a person you would ever meet at a university. He was typically Irish. He just read a lot and had his own good taste. His name was Teddy Millington. So, at that time I started reading everything. I quarrelled vigorously with my father, who called Joyce 'a sewer' and who admired Shaw, whom I always despised — partly because my father liked him. And, besides, I didn't like the Nanny in Shaw; Shaw's always nagging and lecturing. My home life changed at that point.

But while the "teenage leftie" did not hesitate to express his new political and literary tastes, Moore did more than simply indulge his disaffection by becoming a dropout among other dropouts from the establishment world of academic and professional success. He was developing an historical consciousness and a keen interest in contemporary political attitudes. Even more, he seems to have been developing a shrewd sense of how the opinions of people *en masse* are shaped and determined. His analysis of the developments in European politics was also an analysis of how the political opinions and commitments of his father's generation were formed.

What happened was, at that period of history, the time of the 1939 war, people of my father's generation, who had all their lives been anti-British, were vaguely startled by being pro-Mussolini in the early days. Then they became rather pro-Franco because he was keeping the Communists at bay. They woke up overnight to find that they'd been wrong, and that they were on the wrong side, and that the values by which they had lived were shot in a sense. And I think all of England woke up — never mind the Irish — all the English woke up to the fact that they were living in the past, that Chamberlain's "We have dismantled danger, and we have plucked this flower, peace," at Munich had been a sell-out. And that was a terrible blow for that generation to take.

While his recollections focus mostly on the advent of war, and in the end, his feelings about the city were that it was a profoundly depressing place which he must leave if he were to maintain his self-esteem, it appears that for a period he felt himself achieving a kind of peace in his new milieu. At this time, in spite of his frequently voiced memory of how physically unattractive he felt he was, he went out with a girl named Ethna Maguire, a nurse, and so it may be assumed that the course of Gavin and Sally's relationship in *Emperor* captures something of that experience. His friendship with Teddy Millington, his association with the theatre, and his work at the ARP all provided him with opportunities to be someone other than the failure that he had been branded in his final years at St. Malachy's.

He must have found the people he met in the ARP both liberating and disturbing, for, on the evidence of *Emperor*, he learned to observe for the first time and to appreciate a world apart from the closed, middle-class world of his parents. In this way, the novel foreshadows Moore's later career as a traveller, forever trying to confront and capture new cities, forever uncovering the underside of those cities, as if in travelling away from his parents' house, he found a new moral universe. "Strange, how quickly one's life can change. No need to sail seas or cross frontiers to lose your bearings, you can do it here in this room, less than a mile from your parents' home." The first education he received during these years of the phony war — when it was assumed that Belfast would never be attacked by German bombers — was in the widespread forms of failure in this depressed city, so that the word came to mean much more than the middle-class sense of failing to enter university. The ARP was staffed by individuals who were not essentially different from himself in that they were unemployed, yet here he came in contact with a cross-section of the population, Protestant and Catholic, young and old, women and men, and what he observed was not wholly negative.

In an essay on Belfast written before the Troubles boiled up once more in the late sixties, Moore presents an image of the place as a provincial city with its own distinctive working-class culture. His years as a young socialist may have allowed him to imagine that with the overthrow of the repressive establishments, Catholic and Protestant alike, the best qualities of the Ulster character and culture would survive. His affectionate portrait of the city focuses on the colourful talk and the personal charm of the people:

"Can ye stick it?"
"Aye."
The men are Belfast shipyard workers. Their half-facetious greeting is the not-uncommon substitute among the city's working people for the normal exchanges of "good morning" or "good evening." It is at once their recognition of hard fact and their proclamation of defiance. . . . Its people, a mixture of descendants of English and Scots planters first introduced into the area in the beginning of the 17th Century, and of the native Catholic Irish, are, despite the differences they cherish, members of the same down-to-earth race, ironic in their humour, despisers of cant.

This brisk and comic sketch of the city, written while he was working on *The Emperor of Ice Cream*, reflects an optimistic view of a community united by its similarities rather than divided by its differences. His love of the particular detail, of humour and irony, and of the down-to-earth people, "despisers of cant," seems to reflect his own self as novelist and his dedication to the honest portrayal of ordinary people confronting real dilemmas. Indeed, that final sentence may contain a miniature self-portrait, for the characterization of the Belfastman reflects his own declared preference for realism and a plain prose style.

Referring to the opening up of another side of his character in the 1960s — an interest in the metaphysical, the mystical, and the miraculous, so evident in novels from *Fergus* to *Cold Heaven* — he spoke of his suspicion of and discomfort with literary embellishment, "because the Ulsterman, you know, is traditionally hard-headed and doesn't understand any of that stuff." In spite of the self-conscious detachment and generic experimentation that came in the later 1960s, the orientation towards brevity and realism remains. There is a hint here also of his father, for the expression "despisers of cant" seems to reflect the salient qualities of his father's character, which Moore admires and refers to as honesty and a hatred of pretension.

In spite of this later realization, the literary taste that he developed for poetry of the thirties and for the modernists, James Joyce and T. S. Eliot, especially, helped him to imagine himself outside Catholic Belfast and his father's taste and judgement, to imagine himself as a youth of his own time. References in *Emperor* to the leading poets of the 1930s, W. H. Auden, Louis MacNeice and Cecil Day-Lewis, suggest that he appreciated the contemporary note of prophetic distance from the past and its deceptions and obfuscations. He had not yet learned to appreciate the prophetic poetry of Yeats, which would come to mean a great deal to him in the 1960s and later: the work of that Irish poet had been ruined for him by his English teachers at St. Malachy's who provoked the mockery of the boys by chanting soporifically: "I will arise and go now, and go to Innisfree."

It was the discovery of Joyce more than any other that reinforced his commitment to the writer's vocation.

In 1939 when I was eighteen years old I was invited to spend the weekend at the house of parents of a boy I had known in school. Browsing through the bookshelves, I discovered, hidden behind some innocent titles, the two-volume Odyssey Press edition of *Ulysses*, published in Hamburg, Paris, Bologna, and bearing the warning: *Not To Be Introduced Into The British Empire Or The U.S.A.* My friend told me it was a dirty book which his older brother had brought back from Paris earlier that year. As my friend's parents were not present that weekend, I settled in to read it openly in search of the 'hot bits.' It was, of course, a dirty book, more explicit about sexual matters than any other I had read until then. But it was, for me, stimulating in an altogether different way.

I took *Ulysses* home and hid it in my room. Over the next few days I began to read it clandestinely, slowly, and with excitement. There was much in it that I did not understand. But it was stunningly unlike any other Irish (or English) fiction I had read. . . .

From those first readings, *Ulysses* changed, if not my life, then my ideas about becoming a writer. It both inspired and intimidated me. It led to a reading of *A Portrait of the Artist* which, for me as for others of my generation became "our" book, the quintessential Irish *bildungsroman*, set down brilliantly and unimprovably.

Moore found in *Portrait* "the story of one's early life . . . the retreats, the hellfire, the feeling of hopelessness with girls, etc.," and so when he came to write his first novel he did not want to redo that archetypal story of Irish adolescence. The example of Joyce's commitment, however, and the techniques he had developed in *Ulysses* for representing contemporary consciousness in an urban setting became lasting elements of Moore's vocation. That commitment reinforced Moore's own sense of independence from his milieu, and Stephen Dedalus's ringing declaration of his duty to his own self and to his vocation to embrace "silence, exile, and cunning" as a means to becoming an artist undoubtedly fueled Moore's own determination to leave Belfast.

The years between 1937 and 1942 were tumultuous ones in European politics, but for Moore they were years in which he circled his own dilemma, unable to find a definitive way out. This has to be the explanation for an unusual series of confusions in Moore's memories of the chronology of this period. Most remarkable is his frequent ascribing of key experiences to the year in which he was eighteen, in particular his discovery of James Joyce, the extensive bombing of Belfast that destroyed the house on Clifton Street, and the death of his father. In fact, the Blitz struck Belfast in April 1941, when Moore was almost twenty, and his father died almost a year later. In these slips of memory can be felt the desire to compress those years into a single year, as in fact happens in the fictional treatment of them in *The Emperor of Ice Cream*. As in his first two novels of Belfast, in which his protagonists Judith Hearne and Diarmuid Devine seem to travel a circular path, the key psychological states of the young Moore seem to have been of waiting and irresolution, as if during these years time stood still.

Moore frequently returns to these years of his adolescence in discursive comments and in fictional enactments of a bitter father-son relationship. Those comments most often explain the problem in terms of his academic ability, his father's judgement of it, and his father's official role as custodian of the Catholic ethos that enveloped school, home and community politics. Yet, increasingly, Moore speaks frankly of his own personality as the cause of his troubles, his academic difficulties being due to deeper psychological stresses arising from his sense of having lost his faith at an early age, or of never believing, and of having sinned in continuing a charade of confession, communion, and church attendance.

The sense of being an actor pleasing an audience, of, indeed, being many different selves, is a troubling one not unfamiliar to many adolescents, yet, in the case of a young man who grew up to make these very issues of identity his subject and his technical concern as a novelist, it is evident that the events of these years in late adolescence are truly formative. The tension and anguish that beset the youth could only have one release. "I'm absolutely convinced that the reason I left home as quickly as I could, and left Ireland, was because of that. I was living a lie." Although it is surely with real self-understanding that Moore quotes Mauriac's words about the door closing at twenty, he has spent a lifetime trying to prove the statement invalid in his own case.

# 4

# LEAVING
# HOME

For almost two years, Belfast followed the catastrophe of the war from a distance, as if it were happening far away and would never actually touch the city. The "phony war," followed by the collapse of France and the beginning of the Blitz in England, had an air of unreality well captured by Moore in *The Emperor of Ice Cream*, in the attitudes of a wide range of characters. The ordinary routines of life continued undisturbed: "Nothing would change. Out there, in the world, governments might be overthrown, capitals occupied, cities destroyed, maps redrawn, but here, in Ireland, it made no difference. . . . The frozen ritual of Irish Catholicism perpetuating itself in secula, seculorum. . . . Ireland free was Ireland dead." In spite of Gavin Burke's fantasies of dramatic change that would liberate adolescents from the repressions of the past, that change did not happen.

In the Moore household a private war continued between Brian and his parents, and with, it would seem, Séamus. Gavin muses about the lack of understanding shown by his older brother: "How could you explain to Owen the feeling you had before every examination, a feeling that the authorities had somehow predetermined your future?" As in the novel, Brian did enroll for an external degree with the University of London, and completed some of the requirements for a bachelor's degree while working in the ARP. During the year of his failure to matriculate, battle lines had been drawn in the fashion depicted in *Emperor*: "The world of misfits, the A.R.P. world, was a world one could enter only if one belonged there." Father and son appear to have settled into ambiguous hostility, for, as this sentence suggests, the young protagonist suffers more from the feeling that his father withdraws his support because he believes his son lacks ability rather than in anger at the son's wilful indiscipline.

The son can comfort himself with his own thoughts: "His father, who, until now, had decided on everything — schools, holidays, punishments, plans — was unaware that, this morning, all had changed." But, in fact, to believe in that change was increasingly difficult. And worse still, the personal change, the breaking away from the tyrannical routines of religious observance that had sustained him to begin with seemed increasingly hollow: "Although he had left God behind in the dusty past of chapel, confessional, and class-room, the catechism rules prevailed. In both worlds, lack of purpose, lack of faith, was the one deadly sin." The novel captures well the frustration and the absurdities of waiting, especially in the life of an impatient adolescent, but it is not only a *Bildungsroman*, for it shares with many of Moore's other books a preoccupation with purposelessness, personal failure, the unreality of the present, and the yearning for faith and meaning.

Suddenly, all did change. On the night of 7 April 1941, German bombers attacked Belfast. An even more widespread and devastating attack came a week later, and this was followed by two minor attacks in early May. The city was relatively unprotected, anti-aircraft guns were inadequate, and people were careless about shelters and security, officials and civilians having settled into an assumption that such an attack would never happen. The target area was the docks, where war industries were situated, but bombs fell over a wide area, causing much loss of life and extensive damage to residential property and to public and industrial buildings. Almost nine hundred people died and more than this number were seriously injured, many of them trapped in demolished buildings. Forty thousand were homeless, seventy thousand had to be fed at special centres, and one hundred thousand people left the city immediately. The devastation to roads, waterworks, electricity, and gas supplies was massive.

The period of waiting had ended; the reality of war in the city changed Moore's life irrevocably. The family home on Clifton Street was damaged, but none of the Moore family was injured. They moved to another house, 13 Camden Street, on the south side near Queen's University — the street of Judith Hearne's boarding house — and would never again occupy the Victorian home of the novelist's childhood, although more than a year later, they returned to their old neighbourhood, settling on Cliftonville Road, a little to the north of Carlisle Circus.

Dr. Moore and Brian were directly affected by the devastation and death. The novelist has confirmed that the pivotal experience of that grim and chaotic time, portrayed in *Emperor*, reflects what actually happened to him: "I found myself being punched from adolescence into a volunteer job coffining dead bodies for weeks. And that experience naturally had a strong effect on me." What the nineteen-year-old Moore faced in Belfast was more grim than anything he would encounter later in the war-zones of continental Europe:

The city mortuary was unable to cope with the large number of bodies. In an attempt to ease the situation corpses were also taken to St George's Market near Cromac Square and to the Falls Road Baths. In the baths, the bodies initially arrived in coffins and were laid out around the pool. However, the city quickly ran out of coffins and the baths became so full that bodies had to be accommodated in the pool itself. . . . After three days the bodies started to smell due to decomposition. . . . It was decided to remove all the bodies to Mays Fields and lay them out on the grass where they could still be identified. So as to slow down the decomposition process an ARP volunteer sat all day watering the bodies with a garden hose.

While the circumstances depicted in the Blitz chapters in *Emperor* roughly correspond to Moore's own experience of the bombing and devastation, certain aspects of the father in the book do not correspond with Moore's own father, James. The seventy-four-year-old doctor worked at the hospital during the raids, and the Mater itself was at the centre of some of the worst destruction, although only the Nurses' Home suffered extensive damage. Afterwards he frequently stayed at the hospital overnight in case another bombing raid would find him unable to get there. Many people, including the novelist, attribute the elder Moore's death a year later to the stress of his work at this time. A posthumous tribute noted that "his heroic work since the air raids put too great a strain upon his constitution and contributed to his death from heart failure."

If the conquering of fear is one criterion of maturity, there is little reason to assume that the reversal of the roles of father and son, as depicted in the novel, has any basis in fact. Moore's father did not leave the city for the safety of Dublin as Mr. Burke does, leaving space for Gavin to appear in a courageous light. Yet in another way, Dr. Moore was forced to undergo a reversal and an awakening: "My father, who was pro-German, when he saw what the Germans were able to do, when he saw what modern warfare was really like, when they blew up your home, that was all, things were over." James Moore had to admit that his judgement was fallible, and on something of such significance for world history as the nature and effect of Nazi militarism. That realization was, evidently, a tipping of the political balance towards the sceptical truths endorsed by his son. But, in fact, as Moore has noted, this was largely a generational division, and his father's reversal was one that a whole generation had to undergo. It is unlikely that James Moore confessed to having been a fool, as Gavin Burke's father does, or that Brian was given the opportunity for such a magnanimous gesture of forgiveness. What is somewhat surprising, however, is that the service given by Brian in the aftermath of the attack does not seem to have merited acknowledgement by his father.

In Moore's recollections of his relationship with his father at the time of his death, James Moore appears to be frozen in a proud and unarticulated state of disappointment with his inadequate son. Even though the years from 1939 to 1942 had brought great changes, their relationship appears not to have evolved, although it may have been the shock of the death itself that imprinted on Moore's memory this sense of his father's public and unyielding self. "My father died when I was eighteen [*sic*], so he died thinking I was a wimp, that I was a person who wasn't going to achieve anything in life and that was very sad. I've had to live with my father's disappointment. So, actually disapproval is not the word: disapproval you can deal with because you can say, I disapprove of this disapproval. Disappointment you cannot deal with." At any rate, his father's death and its aftermath remain turning points in the novelist's life to which he has returned over and over in an effort to clarify his feelings about his dead father.

Dr. Moore died almost a year after the Blitz, on 1 March 1942. His status in the Catholic community in Belfast and in all of Ireland can be gauged from the notices given to his death in the *Irish News*. For three days a prominent part of what had been reduced in wartime to a four-page newspaper was devoted to describing his career, to tributes from many sources, and to listing the religious, academic, and civil dignitaries from Belfast and Dublin who attended funeral services at church and at graveside.

James Moore was at once a conventional luminary of the Catholic establishment and a much larger and more independent figure than is suggested by that designation. In spite of his crowded professional and public career, it appears that his generosity towards patients was remembered, not simply in a routine formula, "devoted to his religion and to the cause of God's poor," but in the remark that he was popular with patients because he was "kind and courteous to a degree." At his death, a motion was passed by the Workers' Maintenance Committee at the hospital paying tribute to "Mr. Moore's labours for the working classes during his lifetime of service," and another tribute alludes to a class of doctors "who almost resent the financial aspect of their services."

Brian Moore has spoken of the anti-materialist stance of his father as both a mark of his selflessness and of a rather snobbish disdain for business. His lack of concern about the commercial aspect of his profession also meant that many patients neglected to pay him for services. On his death, the small sum of £850 was willed to his wife, leaving her with few resources for running a household of nine children, half of them still teenagers. The household was supported by the two older girls, already working in the civil service. Until his mother's death in 1957, Brian sent regular financial gifts. The idealistic and improvident father with the public aura of status and success may be seen as a shadow following the novelist throughout his life: his anxiety about being a freelance writer and his determination to manage his earnings judiciously are constant concerns, even when it would seem that his earnings from his work would guarantee him lasting security.

While it appears that his father's selfless devotion to his patients was a prominent feature of his character and was interpreted in the light of his religious commitment to Christian principles, Moore's career as novelist is an oblique reflection of this aspect of his parent. In spite of recurring declarations that writing is a "surrogate life" compared with, say, the practice of medicine, the success of the novelist has been won by his "selfless" commitment to the depiction of his characters in their own world, characters who evoke the sympathy of readers because of the painful crises they endure.

This forceful and hard-working father of diverse affiliations, roles, and selves has become the basis of many different mythic figures in Brian Moore's imaginative world, most remarkably as the unforgiving and distant father in "Uncle T," *The Emperor of Ice Cream*, and *Fergus*. He is recalled as a difficult and inscrutable figure in references that hint at Moore's incessant search for understanding of the essential character of his father. "He believed totally in the things he believed in; he was very uncompromising, and he left us at least with that — a legacy of values that I think are very out of date today." This eminent patriarchal figure was a father whose disapproval provided his son with large-scale difficulties during adolescence, yet as the novelist quarried his memories of his father for a series of portraits of such a male type, his feelings towards him clarified into a warmly approving and admiring outlook.

An early remark on his penchant for writing about "failure" and about characters who seem incapable of success in middle-class terms seems to have its obsessive centre in Moore's relationship with his wholly successful father. In searching to understand the doctor's essential core of self-assurance, at once admirably selfless and impersonally "dehumanized," Moore is drawn to characters who contrast with his father, who are, like so many of the women and priests he has chosen to portray — and, no doubt, like himself — vulnerable to inner and outer conditions that instil doubt and fear and undermine the successful and poised sense of self.

The death of his father, following hard on the abandonment of the old home and the collapse of the "Irish Catholic" perspective on the fascists, add up to a decisive end to Moore's youth, yet his memory has focused often on the ambivalence of his feelings regarding the fact that his father should die thinking him a failure. The conflation of these years in his memory may suggest that he is more comfortable with the idea that he was young at that time, so young that he had had few opportunities to prove himself to his father.

But James Moore's disappointment, which crystallized when Brian left school and endured during his father's last few years, has remained a central part of the novelist's own sense of himself. In Moore's interpretation, his father's disappointment in him became the motor of his incessant writing, of his unrequited wish for perfection: "Somehow that feeling of unfulfillment can be a spur to ambition. If you will never gain parental approval, you will keep on writing novels. In any case, I don't think I will ever feel fulfilled. I know what I wanted to do in every work and I know that in no book have I succeeded. That feeling that I haven't succeeded, that every book is a partial failure, is what drives me to write another book." What is evident, however, is that while the novelist will never gain parental approval, the characters of his parents and their attitudes to life, above and beyond narrow parochial and sectarian interests, have been incorporated into his work, and as he has grown older, he appears to move further away from his own youthful stance of rejection.

Moore left the ARP and worked with the National Fire Service in Belfast in 1942. Even after his experience of the Blitz and the death of his father, the only role that the young Brian Moore could imagine for himself was to be a writer, and he continued to be sure that he could not be one in Belfast. "How does a person who has never *written* anything, who has no degree and no prospects *become* a writer in London or Paris or New York? When one is twenty these problems, as Eliot said, 'still amaze, the troubled midnight and the noon's repose.' In my case my *deus ex machina* was the War. I spoke some French and was hired — on a fluke — by the British government to go as a port official to North Africa."

He left Belfast to take up his new job as a civil servant with the British Ministry of War Transport in Algiers, and apart from brief stays between jobs in late 1945 and late 1947, he became a permanent emigrant. Although he has often spoken of his abhorrence of the repressive and bigoted climate of Belfast, something he had to "write out of my system," his sense of the wider political and cultural forces at play in contemporary society has been coloured by the intractable sectarian commitments and violence of his first home. He distances himself from partisan issues, from theoretical or ideological perspectives, and insists that in the creation of his characters, he must be free from all such constraints. He endorses James Joyce's view of the invisible novelist as "a God paring his fingernails." Yet Moore's constantly ambiguous and troubled relationship with his native realm, and his characterization of himself as an Ulsterman even in so intimate a matter as prose style, indicate that when the door closed at twenty the ethos of Belfast had been indelibly imprinted on him.

He has written a whimsical version of his leavetaking in two essays, neither of which touch on the psychic depth of the uprooting revealed in such books as *The Luck of Ginger Coffey* and other novels of adaptation to North American life. "I remember as the ship sailed up Belfast Lough that night, bound for Liverpool," he has written in "The Expatriate Writer,"

I sat among the real emigrants — the poor who worked on English roads and in English kitchens. The last channel buoys slipped past. I felt I was leaving forever. Three young navvies began to sing "The Long and the Short and the Tall," and people joined in, blessing all the sergeants and the double-you-oh-ones. I didn't sing. I remember thinking — I'm not going abroad to fight in the war, not really. I'm leaving home because I don't want to be a doctor like my father and brothers. Because I want to be a writer. I want to write. And, at that moment, a man sitting on a suitcase beside me took out a Baby Power and offered me a drink. "Your first time across the water?" he said. "Yes," I said. "What line of work are you in?" I didn't know just what I was going to do in this British government job. I had bluffed my way into it. All I knew was I was being sent abroad to someplace my French would be useful. So when the man asked what line of work I was in, I began to live out my private lie. "I'm a writer," I said. "A ship's writer?" he said. "No, just a writer." "Would that be good wages?" "I don't know," I said. Perhaps that's the way a lot of people become writers. They don't like the role they're playing and writing seems a better one.

## 5
_____

# WAR AND
# WANDERLUST

It was 1943, and the previous year Algiers had become the base for the First Army in Montgomery's successful campaign against Rommel. Only a few months before Brian Moore's arrival to serve as a port clerk with the British Ministry of War Transport, de Gaulle had established the head-quarters of his Free French movement in this first *département* of France to be liberated. This posting would be one of a series of stopping points as Moore worked behind the advancing front lines, from North Africa to Italy to the Côte d'Azur, and then north to Paris. "I was terribly excited by the war, by the foreign countries I was in, by the disjointed, strange life I led just behind the front lines in a time when you felt you were a living part of history."

In spite of the fact that Moore witnessed in wartime "the great happenings of my generation," he did not choose to write about them: "In Europe I had been a spectator at events that were not my events." What he means is that the significant "events," even in the midst of war, were private rituals — those moments when he transformed himself and freed himself from what he saw as his shameful weaknesses of character. The "disjointed, strange life" would also offer him the most important education for a novelist, the experience of observing a variety of characters and cultures under extreme circumstances. That education in the meanings of European history and of human character would be cumulative, and the distance necessary to write about the Belfast that had made him suffer would be gained gradually.

On a more conscious level, he had to cope with the demands of his work and his new colleagues and to orient himself in the new places he moved on to every few months. He has had little to say about this aspect of adaptation to changing circumstances, except that the French he was taught at St. Malachy's, on the strength of which he had been hired, was less than adequate to the task. His bitterness in later remarks about knowing his French verb tenses but being unable to speak suggests that he may have had a rude awakening. Nevertheless, his first stopping point, Algiers, must have excited him, for not only was it his first French city but it was also an Arab city and a divided one like Belfast. In one of the commercial thrillers he would write in the fifties, *French for Murder*, he would draw on the racist and criminal stereotypes of North Africans in France. Only in *The Statement* and *The Magician's Wife*, written fifty years after he lived in Algiers, does he draw on his knowledge of French-Arab relations to portray racist attitudes in contemporary France and in the early stages of the French colonization of North Africa.

Moore's practical intelligence and his skill for quickly picking up the tricks of a trade — to be demonstrated later in the many kinds of writing at which he excelled — are evident in his promotion to a position of major responsibility within six months. He became an assistant port officer for Naples following the capture of the city by the Fifth Army in October 1943. For six months, he had many responsiblities: the ploughing of ship channels, supplying hundreds of ships with food and water — he has recalled that he debriefed ships' captains, ran a fleet of cars, and found time to open a hotel for merchant seamen. He is modest about all this: "I was suddenly projected, just through a fluke, into a position where I had a terrific amount of responsibility and I was able to hire civilians to work for me and really run a big port operation."

Moore arrived in Naples while military action continued, and he has recalled that he witnessed the Germans fleeing the city and the hospital ships bringing the dead and wounded from the fierce fighting during the Allied landing at Anzio, north of Naples, in January 1944, and from the German counterattacks in February and March. This was Moore's first close-up experience of large-scale death and destruction since the Blitz in Belfast. During these months, the British and American forces made slow progress in the Italian campaign, although Rome was eventually taken in June, and it then became clear that, following the collapse of the Italian regime, the German forces would eventually have to retreat. With the successes of the Normandy campaign in the summer of 1944, and with significant Russian advances into Poland, the Allies opened another front, with landings in the Côte d'Azur from bases in Naples and North Africa. Again Moore moved forward quickly behind Allied lines, coming ashore in France near Marseilles.

The responsibilities of his assignment at Naples "gave me a sort of confidence about the world," he affirms, and then adds, significantly, "for a while, anyway." While his father was not there to witness his accomplishment, it is surely likely that Moore did not deny himself that recognition.

Yet the qualifying phrase, "for a while, anyway," is a typical feature of the novelist's sense of character and of his own identity. Self-esteem is a frail and provisional accomplishment, for change is an inevitable part of human circumstances, and the feeling of success is always vulnerable to the erosions of doubt or rejection.

Like all exiles, Moore brought the concerns of home with him, and an unfinished novel of the mid-fifties focuses on a widowed mother's anxieties and judgements. The circumstances of Michael Russell's departure from home and his trajectory — from Algiers to Naples to Marseilles — parallel Moore's own experiences, except that Russell is a soldier. The focus of the novel is not on exploits in the war zones, however, but on the bond to home, especially to his mother, who is portrayed as worrying unceasingly for both his physical safety and for his immortal soul.

But Moore was not a soldier, and throughout these years, his life was not in immediate danger. This first version of a fiction that would envision the black sheep's separation from, and eventual meeting with, his family explores a different kind of danger — the emasculating power of inhibition, guilt, and morbidity. More than ten years after leaving home he was unable to complete that fiction; it would take another decade before he could write *The Emperor of Ice Cream* and, later, *Fergus*, the novel that examines most directly Moore's familial inheritance. But this unfinished novel reveals that the leavetaking was a long-drawn-out process; although it apparently began with a decisive break when he went away to war, Moore seems to have brought with him into the war zones his own private battle against depression and failure.

Even though he did not write during these years, apart from trying his hand at poetry in the style of Eliot during his time in Naples, it is clear that France was the first place outside Belfast that became sufficiently imprinted on his imagination that he would want to recreate it in fiction. He has recalled seeing collaborators shot on the streets of Marseilles and a "revenge" trial in Paris of a former minister of the Vichy regime. These much-publicized trials took place during the winter of 1944–45, even while the war continued in Germany. Fifty years later, the situation of collaborators and the attitudes of French people towards the Vichy regime gave him the central idea for *The Statement*. Rather than the depiction of wartime experience itself, it is the moral dilemmas that interest him, and especially the shades of Catholic rationalization that allowed church members to conceal a war criminal for decades. In this novel, one can see his continuing interest in the mentality of those Catholics, such as his father, who were prepared to overlook the actions of the fascists because they placed the preservation of the Catholic ethos above politics and the rule of law.

Moore's interest was caught in 1945 by personalities like de Gaulle and Pétain, rather than by the flow of events, because he associates the actions of such leaders with those who are inclined to follow them: "Daddy would have supported Pétain." His anger at an Irish leader like Prime Minister Eamon de Valera who "shamefully" kept Ireland neutral in what was "a just war" is unrestrained: "De Valera was the only leader in the world to sign the book of condolences on the death of Hitler. How was that for pretending that nothing had happened?" His sense of other political leaders is equally caustic: "The Allies liberated France. De Gaulle was far more interested in having a seat at the victor's table than in defeating the Germans. I think de Gaulle is very, very overrated; self-centred." And regarding the collaborator and leader of the Vichy régime, Marshal Pétain: "The hero becomes the stooge." Moore's insights into the self-preoccupied personalities of such conservative leaders indicate his lasting scepticism regarding the heroic images created for them by their adherents.

While the Catholic ethos of French politics fascinated him, the pleasures and freedoms of the culture generally also became part of his permanent attachment to France. After coming ashore near Marseilles, he spent time down the coast closer to Spain in the port of Sète, and this coastline generally became an "emotional territory" to which he would return almost annually in the decades of his success as a novelist. Paris and various resorts and towns in Provence would provide settings for *The Doctor's Wife*, *Cold Heaven*, *The Statement*, and for a handful of thrillers, but it is his feeling for the minutiae of French life, from fine cuisine to historical nuances, that colours his recreation of France.

Moore's imaginative assimilation of French culture has a further dimension. After the success of one of his novels in French translation, he expressed no surprise for, as he put it, "I have a French cast of mind." His love of French literature might have been sparked at St. Malachy's perhaps, or through his awareness of his aunts' education in Caen, or his father's holiday there. At any rate, Catholic France was given a special status in the Moore household. More important in the formation of this "French cast of mind" was his discovery of Joyce, who had lived in Paris in the twenties and thirties and, through him, Flaubert. Through Joyce he came to know other modernists, such as Valéry, and to realize that Paris was the centre of the avant-garde in those decades. Now the war offered Moore a chance to experience this city of his teenage dreams.

Years later, in a review of Malcolm Cowley's book *Exile's Return*, about the "lost generation" of Americans in Paris after the Great War, Moore confesses that "one can't help feeling a touch of envy." In reading this "cautionary tale," he seems to identify strongly with those American exiles: "Escape meant freedom . . . The artist can break the puritan shackles . . . what more could an innocent ask of abroad?" Cowley's book seems to trace Moore's own path into maturity, "the terrifying realization that the country of their boyhood is lost forever . . . returning . . . changed, changed utterly, by this self-knowledge." Writing with an expatriate's sense of loss, Hemingway, Fitzgerald, Stein, and others capture, nevertheless, the atmosphere of "first love," unlike the post-war generation of Americans for whom a sojourn in Europe resembles "a quick time in a brothel." Moore's love affair with Paris has survived for decades, and he writes of "the lingering infatuation of first love" as if the sentimental education of the time had a more than cultural intimacy.

If Moore's dreams of experiencing Paris as a romantic and artistic city were realized in these years at the end of the war, it is likely that his first visit to the recently liberated city was overshadowed by the war itself. Paris was an intellectual centre in which the great issues of conscience and faith were tested in political terms of collaboration and betrayal, resistance and existential freedom. At what point Moore became aware of the writings of Sartre, de Beauvoir, Camus, and Malraux is not clear, but their prominence already in 1945, in the former Resistance newspapers *Combat* and *Libération*, may have directed his attention to their work. Certainly, by the 1950s, when he was beginning his career as a novelist, references to them appear in notes and in print. It is arguable that their kind of political and philosophical fiction, recalled to him by his film adaptation of de Beauvoir's wartime novel *The Blood of Others* in 1983, encouraged Moore's adoption of the political thriller as a medium in *The Colour of Blood* (1987) and *Lies of Silence* (1990).

Moore has said that the politics of the time interested him greatly, and, although he has also said that the great events he witnessed were not his material, he confesses: "Sometimes I'd feel unhappy that I wasn't writing these things down, that I wasn't thinking of my future. My future when I would become a writer." Yet it seems reasonable to conclude that the death and destruction around him and his increasing self-confidence as an administrator were giving him a new sense of his own worth and of the worth of individual lives. Rather than the great drama of the world at war, he was observing the forging of courage as a moral principle: he will call it "endurance" — the confrontation of one's own fear and the feeling of failure.

*James Moore, novelist's paternal grandfather, c. 1870.*

Courtesy Seán Moore

*Wedding of Eoin MacNeill and Agnes Moore (Aunt Taddie), 1898. The novelist's father and paternal grandmother are seated directly to the bride's left.* — Courtesy Seán Moore

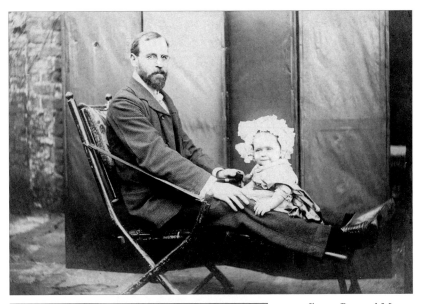

*James Bernard Moore,
the novelist's father,
with niece, c. 1902.*

Courtesy Seán Moore

*Mary Judith Keogh,
the "original" of
Judith Hearne, 1907.*

Courtesy Seán Moore

*Eileen McFadden,*
*the novelist's mother,*
*on left as a member*
*of her "foster" family,*
*the parish priest in the*
*picture being her uncle.*

Courtesy Seán Moore

*Wedding of*
*James Bernard Moore and*
*Eileen McFadden, 1917.*

Courtesy Seán Moore

*Clifton Street, Belfast, looking North towards Carlisle Circus, 1906; the family home where Brian Moore was born is on the right facing the Central Orange Hall crowned with the statue of King William of Orange on his horse.* — Courtesy *Friar's Bush Press*

*Mater Infirmorum Hospital, Crumlin Road, 1906. This hospital administered by the Sisters of Mercy was where the novelist's father worked as a surgeon and where Eileen McFadden worked as a theatre nurse until her marriage.* — Courtesy *Friar's Bush Press*

*The novelist's mother with her first five children: Brian, aged two, is second from the left; also included are Eibhlis, Gráinne, Séamus, and Marie-Therese.*

Courtesy Seán Moore

*Brian, aged seven, on the day he received his first Holy Communion.*

Courtesy Seán Moore

*The novelist's paternal aunt
Maggie, who had been
educated in France and
worked there as a governess;
she lived with the family
and was known to Brian
and his siblings as
"Maximus."*

Courtesy Seán Moore

*James Bernard Moore, c. 1930.*

Courtesy Seán Moore

*Warsaw, January 1946; the view of the central railway station from the Hotel Bristol, where Brian and the UNRRA mission stayed.* — Courtesy Ann Vachon

*John Vachon, American photographer and friend of Brian in Warsaw:*
*self portrait as a private-eye.* — Courtesy Ann Vachon

*Brian in*
*Warsaw, aged*
*twenty-four.*
Courtesy
Ann Vachon

These last two years of the war, when Moore was between twenty-two and twenty-four, took him far from the depressing and limiting ethos of Belfast. The international population of soldiers and administrators that he rubbed shoulders with, and, especially, the gradual enlargement of his milieu to include not only British but Americans and Canadians, introduced him to a world without national or ethnic borders, which made a lasting impact on his imagination and his career. In the decades ahead he would become a Canadian and an American, in addition to being a francophile Irishman whose literary sensibility had been greatly influenced by English literature. In these years were set the foundations of the international person he would become, travelling and living in all his "emotional territories" and setting his novels variously in places where borders and boundaries are fluid.

The bookish and socially awkward young Moore grew into a confident adult, with social skills that allowed him to hold his own in this male world of wartime and to become a successful journalist later. Although Moore has said that he did not write about his own experience in wartime, he did write in the thrillers of the 1950s about the masculine ambience of adventure and isolation, of risk-taking and tests, of smuggling and black markets and commercial sex, of places and character types familiar to him from these years. The formulaic fantasies of male power which thrillers indulge are closely tied to the lonely and competitive arenas of which powerlessness and death are an integral part; the visceral fear which fuels the suspense in those fictions, and in many of the literary fictions also, may have gained its characteristic tension in his wartime experience.

Although he became capable of mimicking the roles of men in wartime, or in similarly isolated and disorienting circumstances, there is reason to believe that he had become a skilful actor, effectively disguising a private self still heavily marked by doubt and anxiety. These qualities are released in different styles into the thrillers and the literary novels, and the many fictions of the 1950s — commercial and literary — elaborate a set of preoccupations focused on the delicate and brittle balancing of the inner self and the public self.

After his post with the Ministry of War Transport became redundant in 1945, Moore took up an assignment in Warsaw with the United Nations Relief and Rehabilitation Administration. "When the war ended, I was listed to be sent on to China. But when I was sent back to London and interviewed to become a Ministry official in China, I was told I was not suitable because I was Irish, and the Irish had a bad record in the Far East. Not trustworthy. Tended to be subversive. Well, having been an

Anglophile all through the war, I became an Anglophobe for a few years after that. I was sent to Warsaw with the UNRRA mission, and I was there for a year and a half." These casual phrases about the time Moore spent in Poland, from January 1946 to November 1947, mask the lasting impact of this post-war experience.

The United Nations Relief and Rehabilitation Administration was established in 1943 to plan on a world-wide basis for the alleviation of mass destitution and for the rebuilding of the physical and economic infrastructures after the war's end. The destruction of the city of Warsaw was so complete, and the economic and social dislocations of Poland so radical — as it became the battleground on three occasions of the German and Soviet armies — that one fifth of all aid resources world-wide was directed there. The official history of UNRRA sets the scene that was being pieced together only gradually as Moore arrived: "Over six million had died; as many more had experienced deportation, forced labour and the concentration camp. Seven hundred thousand were physically disabled. . . . The Germans had, moreover, in their efforts to wipe out Poland as an entity, systematically exterminated the Jews."

Against this background of recent history — and Moore was one of the first to see the camp at Auschwitz — what he was about to witness was nothing less than the Communist takeover of Poland, the installation of the Iron Curtain, and the beginning of the Cold War that would dominate world politics for four decades.

While the business of UNRRA was to administer relief, and his understanding of the larger political transformation of Poland would grow during 1946–47, more immediate images captured his imagination at the start. In spite of the devastation of the city, incongruous signs of other ways of life survived and revived, as he recalled in a memoir of his friend, John Vachon:

A few hotels had been used by the Germans right up to the moment of their departure. We lived in these hotels, some of us in the bombed-out splendours of the Hotel Bristol, once Warsaw's finest. We ate, often, in the once elegant Europa Hotel, its rooms destroyed but its dining room still serving pressed duck, caviar, champagne, and chocolate souffles. In a typically Polish contradiction, the Europa was still under the direction of its former owner, a prince whose ancestors had been Poland's kings. But the centre of our social life was, undoubtedly, the Polonia, which because of its undamaged state was crowded every night, an orchestra playing in the dining room, the bar jammed with foreign correspondents, embassy officials, and convivial drunken Russian officers offering alternate toasts to "Truman" and "Stalin." . . . Here was a frivolous, twentyish world of elegant little tea salons rising from the ruins, at which Polish ladies in felt boots and rakish men's fedora hats, sat eating delicious pastries, drinking Polish tea in tall glasses, and chattering in fluent French as through they were in Paris.

Vachon, an American photographer working for UNRRA, shared Moore's literary interests. "We were both admirers of James Joyce and on spring evenings we walked dark streets, discussing *Ulysses* and *Portrait*, Auden's and Eliot's poetry, and the novels of Hemingway and Dos Passos." This close friendship would survive Vachon's departure in July and would be revived when Moore moved to North America, where Vachon was working for *Look* magazine and living in New York.

Their literary interests led them to see beyond the devastation of Warsaw's streets:

Above all, Warsaw was, for me, as it was for John, an exciting visual confirmation of our readings of Tolstoy, Gogol and Dostoevsky. Here were droshka, the horse-drawn street cabs we had read about in Russian novels. Here were filthy peasants in fur-trimmed coats, driving long carts through the muddy streets; here were Russian soldiers singing gypsy chants, bearded beggars (or were they priests?) begging alms outside ruined churches. Here was the heart-stopping sound of a piano playing Chopin on a quiet Sunday morning in a deserted square.

If *endurance* is Moore's term for the resilience of people in the most extreme states of psychological stress and physical deprivation, Poland is the place he learned the meaning of it in everyday circumstances and on a mass scale. Yet, as this memoir suggests, at such times, the hunger of imagination itself endows meanings to the most unlikely events; while observation and memory nourished Moore himself in this grim place, "no longer a city . . . a grave," many of the people he observed — and his friendship with Vachon, the photographer with a literary bent, encouraged him to observe — were taking extreme risks to invent new lives for themselves.

Shortly after I arrived in Warsaw, I was posted to Gdynia, a Polish Baltic port into which UNRRA was bringing grain, agricultural equipment, locomotives, industrial machinery, and other supplies to help rebuild

the economy. . . . In my first few days in Gdynia I visited Zapot, the
Baltic seaside resort. There, in the Grand Hotel, used formerly by the
Germans as an R and R station, I saw an intriguing mix of black mar-
keteers, most of them Hungarian, who gambled, wined, and wenched
as though this were Monte Carlo. When I asked one of them how long
he would be in Zapot, he held up a fat sheaf of banknotes and said, "I
am here for 100,000 zlotys." Within weeks, I, too, left Zapot and
Gdynia, recalled to Warsaw to work as a "statistical officer," a job for
which I was totally unqualified. Our UNRRA mission had an overall
chief, a Canadian brigadier-general named Charles Drury, and under
him three deputy chiefs, one American, one British and one Russian.
The Russian, Colonel Poulnikov, was in charge of transportation and so
I worked for him.

This experience made it possible for Moore to write the thrillers. Two of
them would have Polish characters and political preoccupations, but this
world of high-stakes risk-taking, of greed and desperate pleasure-seeking,
of visceral responses to fear, and of the absurdity of circumstances perme-
ates all of the thrillers. This political and bureaucratic world would eventually find expression in Moore's "Polish" novel of 1987, *The Colour of
Blood*.

But apart from accumulating such material, the young Moore was also
undergoing change. Speaking of the political sympathies of John Vachon
and himself, he explains how these experiences transformed them:

Like most of us at that time, his politics were left-wing and he did not
want to think that our allies, the Russians, were not the Soviet heroes we
imagined them to be. I, on the other hand, was receiving an unpleasant
education in *realpolitik*. Working with Polish government officials I discovered that Polish communists were almost always as antisemitic in
their views as the rest of their countrymen. I also discovered that to my
communist acquaintances I was something of a joke — a socialist — a
breed they distrusted more than they did the more reactionary members
of our mission.

The political disillusionment of Moore over this period prompted him,
in the end, to write his first journalistic pieces, two articles smuggled out
of Warsaw in the British diplomatic bag in November 1947 and published
in the Dublin *Sunday Independent*.

The two articles were scoops. One provides the background to the sudden disappearance from Poland of the leader of the political opposition, the head of the Polish Peasant Party, Mickolajczyk, and the other presents an interview with an official spokesman for Cardinal Hlond, the head of the Catholic Church, which had also come under severe attack from the newly consolidated Communist government. Not only the content of the pieces but the manner in which Moore had forwarded the articles evoke the atmosphere of menace and espionage in which he operated as a fledgling journalist. While he was sworn to neutrality as an UNRRA official, he had managed to get a press badge, and these first pieces are as much a political act as a journalistic assignment. Both reflect his shock at the ruthlessness of the Communist takeover, and there is surely a pivotal irony in the fact that he should be reporting in this style to an Irish newspaper when, ten years earlier, he had fought with his father over the reporting in the *Irish News* of the behaviour of "the Reds" during the Spanish Civil War.

"The disappearance from Poland of M. Stanislaw Mickolajczyk, leader of the Polish Peasant Party, is the last act in the liquidation of the Democratic Opposition by the Communist-led Warsaw Government," Moore opens his first article.

It also ends a two-year government campaign of sabotage and detraction aimed at destroying Mickolajczyk's popularity inside Poland. The success of this campaign may be judged by the fact that the departure of a leader, who, one year ago, could have had the support of seventy percent of the electorate in a free election, is viewed today by the average Pole with comparative indifference. I myself, having lived in Poland since January of 1946, have seen the methods used and can testify to their efficiency.

This article analyzes political developments in Poland since the pro-Soviet provisional government was created in opposition to the London-based government-in-exile led by Mickolajczyk, and since Mickolajczyk's return to Poland, which had been occupied by Soviet armies following the rout of the Germans in 1944. The second article focuses on the role of the Church at this time: "Many Poles feel that the Catholic Church has unwillingly been forced to assume the role of the Opposition in the struggle for the peoples' allegiance. . . . In this event Poland will become the European testing-ground in the Ideological war between Catholicism and Communism." Moore's observations were, of course, prophetic and mapped out the direction of Polish society for the next forty-five years until the collapse of the Communist regime. The urgent tone of his reporting reflects at once the sympathies of his mainly Catholic readers and his own close study of the ruthlessness of the Communists in their takeover of Poland. In 1950, in his second thriller, *The Executioners*, Moore drew on the circumstances of Mickolajczyk's disappearance.

While these two years in Poland revised Moore's political outlook, making him even more sceptical of leaders, ideologies, and the power of the media — which he observed misleading and brainwashing a whole population — and provided him with a deeply rooted existential sense that an individual life is defined and vindicated through moments of crisis, these years were also formative for another reason. Perhaps more influential and more lasting than this refining of political or philosophical stances was the *éducation sentimentale* he received in his first important sexual relationship.

In Warsaw, Moore fell in love with Margaret Swanson, a Canadian economist from Saskatoon, who was also working at UNRRA. While he has not said much about this relationship with a woman ten years older than himself, or of its duration, he does refer to travelling around Europe with a girl. He did spend three months, in late summer of 1947, after the UNRRA mission closed down, travelling to Scandinavia, but it appears that he also spent time in Paris with Margaret. In fact, this affair seems to have had far-reaching consequences in his life and in the treatment of sexual relationships in his novels. The aspects that seem to be most significant are that Margaret Swanson confidently took the sexual initiative and that she ended the affair against Moore's wishes.

Notes for a novel which appear to date from 1955 convey a sense of what may have happened. The protagonist of the novel is a middle-aged man with a wife and children who discovers in his desk a photograph of a girl taken perhaps ten years earlier in Warsaw. His mind circles back to his love affair with this girl. The protagonist, Moore's brief notes indicate, is to be imagined as naïve, puritanical, and inexperienced, while the woman, ten years older, is American. The biographical notes for the protagonist continue with details of Belfast birth and family background, including a father who is a doctor, which suggests that Moore is the prototype for this young man.

While other references suggest that he envisaged this novel as a satirical fiction of expatriates in Europe, the direction of the narrative and the significance he would wish it to reveal foreshadow many psychological elements in Moore's later characters. Here the abandonment of self to the love affair is, at first, an intensely passionate experience, but soon a power struggle surfaces and reveals elements of desperate dependence in "the weaker" party. The tone of bitterness, associated with rejection and self-hatred, will reappear later in the 1950s, in "Preliminary Pages for a Work of Revenge," but the outsider theme — the theme of defensive loneliness which will reappear in *Judith Hearne* — is here related to wartime experience. The timidity and indecisiveness of what is called the "WW mind" seems to be remarkably contiguous with the Catholic mind Moore inherited.

There are reasons for dwelling on this paradigm of the abandoned lover or spouse — almost always male and a dreamer, a would-be writer, a traveller, a failure. In almost all the thrillers and in the protagonists of the first four novels: Judith Hearne, Diarmuid Devine, Ginger Coffey, and Brendan Tierney, and in later characters such as Fergus Fadden and Jamie Mangan, the end of an affair or of a marriage is the central incident in the plot or the opening situation. Obviously, this situation is always a turning point and a new beginning, in fiction as in life, but the patterns of its recurrence in Moore's novels and its associated themes are remarkably consistent. Most obviously, the collapse of self-esteem is associated with an increase in self-knowledge and honesty and a fevered search for psychological and metaphysical certainty.

It is evident that Moore chose not to join Mailer or Hemingway or Waugh in writing about his wartime experiences in the European battle zones, and the reason is that, as his comments on Irish revolutionary politics indicate, he is not interested in stereotypical heroic scenarios or characters. He is interested in a different kind of moral courage:

> I believe in a real world because I was brought up in it. My experiences — being *dépaysé* and moving around — have made me aware of the awful realities most people face in life. . . . I just feel there is a lot of phony unreality to the novels written by people like Mailer. . . . Ordinary people: it's astonishing the reserves people have and how they make do with small things, inconsequential things. I feel that when ordinary people are forced to examine themselves and when they're lucky enough to have that moment of insight — of seeing themselves — it's astonishing how they manage to get up and go on. It's their endurance I admire, the guts that ordinary people have, the guts that the least likely people have.

His orientation as a writer of fiction was, then, away from the sensational events of military and political history, from "the great events of my generation," and towards what he called, after Joyce, the "celebration of the commonplace."

The end of the relationship with Margaret Swanson came late in 1947, about the time that Moore wrote his articles on the political situation in Poland. By Christmas, he was back in Belfast. The years of war and the years of wandering were over — or were about to begin again, for he had no job, no definite plans, no reason for being in one place rather than another. He was twenty-six years old, and after ten years of attempting to establish a sense of self beyond the terms of his parents' world, in some crucial ways, he was forced to recognize that he still had not left home.

That recognition became a preoccupation of the mature novelist for many decades: the complex overlapping of psychic states, of home and exile, of Ireland and Europe, of Europe and North America, would be explored in many novels of the 1960s and 1970s set outside Belfast, yet the 1950s are punctuated by efforts to write a novel that would confront this issue of the wanderer's return home. None of these novels was completed, but they are so close in many respects to Moore's own experience of the 1940s that they offer a useful mirror of his psyche at this time.

One of the protagonists, who is identified as "self" in Moore's notes, is Michael Russell. The uncompleted draft in which he first appears was probably written in 1954–55. Drafts and notes explore the prodigal's return, his discovery of family secrets, and his effort to help his sister leave with him. The tone is nervous and bitter. His years away have not freed him from the repression and guilt that he feels once he is back with his family. His anger is first directed at the subservient piety of his Catholic community, but soon it is directed at himself for his cowardice and caution. The monologue of Michael Russell sketches a set of psychological states and reactions with far-reaching echoes in many of the novels Moore would succeed in writing later.

Moore has spoken of how depressed he felt in Belfast on that visit home. He was in the limbo of the post-war years, his lack of formal educational qualifications or a real profession coming back to pass judgement on him. It is likely that Moore considered going to university as a mature student, as Michael Russell does. The fictional character decides not to become a student; like his creator, he becomes a wanderer again. The dilemma of the ex-Catholic expatriate, brought into intimate proximity once more with his family, serves to highlight the reasons why he left and the ties that remain and also to underline the situation of a generation of war-weary and alienated males. Moore was already beginning to discover his major preoccupations with identity and selfhood. Michael Russell vacillates, his feelings sharply responding to the paradoxes of exile, yet his fragile state foreshadows many fictions that Moore will write in his recurring efforts to grasp the psychological and metaphysical nature of selfhood.

Brian Moore did not stay long in Belfast. He seems to have known what he had to do. Michael Russell's departure for Canada was prompted by seeing an advertisement "Fly to Canada. Step Inside" posted in London. Moore's own decision was more deliberate. He has given two explanations for his choice of destination. Margaret Swanson had returned to Canada, and he wanted to meet her again; and when he was interviewed at Canada House in London, he was told that it would be easy for him to find work as a journalist. The optimistic visa clerk at the Canadian Embassy offered him an opportunity to believe that he could at last become the writer he wanted to be. During the war years, he had intermittently thought of himself as a writer, but he was now about to put himself to the test. He has said that when he arrived in Canada in 1948, he was ready to begin writing, he adds, "I had lived abroad long enough to know that now, if I went back to Ireland, I would be a spectator there too."

# 6

# SETTLING IN
# MONTREAL

Brian Moore flew to Toronto in February 1948 under a Canadian government scheme for assisted passage. "We were among the first post-war emigrants and the country wasn't really ready to handle us. So the men were marched off to the Salvation Army that first night and we spent the night in dormitory cots. I remember thinking it was the end of the road for me. Or the beginning, I mean, if I were going to become a writer." At the labour exchange the next day, it was decided that Moore should be sent to the construction site of a dam in Thessalon, in northern Ontario, to "write up tallies on earthmovers and caterpillar tractors and dump trucks." He stayed six months, as the long winter turned into a brief spring and summer, and it was in the bunkhouse there "in the wilds" that he committed himself in earnest to becoming a writer.

"When I came to Canada," he recalled later, "and spent my first winter, I was impressed by the magnificence of this country, the extraordinary emptiness of it, and frightening scenery you don't get in Ireland, . . . everything that is human is dwarfed here. The minute that you go out into the wilderness, you could be lost two minutes later. The forests, the scale of things really impressed me."

Those first reactions to the wintry Canadian landscape are echoed in later responses to other bleak landscapes, yet the shock of his arrival, exiled from Ireland and from Europe, left a sense of spiritual and cultural desolation reflected in the experience of many of Moore's protagonists. The disorienting doubt, the sense of lost purpose and identity, and the impotence explored in *Black Robe* — Moore's novel of the Canadian wilderness — are touched on earlier in other novels, among them *Judith Hearne, I Am Mary Dunne, Catholics,* and in *The Mangan Inheritance*, whose protagonist reflects: "Canada: cruel landscape, its settlement a defiance of Nature. Home." The loneliness and abandonment Moore felt in that penitential place in northern Ontario became a spur for the extraordinary energy and determination that mark the next decade of his life.

Before the winter freeze-up returned, Moore set off to make a new life for himself in Toronto. He spent three months in the city, living on a tight budget, trying in vain to find work at a newspaper and "going mad." It may have been at this time that he tried and failed to have Margaret Swanson meet him. Finally, in February 1949, he turned his sights towards Montreal, the Gallic city of North America, intending that it would be his last stopping point on this North American adventure. He was, as he said, "at his lowest ebb."

Ten years later, in an article for *Holiday* magazine, Moore tells a story of how he found himself "falling in love" with Montreal on the afternoon of his arrival. Before finding passage on a ship bound for Europe, he and an acquaintance decided to explore the bars and erotic shows for which this city of forbidden pleasures had become celebrated during the years of prohibition.

The most famous performer was Lily St. Cyr, and they went to see her at the Gayety Theatre:

A baby spot felt its way around the curtains and, to the gut-bucket chuckle of "Sugar Blues," the first stripper strutted onstage with a gait as mannered as a Lippizaner riding horse. "*Baptême!*" yelled the man beside me in hearty, un-Anglo-Saxon approval. "*Tabernacle!*" roared a man down front. There was an explosion of laughter and I pulled at Arthur's sleeve. "Do you realize," I whispered, "they still swear liturgically here?"

When we came out of the theatre, the snowbanks were still filthy, the gruel on the streets more watery than ever. The neon lights of the Boulevard Saint Laurent stretched before us, a midway in midafternoon. In a restaurant named *Le Roi des Frites*, we sat down to french fries and an excellent meat pie called *tourtière*. Above us a sign read *Chiens Chauds* — Hot Dogs. I was falling in love.

This cultural mélange of the American and the Parisian in a wintry setting — which Moore's later alter ego, Ginger Coffey, would say conformed to his impressions of Moscow — apparently seduced him. But this magazine report of his love affair was written for armchair tourists, and these first impressions are contrived by the seasoned eye of the much-travelled writer.

There is another story of how the traveller came to settle in Montreal. Having failed to find a job in Toronto, Moore managed to have a family friend set up an interview for him at the *Gazette*, the city's second English-language morning newspaper. The new career as journalist, which he had associated from the beginning with emigration to Canada, actually came to be because of that last-chance interview. His luck turned. He was hired, as Ginger Coffey would be in the novel which reflects these experiences, for the lowly position of proofreader. Moore has pointed out that his first paycheque was for $30, one-third of the earnings of the unionized compositors. The autocratic managing editor, Harry Larkin — McGregor in *The Luck of Ginger Coffey* — quickly recognized Moore's talent, and he was given the opportunity to become a reporter. His first stories with his own byline appeared in April 1949, and he quickly established himself as a versatile journalist.

The *Gazette* was one of three English-language dailies and had been in existence since 1785. In spite of its longevity, it was overshadowed in prestige by the *Montreal Star*, while a lunchtime newspaper, the *Tribune*, occupied the tabloid slot. There was also a weekly newspaper, the *Montreal Standard*, in addition to several French-language dailies and magazines. Print journalism was still the primary medium of information, for television would not come to Canada until 1952, and Montreal, with a population of a million and a half was the country's largest and most cosmopolitan city. It was a lively centre of journalists and writers, and Moore quickly found his place there.

Bilingual and bicultural, Montreal was certainly a place of dramatic contrasts. A very successful novel by Canadian writer Hugh MacLennan, published in the year of Moore's arrival in Canada, had characterized the relationship between Montreal's French majority and English minority as "two solitudes," yet from the mid-nineteenth century, this English-French distinction had been eroded by the arrival of immigrant populations, beginning with the Irish, followed by Jews from eastern Europe.

The Montreal of many pleasures that Moore evoked in his article for *Holiday* was a stereotypical picture that many North Americans would recognize. Since prohibition in the 1920s, it was known as a city of sin, where brothels, bars, and gambling dens rarely closed, and there was a thriving jazz and dance-music scene. While the Catholic Church and its many lay organizations made frequent efforts to have these twilight businesses curtailed, there was widespread corruption among the city politicians and the police. In fact, there was a tightly organized criminal network which collected protection money, and there were close connections between the New York and Montreal underworlds. Soon after Moore's arrival, he would witness the public unveiling of this seedy underside of the city in hearings of a commission of enquiry into organized crime. This Pigalle of North America would provide him with a ready-made setting for his first two thrillers.

Moore's earliest contributions to the *Gazette*, in April 1949, show that he had a fascinated and oblique angle of vision on the world in which he had landed. His first piece, for instance, on a visit to a baseball game, uses an extended, playful comparison of this North American game, of which he pretends to know nothing, with bull-fighting in Spain. This *faux naïf* double perspective of Europe and North America illustrates his talent for the precise observation of significant local colour from the perspective of an outsider.

These early pieces already reflect a literary talent and stand out for the deft shorthand of telling details. The scene and the story are often shaped with rhetorical flourishes of repetition and dramatization. His training in the five Ws of the professional reporter — Who, What, When, Where, and Why — developed and reinforced a dramatic talent for identifying the unique voice and the moment of crisis. As a reporter, Moore worked on the city desk, and a colleague has provided a sketch of his routine: "He was enterprising, accurate, and — above all — fast. He'd come into the office from an assignment at high speed and seemed to start typing while still in the process of sitting down at his desk. He'd have his story finished while the rest of us were still staring blankly at that old Underwood, and adding more sugar to our coffee. Needless to say we all hated him for the spectacular nature of his performance."

Moore seems to have found congenial reporting assignments, which he has said gave him "a crash course on North American life." Yet the divided city of Montreal also reminded him of Belfast. "In the 50s, Montreal was repressive. The French were looked down upon, and the English wanted no contact with them. There was a colonial feeling to it." Moore's youthful socialism survived in his refusal to adopt a superior "British" attitude, and at a time when English-Canadian publications devoted much admiring reportage to the British royal family and visiting aristocrats, he penned sly articles that did not conceal his antipathy. He also discovered the conservative politics of the newspaper when his report of a speech by F. R. Scott, McGill University law professor, poet and founder of Canada's first socialist party, the CCF, was censored; he later told Scott: "You won't get your name in the *Gazette* unless you rape a girl on the corner of Peel and St. Catherine." If the autocratic nature of the managing editor or the trivial and conservative orientation of the paper's content irritated him, he accepted these conditions because he was conscious that he was receiving a professional training.

For a period, he covered the shipping beat, which often entailed going a day downriver from Montreal to await incoming passenger liners from Europe. "I am passing a reposing day at the Hotel Château Blanc," he wrote in spring 1951 to a former colleague, freelancing in Europe. . . waiting for the cutter *Citadelle* to take me out to the *Empress of France* when she arrives from Europe tomorrow morning at 7 A.M. to open the passenger season on the St. Lawrence. Aboard is Prince Sayn-Wittgenstein, cousin of the Czar of all the Russians, who will be interviewed by *L'Evénement Journal, Le Soleil,* and *La Gazette.* The Prince has no money and is going to be an immigrant. Wonderful country, Canada. Why don't you come back to where you came from?

He has confirmed that these trips up and down the St. Lawrence stayed with him until he was able to draw on them during the writing of *Black Robe.* But if the seventeenth-century missionary of that novel feels disoriented and alone on his river voyage, Moore's reports of this time reflect his lively mind playing over his mundane material; the challenge offered him was accepted with enthusiasm. Unlike the recent immigrant, Ginger Coffey, who throughout his life had waited for "his ship to come in," Moore followed the advice of Vera Coffey: "You have to make your own miracles."

The three years he would remain at the *Gazette* gave him material for fiction, as well as the training in techniques of scene setting and narrative; most importantly, it gave him the habit of writing every day. "The discipline of newspaper work and of writing for a definite market has been invaluable to me and I imagine it would be the same for any writer," he said in an interview in 1955. His quick promotions to rewrite man and writer of features indicate that his talents were recognized and valued, and his ability to write quickly and with flair was as remarkable as the speed with which he settled in the city.

Soon after Moore began to work at the *Gazette,* he met William Weintraub, a Montrealer of Jewish background with literary interests. This talented reporter became one of Moore's life-long friends. He was five years younger than Moore, but since he had worked part-time at the *Gazette* during his student days at McGill, he had been moving in journalistic circles for a few years already. In 1950, he was dismissed by the notorious managing editor, Harry Larkin, and left Montreal to spend two years in Europe.

Before he left, William Weintraub introduced Moore to Jacqueline Sirois, a staff writer at the *Montreal Standard.* She had been born Jacqueline Scully in 1921, the daughter of a doctor whose Irish ancestors had emigrated to Montreal generations earlier and of a French-speaking mother. While her parents straddled the linguistic divide of Montreal, a marriage between Irish Catholics and *Québécois* Catholics was not unusual. What was unusual was that her father had a medical practice that included many patients from the "Anglo" establishment and that he moved in Montreal high society. Frank J. Scully, the antithesis of Moore's own father, catered to the needs of the rich. He was known as the doctor who would discreetly take care of sexually transmitted diseases or unwanted pregnancies. He was heavily dependent on alcohol, and at the time Moore met Jackie, he was living at the Ritz-Carlton, Montreal's classiest hotel.

Jackie's parents had separated and divorced during her childhood, and she and her brother, William, were raised by their mother. Camille Scully had little money to spare, but she later married Arnold Wainwright, a member of one of Montreal's elite families. Jackie was sent to finishing school outside New York City, and, at the age of eighteen, she was a debutante.

Jackie was a strong-willed, talented, and personable woman who, at an early age, recognized that she would have to find her own way out of her precarious family situation. Her first way out was to marry, which she did, in the fashion of her class and time, at eighteen. Her husband was Bernard Sirois, who, like her father, was an alcoholic. Life with the abusive Sirois was not a way out, and the couple separated, but journalism was, and her ambition and energy had combined with self-discipline to make her a successful journalist before she met Moore.

It is evident that both of them were ready for a new beginning in 1949. If he represented to her a much-travelled European with a quick wit and curiosity, she may have represented the free-wheeling Montreal he fell in love with and was eager to establish himself in. Jackie possessed a North American savvy and had deep roots in Moore's adopted country. These two hard-working, self-reliant writers were drawn together because both had had to improvise their own way out of difficult family situations.

Moore and Jackie were active participants in a lively journalistic scene through the next few years. They were known as party-givers and party-goers. Possessing his mother's "wicked tongue," Moore seems to have enjoyed mimicry and role-playing — dramatic talents he believes are part of the basic equipment of many good novelists. Moore earned an ambivalent reputation for his sharp and unrestrained commentary on colleagues and acquaintances. His wit and energy were appreciated widely, but his independence of spirit and iconoclasm were sometimes abrasive.

Soon after Moore settled in Montreal, the campaign to rid the city of corruption succeeded in having a judicial enquiry established. In September 1950, this commission began to hear testimony from hundreds of people active in underworld businesses. Many of the underworld figures were known in journalistic circles, and reporters were themselves called as witnesses. On one occasion, Jackie was called to testify, and when she refused to divulge her sources, she was sentenced to jail for contempt. The lurid personal testimonies of coercion and exploitation in this twilight world provided a would-be writer of crime novels with all the ambience and colour he could wish for. In October 1950, Moore signed a contract with Harlequin in Toronto for two crime novels, which were published the following year.

Yet for all its risqué reputation, 1950s Montreal was not unlike Belfast. The province of Quebec outside of Montreal was uniformly conservative and Catholic, and the power of the Church was felt in the metropolis, too, especially through the schools and the press. At this time, the provincial government had been run for almost two decades by the reactionary and corrupt Maurice Duplessis, who made obeisance to the Catholic Church and to Anglo-Scots and American business interests. His supporters bribed newspaper reporters routinely, as Moore discovered, and coercion at election time ensured that Duplessis was returned to office.

During the war, many establishment figures in Quebec had shown sympathy for the Vichy regime, and as soon as the war ended, they were prepared to provide a refuge for collaborators. In Moore's early days in Montreal, a public furore raged regarding the fate of a collaborator who had been unmasked. In late 1946, the Count de Bernonville had entered Canada disguised as a priest and using a false name. In 1948, his true identity became public: he had been a member of the Nazi Waffen SS and of the Milice, its Vichy equivalent, which had tortured and murdered members of the Resistance. The government of Canada ordered him deported to France, but the mayor of Montreal, together with many influential public figures, opposed this, and there were legal challenges and petitions. The public was active also, and there were marches and street demonstrations, with English-speaking and Jewish Montrealers supporting the government side. In the end, in August 1951, de Bernonville left Quebec and joined some of his former colleagues in Bolivia, where he lived, undisturbed, for decades.

This case resembled debates about collaboration and resistance that Moore had witnessed in Paris in the winter of 1944–45, when the first trials of collaborators were held. It would be forty years before the cases of collaborators who had evaded the police and had lived in hiding in religious houses in Provence came to public attention in France. Moore's novel of 1995, *The Statement*, based on one such case, examines the mentality of those who protected the *miliciens*. It is evident that embedded in his memory was not only the outlook of his own father in the late 1930s, but of Montreal and Quebec when such a case had been the talk of the town.

Brian and Jackie married on 28 February 1951, exactly two years after his arrival in Montreal. Their honeymoon took them on an ocean liner to Europe, his first visit back since emigrating to Canada and Jackie's first transatlantic voyage. Paris was their destination. There they met up with William Weintraub, who had been living "precariously" as a freelancer in Italy. Paris had also become the base of Mavis Gallant, a former colleague of Jackie on the *Montreal Standard,* whose first short stories had been accepted by the *New Yorker.* Mordecai Richler — who had dropped out of university in Montreal the previous year — stayed in Paris before moving south to Spain, where his first novel would be written. Gallant introduced Richler to Weintraub who, in turn, introduced him to the Moores. Richler would return to Montreal for a year in 1952, and he and Brian became close friends, a friendship that was maintained by regular correspondence for two decades. In 1951, Paris was the post-war city Moore had known, still the literary centre, still a magnet for North Americans with literary ambitions, but Moore seems to have had no desire to join them, and one of his thrillers includes a satirical treatment of this expatriate crowd.

After their marriage, the Moores settled into a more domestic routine. In the early 1950s a core group of friends formed — Brian and Jackie Moore, Bruce and Dorothy Ruddick, Alex and Gloria Cherney, Philip and Margaret Surrey, and Bill Weintraub — and this group remained together for the most part throughout the decade. Most of these couples began to have children in the early fifties, and this contributed to their cohesiveness. Brian's younger brother Seán was also in Montreal. After completing his medical studies in Belfast, he arrived in late 1951 and became a resident in pathology at McGill University. Seán lived with Brian and Jackie during his years as a student, and from this point on, the two brothers — who had not until now known each other as adults — remained in close contact.

The circle that formed at this time repeats some features of the circle Moore had entered in Belfast during his time in the ARP: these friends were largely independent-minded, Jewish, and cosmopolitan, and even though they were not drawn together by common membership of a political party or theatre group, they were mostly left wing and had a liking for self-dramatization. Weintraub, Cherney, Ruddick, and Richler were children of eastern European immigrants; some were of Jewish working-class background, while Alex Cherney's parents were intellectuals from Czarist Russia, and Moore enjoyed the company of these older émigrés. Other outsiders included the Americans Dorothy Ruddick, from New York, and Gloria Cherney, from California. One of Moore's thrillers, *This Gun for Gloria,* borrowed his friend's name.

Brian and Jackie's larger social circle was formed of colleagues from *Weekend* magazine. On Weintraub's return from Europe, he worked there as an editor, before moving on in the later 1950s to write scripts and to produce films for the National Film Board, and Philip Surrey was the graphics editor. Surrey, a decade older than the others, was also a successful painter. Moore himself eventually worked in the visual media of film and television, and the fact that so many of his friends, beginning with John Vachon in Warsaw, were connected with the world of visual images is striking. Moore acted as a photographer for *Weekend* on a few occasions, and it is tempting to see here a connection with his father's pastime as photographer. Recollection of the protagonist's father as a photographic image appears in more then one of Moore's novels.

Dorothy Ruddick remembers Moore having encouraged her in the mid-fifties to commit herself to a career as a painter. She also remembers that other painter friends had a costume party which guests were invited to attend as their favourite painting; Moore attended as Toulouse-Lautrec's "Oscar Wilde." The Ruddicks also had a costume party to which they invited people to "come as your favourite dream," and on this occasion, Moore attended dressed as Napoleon.

The inspiration for the Ruddicks' theme was that Bruce Ruddick was a psychoanalyst. In his McGill days, he had been actively associated with the avant-garde literary magazine *Preview*, founded in 1942. He has been described as "a wonderfully rambunctious, outspoken, humorous, larger than life character" and, apparently, an intellectually provocative companion. Freudian ideas were still novel in Montreal in the 1950s, and a source of considerable comic relief at parties, an interest that Ruddick promoted with outrageous Freudian interpretations.

Moore's antipathy to the Freudian notion of creativity as regression to childhood fantasy, and to "the whole damn priesthood" of the psychoanalytic movement, is made clear in comic scenes in *An Answer from Limbo*, and in Mary Dunne's imagined encounter with Freud in Central Park, yet it is also clear that he absorbed some of this approach to understanding character. Fantasy, dream, the relativity of mental states and the condition of breakdown are preoccupations in Moore's novels; while he insists that the intellectual and social ethos of analysis is little more than a passing cultural phenomenon, his own experience of anxiety, stress, and "failure" surely underlies the psychological intensity of his fictional portraits.

In addition to Ruddick, he was also friendly for some of these years with Alistair McLeod, another psychiatrist and psychoanalyst, whose help he sought in coping with his ulcers. The novelist and the doctor's son was certainly interested in ideas that might explain his family's propensity for ulcers — both his father and Seán also suffered from them. According to the common understanding of the time, ulcers were psychosomatic in origin. In addition to gaining an understanding of his own condition, and freedom from pain, the novelist was surely interested in the mysterious interdependence of mental and bodily states. Psychoanalysis affirmed that the wellsprings of behaviour lay embedded in the individual unconscious, and although Moore did not interest himself in theoretical or clinical reading, the general concept encouraged a notion of the autonomy and primacy of the self.

In this circle, dinner parties at each others' houses became known for their heavy drinking and animated talk. Apart from disguise and fancy dress, they favoured role-playing games. They were people-watchers and gossips, determined to focus their curiosity and excitement about the variety of human character in more intimate settings and through provocative social rituals.

In 1951, when the *Standard* became the *Weekend Picture Magazine*, Moore began to contribute stories to it, in addition to his work at the *Gazette*. Eventually, in 1952, he decided to leave the newspaper and become a freelance writer, and husband and wife became regular contributors to *Weekend*, Brian as a contributor of pulp fiction and occasional features, Jackie as a staff writer. The decision to resign from the *Gazette* was intended to provide more time for writing a literary novel, and Moore has explained that this was only possible because Jackie continued to work. Her salary was complemented by his income from *Weekend* and by his earnings from the thrillers and pulp stories his agent in New York, Willis Kingsley Wing, had begun to place internationally. In 1955, he reported that he had sold stories to "*The American Magazine, Bluebook, Lilliput* (London), *Everybody's* (London), *Northern Review* (Canada), *The Montrealer, Mayfair*, etc. I have also had my short stories reprinted in Swedish, Danish and Belgian magazines and one was reprinted in Braille."

Moore's work diaries from the mid fifties reveal that Brian and Jackie had become an efficient and professional team. Jackie was typist, proofreader, and advisor for his commercial work, even as she continued her own taxing career. It is evident that she entered wholeheartedly into the development of his writing talent, and that they shared a comfortable domestic partnership.

The birth of Michael Brian on 24 November 1953 does not seem to have disturbed this pattern of intense productivity, made possible, in part, by the help of a domestic servant. From Michael's earliest years, there are signs that Moore took his role as a father seriously, yet it is also clear that Moore's work schedule could not be interrupted. At the time of Mordecai Richler's marriage in London in 1954, he wrote, "When will we swap photos as fathers. Little fellers are great." Michael was, however, to remain an only child.

Moore's fiction rarely discusses children or parenthood other than his memories of his own childhood in Belfast, yet it seems from his repeated efforts to write a novel about the Russell/Kelleher family during the 1950s that Moore was beginning to reflect not only on his own experience but on the dynamics of the family itself. What he calls "the grammar of emotions," which is embedded in the child during its first years, assumed a central importance for his psychic economy; as many critics of Moore's novels have observed, that primal "grammar" seems to be pitted against other later grammars, formed by experience outside the family, and commands an allegiance which even marriage cannot displace.

Moore's extraordinary success in his early years in Montreal might not have happened if he had not fallen in love with Jackie and with her city. Even though he and Jackie would eventually leave the city, Montreal does have a special place in his imagination, second only to Belfast: "This is, in fact, the only place where I had a real job and lived in the real world. It was an important formative period of my life. I married here, I had my one and only child here, and I made life-long friends here." Montreal is where, at last, Moore would know with confidence that he had made a success of his life.

A glimpse of his new self-confidence may be found in a *Weekend* article of May 1953 on the "New Canadians," the more than eight hundred thousand emigrants who had come to Canada since the end of the war: "Immigrants are people who risk the unknown to find improvement. Their critical spirit, their desire for freedom, their ability to live with other peoples of different races are the things which have helped to make Canada a great and growing country." These words were written the month he began to write *Judith Hearne*. In November 1953, shortly before his son's birth, Brian Moore became a Canadian citizen.

# 7

# FORMULAS AND FANTASIES

In 1955, Moore explained that he raised the money to live on while writing his first "real" novel, *Judith Hearne*, by writing six "pocket books" — thrillers published in cheap format paperbacks — "which have sold nearly 800,000 copies." Pleased with his accomplishment, he seems to reveal, nevertheless, a tender conscience in his comment on writing for this market: "This is not because I'm particularly ashamed of commercial work. You make me pontificate in public about artistic integrity and that guff and I'll break your neck." He adds that "Canada is a good place to get a start. In Europe you starve to death doing literary reviews and so on while working on a book. Here there is a mass of commercial work that you can live from while the big one is in gestation."

*Judith Hearne*, Moore's first literary novel, was such a critical success that it became for him the opening of the canon by which he wished to be known. The years of apprenticeship in the craft of writing "page-turners" he wished to dismiss, for in truth many of the lessons he learned were of little use to him in the painful round of false beginnings and rejected drafts that characterized his searching for his subject and his style in the novels after *Judith Hearne*. Unlike the pot-boilers, written to an editor's formula, with which he began, each literary novel was a new experiment in blending genres and styles. Gradually and consciously, however, from 1980, the novel of suspense became a fictional vehicle for serious literary purposes, and so, in a curious way, his work returned to many of the narrative formulas of the earliest fiction.

Moore has repudiated those novels of the 1950s — two of them actually published and later reprinted in new editions under his own name and five others under pseudonyms. "The best-seller is the day-dream which leads us into a happy fantasy and, rather like the books we read when we were boys, books of adventure, we know we're never going to be let down. . . . Books which lead people to re-evaluate their position intellectually are not popular." This distinction he affirmed at many points in his career, and yet he has also said: "The novel tells a story. . . . The story is fiction. It can never be true, but to succeed as art it must inspire belief." Moore's insistence on the purely commercial nature of the pulp stories he wrote for magazines and of the thrillers disguises the ways in which his talent developed through this work and the way his own earlier experience was transformed for fictional purposes.

The novelist's reluctant recollections of this part of his career are usually misleading both in the chronology and in the accomplishment.

When I wrote those stories in Montreal, I had quit my job on the newspaper deciding that I would live as a writer. One of the reasons I decided that was I had already sold a pulp story, and I said, 'Good God, I must be intelligent enough to write a pulp story in a week out of every month and live on the proceeds,' because they paid, I think about three hundred dollars. And I did it for a little while but it became too difficult, and I was never successful trying to write for the pulps. And so it's interesting, I think, that you can only write them if you believe the message. I was always trying to write these things as a pastiche or with my tongue in my cheek, and I was always terribly pleased that an immigrant boy could pass himself off as an American writer. But it didn't really work. . . . These mystery novels were exactly the same thing. My idea of writing mystery novels was this: I was told they would pay in advance, and I thought that way I could go on writing *Judith Hearne*. I did all these things to finance *Judith Hearne*.

The novelist's memory may be misleading him when he says he was not able to write thrillers with ease or that they had little success; in fact the opposite is true. The first two, *Wreath for a Redhead* and *The Executioners*, written for Harlequin, a Canadian house now internationally known as publishers of romance fiction, appeared a few months apart in 1951, before he left his job at the *Gazette* or began to write magazine stories. These novels were reprinted by a large New York-based company two years later, and his agent appears to have had little difficulty selling his work to two of the major series of the time. Although he did not join the ranks of Dashiell Hammett and Raymond Chandler, Moore did have considerable success. *Intent to Kill* was reviewed in the *New York Times*, and for a time there were plans to make a film of it. He has mentioned that he read some of the classics of American "hard-boiled" fiction to understand the formula and clearly drew on Hemingway's *To Have and Have Not*. In fact, though, it is more likely that Moore's long-standing interest in Graham

Greene had included a reading of "entertainments" such as *A Gun for Sale* and that the appreciation of Greene, and of his master Joseph Conrad, lies behind Moore's first, more spontaneous efforts.

It might also be that at the back of his mind Moore had memories of reading his father's favourite fiction, something that had provoked his adolescent condescension. At first he had been an avid reader of his father's books, but as he developed literary ambitions and became aware of Joyce, he had grown away from his father's taste in fiction. He had come to think of best-sellers as a measure of his father's imaginative and intellectual obtuseness. Speaking of this "hack writing," he recalls his father: "I hated detective stories — my father read them all the time. . . . But all writing teaches you something. They taught me the genesis of the thriller, which I've used years later." It is hardly without significance that Moore's first fictions should be written for a male audience and that *The Executioners* is heavily indebted to the political circumstances in Poland he had already written about for the Dublin newspaper. Just as he will recreate his mother's world in his first serious novel, *Judith Hearne* — a novel which reached a large and appreciative audience of women — Moore's first fictions may recreate, in an indirect way, the inner world of his father's fantasies.

Moore's first two thrillers, contracted in October 1950, were written for a Canadian audience. Both are set in Montreal and have Canadian protagonists. A later thriller also had a Montreal setting, so it is evident that Moore felt comfortable recreating the atmosphere of his new city long before he wrote *The Luck of Ginger Coffey*, his first literary novel to be set in Montreal.

In *Wreath for a Redhead*, written at the end of 1950, John Riordan — a young drifter with an Irish name — tells the story in the first person. He introduces himself as a sailor on leave who is heading to Montreal when he meets a mysterious and sexually alluring woman on the train. Riordan becomes fascinated by "the redhead," but his sexual adventure quickly turns into a murder mystery when she disappears from their hotel, is later revealed to have been murdered, and he is identified as the suspect. The plot becomes one of the hunter turning into the hunted. The tense chase involves intrigue and false leads, concealment and assumed identities, and along the way the reader discovers that "the redhead" is the collection agent for an extortion ring. The many characters Riordan had contacted in his search for her, based on a list he conveniently found in her notebook, turn out to be her blackmail victims, all having something in their past they want to keep hidden.

One of these is Simone Fortier, a young law student of mixed Irish and

French-Canadian background. At the end, the intrigue unravelled, the chase over, Riordan marries Simone. According to the formula and the fantasy, in the concluding passage of the novel the lonely drifter decides to settle for a more stable life with a woman he respects. The sexual subplot in *Wreath for a Redhead* reveals the transformation of the male adventurer at the end of his bachelor life. Riordan's anxious masculinity and self-consciousness are transformed into an acceptance of self and of a relationship based on equality of regard.

*The Executioners* follows the classic formula of a gang of hired guns hunting down a venerable elder statesman, a formula that Moore used again in *Intent to Kill*. Here, Mike Farrell is hired as a bodyguard by those close to the "old man," an exile from an Eastern Bloc country who is hiding out in Montreal. The gang is in the employ of the ruthless leader of the Soviet Secret Police and his British collaborator, and its goal is to stake out the house until the statesman is joined by the leader of the underground resistance to the Communist regime, which has gained control after the war. Farrell is unaware of the various forces that are converging on Montreal and is soon caught up in a fast-paced and bloody sequence of events, which includes the kidnapping of the stateman's niece. Farrell becomes instrumental in helping the "old man" to escape by air to an unknown new hideout in Europe, while the niece, in a very unlikely closing scene, becomes Farrell's wife.

Like most of Moore's thrillers, *The Executioners* is a first-person narrative. Its opening lines are designed to draw the reader into the protagonist's "hard-boiled" world, but they also refer to his being at the mercy of ulcers and curiosity, aspects of Moore that have an eerie, prophetic ring for the years ahead. Moore was to have near-fatal crises with bleeding ulcers, and friends from this period of his life speak of his remarkable curiosity as the quality that made him an effective reporter and an inventive novelist. In chapter two, he raises these issues again: Farrell wonders why he is a victim of an irrational drive that runs counter to his practical and masculine self.

Although Farrell has limited historical and political perspectives, his experience of the war and the subsequent turmoil in Europe provides an atmospheric setting for the aimless life of the typical male loner, for masculine adventure which is a test of resilience and physical courage. Yet if those clichéd elements of the genre are novel because they are set within the careful detailing of contemporary Montreal, the most remarkable aspect of this fiction is the extent to which Moore uses his knowledge of post-war Polish politics to create a Cold War thriller. In doing so, he links his two most recent "emotional territories," Montreal and Warsaw.

The characterization of the statesman follows very closely that of Stanislaw Mickolajczyk, whose disappearance from Warsaw in late 1947 Moore had already reported on for the Dublin *Sunday Independent*. The threatened political leader is simply a hinge for the formulaic plotting, yet Moore cannot resist making him a more complex character, and in doing so, he foreshadows the political parables he will write decades later, in particular *The Colour of Blood* and *No Other Life*. Moore has already discovered the figure of the patriarchal liberal trapped between political extremes, a type who will reappear under many guises.

In this novel, the young male protagonist with the Irish name is the fantasy hero who manages to cut through the tightening nets of political commitments and espionage. The "fairy-tale" dimension of the thriller formula allows for the ritual test and for a clear triumph. While the novel opens with a chapter set in a lurid sex club, there is no sex in the novel, and the boy-hero wins the hand of the Polish exile. Her character is under-developed; she is simply the damsel in distress who is rescued by the courageous hero, while her uncle disappears into the European labyrinth for another round of intrigue and danger with high ideals and political stakes.

It is the contributions of pulp fiction to *Weekend* that Moore referred to when he later spoke of being able to earn enough in a week's work to support him for a month. This magazine was a highly successful journalistic enterprise, eventually carried by forty-one newspapers across Canada, with a circulation of over two million. For three years he wrote either a feature article or a story roughly on a monthly basis, and this became a more regular routine after he left the *Gazette* in 1952. His first story, a romance with a Canadian husband and wife on holiday in Stockholm, is entitled "You Never Give Me Flowers." The author is introduced as "a Belfast-born newspaperman whose travels have taken him to 17 countries." Moore could earn $250 for these formulaic contributions, which he could sometimes complete in a day.

As in the case of the first two thrillers, Moore's writing to formula for a wider audience than the readership of the *Gazette* surely enhanced his sense of himself as a professional writer with a national audience. That audience expanded to become international in 1953 when Phoenix Publishers in New York republished the two thrillers, *Wreath for a Redhead* appearing with the new title *Sailor's Leave*. Willis Kingsley Wing also succeeded in reselling some pulp stories in other countries. Moore was also trying to place his literary stories with American magazines such as the *New Yorker* and *Atlantic Monthly*, although without success.

Moore's friendship with Mordecai Richler begun in 1952–53, when Richler was back in Montreal, became close after he moved to London in 1953, and was cemented by an almost weekly correspondence, especially in the first decade of Richler's residence in England. They also met in London after Moore's success with *Judith Hearne* in 1955 allowed him to make almost annual visits. Richler remembers the Moore of those times as a "great raconteur" and "a loyal and entertaining companion." An early letter to Richler gives him advice on how to write a pot-boiler. Moore encloses a detailed chapter-by-chapter outline adapted from *Wreath for a Redhead* for a thriller that Richler proposes to set in Germany. Paragraphs must be short, Moore advises, and chapters no more than ten pages. "Imitate Hemmy [the Hemingway of *To Have and Have Not*] with more sock and bash!" He indicates to Richler how to adapt the setting and maintain the essential elements of the narrative formula.

It is not clear if "Mort" actually used Moore's summary for a thriller, but a later letter from Moore returns to the theme of being a professional writer: "It just seems to me we're in a losing battle. Anyway, I'm glad to be in it. But once and for all I've given up the idea that anyone can make even the ghost of a living by serious writing. The Hemingways are only the exception, not because they are good, but because as 'personalities' — that great modern word — they catch the public fancy. I need some encouragement at this time." This letter was written after *Judith Hearne* was published, but it is representative of many in which the two aspiring novelists articulate their struggle to find ways to preserve their creative talent for writing fiction and at the same time be efficient commercial writers.

In all these ways, Moore's professional confidence was growing and the time was drawing near to begin the literary novel that had been his goal since his arrival in Canada. His plan was to have saved enough money from commercial work to be able to concentrate exclusively on the novel for a few months. Alex Cherney's parents loaned him their summer cottage on Fourteen Island Lake in the Laurentian Mountains north of Montreal, and so in May 1953 Moore retreated from the city to work alone. The Moores did not own a car, nor did they drive, and he was on his own except when Bill Weintraub drove up with Jackie on the weekends.

After five years in Canada, Moore was putting into effect the vow he had made in the isolation of his first winter in northern Ontario. In those five years, he had gone from his "lowest ebb" to a position of considerable professional success, but now, having feared for many years the standards set by Joyce and other literary mentors, he was putting himself to a very lonely and risky test. Did he have the talent to create a work of literature? Later, in *An Answer from Limbo*, the key personal quality for becoming a successful novelist is said to be "ruthlessness, sheer goddamn ruthlessness." Moore withdrew from the companionship of friends and from the domestic security of his new home, leaving behind his newly pregnant wife. It was in these circumstances in the Laurentian cottage that he made the discovery he has recognized as the foundation of his writing career: "In that first novel I discovered a subject which was, over the years, to become central to my writing. It is loneliness. It is, in particular, that desperation which invades the person who discovers his life has no meaning."

It was at this point, when he had been writing for about two months, that the urgency of his theme and, indeed, of his own decision to commit himself to the novel, was affirmed in an unexpected way. Swimming in the lake in mid-July, "I was hit by a motor-boat on the head and I had six skull fractures. I was taken to the Montreal Neurological Institute, and I was in great danger of death. I was also in great danger of losing my powers of speech. I couldn't write, I couldn't do anything." Luckily, he did not lose consciousness and fall into a coma, and he was fortunate also to receive advanced medical care at this research hospital. Never at a loss for accumulating fictional material, he would later use the setting of the hospital for the thriller *Intent to Kill*.

Recovery took about six weeks, and he did regain his verbal faculties. He was able to resume writing, but the experience left a profound mark. He "grew up," he says, as if his earlier exposure to death and destruction in wartime had not touched him. "I said, I don't have an eternal ticket. Life isn't going to go on forever; I could be struck down at any moment. And so I think that crisis made me focus on the fact that I just didn't want to write a lot of journalism, or make a lot of money, or write films or whatever. It made clear to me what I really wanted to do, which is to write novels." The accident and his almost miraculous recovery in the middle of writing a novel about the loss of faith by an ordinary woman had the effect of concentrating the energy and imagination of the writer to articulate his personal vision.

During August and September, as Moore regained his ability to write, it became clear that the time set aside for the novel would no longer be enough. He would have to buy more time than his occasional contributions to *Weekend* magazine earned him and finish the novel later. There was another, more pressing need for him to earn money, for Jackie was due to give birth in November. This event does not seem to have retarded the productivity of the determined novelist, for judging by the timetable for completion of work, he can scarcely have paused for breath in the months after his recovery.

Starting in September, Moore returned to his métier as a writer of thrillers, this time, as he has said, "pretending to be an American," and it was in these months at the end of 1953 that the pseudonymous "Bernard Mara" was born. Mara's debut as author was *French for Murder*, the first of three novels placed by Willis Kingsley Wing with Fawcett in New York, and it was published in May 1954. The "Gold Medal" series of thrillers had print runs of 200,000 copies, and novels were regularly issued in sets that were distributed to mass-market outlets across America. *A Bullet for My Lady* appeared in March 1955 and *This Gun for Gloria* a year later. As "Michael Bryan," Moore contributed the novels *Intent to Kill* (1956) and *Murder in Majorca* (1957) to another prestige series, "First Editions," issued by Dell.

In *French for Murder*, Noah Cain is the narrator and protagonist of a tale set in post-war Paris, Marseilles, and the Provençal town of Cassis. He is a former G.I. in his late twenties, now back in Paris, attempting to survive as a tourist agent. Cain has fallen in love with Paris and its romantic ambience, yet there is another Paris that he is forced to acknowledge. Financially destitute and on the verge of homelessness, he feels an impulse to be reckless and to chance his luck, but he unwittingly stumbles into a hotel room where a murder has just been committed. He becomes both the pursuer and the pursued, police and criminals closing in on him as he tries to find the woman who will exonerate him.

The fast-paced, episodic narrative, which takes Cain through the lurid surroundings of sex clubs, bars, and brothels in Paris and then to a luxury villa and into the world of double-crossing shipping agents in Marseilles, reveals that he has unexpected resources for survival. The innocent and inexperienced loner turns out to be courageous and cunning, a match for undercover intelligence men, thugs and wily scam artists: the fantasy that feeds and controls the suspense and the visceral energies evoked are skilfully contrived according to the formulas of the genre, but beyond these it is worth drawing attention to some of the imaginative strands in this "fairy-tale."

The war gave Moore a touchstone for this hard-boiled world of loners. The novel's policemen and godfathers, intelligence agents and middlemen, and Cain himself, have all experience surviving in the ambiguous zones of wartime, Occupation and Resistance, of political manoeuvring and asocial lawlessness. Moore's experiences in Warsaw, and earlier as a port official in Naples, had introduced him to the twilight world of import-export and international shipping, but the surprising twist in *French for Murder* is that the smuggling, which the reader assumes to include drugs, turns out to be connected to Cold War espionage. The criminal milieu and the political realms of intelligence and espionage overlap with the experiences of destitution, desperation, and ingenuity that Moore himself had come to observe in the war. The literary novels will treat in psychological terms a similar ritual of testing and endurance.

This lawlessness has another aspect: the homelessness of characters may be part of the genre, yet the uncertain affiliations of the characters and their dissolving identities and changes of name as they disguise their pasts have an element of existential loneliness shared by many of Moore's literary protagonists. The sex interest in the novel gives way to a love interest in the case of Cain. He meets Helena Plater, a Polish girl, at the villa, but, in the end, Cain's character as a loner is revealed and, gripped by "wanderlust," he moves on.

The "cure" of moving on is surely a cliché of the single man recognizing the end of one adventure. The novel, written principally for a young American male readership, strikes the note Moore says he discovered in writing *Judith Hearne*: loneliness. Moore's wartime experience is what links the two novels, the sense of a tough outer world in which surviving and making it into a financially secure class do not heal the cosmic loneliness that overcomes men and women at times of crisis.

# 8

# THE WRITING OF
# *JUDITH HEARNE*

During the first half of Moore's decade in Montreal, the years of his success as a journalist and a writer of thrillers and pulp fiction, he still held on to his ambition to win respect as a literary artist. In the isolated camp in northern Ontario in 1948, he began to work on literary stories and, after some time in Montreal, to send them out to magazines. Only one of them was accepted for publication, but the apprenticeship continued, with Moore constantly searching for his subject and improving his style until, in early 1953, he made up his mind to attempt a novel.

In my twenties, before I began to write myself, Joyce was already, for me, the exemplar of what a writer should be: an exile, a rebel, a man willing to endure poverty, discouragement, the hardships of illness, and the misunderstandings of critics, a man who would sacrifice his life to the practice of writing. If it seems romantic and childish when I write it down now, that example, the *seriousness* about writing which seemed to prevail in Paris in the days of Shakespeare and Company, did affect my later attitudes to success. In short, while I was still young, Joyce became for me the possessor of what Auden has cited as one of the few kinds of literary glory worth winning, becoming as a writer "an example of the dedicated life, being secretly evoked, pictured and placed by a stranger in an inner sanctum of his thoughts so as to serve him as a witness, a judge, a father and a hallowed mentor." It was not until the immediate post-war years when, having chosen exile, I began to read Hemingway, a dangerously imitable mentor, that I gained the courage to write short stories.

The mention of Hemingway as a model suggests that it was not merely a technical apprenticeship that attracted Moore to him, but Hemingway's success in drawing on his European experiences for fiction. "I made a very grave mistake — in short stories I was very fond of Hemingway so I started imitating him. Those first stories were Hemingway clones, a pastiche.

I'd written about this girl I'd been running around Europe with and [was] in love with. But they were the wrong thing." If Moore's recent experiences with Margaret Swanson might have encouraged him to attempt an imitation of *A Farewell to Arms*, he seems to have concentrated his literary ambitions in these first years on writing short stories. "I had to exorcise Hemingway through a series of rejection slips," and it appears that whatever the technical gains from this Hemingway period, he quickly refocused on his Belfast material. "I found myself writing . . . about Ireland, about Belfast, about that place, those people, that life I had fled. For that *was* my life, the life I had lived and wept about and remembered in a way I would not forget."

In 1951, his first literary story, "Sassenach," appeared in the *Northern Review*, one of Canada's two literary magazines at that time. The story is a sketch of a Cockney performer on a Belfast street and captures his wit and desperation, as well as the wonder and disbelief of the onlookers. The situation resembles that of his first "North American" story, "Lion of the Afternoon," a tale of handicapped performers in Montreal, published six years later, after *Atlantic Monthly* had republished "Sassenach." Both are stories of pathos and local atmosphere and possess the characteristic Moore notes of early novels such as *Judith Hearne* and *Ginger Coffey*. The hidden allegory of the artist as performer recalls the memory of the puppetmaster in Alexandra Park who had inspired Moore's interest in theatre. Yet the stories also echo the inner sense of failure and exile of those novels, and in spite of the success of these first years in Montreal, a preoccupation with failure as the material of his fiction remained.

In spite of a hectic life as a full-time journalist and a writer of thrillers, he managed to find time to continue to work on literary stories. *Atlantic Monthly* rejected stories it would publish later, after the success of his first two novels, although he was encouraged to develop "A Friend of the Family" into a novel. He received encouragement also from Hollis Alpert, an editor at the *New Yorker*, but as the decade went on, Moore recognized that his true talent was for writing novels rather than short stories, and his manuscripts from these years show how he began to plan longer, more complex fictions.

Before he discovered that literary novel writing would be at the centre of his artistic career, Moore appears to have considered models other than Joyce and Hemingway. The considerable success of the Irish short story writers Frank O'Connor and Seán O'Faoláin did not escape his attention, especially because their careers became centred increasingly in the United States in the late 1940s and early 1950s, O'Connor being a regular in the

*New Yorker*. He had defined himself against their example in the late 1930s, when their reputations were made in Britain and Ireland as realists who explored the revolutionary period of Irish nationalism. Now it seems, he again had to discover his native talent and vision in a way that differed from that of these "*croyants*," who were willing to "subordinate their art to the demands of their faith."

Another short-story writer whose career he followed with a more positive interest was Mavis Gallant. Following her departure from Montreal at the end of 1950, her stories appeared regularly in the *New Yorker*. Throughout the decade, references in his correspondence with Mordecai Richler indicate that they liked to think of themselves as a new generation of cosmopolitan Canadian writers. On one occasion, in his playful correspondence with Richler, Moore signed himself "Mavis Gallant," and that impersonation hints at his efforts to write a "European" novel set in Spain, its style to be "Mavisian."

But it was Joyce's method of capturing the essence of his Irish experience in *Dubliners* and *Ulysses*, rather than Hemingway's or Gallant's European expatriate world, that finally asserted itself as the true model for Moore's early fiction. Even a story of Montreal such as "Lion of the Afternoon" bears the stamp of *Dubliners* and of Leopold Bloom: the central characters are urban loners, marginal people seeking comfort or love from an unsympathetic society. Moore's experience of arriving in Canada and ending up at the Salvation Army hostel, followed by a term in "the wilds," confirmed his sense of himself as "a misfit." His chosen characters and situations in these stories, and in *Judith Hearne* and *Ginger Coffey*, reflect the central preoccupation with loneliness and failure that is his signature from the beginning. It is "a matter of style . . . always a matter of the writer's view of life," as he has said, commenting on the fact that "no matter where Graham Greene travelled in the world, he always wrote in Greeneland."

Moore has recalled that "when . . . I quit my job as a newspaper reporter and retired to a cabin in the Laurentian mountains in Quebec to write my first novel, I again chose Joyce to be my guide:"

> I wanted to write about my own loss of faith, but did not want to risk adverse comparisons with him by describing the loss of faith in a young Irishman. And so, I thought of Bloom rather than Stephen and attempted a characterization which could in no way be described as autobiographical. I decided to write not about an intellectual's loss of faith but of the loss of faith in someone devout, the sort of woman my mother would have known, a "sodality lady."

His pivotal decision was to return imaginatively to Belfast. He turned away from the macho milieu of the thrillers, from the stories of politics and power that make up journalism, from the intellectual and professional preoccupations of his father to an almost invisible figure on the margins of the Catholic middle-class domestic world inhabited by his mother.

Back in 1948, when he first attempted to write literary stories, Moore had written "A Friend of the Family":

> I was trying to write short stories and I thought of this old lady who used to come to our house. She was a spinster who had some Civil Service job to do with sanitation and she lived most of her life with her "dear aunt." They'd not been "grand" but they had pretensions, and she had very genteel manners. So I wrote a story about her; but when I'd finished I wasn't really happy with it. I can't tell you at what point that became my first novel. I know I then wrote a number of stories that weren't finished and, when I finally sat down a few years later and decided I wanted to write about someone losing their faith, it was then I remembered Miss Keogh — Mary Judith Keogh was her real name — and I remembered that little story about her. I could hear her voice, I could envisage where she lived.

Already Moore's interest in such a character and her world singles out her precarious status in this bourgeois world of "pretensions" and "genteel manners," and if that suggests that she has created a fanciful public image of herself, the Joycean touch of the proper unmarried woman who works in the sanitation department hints at the central theme of the conflict between illusion and raw reality.

The story Moore had based on his memories of Miss Keogh is set in middle-class Dublin. The elderly spinster lives in a genteel hotel in the centre of the city, and while she is an eccentric and colourful figure who dresses in many shades of red, she suffers no crisis of faith or dramatic breakdown. Essentially a sketch of Miss Keogh's relationship with the Brannigan family, based on Sunday afternoon visits, the slight narrative turns on the discovery by Mrs. Brannigan that Miss Keogh is a secret drinker. The secret is kept, in spite of earlier indications of rivalry and subtle hostility between the women.

The story is notable because in many aspects it already captures the atmosphere of the Moore/O'Neill home of Judith Hearne's Sunday visits, the attitudes of the children and of Dr. Brannigan and other details becoming part of the novel. Yet in transforming the figure of Miss Keogh for his novel, Moore ignored much about her that was poised and accomplished. Having asked his sister Eilís to write out her memories of Miss Keogh, he received a lengthy and methodical reconstruction of Miss Keogh's life and career of public service, which he then chose to disregard. In its development, the fiction comes to embody much more of Brian Moore's own experience than that of Miss Keogh.

The initial idea for *Judith Hearne* — to explore Moore's own youthful loss of faith by projecting the experience onto a non-intellectual middle-aged woman living in Belfast — automatically drew him back to his own home and to his Catholic experience. His recollection of his past, and his insider's knowledge of the situation, ensured that autobiographical feelings would colour the world of Judith Hearne, but the process of writing uncovered its own surprises.

> I began to write about Belfast, not the Belfast of the day, but the Belfast of my past. It was a lonely and somewhat frightening decision. I had had reason over the years of exile to question every belief I had formerly held. I had few friends, many doubts. In exile, in a summer cabin in the Laurentian mountains of Quebec, I began to make the pilgrimage back in my own mind to the house I had been born in, to the people I had known as a boy.

The urbanity of Moore's distance from that silly spinster in the red hat evaporates as his own past feelings of failure, doubt, and loneliness come to animate Judith Hearne's "voice."

In Moore's comments on Graham Greene, it is easy to catch a glimpse of his own values as a novelist. "When he embarks on a new novel it is, for him, a journey of discovery as he seeks to illumine the secret lives of his characters. His greatness as a novelist depends on this. His plots develop from the nature of those he writes about." It is as a novelist of character that Moore most esteems Greene. When he praises Greene's technical skill and the "astonishing variety" of his work over many years, he returns to what he sees as the centre of Greene's accomplishment: "He walks each new fictional tightrope, never putting a foot wrong because he knows how to *become* his characters." These comments are an echo of what Moore has written of elsewhere as his own experience of writing. Moore's intuitive discovery as he worked on *Judith Hearne* — that the novelist must lose his everyday identity through the discovery of the "voice" of his character — became a method and a central theme of a large part of his later career.

What facilitated the discovery of his character's authentic voice, and how it honed Moore's technique as a novelist, can be understood from Moore's later comments on *Judith Hearne*:

> To my surprise I discovered in writing it what I really felt about my past. I left Ireland with the intention of not going back, but my reasons became clear only when I wrote that first novel. It was then that my bitterness against the Catholic Church, my bitterness against the bigotry in Northern Ireland, my feelings about the narrowness of the life there, and in a sense my loneliness when living as an exile in Canada all focused to produce a novel about what I felt the climate of Belfast to be.

That climate had become part of him at an early age, and it was that climate that had caused him anguish and loneliness, that had led to his determination to leave it all behind. Whatever new disillusionments about himself or the world followed during his years in Europe or Canada, whatever loneliness he had to endure, whatever failure he had to acknowledge and survive, all those later feelings had their origin and could be recognized in that first climate.

Moore was bitter because he had suffered, and the writing of *Judith Hearne*, he realized later, was an attempt "to write Belfast out of my system." That bitterness can be sensed in the description of the rain-sodden streets, in the nuanced depiction of minor characters such as the Catholic bigots Lenehan and Miss Friel or the Unionist racist Major Mahaffy-Hyde, in the mechanical routines of church attendance and deference to clerics and, most of all, in the deterministic trap from which Judith Hearne is incapable of extricating herself. This portrayal of the climate of Belfast has been seen as prophetic: "If in a book like *Judith Hearne* you can delineate the sources of these community antagonisms, the feelings people had before the situation became overtly political, then I feel you have done what a novel should do." Moore is looking back here after almost a decade of the Troubles that have engulfed Belfast since 1969, and appears to be glad to acknowledge this realistic dimension to his fiction, but, in truth, his interest in the climate of the city came first from the way in which his own life had been touched by it, and it was that experience that he gave to his protagonist.

While bitterness and anger made their way indirectly into the texture of the novel, Moore's imaginative recreation of his protagonist was possible because he only partially identified with Judith Hearne, because he had, in fact, done what she was incapable of doing. He had found in himself the psychic resources to overcome the deterministic and enveloping climate of

Belfast, whereas Judith Hearne was trapped by her formation: "She was trapped by emotion into making that promise to stay. That was what made her one of life's losers." Yet by going back in imagination to his own first home, he uncovered "without knowing it" archetypal elements of the experience of being a "lonely woman," and it is those he was able to communicate to his audience through the "voice" of Judith Hearne: "It touched some very raw, sensitive nerve among women and especially among lonely women or women who feared they would be lonely." That ambivalent relationship with the character that Moore himself feels — fearful identification and compassion from a certain distance — is also shared by the reader.

The memory of Mary Judith Keogh gave Moore more than the general sense of character and place. In trying to imagine how such a character would lose her faith, he remembered something about Miss Keogh that supplied him with the first half of the plot-line.

It helped enormously that the book was based on an actual person, who in fact used to come to see us every Sunday. She was an old lady; she wore red, she was perfectly happy. She had tried to marry someone years ago and when I knew her she was in her seventies and she always regarded my mother as an older woman — my mother was much younger than she was — because my mother was married and had children. So she belonged to another era and she was sort of a comic figure, but I used her speech and her mannerisms. I think she had a little weakness for the bottle, which was hidden, and as a boy once I was talking to her and she said, "Well, my brother-in-law who was-to-have-been," and I said, "What do you mean by that?" and she told me then with no sense of shame that she had once been engaged to be married to a man and he had thought she had money and she had felt he had money and when they discovered neither of them had any money, they didn't go through with it. It was probably her only effort to get married.

Moore took from Mary Judith Keogh the dilemma of his central character and the inner tensions that were released in her crisis: the unmarried woman with social pretensions, taking care of her aunt most of her life, and a failed opportunity to marry based on the illusory assumption of financial security, resulting in secret drinking. While Judith Hearne's isolation and loneliness are heightened by her introduction into the O'Neill household — the image of everything she is missing in her life and modelled on Moore's own family — it is the final loss of her religious faith, her refuge on a daily basis from the truth of her situation, that becomes the central crisis. Moore has remarked on ways in which the crisis he "manufactured" from this given material has two further catalysts: the insensitive religious "administrator," Father Quigley, to whom Judith Hearne turns in vain for comfort and reassurance, and the sceptical "devil's advocate," Bernard Rice, who articulates in blunt and extreme forms her own religious doubts. "I realized when I was writing it that he was probably my voice at the time — my youthful voice — and at the same time because I wasn't filled with self-love I made him sort of the villain and an unpleasant-looking person physically."

But if Moore's own thoughts are represented in the novel in the voice of Bernard Rice, and his childhood home and family are depicted in the O'Neill household, he is even more intimately present through his identification with the lonely outsiders, with the character of Judith Hearne herself and the fictional world he created to capture "her voice," and also with the character of the returned emigrant, James Madden. Recalling Miss Keogh's remark on her fiancé, Moore says, gave him the idea of Madden: "That phrase popped into my head and out of that the whole idea of Madden and the Irish-American returning and believing she had money — it just came back." In fact, the presence of Madden in the novel, a counterpoint and male version of Judith Hearne's failure, introduces further strands of Moore's complex and unresolved feelings about his own exile. If the idea is paradoxical that a married, successful writer and bon vivant traveller should be the creator of intensely realized failure in the character of a lonely provincial spinster, Moore's remark on his own loneliness as he wrote should be associated with Madden, the prototype of the male "misfit," the outsider, who is the recurring alter ego in many novels.

*Judith Hearne* appears to be securely bounded by the world of Belfast, yet in that first novel Moore had already taken a major step away and towards an imaginative engagement with his North American and exiled experience. Chapter three dramatizes one day in the life of James Madden and begins, "Shoes shined, clean white shirt, tie knotted in a neat windsor, suit pressed, top o' the morning, James Patrick Madden went in to breakfast. His good humour fled when he saw them." With these few phrases, Moore alerts the reader to Madden's fragile sense of self-esteem, his desire to create an impression on his fellow boarders that will mask his anxiety; he is a mirror image of Judith Hearne herself. Yet, as a character in his own right, as a returned Irish-American, he engages Moore's interest in a significant way.

This heightened engagement may be surmised because the precise situation, and the cadences of those phrases that establish the inner voice of the character, anticipate exactly the opening paragraph of Moore's third novel, *The Luck of Ginger Coffey*, the first to be set in North America:

> Fifteen dollars and three cents. He counted it and put it in his trouser pocket. Then picked his Tyrolean hat off the dresser, wondering if the two alpine buttons and the little brush dingus in the hatband weren't a shade jaunty for the place he was going. Still, they might be lucky to him. And it was a lovely morning, clear and crisp and clean. Maybe that was a good augury. Maybe today his ship would come in. James Francis (Ginger) Coffey then risked it into the kitchen.

Both Madden and Coffey are isolated males on the edge of despair, clinging to the vain hope of concealing the truth of their real situation by making a good impression. But they have something more important in common: Madden is a recently returned Irish emigrant who has spent almost thirty years in New York City, and Coffey has recently arrived as an immigrant in Montreal. Both are mid-Atlantic exiles, displaced males, at home in neither of the places they inhabit.

As the boarders sit around the breakfast table in judgement of Madden, Moore expertly weaves a variety of Irish attitudes towards the stereotypical "returned Yank" and towards the immigrant's version of the American Dream. Moving beyond the satirical edge of such caricatures, Moore makes the reader enter Madden's consciousness by evoking the competing claims of nostalgia, pride, and loss that govern the condition of the exile. While Madden is characterized as a homeless outsider, the novelist also dramatizes the irresolution of his life with insight and compassion and situates him in a social and cultural no man's land between Ireland and New York. If *Judith Hearne* embodies Moore's loneliness in Montreal, as he has said it does, the depth and meaning of that loneliness may be felt not only in Judith Hearne's crisis, but in the homelessness of Madden. This characterization is Moore's first version of his own personal struggle to find his place in North America, this first version of the immigrant's story foreshadowing in remarkable ways *The Luck of Ginger Coffey*, *An Answer from Limbo*, *I Am Mary Dunne*, and *Fergus*.

In spite of the boating accident in July, and the writing of *French for Murder*, he completed a first draft of *Judith Hearne* by Christmas and went straight into the next draft in January. "I was obsessed with the feeling that unless I got the book out, I would have to let it sit for a while again while I did some more hated 'commercial' work." At this point, it was untitled, although two possible titles were *House of Gold* and *The Eloquent Silence*. This final draft was completed in two months.

The composition of *Judith Hearne* was easy in comparison with the writing of later novels. "It would be marvellous if every novel you write could be your first novel, because then you do not know the mistakes you can make, and everything seems terribly easy for you. You're often more daring than you'll ever be again." While Moore used technical devices that were daring — some of which, such as the "round robin of interior monologues," he now regrets — the writing was less onerous because of the easy discovery of tone.

> I was lucky when I wrote my first book. I got a tone in it, and was quite excited because I realized it had a tone. The first part of the book, when she's having these illusions and she's meeting this man and everything is working, everything's happening for her, is all bubbly and there's a certain tone in the writing which sustains the illusion. Then boom! it starts coming down. I realized that was just luck, but because it was so important in that book, it was a lesson to me in all my other books. I always consciously put the tuning fork up and looked for the tone ever since.

Elsewhere, he has commented on the skill of the opening scene, which brings the reader directly into key aspects of Judith's character: that she is in the habit of concealing the truth from others and from herself, that she is a victim of carefully wrought illusions, and that the pictures of her aunt and the Sacred Heart are symbolic of the forces in her past that have trapped her. If Moore was conscious of using certain details in a symbolic fashion, he warns against attaching too much significance to details. Intuition matched by craft is the secret of narrative technique, and while Moore emphasizes the luck of intuitive associations that governed the "voice" of the novel, he also worked at the craft. A surprising model was Thomas Mann: "I studied *Buddenbrooks* for style in chapter beginnings and endings. . . . He bridges large gaps in time by ignoring them, then producing the character as descriptively older. He works each incident for climax. . . . Next chapter starts on a quiet note."

*Judith Hearne*'s economy of drama is possible because it is a novel of one character's crisis and her awakening to a new truth. "Judith Hearne believes that if she prays to God and if she lives a certain kind of life, at some point she can make the ultimate test of her religion by asking God to help her. When this illusion seems to work, she immediately goes into a sort of manic phase, but when she discovers that God has not provided her with a man, she depressively begins to examine her friendships and her life with other people." The collapse of Judith Hearne's religious faith is accompanied by a recognition that all along she has concealed from herself her essential loneliness, and that, just as she has been free to fantasize, she is equally free to rebel against the hypocritical conformity that has repressed her freedom to think for herself. Hers is a desperate, drunken and failed rebellion, and, in Moore's view, that is true to the way most rebellions are aborted in life. In the course of her "lonely passion," however, she has achieved a new honesty with herself.

Moore has spoken of the discovery of loneliness as a theme to which many people responded, especially women readers, and it is that loneliness, rather than loss of faith itself, that looms larger in the overall vision of Judith Hearne's life. The final image of the novel — Judith, after her crisis and breakdown, friendless and alone — reaffirms a truth of human experience that Moore claims is essential to his sense of what a novel should capture:

> One of my beliefs in writing that book and of the beliefs I've always had is that most ordinary people do not seek extreme solutions to the problems at hand. Ordinary people don't commit suicide or do the dramatic things that people do at the end of novels because life isn't like that. So a woman like Judith Hearne, after her sacrilegious behaviour, running into a church and disgracing herself, losing faith, if you like, with everyone she knows, is then forced to pick up and resume the business of everyday living.

That resumption of everyday living is indicated symbolically by the putting up of the pictures in the closing scene, as she had done in the opening scene.

> The aunt's picture and the picture of the Sacred Heart are real to her. The photograph of the aunt is a real person whom she remembers now only through a picture. The Sacred Heart to her is a real person, God, whom she knows is an image in a picture so that that is a symbol that is actually a real symbol which she put on the mantelpiece. The two pictures are used symbolically throughout the book, I think successfully, because they open the book, they close the book in both the symbolic and the real sense. Behind that picture lives her aunt and everything that her aunt had done to her and behind that picture of the Sacred Heart lives the Church and the presence of God or the absence of God.

The ending of this novel became a hallmark of Moore's sense of what an ending ought to be and of the central tenet of his method: that he must not predetermine the ending or even know the outcome of the crisis into which he places his characters before he has discovered the inner logic of their emotional world:

I never know what the ending is, and I think death is a cop-out. Another sort of vague theory I have is that ordinary lives do not end; life does not really end in death, and that's an Irish-sounding remark, an Irish bull. But people do not commit suicide or suddenly change in an enormous way. . . . We, as writers, are losing sight of that real world in which our parents and relatives still live. . . . Most people still live in the old-fashioned world of the nineteenth-century novels. . . . I'm terribly anxious to preserve those strong links with the real world where, when people go mad, they may have a little bad turn, but most of the time they just sit and look at television. . . . There are endings, yes, but they're harder to achieve. They're emotional endings, perhaps a change of thought, or a slight turn of direction. They're what happens when you lose your illusion or your illusion changes.

Such lonely endurance is central to Moore's sense of the commonplace experience of most people living their unheroic and undramatic lives, yet in focusing on it with such precision and compassion, he makes this resilience of character, even of those who fail, seem heroic:

Ordinariness is one of my main concerns in writing. The very ordinary person who lost her faith: Judith Hearne, how would she face up to this absolutely shattering thing, this complete loss of her beliefs and illusions? Everybody says, you know, that we've no more great drama, we've no more kings and heroes, but a situation like that is absolutely in the kingly Greek tragic vein, even if it is about a silly spinster, because the loss of illusion is a great loss.

# 9

## SUCCESS

At the end of 1953, Mordecai Richler returned to Europe, this time settling in London where British publisher André Deutsch had accepted his
first novel, and it was Richler who brought the manuscript of Moore's
novel to the attention of his publisher. Moore recalls that "after some little delay it was read by Laurie Lee, an English poet; he said that he found
it one of the most depressing books he'd ever read, and that he would
hate to read it again; but he strongly urged that they publish it." Diana
Athill, at André Deutsch, took Lee's advice and, in June 1954, contacted the author.

Moore was living in Spain. Well known as a cheap place to live, Spain
had been attracting writers for decades, and Richler's first novel, *The
Acrobats*, had been written there a year earlier. In March, Moore had sailed
for Europe alone and installed himself in Barcelona to plan, it seems, a new
thriller and a new literary novel. Unable to meet Deutsch and Athill in
London, he wrote a letter about himself and his intentions:

Miss Hearne is perhaps a joyless book, but it is one which has been in
my mind for a very long time and which I feel I had to write. I chose a
difficult type of heroine, I admit, but I wished to avoid the autobiographical type of first novel and I feel very strongly that if you write you
should progress in each book, not repeating yourself but tackling new
problems each time. James Joyce has been my main literary influence
and *Judith Hearne* is a Joycean type of book. I tried to show in a dramatic form the dilemma of faith which confronts most non-intellectual
Catholics at some time or other in their lives. . . . It is also a book about
a woman, presenting certain problems of living peculiar to women. I
wrote it with all the sympathy and understanding that I am capable of.
. . . I make no apology for its being about an uninteresting woman.
Miss Hearne is meant to bore and irritate the reader at times. Real people do. There's far too much of a vogue at the moment for books about

one-eyed men, whores and other assorted weirdies — for phony sensationalism — which I feel has little or nothing to do with life as it is lived
by most of us.

In spite of the paradox that at this moment Moore was masquerading as
Bernard Mara and preparing another instalment of "phony sensationalism," Moore declares his commitment to an art of dramatic realism. This
letter initiated a warm correspondence between Moore and Athill, and a
friendship grew that endured for more than a decade. This friendship
between author and editor initiated a pattern that would be repeated with
some of his other editors whose literary judgement and advice he trusted,
notably, in the United States, Seymour Lawrence and Aaron Asher. Athill
was Richler's editor also. His second novel, *Son of a Smaller Hero*, was published in spring 1955, followed a year later by Deutsch's publication of the
first collection of stories by Mavis Gallant. All three Montrealers took this
as an endorsement of their common idea that they were a new generation
of cosmopolitan Canadian writers.

As soon as this breakthrough occurred in London, Moore returned to
Montreal, "quite buoyed up," he recalls, in the belief that the novel would
quickly find a publisher in New York. "I hoped it would be published in
America. It went to ten American publishers, including I think some of the
best-known names, and it became in its time quite a literary scandal in
New York because every editor who had turned it down felt that he had
missed something." This stalemate in the United States persisted until the
summer of 1955.

In the meantime, Moore settled into a gruelling schedule. The work
diaries he kept during the 1950s document his daily progress, and the self-
disciplined focus on productivity of commercial work contrasts with the
method of trial and error that marked the evolution of drafts of literary
novels, many of which never reached completion. The efficiency of Moore
the commercial writer is stunning, while tentativeness and frustration
mark the creation of his serious fiction. The picture of the novelist is of a
man who never stops writing, and who concentrates obsessively on one
piece of writing at a time. The diaries sometimes note a schedule that
divides the day into three periods, and frequently he worked through the
night to meet self-imposed deadlines.

In June 1954, as soon as he arrived back in Montreal, he began to work
in earnest on "Die Amigo!," his second "Gold Medal" opus. He quickly
revised the chapter by chapter synopsis he had prepared for Fawcett's editors, and the book was written by the end of August. It is clear that his

primary wish was to return to his next serious novel as quickly as possible, which he did in September, yet the need to balance commercial and literary work may be highlighted by his income at this period. The advance offered by Deutsch for *Judith Hearne*, to be paid six months later, was recorded by him, after exchange, as $227.30; in contrast, *French for Murder* had earned a $2,500 advance the previous year, and he was paid $275 for a pulp story written in a day for *Weekend* magazine. This dependence on commercial writing for his real income would continue in one form or another for two decades, yet he also commented that after a decade *Judith Hearne* had earned him more than any other book, with reprints, translations, stageplay, and screen rights.

His fourth thriller drew on his time in Spain for the primary setting, although the plot involves jewellery smuggling, and the setting also includes Paris and Amsterdam, with much travelling in aeroplanes and boats. It opens with two post-war drifters, former USAF and commercial pilots, arriving at the airport in Barcelona. Josh Camp is the American narrator, and he and his buddy are members of an international population of British and American ex-servicemen who have been hanging around Europe trying to survive by doing shady business deals. Once again, the formula accommodates Moore's themes of the wanderlust and post-war displacement of young men.

The story follows predictable twists and turns, mixing scenes of sex and violence with suspenseful plotting, and ends with the hint of growing up, which eases the reader out of the tense fantasy world of the fiction back, to a degree, into the more predictable or routine world. The novel was published in March 1955 under the title *A Bullet for My Lady*.

As soon as Moore had this thriller off his hands, he settled down to work on a serious novel, which he referred to by the Gaelic family name of "MacEoin." Its protagonists are two young Irishmen on a vacation in Majorca. What begins as a study of two men of Catholic background and contrasting personalities in search of experience, written in the style of Hemingway, soon changes into a more autobiographical study of exile. The work diaries reveal the process. Beginning in September, and for six months, Moore tries over and over to find a way into a body of material that resists him, four times writing drafts of more than a hundred pages before abandoning the effort.

In mid-October, he decides to switch the setting to Ireland and also takes a week off to work up an old pulp story as a TV script for submission to CBC. In the following month, he approaches the novel by writing a synopsis of the first fifteen chapters, his method for the thrillers. He then writes a new draft of 150 pages but abandons it at the end of December. Beginning again, this time with the protagonist as Michael Russell, he writes optimistically to his agent that he hopes to finish a first draft by the end of February 1955, but towards the end of January he rereads what he has written up to page 146, and the verdict is "unsatisfied." He begins once more but stops work at page 130 on 20 February. The working title he considers in early January seems to refer to his own state: "On the Tight Rope."

The action of the novel focuses on the return home after many years of Michael Russell, on his difficulties as an estranged exile, and on the conflicting identities and roles that different family members impose on him. The many drafts of this Russell material seem to have dissatisfied him because he was unable to distance himself sufficiently from the autobiographical material, or, conversely, discover its essential truth. The dramatic realism that had allowed him to write *Judith Hearne* with such poised sympathy was possible because the circumstances of the Belfast spinster were so different from his own; he was recreating a world that was no longer his, and so he could envision it in almost ritualistic terms. The material that comes into the drafts — the war years, the after-war years of international travel, the North American scenes of settling — suggests that the time had not yet come when Moore would be able to find the authentic "voice" of these experiences. In fact, it would take another five years until he would be able to dramatize an Irishman in exile, in *The Luck of Ginger Coffey*.

Moore gave himself precisely six months to get this second literary novel launched, but he had to give up. One day after abandoning "Michael Russell," he began the first of two thrillers, both of which he would complete before the end of August, a few days short of another six-month period. Writing as Michael Bryan, he began his first book for Dell on 22 February 1955. Within three weeks, he mailed a synopsis and five chapters to his agent, and then prepared a synopsis and five chapters of his third Gold Medal book for Fawcett. This he completed in four weeks, and then he took a week off to try his hand at another CBC script based on a pulp story. By mid-May, he had signed a contract with Dell for $3,000 for *Intent to Kill*, which he would complete by mid-July. Without a break, he resumed work on *This Gun for Gloria*, and it was finished by 21 August.

*Intent to Kill* is an expansion of a situation first sketched in a pulp story, "The Gift," two years earlier. The main plot concerns the attempt of three hired killers to assassinate the president of a South American country who has arrived in Montreal for emergency neurosurgery. This third thriller with a Montreal setting draws on Moore's own experience in the Neurological Institute following his boating accident, and it also echoes the situation of the "old man" from Poland in *The Executioners*. In addition to the characterization of the patriarchal political figure of President Menda, the novel is also remarkable for its treatment of marital discord. Although the hard-boiled, action-packed narrative blends the required elements of suspense, violence, and sex, and the conflict between husbands and wives is viewed through a male perspective, there is a surprising degree of foreshadowing here of Moore's preoccupations in many of his literary novels: sexual incompatibility, failure and crisis, religious faith, doctors and death.

In moments of self-awareness and self-evaluation, Robert McLaurin, a thirtyish doctor, and the aging president reveal a psychological complexity and identification that suggest that it was a struggle for Moore to keep his "flat," formulaic, characters from becoming "rounded" — ideas on characterization he was familiar with from his reading of E. M. Forster. In addition to being surrounded by a rogues' gallery of thugs and political opportunists, these two honourable men are also betrayed by their wives. The doctor's American wife, Margaret, wants him to move to the United States to live and schemes to discredit him in the eyes of his chief, who significantly is named Dr Jamieson MacNeill. Apart from borrowing the names of his father and his admired uncle, Moore has also recycled the name of the professor in *Judith Hearne*. The name Margaret also has important autobiographical echoes, and all of these characters are related through the plot in ways that suggest that an autobiographical compulsion has governed these apparently casual coincidences.

Margaret threatens to blackmail her husband by telling his chief that McLaurin is having an affair with another doctor, Nancy Ferguson. Margaret is contrasted with the innocent Nancy, to whom McLaurin is forced to reveal the blackmail plan, and to whom he is increasingly attracted. Carla, wife of President Menda, has a sexual liaison with one of those who is plotting to have her husband killed while he is still under anesthetic in the recovery room. In words that anticipate the serious political thrillers of the eighties, *The Colour of Blood* and *No Other Life*, Menda prays. The images of paternal stability and dedication and of an unselfish, young man, whose vocation comes before all else, will be recurring images in Moore's later work, and there is often a paradigmatic coincidence of the two — most overt in the figures of the two priests in *No Other Life* almost forty years later.

The marital difficulties of McLaurin and Margaret arise from a mutual disappointment that has eroded their love. Prompted by the confidences of Menda about his own worries, McLaurin realizes that Margaret's expectations of becoming wealthy as a doctor's wife conflict with his own idealistic commitment to the practice of medicine. This conflict clarifies further his own disappointment and his sense of having failed. He must now free himself from the feelings of guilt and self-pity for having married the wrong woman.

Such reflections of Moore's own preoccupations seem to have surfaced in the formulaic fiction in a subliminal and almost prophetic way. Only in the later literary fictions will he return to dramatize directly these situations and images which become central to his work, and they do not recur in *This Gun for Gloria*, the second thriller of the summer of 1955.

This novel is set in Paris, and the protagonist, Mitchell Cannon, a recently divorced and down-and-out freelance reporter, becomes embroiled in a seamy plot while searching for a young American, Gloria Gay, who has disappeared. In fact, Cannon is just as "lost," another one of the wandering males in these fictions who is drawn by circumstances into dangerous actions far beyond his original intentions. The texture of post-war Paris is elaborately observed behind a plot that involves drug-smuggling Arabs and Africans, but Moore's real interest seems to be the naivety of expatriate Americans. The Latin quarter of cafés and music clubs, the streets of St. Germain des Prés, and Pigalle with its sex shows are evoked, along with other well-known tourist sites. There are tart comments on "existentialist types" and tourists sitting at cafés on the Left Bank. It seems that within the formula and the fantasy Moore is self-consciously writing a fiction of characters who take on roles and identities, much as actors do on a film set.

The Paris of *This Gun for Gloria* was one that Moore had visited on many occasions, and he had met members of that expatriate colony of writers, but he was also aware that Mavis Gallant had dedicated herself to exploring "that other Paris" behind the tourist settings. Mordecai Richler has written an evocative memoir of those times in which he comments on this Parisian phenomenon: "At times it seems to me that what my generation of novelists does best, celebrating itself, is also discrediting. Too often, I think, it is we who are the fumbling, misfit, but *unmistakeably lovable* heroes of our very own fictions, triumphant in our vengeful imaginations as we never were in actuality. Only a few contemporaries, say Brian Moore, live up to what I once took to be the novelist's primary moral responsibility, which is to be the loser's advocate. To tell us what it's like to be Judith Hearne."

Richler's memoir was written in 1968, but his retrospective view of Moore's work is correct and also prophetic of its development. Above all,

Moore wanted to avoid casting himself in a heroic light in his fiction. From the beginning, he discovered the core concern of his later novels — the search for authenticity in a self-conscious culture of roles, styles, and formulas for living. Richler puts his finger on the way the down-to-earth Belfastman enters into the refined lifestyles of cities like Paris, Montreal, or New York and remains sceptical of self-dramatization.

While Moore's satirical edge and his love of Paris may be detected in this thriller, the hard-boiled tone and extravagant plotting conform to the demands of the genre. In the end, the protagonist regains his self-esteem through his courageous pursuit of the truth about Gloria. In the process, he regains his role as a journalist, but rather than exploit his coup in breaking a big story, he settles for an agency job in Ottawa. As usual, this thriller follows the pattern of the undomesticated male testing himself recklessly in the world of the tough guys, and then yearning for stability, order, and a lasting relationship. At this level, the ritualized plot echoes Moore's own life.

Midway through the writing of these two thrillers, *Judith Hearne* appeared in London in May to uniformly enthusiastic reviews, the *Sunday Times* reviewer, Oliver Edwards, describing it as "an almost classic example of the power given by unity of theme — the range narrow, the craft immense." Moore recalls walking to Westmount Park in Montreal in June 1955 and sitting on a bench with a handful of reviews; he quickly realized that the novel was an extraordinary critical success. This first novel established a loyal audience among critics and readers in Britain for Moore's fiction, and his work has continued throughout his career to win high praise and recognition there. The novel was also published in Canada by Little, Brown in August 1955, and received very favourable reviews, notably from Robertson Davies, Claude Bissell, and Robert Weaver.

On the strength of that success and with the income from the two thrillers he had just completed, the Moores made a decision to buy a house, a handsome grey stone house on Lansdowne Avenue in Westmount, Montreal's wealthiest district. This house will be the model for the childhood home of Jamie Mangan, to which he returns in chapter two of *The Mangan Inheritance*. This section of Westmount is traditionally home to successful English-speaking lawyers, doctors, and businessmen, and it might be noted that the rebellious young leftie of fifteen years before — now the father of a young child — had settled in a neighbourhood and in a social class that would have won his father's approval. By the external measurements of upper middle-class accomplishment in Montreal, Brian Moore had arrived.

Only after the publication of *Judith Hearne* in Britain did it find a publisher in the United States. Seymour Lawrence, an editor at Atlantic Monthly Press, was in England in the summer of 1955, saw the reviews there, and approached Moore for the novel. Lawrence persuaded his reluctant directors to offer Moore an advance of $500, and so, in spite of misgivings about the content of the novel and its marketability, Atlantic /Little, Brown published it. Moore and Lawrence became close friends; Lawrence visited Moore in Montreal, and on a number of later occasions they holidayed together. He was instrumental in having Moore's stories placed in *Atlantic Monthly*, and Moore relied on his appreciation and support for many years. The novel, now retitled *The Lonely Passion of Judith Hearne*, appeared in Boston a year later, and in the United States it was widely acclaimed, receiving appreciative reviews across the country.

An early "review" in summer 1955, perhaps more interesting to Moore than the rest, was contained in a letter from his mother: "I would have liked your book much better if you had left out the part about Bernie and the maid also Mr Madden in some of his moods. You certainly left nothing to the imagination, and my advice to you in your next book leave out parts like this. You have a good imagination and could write books anyone could read. Perhaps you will think me rather hard and critical, but this is exactly how I feel no matter what anyone thinks." While this forthright criticism is focused on the sexual passages in the novel, it is surprising that his mother could have missed the attack on the Church: "I am glad to find you were kind to the Church and clergy."

His mother's sanguine view of Moore's treatment of the Church notwithstanding, the novel was banned for indecency by the Censorship Board of the Republic of Ireland in August 1955. And so this novel, which captures so accurately the repressive climate of Catholic, nationalist Belfast and of Ireland, fell victim to the self-righteousness of those who officially perpetuated that climate south of the border. While he has shrugged off the significance of this ban, he has also commented with chagrin on the fact that he was not recognized as an Irish writer for more than a decade, and the unavailability of this novel and the next — which was also banned — undoubtedly contributed to his status as a writer without a fixed national affiliation.

It may be that the banning of that first novel rekindled his bitterness, for it is evident that he needed to "write Belfast out of his system" once more. On 3 October, he began the novel *Devine*, which eventually became *The Feast of Lupercal* when it was completed eight months later, and was an even more abrasive rendering of that repressive climate than *Judith Hearne*.

The reference in its title to a Roman bacchanalian ritual, in which virgins were whipped, was a gratuitous affront to the censorious.

Moore has spoken of the way in which *The Feast of Lupercal* grew out of the writing of *Judith Hearne*:

> I felt that in *Judith Hearne* I had written about somebody losing faith and it then occurred to me to ask what was the education, the religious education and the background, which maybe destroyed that woman's life — she was a "Sacred Heart" girl. And so I became interested in the schoolmaster character and in how much that kind of education makes cowards of us all — because we have to live in the community; we can't just walk away from it. That, I think, was the real background to the end of *Judith Hearne* and the beginning of *Lupercal*.

That realization drew his imaginative energy to memories of his own adolescence in St. Malachy's College, but he chose as his protagonist a teacher, a graduate of St. Michan's where he teaches, who comes to see the school as a psychological trap from which he has failed to escape.

Devine, a thirty-seven-year-old celibate bachelor, is "an absolutely invented character," as is the Protestant girl, Una Clarke, whose "moment of love" with the ineffectual and humiliated Devine becomes the inspiration of salacious speculation among the students. The scandal that follows exposes Devine to even greater humiliation, when the clerical and lay establishment join forces to control the damage the incident will cause to the boys and to the school's reputation. Devine's "weakness of character" in the face of the wrath of this establishment is what interests Moore, and in this sense Devine is a male version of Judith Hearne:

> I saw then and I see their dilemmas now as the result of weakness in their characters; people have had to confront more dreadful obstacles and they have survived and surmounted them. But the climate of Northern Ireland then, and — as far as I know — the situation there today, is such as to encourage weakness of character. Judith Hearne and Diarmuid Devine are in the straightjacket of the narrowness and bigotry of Ulster, but that straightjacket is their cradle and their cushion.

The masochistic passivity that breeds anxiety and fantasy, and leads finally to an uncontrollable sequence of humiliating events, is common to the conception of both characters, but Moore also saw Devine differently. To begin with, he is male and therefore is not a victim of the bias against gender Judith Hearne suffers; in such a society, the male is free to take social and sexual initiatives that are impossible for women. "The interesting thing about Devine was, compared to Judith, who had all the bases loaded against her, he has some choice and therefore he is a less admirable character, because you feel he is in some way master of his fate, which she really wasn't. . . . I wanted Devine to be a character who had choice, and who had failed in the choice. I wanted him to be a victim of that school system."

In this sense, although Moore does evoke compassion for this child-like man in middle age, he is also interested in how the school functions.

> I tried to use him to show what I feel to be the truth about that system. He finally makes his breakthrough, he finally does rebel, but his rebellion is futile because it comes too late. His rebellion is passed over, ignored. He is treated like a schoolboy by the priest, his masters, becoming thereby a victim of the system he as a teacher has helped provide. The headmaster, whom many critics mistakenly took for a kind old man, is to my mind the very spirit of authoritarianism and Catholicism at its worst. He is *Realpolitick* all the way. He doesn't give a damn for anyone but the good of the school. He is the person I think one should be most frightened of.

The novel was written quickly, the first draft completed in four months by the end of January 1956. On 1 February, Moore took stock of what he had written, and these comments *in medias res* are a fascinating glimpse of Moore "becoming his character."

> When I began to write this draft I had in mind a man somewhat like my father, solid, honourable, dull, semi-virgin and pompous. Kind also and easily hurt. But as I went on writing the character evolved as a man of doubts, then became a man who was weak and easily swayed by others. These factors remained constant: dislike of having his feelings exposed; a certain hypocrisy in his love of privacy and propriety. Thus the man I finished the book writing about bore little resemblance to the original character. At first I had wanted to show how the forces of Ireland, religion, conventional middle-class morality and finally, the Catholic puritanism towards sex, prevented this honourable and well-intentioned man from attaining his due in life — Una.

Attempting to write a somewhat detached portrait of his father, Moore explored in the character of Devine not only his father but himself too, a

portrait of the kind of failure he might have been. It is surely not coinci-
dental that in September 1955, just before he began *Devine*, he had spent
a few weeks sketching a novel of another affair, a failure in Moore's own
life, the affair in Warsaw with Margaret Swanson.

His thoughts on the first draft of *The Feast of Lupercal* continue in a vein
that foreshadows some of the psychological and cultural generalizations
that are background to the later novels of ideas, such as *Catholics, Cold
Heaven*, and *No Other Life*:

> In the end I was forced to admit that what held him back was primarily
> his weakness, his willingness to sit in this hell he had been born into.
> That it was Catholic thinking which was the real villain — in this way.
> Catholics, born under a belief that something from without controls our
> destinies, are unwilling to act themselves. Protestants, born under the
> Reformation ideals, believe that their moral duty is to act themselves.
> Free-will versus God's will. The book has resolved itself into these issues.
> The girl represents, not only Protestantism, but youth, youth's foolish-
> ness and pride and power. She may be a fool, but she dares everything.
> Devine represents Catholicism, with its fear, and also he is age, age with
> its softness, its love of small comforts, its habit of shutting out unpleas-
> ant reality. He could dare more than she, but dares nothing because he
> never has, because having never, he has the premonition of failure. In the
> second draft, now to be written, I must clarify these conflicts, correct my
> own ambivalence towards Devine. He is the hero as weakling. We are all
> hero weaklings, therefore he should reach our sympathy. But the weak-
> ness should also inspire the reader in a desire to kick Devine, to say, get
> on with it, risk your money for God's sake.

A second draft was started right away and completed in two months, by
4 April, and a further month from mid-June was spent on a final rewriting. Moore's comments on the writing of the novel show him moving from
the almost spontaneous composition of *Judith Hearne* to a more self-conscious craftsmanship, especially in the choice of the appropriate point of
view for the revelation of character. "In *Lupercal*, I saw some of the mistakes I made in *Judith Hearne*. I tended to exaggerate them at that time,
and therefore I wanted to be more my own man — I felt that I might have
been derivative. I felt that parts of it hadn't worked for me so there was a
sort of natural pulling back in the second novel." He decided to keep a
more transparent perspective on Devine and developed more consciously
his "invisible" technique of narration, a style which never draws attention
to itself or to the presence of an author.

He also thought of the plotting and characterization in a more low-key way:

> I felt it was a less artificial plot than in *Judith Hearne*. When you think of it, *Judith Hearne* is a pretty melodramatic story with a woman winding up in a church tearing at the tabernacle, and suffering a depression. It also hinges on a misunderstanding — she thinking a man wants to marry her, and he thinking she has money, which is also a contrivance. . . . I feel, in the sense of construction, that *Lupercal* is honestly constructed because there is nothing in it essentially which is melodramatic. It is anti-melodramatic.

Yet if the character of Diarmuid Devine remains less sympathetic and engaging than Judith Hearne because Moore wanted a more "honest" construction, he also seems to have realized later that the emotion *Judith Hearne* evoked was a necessary kind of emotion: "I've been accused of treading a borderline close to sentimentality. I think that life itself is very close to the sentimental, and the line between melodrama, sentimentality, and real emotion and the real truth of life is a very thin one. If you're good, you must be willing to go right up to that line and risk overstepping it."

Moore has said with regard to the influence of Joyce on his early work that in *The Feast of Lupercal*, "the ghost of Joyce stands by the reader's shoulder." If the conception of the characters of Devine and Judith Hearne is that they are "painful cases" out of *Dubliners* — Devine like the masochist Duffy, Judith more like Eveline or Maria — Moore's novels prompt a question that the more naturalistic frame of Joyce's stories does not allow. Moore agrees that both his characters attempt to rebel and their rebellions "fizzle — he couldn't change. For the rest of his life he'd go on telling people what they wanted to hear." But the question of how to become free of one's formative environment is implicit in the narrative.

The novelist has recalled the words of Seán O'Faoláin, who had argued in the late 1930s that the only possible dénouement of an Irish novel was that "the hero gets on a boat and goes to England," but Moore didn't want Judith Hearne to do that, and the "weakness of character" of his first two protagonists ensures that they are not capable of such a step. It is their weakness, however, that makes them vehicles for the overwhelming feelings that Moore still carried imaginatively from that first home. In a way not absolutely true of Moore himself, the door did shut on the lives of his characters at an early age, and that is their tragedy.

A further light is thrown on Moore's temperament and the conception of his characters in a correspondence about the novel with Diana Athill.

The typescript had been sent in mid-September 1956 to Seymour Lawrence at Atlantic Monthly Press and to André Deutsch in London. Lawrence and his readers reported quickly and enthusiastically, and Moore heard on 9 October that Atlantic planned to publish the novel in May 1957. But he had to wait a few months more before he heard from Deutsch. He had been forewarned by Richler that the British readers had found his treatment of Devine "cruel," and already anxious about his ability to live up to the expectations created by *Judith Hearne*'s success, he now confessed to being "thoroughly depressed" by their reaction. When Diana Athill's letter of acceptance came in early February, he responded in a reflective and frank mood and revealed in unexpected ways how intimately he might be associated with the vision of the novel and with its central character:

> You really are my best critic. You detect the very nuances which worry me and which so few other readers ever mention. For instance, my habit of making whipping boys of people like Dev and Miss Hearne and your comment that such people can never be truly tragic because they start out with so little human dignity. This is awfully true. I think it has something to do with "realism" as the New Critics call it. I always want to give my character more diversity, more intellectual strength — something of that wonderful Dostoievskian quality of the unexpected, which, on examination, turns out to be the logical, the underlying truth in their behaviour. But, so far, each time I simply lack the ability to bring this off and, lacking it, settle for what my pessimism and my experience tell me is possible. So the characters become smaller, duller in a way and without the stature of tragedy. Perhaps I can make this more coherent by telling you that each of these books is a failure in terms of what I would have liked to do with them at the beginning, but that their development seemed to be forced on me by some pessimistic sense of truth about human behaviour. This I know is a failure of my imagination and leaves me dissatisfied at the end. But then I miserably cheer myself up by thinking that I cannot conceive of my being completely satisfied by anything I would ever write. . . . As you also noted, I have a sadistic streak in my writing. Do you wonder, after a school like Saint Michan's?

And so the struggle between the "pessimistic" or "Catholic" side and the "intellectual strength" or "Protestant" side of Moore's imagination came to the surface as he wrote this novel. At first, he seems to have envisaged them as the elements of conflict between the principal characters, Devine and

Una, but it appears that he was beginning to become conscious of elements within his own temperament that drove him paradoxically to invent technically controlled fictions that dramatized the loss of control, the loss of free will to the enveloping ethos of family and community, and, perhaps, even to a sense of tragic destiny.

By the time Moore was writing in this sombre mood to Diana Athill about *The Feast of Lupercal*, he had spent a year celebrating the widespread recognition of his accomplishments. Even before this second novel would confirm his emergence in Britain and North America as an important new literary writer, 1955–56 marked the taking off of his career in many different ways. In May, he travelled to London to be feted as the winner of the Authors' Club of Great Britain Annual First Novel Award. He also visited Belfast and Paris during his three-week trip. Earlier, he had been awarded the Beta Sigma Phi Award for the best first novel published in the previous year in Canada, and the annual Quebec Literary Prize in 1955. *Intent to Kill* appeared just before *Judith Hearne* in the United States and was reviewed so favourably in the *New York Times* that film rights were bought for $3,000. *Judith Hearne* was reviewed extensively, with features in the international editions of *Time* and *Newsweek*, and headlines such as that in the *Washington Star*, "Discovery of the Year." The immediate effect was that paperback rights were sold to Dell, theatre directors began to talk of a stage version, and not long after, film rights would be sold to John Huston.

The publication of *Lupercal* in London was held up for many months in 1957 by fears of libel. In an effort to deflect a libel suit from St. Malachy's, Moore considered including this statement following the title page: "Saint Michan's is an imaginary college. The characters in this novel are fictional. No reference to persons or institutions past or present is intended. However, corporal punishment, conformity and cowardice were and are complementary and continuing factors in the education of most Irish Catholics." The statement is a measure of Moore's intense involvement in the issues, although he, rightly, doubted that his old school would admit to recognizing itself, and so there was no libel action. A remark of the school principal was reported to him, and it is eloquent testimony to the impulse behind the novel: "This boy is merely biting the hand that birched him." Years later he could laugh at the irony, yet his raw feelings from the 1930s fuelled the writing of the novel.

Thirty or forty years after he had left the school, Moore would still speak angrily about it, but in an odd way the writing of the book enabled him to free himself from some of his memories, so that when he returned to his adolescence in *The Emperor of Ice Cream*, he could adopt a more comic tone. "I had nightmares after I left school and when I grew up. I'd start calling to myself, 'Listen, I'm married, I'm thirty years old, I have a wife and child, I'm wearing a Brooks Brothers suit, I live in Canada. Leave me. You shouldn't be caning me,' and he'd say, 'Out with your hand' and cane me. And then I used the caning incident in the novel and after that I never had the dream again."

Following the completion of *Lupercal*, Moore had begun work on what would be his final thriller, known before publication as *Free Ride Home*. This work was done in his usual efficient fashion, and he sent off the manuscript to his agent Willis Wing in early August, more than a month ahead of Dell's deadline. *Murder in Majorca* was published in August 1957 and is set in Paris and Spain. The plot concerns diamond smuggling with a naive "courier," Isabel Kenner, falling victim to a gang. She is the estranged wife of American freelance journalist Chuck Kenner, and apart from the complications necessary for plotting, the novel traces the growth of her relationship with another innocent but world-weary American, the photo-journalist Gregory Fall, a characterization probably borrowed from John Vachon, Moore's friend from his days in Poland. This novel is notable for the experiments with point of view, but the speed with which this last thriller was written and his later dismissive comments on this commercial work indicate that the success of *Judith Hearne* had freed him into writing only literary fiction from this point on.

# 10

## UPROOTING

Moore's second novel was written by the time *Judith Hearne* appeared in North America; it was published first in Boston, in February 1957, in Toronto two months later, and in London by the end of the year. *The Feast of Lupercal* also won wide critical praise, but it is likely that the response that interested the author most came from Graham Greene in a letter to Seymour Lawrence. "I have just finished reading *The Feast of Lupercal* with enormous pleasure," Greene wrote. "*Judith Hearne* seemed to me to be one of the best first novels I have ever read and this is certainly one of the best second novels — always a more difficult feat. There is a quality of realism in Mr. Moore's writing which gives the reader a kind of absolute confidence — there will be no intrusion of the author, no character will ever put a foot wrong."

The attention of eminent writers such as Greene, and the interest of American producers in filming and making a stage play of *Judith Hearne*, brought their own anxieties and doubts. In the summer of 1956 Moore wrote to Richler: "What do you really think of all this criticism of J.H.? Right now I am very sick — and I mean pains, ulcer pains — going through something that is fairly common with people who feel they have had one success. You get worried sick and feel rotten about the future. I'm sure you're one of the few people who will understand this. . . . I, of course, want my next one to be better — I do not rate the book as successfully as the critics."

Moore has often referred to his personal criterion of success, the ten-year test — that a book must remain in print for at least ten years. Closely associated with such comments is a consideration of the qualities that ensure classic status for a novel, or, in other words, the question of writing for the larger audience beyond contemporary success. In Moore's mind, writing for posterity has a spiritual purpose; it substitutes for those religious beliefs and practices that promise the immortality of the soul. The anxious sensibility of the ex-Catholic was fixed not on commercial success, but on immortality. Yet it was not easy either to separate or combine those two goals as a writer.

If Moore felt that in the late 1940s and early 1950s he had had to struggle out from under the smothering accomplishments of Joyce and other modernists, his talent was now unmistakeable. His private evaluation of that talent and of his promise as an artist began to be a continuing source of anxiety and is inseparable from other personal and circumstantial issues. The difficulties of this long period of taking stock and of false beginnings should not be understated. If the three years, 1953 to 1956, are taken as a measure of his productivity and success, then the weight of anxiety during the following three years must have been heavy. Between 1953 and 1956, he had written *Judith Hearne*, *The Feast of Lupercal*, and five thrillers; in the next three years, he did not complete a single novel, nor was he doing much commercial work. Only at the end of this period, in winter-spring 1958–59, was he satisfied that he was on the right track with his third novel, *The Mirror Man*, to be published as *The Luck of Ginger Coffey*.

The depth of his troubling reflections on his temperament as artist, hinted at in that letter to Diana Athill but rarely revealed in his otherwise more urbane and buoyant public utterances, can be seen in the occasional jottings in his Commonplace Book and scattered throughout the working notes for the novels from this point on. In particular, brief quotations from other writers on the activity of writing or on the artistic character become the starting point, and his reading of French writers, especially, often touches on these issues, yet these reflections are always linked to the working out of a literary problem, a question of characterization or technique.

In spite of the literary success of his first two novels, many readers found them depressing or despairing books — "downers," as Moore would later call many of his books. It appears that the jovial, energetic party-goer known to his friends and colleagues of these years had another side. His comment to Athill on the underlying pessimism of his character is developed in a consideration of French existentialist writing, focused on the issue of suicide. Extensive notes for a version of the "Michael Russell" material, possibly to be entitled "Suicide of an Honourable Man," reveal how he was defining his position in the light of what he called Protestant and Catholic responses to "the senselessness of living":

*La Nausée*, *L'Etranger* only touch the first belief, *e.g.*, the suicidal Protestant desire "all is nothing therefore I wish to die." The new book and new theme were touched on in "Godot" but there was an element of *croyant* there. The really great theme would be: How does the successful,

gifted, honest, driving man react to that moment of terror when he realizes that it is all a game and that he does not know the afterlife's answer?
The fear of everlasting life: To turn to an unknown unloved God through
fear seems base. To live differently for one's fellow men? To ape a Godlike
behaviour would seem the answer. But the moment it occurs that this also
is done from a base motive — fear is the motive, not love — then is this
too not base? Great saintliness must surely consist in resisting the apple of
religious consolation even at the moment of greatest terror?

But if the religious theme, which is such a recurring preoccupation in the
work of this declared unbeliever, developed out of his writing of the Belfast
novels and out of a recognition of the fatalistic Catholicism imprinted on his
own temperament, it is also a broader literary theme. In these same notes,
Moore quotes Rimbaud on belief, "*Si vous gagnez, vous gagnez tout. Si vous
perdez, vous ne perdez rien,*" and glosses the comment: "Development of this
is perhaps that in our baser instinct it is not the prospect of losing God that
terrifies us — it is the prospect of losing eternity — for we cannot be afraid
of losing that (God) which we do not believe in." The ground of his inves-
tigations from *Judith Hearne* on — "the *croyant*'s wish, the terror of life's ending, underneath it is a guilt" — fuels not simply the religious and philosophical speculations, but the narrative drive of the fiction.

The suspense of those short haunting novels and the yearning embodied as sexual desire and aesthetic pleasure have a heartfelt grounding in
that "terror of life's ending." Moore's work is marked by a sense of
"Time's winged chariot hurrying near" and of existential urgency, but it
is also rooted in the turn-of-the-century Catholicism of Belfast; from the
thrillers to *Cold Heaven* and on to *No Other Life*, the well-known
Catholic poem of his father's culture points up the peculiar *frisson* of
Moore's search:

I fled Him, down the nights and down the days;
  I fled Him, down the arches of the years;
I fled Him, down the labyrinthine ways
  Of my own mind.

Francis Thompson's poem "The Hound of Heaven" characterizes an ethos
at the root of Moore's earliest formation, and, although he speaks only of
his admiration of the technical skill of Graham Greene and also Evelyn
Waugh, it is not irrelevant that they consciously absorbed the same ethos
of English Catholicism.

Although the novelist hoped in the mid-fifties that he had written Catholic Belfast out of his system and could move to other characters, places, and issues — to Montreal and to exile, in particular — these larger religious questions and feelings remain inseparable from others that form the nexus of Moore's imaginative life from this stage on. Following his existentialist musings on the instinctive fear of the loss of eternity, for instance, he continues: "The foregoing forms an underlying theme which might give a real support to something quick with the elements that make up living: Humour; Coincidence or the lack of it; Sexual drives and success joys." The novelist's focus on the drama of living, on the surfaces of daily experience, and on sexual experiences, as well as on the depths of introspection — in fact, on the interplay of those contrasting fictional textures — is constant in these notes, and one can foresee already the form of *I Am Mary Dunne* or *Fergus*: "The small things of the past coming up in a variety of scenes against a present background of the exciting: this is an old idea of mine, the two novels in counterpoint." It is as a novelist that he reads and speculates, the insights of others and his own autobiographical material all grist for the fiction-maker's mill.

Moore returned to the "Michael Russell" material in 1957, after a two-year break, and for much of that year worked on a novel about an Irish-Canadian family named Kelleher, set in Montreal. A number of plotlines from the Russell novel were developed. Then he considered travelling to Dublin with the intention of setting the novel in that city, but eventually he moved the Kelleher family to Belfast, and adopted a more intimately autobiographical tone. While the Kelleher novel in Montreal had a more contemporary time frame, the Belfast version fuses the period of his father's death — in dramatic terms the reason for the son's return home — and later visits that Moore paid to Belfast, especially, at the end of 1947, after his Polish experiences. The opening chapter is written from the point of view of the mother anticipating her son's arrival, and that chapter was eventually polished as a story for *Atlantic Monthly*, where it appeared in August 1959 under the title "Grieve for the Dear Departed."

Although he failed again to find a satisfactory way of situating the exiled son and the family in a novel-length narrative, this story did point a way forward, for the characterization of the mother foreshadows Mrs. Tierney of *An Answer from Limbo*, and that universally praised characterization seems to have freed him to write the novel of his adolescence in Belfast, *The Emperor of Ice Cream*. In fact, *Limbo* seems to have uncovered indirectly the solution Moore needed for dramatizing this meeting of black sheep son and Irish family. The solution was not to return home, but to bring "the family" to North America, specifically, to New York in *An Answer from Limbo*, and to California in *Fergus*. Many of the characters from the Russell/Kelleher drafts of the mid-fifties find their way into *Fergus*, ten or fifteen years later — not only characters, but also a deepening sense of the psychological and metaphysical aspects of what he recognized as a Catholic sensibility.

The distillation of the mother's voice from the Kelleher novel and its concentrated focus in "Grieve for the Dear Departed" are almost certainly due to an extra-literary consideration at this time. Moore's mother had been in declining health for some time; in October 1956, he wrote to tell her of the dedication "To My Mother" for *The Feast of Lupercal*, although he expressed his fear to Seymour Lawrence that she would not live to see it. She had taken an active interest in his career and had sent news of any recognition *Judith Hearne* received in Belfast. He wrote to her regularly and, as his diaries reveal, sent financial gifts a few times a year. Brian, Jackie, and Michael spent July and August 1957 in Provence, and he brought his mother for a short holiday there. Later comments, after the writing of *An Answer from Limbo*, indicate the lasting impact of this visit.

Eileen McFadden Moore lived on to know of *Lupercal*'s publication in North America in 1957, but before it appeared in the Belfast bookshops she had a major heart attack. In October 1957, Brian flew from Montreal to be with her during her last days, and Seán flew from New York, where he was on a medical fellowship. He recalls his mother's characteristic wit: "Wouldn't it be terrible if you came all that way and I didn't die!" In fact, she did die a few weeks later, after she had appeared to recover and her sons had left Belfast for North America. The situation in "Grieve for the Dear Departed" — the father's death and the mother anticipating the exiled son's return — draws on much more recent memories of bereavement than the "Russell" drafts, and, in fact, the story is a moving interior monologue of a woman reflecting on her life as a wife and mother.

If this story represents Moore's first recreation of his mother as a more complex character than the kind professor's wife in *Judith Hearne*, it resembles the retrospective thoughts of Mrs. Tierney in *Limbo* and Mrs. Fadden, the doctor's wife, in *Fergus*. "Why had she cared more for them, her children, than for him? He had not been all she wanted . . . righteous as a pharisee, an old man full of hate and pride and caring for no one, not even her. . . . But he was my children's father, he never did any disgraceful thing, his weaknesses were small and I knew them, I forgave them, I stayed with him." This situation of the mother's loss of faith in her marriage to the doctor foreshadows the situation of *The Doctor's Wife* twenty years later. In that novel, a Belfast woman, of a later generation than Eileen McFadden, travels to Villefranche and decides to abandon her husband and son and find a new life.

But there is another loss of faith that is, perhaps, more significant. On the publication of *No Other Life* in 1993, Moore claimed that a scene of the protagonist by his dying mother's bedside is actually based on a real incident his own mother lay dying. "Do you remember when you were a little boy and did something bad? I would say to you, 'Remember, Paul, the Man Upstairs is watching you.' . . . I was wrong to tell you that. . . . There is no one watching over us. Last week, when I knew I was dying, I saw the truth. . . . There is no other life." In this pivotal dramatic moment in the novel, the dying mother goes on to plead with her son, who at her urging has become a priest, to abandon his vocation. Even if this confession of doubt did not actually take place as Moore's own mother lay dying, his telling of the incident appears to reflect his sense of his mother's character. In writing an interior monologue of the mother's ambivalent feelings towards her husband, and in using this scene to give focus to *No Other Life*, he is identifying the mother's central impulse: to be honest in expressing one's feelings no matter how painful the truth may be.

Another aspect of Eileen McFadden's death seems to have had a similar significance. The characterization of the mother in *An Answer from Limbo* drew some of Moore's most positive critical accolades. Yet it is the truth-telling of the writer's own attitude towards the mother that is encapsulated in the closing scene at her graveside:

> I remembered that I had not wept, would not weep, for what I felt was guilt, not sorrow; shock not loss. . . . I asked myself if my beliefs are sounder than my mother's. Will my writing change anything in my world? To talk of that is to believe in miracles. Is my motive any different from hers? Is it not, as was hers, a performance of deeds in the expectation of praise? . . . As for the verdict of posterity, is it any more deserving of belief than a belief in heaven? . . . And, as for the ethics of my creed, how do I know that my talent justifies the sacrifices I have asked of others in its name?

These words were written five years later, and there are many circumstantial parallels in the lives of Brian Moore and his protagonist, the novelist Brendan Tierney; what is important here, however, is the self-lacerating truth about himself the novelist is forced to face, and it is the mother's death that forces this awareness on him.

The failure to complete the Russell/Kelleher novel on which he had worked between *Judith Hearne* and *The Feast of Lupercal*, and to which he returned for much of 1957, confirms the difficulty Moore had developing the theme of exile. Other fictions started in the year before he began *The Mirror Man/The Luck of Ginger Coffey* suggest a confusion of overlapping concerns that focus not on the values and beliefs of home, but on the cost of "liberation," of adaptation to North America, and of a possible betrayal of self or of others.

Part of the Kelleher material that is set in Montreal is a preliminary sketch of the newspaper milieu that he will go on to develop in *Ginger Coffey*. A scene in which the young man, newly arrived in Montreal, meets an incarnation of himself in the person of an older journalist foreshadows Ginger's meeting with Old Billy, the Irish emigrant who has failed to make it. In the drafts of the Kelleher material, there are a number of versions set in Ireland and in Montreal of a young and rebellious exile meeting and recognizing his kinship with an "Uncle Peadar." That uncle appears to have been involved in an incident of sexual assault, although the family has concealed the truth and does not wish it to be known. The young man discovers the secret cause of the uncle's subsequent alcoholism and decline, and there is between them an ambiguous relationship of sympathy and rivalry. In some versions, the young man discovers the uncle's suicide. In elaborating this material, Moore's interest seems to have shifted to the suicidal uncle so that a manuscript referred to as "Uncle Billy" took over from the Kelleher novel. He is the outsider, anti-hero, who has distanced himself from guilt and repression only to fall victim of his own "lack of faith, lack of purpose."

It is evident that these drafts and notes are a way of beginning the transition to a North American fiction of an exiled Irishman, and in this sense the movement forward in Moore's development can be signposted. The abandoned "Uncle Billy" material will be polished later, the setting now moved to New York, and it will became the story "Uncle T" in *Gentlemen's Quarterly* in November 1960. Ginger Coffey is also a development of Uncle Billy, whereas Brendan Tierney, the protagonist of *An Answer from Limbo*, is an elaboration of the younger exile, the character called Vincent Bishop in "Uncle T."

All these fictions explore the dilemma of an exiled Irishman — an ambitious young man or an older, failed man — especially in the conflict regarding his loyalty to his wife or to his "Irishness," which represents his temperament and innate talent. In "Uncle T," that conflict is signalled by the uncle who recalls, "My old mother used to say you should never give an Irishman the choice between a girl and the bottle," but the seductiveness of alcohol in the story only facilitates a complex drama of betrayal in which young Vincent is drawn away from his new wife and chooses to stay with his uncle. The psychological layers that surface in one evening — of guilt and forgiveness, loss and yearning, self-centred fantasy, failure, and shame — underlie the larger drama of personal and sexual incompatibility that lead to profound marital crises in the novels.

Moore's own experiences during the war years and his first year in Montreal are woven into a long flashback for the characterization of the young Michael Russell/Kelleher protagonist. In a note to himself he comments that the subliminal ties to family are more powerful than any later relationship, even marriage, because the emotions were formed on a level below the intellectual or the conscious. This is the first summing up of Moore's thoughts on what he later calls the "grammar of emotions" that underlies the novels of exile, which culminate and reach a resolution in *Fergus* when the ghosts of his childhood revisit the protagonist in his Californian retreat. Moore appears to conclude that his imaginative impulses are rooted in the inherited or most deeply embedded traits of his character and that his single-minded commitment to developing those impulses leads to a guilty detachment from the present and even from his most intimate relationships.

In addition to the preoccupations with alienation from family and the character of the outsider, Catholicism, pessimism, and guilt, perfectionism and failure, the false starts of the years 1957 and 1958 focus also on the world into which the writer/exile has fallen. This material is equally interesting as early foreshadowings of what will be worked out later in *An Answer from Limbo* and *I Am Mary Dunne*, both novels that explore an intense and disturbing nexus of collapsing identity, the anxiety of being a writer, and sexual betrayal and incompatibility. Many of these concerns appear first in a story called "Preliminary Pages for a Work of Revenge," published in the winter of 1961 and incorporated in part into *An Answer from Limbo*, but early versions of the bitter and disoriented "Notes from Underground" appear to date from 1957. Versions of a piece called "Dear Booby," which Moore has said is the origin of "Revenge," dramatize, in direct address, drafts of an unsent letter, the disillusioned and cynical thoughts of a distracted "woman of no identity."

One of these versions, obviously set in Montreal, seems to foreshadow directly the Montreal period of Mary Dunne's life, and resembles *Fergus* also, in the sense that it is an attempt to lay to rest the ghosts of the protagonist's past. Written almost ten years before *I Am Mary Dunne*, the piece focuses is on a female protagonist who has changed her city of residence too often and no longer feels attached to a home. She addresses herself to an old lover, and her disorientation appears to be due to her realization that they had changed and fallen out of love almost unawares. The unsettling sense of time, change, and the relativity of perception are distinct from the Montréal setting, yet this period of unease in Montreal pointed the self-exiled Moore's sense of cultural displacement in specific directions. He experimented with a satirical story of affluent Westmounters in the style of Gallant's "Bernadette," and he appears to have considered further "Westmount" material for a novel or a play.

A fragmentary typescript of a play to be called "The Game" introduces a fierce satire of a Westmount hostess and her guests at a dinner party during which they play a cruel game of "odd man out." The hostess is to be developed "à la Judith Hearne," finally alone, drunk, and abandoned in spite of the comforts and resources of her wealth. The abandonment of this older woman is seen as a judgement on the younger self-preoccupied characters. While this bitter scenario anticipates *An Answer from Limbo*, it also reflects Moore's mounting disillusionment with a particularly egocentric social set.

Brian and Jackie Moore played "the game" with their Montreal friends, a somewhat darker aspect of the excitement generated by role-playing parties, yet this effort at recreating it for literary purposes suggests that he saw an unpleasant truth about personal identity in his Montreal milieu. While he has said that these were the years in which he made lifelong friendships in Montreal, and for a time, while he had a job, his life was "real," it does seem as if the high tensions of these years led to profound alienation for Moore. Later he would refer to "the scars" left from the Montreal years.

Moore's restlessness and the many false starts in 1957 and 1958 may have arisen from exhaustion. He had become a writing machine, working almost non-stop as he turned out thrillers and magazine stories, with breaks to write his literary novels. As the diaries record, Moore was also becoming a manager of an increasingly busy career that involved extensive correspondence and accounting.

The energy and the enlarged ambition generated by his success had undoubtedly concentrated his attention on his work, and the diaries also show that Jackie typed and proofread all seven of these novels, in addition to continuing her own career as a magazine writer. This work required her to travel on assignment, and there are references to periods away in Vancouver, New York, and Chicago. Coupled with Moore's own promotional and holiday trips to Europe, New York, Boston, and Toronto, the glimpse given by the diaries is of a life driven to a compulsive degree by ambition and anxiety, as is the case of most young writers.

The domestic scene reflected in the work diaries is of two professional writers working to the limit of their capacities — and perhaps beyond, for there are days in the diaries marked, simply, "Sick." The most recurring references are to his ulcers. Although his heavy drinking was probably a continuation of habits developed in the war years and in the journalistic world of the earlier years in Montreal, the tone of this later comment to Mordecai Richler is ominous: "Mr. Weintraub and I drink 3 or 4 gins and tonics each night at five in my house. We observe this ritual in a strictly kosher fashion seven days a week, allowing no tainted outsiders to join us. I have not been going out anywhere at all recently, and am now prepared to hibernate for the winter." These remarks were written in September 1958, at a time of intense frustration with *The Mirror Man*, the novel that was slowly, over a period of two years, becoming *The Luck of Ginger Coffey*.

While this soul-searching continued, the playscript of *Judith Hearne* went through many revisions in a vain attempt to satisfy the New York producer, Dan Petrie. Moore expressed great frustration with the process, during which he moved regularly between Montreal and New York for working sessions, and he entertained his friends with stories of the fatuous behaviour and attitudes of the self-absorbed theatre set. Still, New York began to cast a spell, and Montreal gradually began to feel more like a "colony" to him than a "free" place. The stress generated by success and by his own high expectations, may have been part of the desire to move on, yet it also appears that a pattern was establishing itself: as he had to move on from Belfast so, as the 1950s came to a close, he had to free himself from Montreal.

Apart from getting an American agent in the early 1950s and writing thrillers for American publishers, Moore had many personal connections that directed his attention south of the Canadian border. The friendship with John Vachon from the Warsaw years continued with regular correspondence, visits, and family holidays together in Cape Cod. His cousin Máire MacNeill was married to John Sweeney, a professor of English at Harvard. Vachon and Sweeney were among the first to see the manuscript of *Judith Hearne* in early 1954, and Moore valued their advice on minor changes. His new friendship with Seymour Lawrence in 1956, and his increasing awareness of the American literary and critical field — he spent a brief period at Yaddo, the writer's colony in New York state — seem to have convinced him that his career would benefit from a move south. In Jackie's childhood and in her professional life, she had been a frequent visitor to New York and welcomed the change.

But it was the Ruddicks who facilitated the making of concrete plans. In 1957, Bruce and Dorothy Ruddick moved back to New York, where Bruce had trained as a psychoanalyst. In summer 1958, they rented a house on the beach at Amagansett, Long Island, and the Moores came to visit. Moore fell in love with the ocean, and instantly declared that he wanted to move there. In characteristic fashion, he set about making his dream come true. His intention was to rent a house the next summer. He applied for a Guggenheim Fellowship for the following year, but before the news of the award came in June 1959, the family had already moved to Amagansett, where they were renting a house in the village. The terms of the Guggenheim required Moore to reside in the United States and so, having rented out their house in Westmount, the summer by the ocean turned into a more permanent step. At the end of September, they moved to an apartment on the edge of Greenwich Village, and established a pattern of moving between Amagansett and Manhattan that continued for five years.

During that period of preparation, references to the anxiety generated by success and to ulcers continue: "Much worse than usual this year," he reports to Richler in 1958. This stress came to a climax soon after the move to New York when Moore had to have surgery for a bleeding ulcer. "The doctor says it is large and there is lots of evidence of old scarring and so I think it may be some time, months perhaps, before I can take a drink again," he wrote to Richler. "Actually, once off it, I don't miss it. Can't stop smoking though. I am to go in for another X Ray in three weeks time. . . . The depressing thing is that ulcers are all in your head, doc, and if you're like me, you will get one again. And if I bleed again — surgery etc. . . . So I am face to face with the facts of life, as they used to say." Unlike his earlier brush with death in the speedboat accident, this sickness could be ascribed to his temperament and lifestyle, and may have drawn his attention to his own mortality in a new way; although he was only in his late thirties, it is striking how often from the time of his mother's death he speaks in his letters of feeling old.

In spite of his health problems, the prospect of moving seems to have jolted Moore into a new beginning on *The Mirror Man*, which finally began to take shape in early 1959; "this bloody novel which has only been thirteen months in writing," he wrote to Richler. In fact, the tone and energy of Richler's recently published novel of Montreal, *The Apprenticeship of Duddy Kravitz*, may have helped Moore out of the doldrums. Writing to congratulate Richler in February, he discussed *Duddy Kravitz* in a way that seemed to define his own path out of the material that had frustrated him:

At the end of the book, I was left unsatisfied about one thing. I some-how felt that one of the most important things you were trying to illu-minate was the hold which family relationships have on members, a hold which is greater than any other holds later in life. I am a child of nine kids . . . but in my experience, 14–20 is the period when family mem-bers betray other family members for outside friends, in a breaking away revolt. Later the ties reassert themselves, often with frightening strength, so that a husband hits a wife when she insults his brother.

This is Moore's "grammar of emotions" at its most primal level. In mak-ing such an extreme statement of the atavistic pull of his past, and his alle-giance to it, Moore is apparently detaching himself from his marriage and his life in Montreal, as he once again embraced a new beginning in anoth-er chosen place of exile.

# 11

# A CANADIAN NOVELIST
# IN NEW YORK

The writing of *The Mirror Man* continued without pause through the transplanting from Montreal to Amagansett in May 1959. It is probable that this first novel set in Moore's second home could be written only by detaching himself from the city, by moving away from Montreal, as he had done from Belfast. While the pattern is not without exception, the experience of living away from home for extended periods would become an essential ritual associated with the completion of many novels. In later years London, Paris, Nova Scotia, and Ireland would be his temporary workshops; for a writer who is so methodical and disciplined, it is remarkable that the mysterious breakthrough that gets a novel on track or makes it possible to envisage the ending was facilitated so often by displacement to a series of rented houses, hotel rooms, and borrowed apartments.

Whenever Moore speaks of a pattern in the evolution of his fictional world, he relates it to this displacement: "In my third novel, *The Luck of Ginger Coffey*, my character and I emigrated to Canada and later my novels followed the course of my emigration, moving on with me to New York and California." While this is true of the sequence of books Moore wrote in the 1960s, apart from *The Emperor of Ice Cream*, it is a very simplified version of those literary experiments and of his imaginative probing of his own responses to his nomadic condition. Each of those novels, *The Luck of Ginger Coffey*, *An Answer from Limbo*, *I Am Mary Dunne* and *Fergus*, is remarkably distinctive in style and characterization — so distinctive, in fact, that the different places which are "characters" in the novels are less important than the evolving sense of the self in exile at the heart of this new phase of Moore's work.

His first efforts to get started on a novel that would encapsulate his North American condition were made in the early 1950s, probably even before he wrote *Judith Hearne*. The earliest notes identify his first job as proofreader at the *Gazette* as a situation of awakening, and the managing director is actually named: "The Irish drifter of no past — No future

— Larkin and the proofreaders — Old blind man cry — fired — he thinks there must be more to life than this; cheap boarding house; Honey Dew Café; Peasant values — old battle cry in new environment." The situation in which Moore found himself on arrival in Montreal, "at his lowest ebb," seems to have defined the limbo of last resort that he wanted to study. Perhaps more desperate even than Judith Hearne or Diarmuid Devine is the homeless drifter, and while the figure of Ginger Coffey will only approximate to that condition, the elements noted above will remain and be developed in the novel as the backdrop against which he must define himself.

Further notes indicate that Moore envisaged actually beginning the novel by drawing on his experiences in northern Ontario: "Hero arrives at camp — flashback to leaving, emigrating, reasons for — to camp again — in camp meets others — life of camp." This fiction did not get beyond these first notes, and it appears that the Russell/Kelleher material that he worked on intermittently through the middle 1950s took over as the focus of his investigation of "the Irish drifter." A character who makes recurring appearances in the many drafts of that material is the "uncle," the image of what the young, exiled drifter may become: "A middle-aged man leading a mediocre existence"; "Uncle Peadar is a drunk who lived for a time with sister-in-law and her daughter"; "He is a man who has floated about from one small job to another, on the fringe of great events, never doing work that has any real validity: he is a symbol of the fifties — faceless — nothing left to believe in — the dispossessed peasant sent to the city (in this case Ireland and the wide world) where he is put to a meaningless job. . . . When he loses his faith he does not have the courage to admit it"; "Young man has to find a job and is hired as a reporter by the same newspaper that would not hire his uncle."

Through the many different fictions of the 1950s, some set in Ireland, some in Montreal, the character type recurs, often in counterpoint to his younger self, and, indeed, young or old, this male "failure," a character in limbo, becomes one of Moore's constant concerns. Members of this family of characters include Madden in *Judith Hearne*, Uncle T in the story of that title, Old Billy Davis in *Ginger Coffey*, and Ginger Coffey himself. Later, on a higher social level, this type will remain in the characterizations of Fergus Fadden and Jamie Mangan, and, of course, many of his women characters may be seen as versions of this same condition. Indeed, few of Moore's characters do not enter such a state of mid-life doubt and drift when the dramatic crises of the novel force them to question the structures of belief and social position that have hitherto sustained them.

Moore is quick to admit that he identifies with the "misfit" Ginger, but is also aware of his character's representativeness:

A part of him is an amalgam of many people I have known. Also I think he is a classic Irish type. And if you wanted his literary genesis, it's in Joyce's father. Stephen said of him, he was a public relations man in the distillery, a sometime tenor, a something else and a something else singer, and "at present a praiser of his own past" — which I think is a beautiful phrase. . . . I didn't think of it consciously, but as I was writing I realized that, yes, he is the type of the gay, feckless Irishman. Not so gay, of course, in real life. . . . I always suspect a man who buys drinks for the house. I always suspect he has nowhere to go home to. And that's a type I think is more universal than Irish.

Moore's challenge in writing his first "Canadian" novel appears then to have been to define an attitude towards this type. He situates the feckless Irishman in the larger category of the emigrant, and that category in turn in the more universal category of the homeless. He wanted Ginger to be seen as more than an exiled version of Judith Hearne or Diarmuid Devine. He wanted to understand how he could be both a failure and a survivor. "The covering up of weakness helps propagate it," he wrote in his notes for "Michael Russell," as if he were thinking of Judith Hearne and Devine, but he goes on: "The unrealistic aspect of last end, preparation for God, etc. is Ireland's weakness. Shuts its face to the outside world." The challenge was to face the "outside world," the world unconcerned with Catholic fatalism and the formulas of religious practice, and to become strong by acknowledging the truth about one's former beliefs, self-deceptions and pretences. That is why the new novel was to be called *The Mirror Man*, for it was to trace the gradual process of self-recognition and to find in that process strength rather than despair.

It is evident that Moore's eventual enriching experience as an emigrant in Montreal quickly obliterated his own first year of despair. The decade that followed found him most often in his literary work looking back to those "weaknesses" of Irish culture that had been imprinted on his own personality, yet he was also overcoming them through a variety of experiences. While Ginger Coffey's situation reflects his own in the early months of 1949, he moves the action forward to January 1956; and the writing in 1959 would experiment with mixed genres and modes in a way that reflects an even later stage of his own imaginative evolution. One major difference between the earlier fictions written closer to his situation in

1949 and the novel of 1959 is that he grafts a portrait of a discordant marriage onto the portrait of the middle-aged drifter. The truth of his character is revealed through the crisis in that marriage, but even if Moore later declared himself dissatisfied with the portrayal of the marriage of Ginger and Vera, attempting it was the essential step forward.

Leaving aside for now the single and celibate protagonists of the first novels, Moore enters more fully into the world of *Ulysses.* If *Judith Hearne* and *The Feast of Lupercal* are Joycean in their portrayal of marginal characters trapped by their city and its life-denying culture, Ginger Coffey is portrayed as a marginal character whose relationship to the city of his present, Montreal, is the oblique, buoyant, comic attitude of the survivor. From the late 1930s, Moore had been reading Joyce as an Irishman, but during the 1950s, he began to read him from an evolving North American perspective. In making Bloom a Jew, Joyce had deftly suggested the ambiguous identity and sense of belonging of the individual in modern urban culture. Jewish writers had been among the first to champion Joyce's work, and his influence had been absorbed by a generation of American writers.

If Moore became interested in American literature because it is a literature of immigrants, of survivors, he was especially interested in Jewish Americans:

> Evelyn Waugh is to me the most important living English novelist on the basis of his first six novels. Graham Greene is a first-class novelist. But the exciting novel-writing is being done in the U.S. today. And the most interesting feature there is the breakthrough of the younger Jewish writers. Their work represents a new stage in the evolution of the American novel. First, there were the New England writers; then the 'immigrant' novelists represented by Dreiser; then, I suppose, the Irish — Scott Fitzgerald. Today, the Jewish novelists are getting a hearing.

And so this immigrant tradition, especially the early work and outlook of Montreal-born Saul Bellow — Moore considered *Seize the Day* to be one of the most important novels of the 1950s — may be more significant than his Canadian residence in attempting to understand the Americanization of Brian Moore's sensibility and literary technique in *The Luck of Ginger Coffey.*

Moore had begun his intellectual emancipation in the late 1930s by participating in the Jewish Institute Dramatic Society, and in Montreal had been energized by the extent of the immigrant Jewish culture he had found there. Through his close friendships with Weintraub and Richler, the Ruddicks and Cherneys, he became aware of the two-generational transition of their people from Eastern Europe to North America and of the tensions of exile and assimilation. His move to New York was a further step into an even more vibrant Jewish-American milieu. At Amagansett "there were a lot of writers and painters there in those days. [Jackson] Pollock and the *Partisan Review* people. I was the house goy in a whole Jewish literary atmosphere." The Moores quickly found themselves in a circle of writers and artists who moved between Manhattan and the Hamptons.

The Ruddicks were there, and among those residents of Amagansett who befriended the Moores were Philip Roth and Neil Simon. Like Moore, Roth was a Guggenheim fellow in 1959–60: his *Goodbye, Columbus* won the National Book Award in 1960. Moore greatly appreciated Roth's lively company and especially his wild comic talents. He became friendly with others at the beginning of their careers who were not destined to become as well known as Roth. Josh Greenfeld remained a friend for many years, and in the 1970s he ended up living in Los Angeles, close to Moore. In the circle also were Wallace Markfield and Ted Solotaroff, later editor of the *New American Review*, which later published work by Richler, Weintraub, and Moore. The artist and illustrator Tomi Ungerer was a regular at parties that seem to have rivalled the costume parties of Montreal for their liveliness.

It would seem that Jackie, no less than Brian, entered into the buoyant spirit of this new situation. In early 1960, she wrote to Richler: "Life in New York is great. We both love it. Not so hot for Mike though. No green grass, lots of perverts, child can't be let out alone." Amagansett, with its colony of established artists and writers, was far from bohemian, and their lifestyle in New York City was similar to what the family had enjoyed in Westmount. Michael went to private school, and their addresses on the edge of the Village and on the Upper East side suggest the wealthy New York ambience later recreated in *I Am Mary Dunne* and *The Mangan Inheritance*. Manhattan was to be Moore's home for almost six years.

As a successful novelist, Moore had a place in literary circles in New York from the beginning. Jackie felt at home there also, and so Ginger Coffey's tenuous situation in Montreal bears little resemblance to the chosen and comfortable exile of Moore. In fact, it looked as if New York was the logical place for an ambitious novelist to be, and Moore has said that he assumed for a time that he would always live there. All about him were writers and critics and editors — Moore would capture that world in his next novel, *An Answer from Limbo* — and he was quickly regaining the confidence and energy that were at a low ebb during his last months in Montreal.

In portraying a character determined to be free to create his own life and to leave his past failures behind, Moore was not simply writing a novel of an emigrant in search of the American Dream. He was also writing a more probing study of a man like himself who, as recurring patterns in so many novels suggest, is aware of the precarious edge on which self-esteem balances. While the earlier portraits of failure exhibited the self-defeating trap of delusion and rationalization, Ginger Coffey learns to look in the mirror, to recognize the "sad imposter," and to move from his self-serving fantasies to an acceptance of "humble circs." Moore is attempting to capture those personal meanings and cultural influences that are the origin of both failure and survival. Not surprisingly, his portrayal of Ginger Coffey is ambiguous.

Taking the measure of Montreal and creating a dynamic relationship between Coffey and the city were easy for the trained reporter. He recreates an inhospitable, wintry cityscape in a great variety of settings — offices, taverns, cafés, hotels, apartments, the YMCA — and a correspondingly varied gallery of Montreal's multicultural population — Anglo-Scots, French Canadians, Jews, and post-war immigrants. It is not a flattering image of the city, for the prevailing atmosphere is drab, a combination of complacency and frustration, yet Moore countered the criticism that the Montreal he depicted is less itself than it is the Belfast he had evoked in the first two novels: "I suppose I am attracted to the underside of cities. I know that I still think the most fascinating street in Montreal — and no other street compares with it or has anything like its colour and variety — is St. Lawrence Main, which is the Skid Row of Montreal. I think the rest of the city is dull by comparison." Moore conceded that there is a similarity between Northern Ireland and Canada in that they are "both provincial societies . . . both maintaining an identity which is being encroached upon by a much larger country," and that Calvinism pervades both cultures.

Moore's strategy of choosing to see Montreal from the limited perspective of an immigrant was necessary not only because he wanted to draw on his own experience but because "this is my character's view:"

This book was a first-person novel written in the third person. In other words, I tried to have everything seen through the eyes of my central character. That's very limiting, but it was interesting to try, technically, and it also gave the book a unity. I came to Toronto as an immigrant. . . . and I hit Bloor Street at eight o'clock of a very cold February morning with lots of snow. I later arrived by bus in Montreal . . . and I came out of the

Dorchester Street bus terminal into the same sort of snow and gloom. The immigrant who comes to Canada really sees the country much more as a whole. He sees industrial Canada and he sees great raw cities, with some old buildings.

A handful of characters in *The Luck of Ginger Coffey* occupy positions of power and privilege in a large and thriving city — chiefly the managers of businesses whom the unemployed Ginger visits in the hopes of finding a job, and Grosvenor, the representative successful journalist — but a wide cast of characters evokes the underside of Montreal. Coffey's colleagues at the *Tribune* — the newspaper at which his fantasies of becoming J.F. Coffey, Journalist, are woven — are the proofreaders, the "galley slaves," "the lame, the odd, the halt, the old," who collectively suffer under an exploitative and humiliating boss, MacGregor. In 1949 Moore, like Ginger, was lucky to get a foot in even as a proofreader, for he too had been at the point of leaving "the land of opportunity," his gamble on "a horse coloured Canada, which now by hook or by crook would carry him to fame and fortune," having left him down and out.

The anti-capitalist stance of the young Moore was reinforced by his experience at the *Gazette*. Although Ginger is sympathetic to such views, it is a minor character, Fox, who articulates a socialist critique of the Canadian economic system and the poverty of the American Dream: "Money is the Canadian way to immortality. . . . Money is the root of all good here." Yet a sense of the arbitrariness and fundamental injustice of much of life's experience is reflected not only in the sympathetic depiction of that underclass of Canadians but in the portrayal of the American Dream itself and of its many victims. At a moment of intense isolation and loneliness, Ginger realizes that "the filmed America no longer seemed true. He could not believe in this America, this land that half the world dreams of in dark front seats in cities and villages half a world away," and in his fellow proofreader Old Billy Davis, he sees his own future self: "Would Ginger also end his days in some room, old and used, his voice nasal and reedy, all accent gone?"

Moore's interest in the novel is to investigate the ways in which public myths reflect and encourage private fantasies. The true challenge and test in life resides in the private domain, in intimate relationships, and it is for this reason that the central drama of the narrative, which is intertwined with Ginger's search for wealth (or simply work) and public recognition in the New World, is the collapse of his marriage to Vera.

Some critics have found the treatment of Vera and of her abandonment of Ginger for a potential relationship with Gerry Grosvenor a weakness in the novel, and Moore seems to have realized that readers would be dissatisfied with it:

> I've always been afraid of what happens in first-person novels because you cannot really do anything with the character's own perceptions. I said to myself, Ginger wouldn't understand what his wife thinks about things; therefore I won't have to put it in. Then I was attacked by critics and readers for making the wife a flat character because I wasn't able to come in and say, "This is the author; in reality, she thinks this," which of course Thackeray would have done. So first person is very limiting.

It may be that this experience led to the experiments with interior monologue, stream of consciousness, and first-person point of view that Moore undertook in his next four novels, and his frustration with the limitations of his characters' insights possibly led him to choose more educated and perceptive protagonists in later books.

Although he described his protagonist as "a relatively stupid man," Moore bristled when a reviewer called Coffey a dolt: "I don't think anybody's a dolt. *Dolt* is a pejorative word. The hero who is alienated from his culture seems to me to be the classic pattern that's emerging today. Starting on the highest level — I think Camus brought the alienated hero to an international public. Maybe even, it was done by someone else before that — Kafka possibly." The more obvious example, which Moore certainly had in mind although he is not mentioned here, is the Jewish-Irish anti-hero Leopold Bloom. *The Luck of Ginger Coffey* is a further effort to do as Joyce had done, to "celebrate the commonplace," and it now begins to appear as if, by that, Moore means the ability of the alienated or marginalized character to endure.

In taking such a type for a further investigation of failure in the new circumstances of North America, Moore recognized in retrospect that the creation of Ginger extended an investigation that he had started in the first two novels: "Yes, if we're talking now of failed moments in life, his fault — which is so many persons' fault — is that he doesn't see the moment when it comes." Ginger is offered many opportunities not available to Judith Hearne or Diarmuid Devine, yet he is limited: "He is unrealistic to the point that he deliberately turns down what might be best for him, like the job in the laundry — the things he should do. He has insight at the end — insight into the reality of his marriage; it's like Devine, it's an insight into his own limitations. So all of these characters move away from Judith

Hearne in that they become people with more and more alternatives."

These general comments on the protagonists of the early novels — on their common condition as "all in a sense losers" with limited choices, on their earned insight through experience, and on the degree to which the reader might identify with them in their "commonplace" dilemmas — are retrospective. In the actual writing of *Ginger Coffey*, Moore appears to have wanted to affirm a comic and buoyant mood against such a traditional novel of moral realism. "I did want to break away from realism, and if you are writing, as you know, you're always interested in experimenting, and not standing still. I tried to mix three styles in this novel: realistic style, comedy, and tragedy, and to do something that actually could happen realistically in certain scenes in the book in a farcical way. To lift it out of flat realism." This uneasy mixture of genres and an increasing complexity of vision run through the novel and are especially noticeable in key scenes towards the end — the farcical humour of the arrest and acquittal, the mystical intuition of freedom on the courthouse steps, and the reconciliation with Vera.

Moore has spoken of these scenes and the difficulty he had in writing them:

> I felt the ending was not as good, certainly, as it could have been for two reasons. While I was writing it, over a period of nearly two years, it came to me so many times, as it has come to me so many times in my life, that if we talk about the pursuit of happiness, true happiness comes to you fitfully and accidentally. It has nothing to do, as I said in the book, with wealth, fame, success, anything else. They're almost Zen, they're almost mystic. We don't know why they happen. Something ridiculous can make us happy. I wanted to try and write this. That was the hardest paragraph in the book — to give this sensation as he stood on the courthouse steps when he'd been released. That would be a very good moment for a feeling of release — an almost mystical feeling that you're happy now, but realizing that this true happiness can't be captured again.

The novelist has often returned to his dissatisfaction with the reconciliation of Ginger and Vera, and he had a running quarrel with the critics about it. He seems to have felt that in some way he betrayed his imaginative integrity in failing to translate his intention into the actual writing:

> I wanted the ending — the so-called happy ending — to be an ironic anti-climax. I saw it as an ending, a doomful ending, but many critics

didn't. I saw that he had dreamed that his wife was terribly attractive because he couldn't have her, and he walked in and saw, with the eyes of reality, after this mystical moment, the true fact of his wife — a middle-aging woman; and that he was in a way stuck with her and she was in a way stuck with him, but perhaps this was reality he was facing. I didn't mean to imply, and perhaps I was wrong there, that he would not be Ginger again. That he was changed for life. But I do think we all have moments of self-realization.

Yet his ambivalence about the character of Ginger and the happy ending surely reflects his own uncertainty about the natural fate of such a character and the recurring conflict that emerges in later novels between being alone — and true to one's self — and being married.

Through the pain and anxiety of living on the brink, of facing rejection and destitution, Ginger Coffey becomes more of a New World realist. This growth in self-knowledge and the prevailing tone of the book underwrite the fundamental instincts and energies that allow an individual to endure in a new place. The ending celebrates a democratic vision of the commonplace, of that spirit of survival and the capacity for a mystical intuition of meaning in an ordinary person of limited intelligence and imagination.

The novel was a critical and commercial success when it was published in London in April 1960 and in Boston and Toronto two months later. This was especially true in Canada, and it was this book, written at a time when Moore was loosening his ties to Montreal, that paradoxically drew the attention of a wider audience of Canadian readers, publishers and critics to his talent. Robert Weaver of CBC Radio, who was becoming a prominent figure in the promotion of an indigenous literary culture, invited him to contribute a story to a series that included the major figures of the "new generation of Canadian writers . . . the most diverse, professional, and mature generation of writers we have ever had." "Off the Track" — a story that reflects a holiday Brian and Jackie took in Haiti in the mid-fifties — was broadcast in 1960 and then published in the collection *Ten for Wednesday Night* beside the work of Mordecai Richler and Alice Munro, and older established figures like Gabrielle Roy and Morley Callaghan. Significantly, that collection was published by McClelland and Stewart, one of the company's first publications under the direction of Jack McClelland, who would soon become Moore's publisher, a partnership that would endure for almost twenty-five years.

With this novel, Moore was adopted by the Canadian literary establishment, which was creating in the 1960s the conditions in which the country's literature would flourish over subsequent decades. The Guggenheim Fellowship, which had taken Moore to New York in 1959, was now followed by Canada's most distinguished literary prize, the Governor General's Award for Fiction. The award was announced on 25 February 1961 and was followed two days later by a major grant of $4,500 from the Canada Council. In the early summer of this year, the CBC produced a televised version of the novel, and Moore himself prepared a filmscript. That script would eventually become the basis for the shooting of the film, in Montreal and Ottawa, in February/April 1964, directed by Irvin Kershner and produced by Leon Roth and Ottawa-based Crawley Films.

The first critical essay to survey Moore's accomplishment appeared early in 1961 in *Canadian Literature*. Its author, Jack Ludwig, referred to Moore as "Joyce's heir in fiction": "Ginger Coffey is out of Leopold Bloom and *Ulysses*; Moore has pared away the literary devices and touched the core of that novel, the lonely passion of the uninvited-to-the-feast unlucky man, Leopold Bloom turned into a celebration of the human spirit doing what it does in moments of magnificence — liberate itself from the *facts* of life." Ludwig described *The Luck of Ginger Coffey* as "probably the finest novel Canada has seen."

# 12

# AN AMERICAN NOVELIST
# IN LONDON

The summer months in Amagansett in 1959, during which *The Luck of Ginger Coffey* was brought to a conclusion, and the months that followed as the Moore family settled in Manhattan were also a time for Moore to take stock of his new situation. He had moved to be by the sea, to break the routines that had hardened around his life in Montreal and to gain advantage in his career from being close to the centre of publishing in North America. But his move to New York also implied that he wanted to take on imaginatively the burden of being American.

The Jewish writers and intellectuals he met in Amagansett and Manhattan were committed to defining their personal and cultural identity in American society:

> Some of the best young writers in America today are Jewish because they have a tradition, something to revolt against; they have a religious tradition to revolt against, and they have a racial tradition to revolt against if they want to, or discuss, or make a dialogue of it anyway. . . . I feel there's something of that in Irish culture. I'm interested in Catholicism in a non-religious way. I'm interested in the traditions it sets up, and the conflicts.

His sense of his own personal conflicts as Catholic exile and conscientious artist would soon become grafted onto a reading of the cultural and spiritual condition of America. "Philip Roth is my neighbour," he wrote to Richler, "and we are friendly despite the fact that he does not care for my work, it seems. Very parochial, it is over here among this group of young Jewish writers." The Jewish-American writers provided him with models of response to his own ambiguous situation, caught between an overly articulated and codified past and an amorphous and unarticulated present.

Nineteen sixty was an interesting year to immerse himself in American life; it was the year of a presidential campaign in which John F. Kennedy would be victorious. The spirit of Kennedy's campaign was one of optimism and renewal, yet the east-coast literati who came to prominence in the 1950s — J. D. Salinger, Saul Bellow, Norman Mailer, and cultural critics like Lionel Trilling and others clustered around *Partisan Review* and *Commentary* — expressed alienation and frustration. Philip Roth was keenly aware of this adversarial inheritance, and his thoughts from that year, "Writing American Fiction," serve to set the intellectual ambience Moore entered:

> The American writer in the middle of the twentieth century has his hands full in trying to understand, describe, and then make *credible* much of American reality. It stupefies, it sickens, it infuriates, and finally it is even a kind of embarrassment to one's own meager imagination. The actuality is continually outdoing our talents, and the culture tosses up figures almost daily that are the envy of any novelist. . . . The daily newspapers, then, fill us with wonder and awe, also with sickness and despair. . . . Recently, in *Commentary*, Benjamin DeMott wrote that the "deeply lodged suspicion of the times is that events and individuals are unreal, and that power to alter the course of the age, of my life and your life, is actually vested nowhere." There seems to be, said DeMott, a kind of "universal descent into unreality."

These words were written as Moore worked on the first drafts of the novel that would become *An Answer from Limbo*. Two years later, when he had finished the book, he would write a review in which such ideas reappeared.

The book he reviewed was Mary McCarthy's *On the Contrary*, and certain essays in it interested him for their articulation of the meaning of fictional realism. Although he does not agree with everything McCarthy says, nor does he find her fiction praiseworthy, he considers that two "fascinating and controversial essays" almost earn her a place "beside E. M. Forster and Edwin Muir in a discussion of the novel which seems to have a real bearing on the subject." Contrasting the "quality of veracity" one finds in classical realism with present-day fiction,

> McCarthy shrewdly puts her finger on what would seem to be the real difference when she points out that the nineteenth-century novelists "knew everybody," whereas today's novelist is like a *machine à écrire* who sees only other writers. . . . Rightly, she offers no panaceas; the problem, I feel, is one which calls for radical individual decisions: few writers have the courage to disappear from the literary scene in search of their own salvation.

This isolation of the writer from his community, his narcissistic alienation from "the commonplace," is a recurring topic of concern to Moore, and McCarthy's thoughts on the subject echo down through succeeding decades until Moore repeats these ideas as his own in "Imagination and Experience" in 1992. Her thoughts are in an essay on "The Fact in Fiction," which touches on the fundamental principle of the novel that it is "an accurate report of conditions as they exist," but Moore comments: "Our world has become so irreal we no longer believe in it." It is a remark surely prophetic of his own movement away from literary realism into fantasy at the end of the 1960s.

Thoughts on this double unreality, the social and the personal, are focused in a further essay by McCarthy, "Characters in Fiction," and she endorses Joyce's development of the interior monologue as the innovation that preserves the reality of character in a century when "the novel lost interest in the social." Moore disagrees with her when she says Holden Caulfield, Augie March, and Humbert Humbert are "not quite the real thing" because Salinger, Bellow, and Nabokov do not "identify sympathetically" with their protagonists. Instead, he argues that the success of these novels comes from a close identification of author and a protagonist whose "dreams and desires" resemble their own. While Moore continues to argue that the reality of character and the ability of the author to "become his characters" are the defining criteria of good fiction, one can see that in writing *An Answer from Limbo* he wanted also to make a moral statement about the spiritual and cultural condition of America:

> My fiction begins to move, I think, in *An Answer from Limbo* toward a different world — first of all, really, an American world, and also toward the concerns of the so-called artist, the person who has an illusion that he will do something great, or a hope that he will do something great and his constant fear that this may be an illusion. The other books were about failure. In *An Answer from Limbo*, I tried to go a little into how success de-humanizes people. Failure makes you more intensely yourself; you have to fall back on whatever you are and you may become an eccentric, but your eccentricity will be a distillation of that peculiar person you were before, whereas success de-humanizes people and changes them into something they were not. In other words, they become their public persona, or their image of themselves, and in that sense they're dehumanized.

It is hardly surprising that the recipient of awards, grants, critical acclaim, and respect from fellow artists should begin to examine the effect of such success on one's art and life. In his own first interview upon the publication of *Judith Hearne*, he is cautious about the public role and persona he should adopt. "I have never been a member of any writing group, national or otherwise. I am a loner . . . I dislike personal publicity and I have contempt for those writers who become 'personalities.'" From this time on, a measure of an artist's accomplishment for Moore appears to be the extent to which he can refrain from being the hero of his own novel, as character, or as moralizing narrator, or as an exhibitionistic stylist who draws attention away from the autonomous life of the fictional protagonist. "I think with Flaubert," he wrote to Richler, "that if material is presented so that the author is inside each character, setting down with understanding and truth each detail which makes a whole truth, then explanation is unnecessary, the values show themselves." As in the case of Judith Hearne and Diarmuid Devine, whose selfhood was distilled by their failure, so also with successful characters; the truth of their success and their values must be incarnate in the characters themselves.

As a successful novelist, Moore had been selected by the Guggenheim jury to join the company of America's most esteemed writers, and yet he experienced disillusionment:

> I lived in Greenwich Village at the time of writing *An Answer from Limbo*, and I noticed that the serious writers there — the serious writers, mind you — were quite interested in best-sellerdom, publicity, immediate personal fame, that they were, many of them — like Capote and Mailer and so on — shameless little puffers-up of their talents and muggers-in-public for anyone who would write them up. No different from people I had interviewed years ago as a reporter — show-business people. I think the temptations for the serious American writer today are fame and fortune. Nobody understands the old idea — that there should be a company of the good, and the fact that your books don't sell a hundred thousand copies, or fifty, or forty, isn't the real answer.

Moore's preoccupation with questions of integrity and the conscience of the artist reverberate back to his adolescent confrontations with his father in the late 1930s and his idealization of Joyce's dedication to his art. New York forced this issue of conscience to the front of his mind:

> When I went to live in America, in Greenwich Village, I was, for the first time in my life, plunged into a literary milieu. I had a lot of friends there, writers, mostly Jewish, all of them extremely ambitious in the

American way, all of them imbued with the American sense not of being one of the company of the good, but of wanting to be the heavy-weight champ. I saw an enormous amount of that sort of fear and that sort of self-doubt enter into their lives. I think it enters into the lives of many writers.

Brendan Tierney, alias Gildea in the first draft of *An Answer from Limbo*, is doubly preoccupied with success, as an aspiring American novelist in the literary marketplace and also as an ex-Catholic European with yearnings for immortality. This character is at the centre of a portrait of the artist that aims also to be a study of American mores and values through the dramatization of a marital crisis and through a contrast between the Manhattan world of Brendan and Jane Tierney and his former Irish Catholic world. The literary milieu of Greenwich Village is used as setting but also as metaphor for a cul-ture caught in the moral and spiritual contradictions of the American Dream, of placing personal success above all else — a contradiction Moore acknowledged and has struggled throughout his life to accept.

"When does youth end? In a year or in an hour, in a birthday or a mourning?", an early draft opening for the novel begins.

Or do we lose it as we lose a familiar object, its absence unnoticed until one day we can no longer find it? Did it end for me one summer morn-ing on 44th Street in New York or later that day at Saint Vincent's Hospital? Had it been lost a long time before I discovered its absence? I do not know. I know only that in its losing I played hero and villain, saint and self-deluder, tragedian and buffoon. I was all these things because all these persons are related to me. My struggle is to survive them.

How shall I begin? I shall establish the place as an apartment on the fringe of Greenwich Village, the time as eight o'clock on the morning of July 25, 1959. . . . I lie naked on the bed. . . . It is the body of a man in the last months of his twenties, a man born in another country and still on the run from it, a man who wakes now from a dream of home (that large house where, with my parents, my sisters and brothers, I lived through forgotten events which according to the authorities of our time, fix and pre-determine my present actions). I awake, as always, in the stammer of memory, which is to say, in fear.

If such a sketch recalls the character of Ginger Coffey, the recollection is not misplaced, for Coffey initiates a sequence of characters who are self-deluded and whose self-delusion is revealed through a dramatization of the burdens of success. The loss of youthful identity and certainty, the exiled state of being in limbo, was very much on Moore's mind as he began what he thought of as his most ambitious novel to date, and that loss remained central for more than two decades.

Brendan Tierney is an autobiographical portrait to the degree that Moore had personal and intimate experience of many of Tierney's professional compromises and of his artistic and ex-Catholic consciousness. The Irish background and North American career of Brendan Tierney, sketched in the first few chapters of the novel, draw on Moore's own earlier life. Passages of the story "Preliminary Pages for a Work of Revenge," on the childhood dream of being a poet and the later motivations of "rage and revenge," are incorporated directly into the novel. More surprisingly, other passages which etch in Brendan Tierney's youth are reprinted more than a decade later in an autobiographical essay on "The Expatriate Writer" as descriptions of Moore's own youth.

Yet, as he has said, he would not have been able to write of these dilemmas of artistic ambition and exile, and of the New York literary milieu in which they are set, if he had not at the same time been an outsider and able to distance himself from what he dramatized with such intimate knowledge. "That's a problem when you are trying to write a book about a writer. The reviewers tend to think that you are writing about yourself. I wanted to show that Tierney's view of art is flawed and it is selfish; he doesn't know whether he is trying to create art or trying to become famous and the dichotomy in his own mind hasn't really been resolved."

An appropriate distance from Tierney became possible when, during the writing of the novel, Moore moved away from New York. In June 1961, the couple sailed for Ireland, to spend June and July in a rented house in Connemara. Moore wrote a whimsical account of this holiday for *Atlantic Monthly*, and he has spoken elsewhere of his awakened attraction to this bleak landscape, a part of Ireland with many literary associations through the work, notably, of Synge and Yeats. Yet, if it touched the writer deeply and in a lasting way, this stay was overshadowed by extreme tension and marital discord. "We have to get out of Bleak House and this land of my fathers before we all go off our rockers," he wrote to Richler in London. "I have been sick since I came and forced through some work on the novel, then the piece on Belfast for *Holiday* but am now at a halt and what the psychiatrists describe as 'tense and anxious.' Not good. I really think it was the return here after so many years that did it."

This was Moore's first visit to Ireland since his mother's death. He would speak in the 1970s of feeling depressed whenever he returned to Belfast and that Connemara offered him relief from those feelings. And he would associate that relief with the "unchanging" world of his parents. This first phase of the year the Moore family planned to spend away from New York seems to have brought into focus, unhappily, some fundamental conflict in Moore's marriage.

Early notes for *An Answer from Limbo* focus on the Tierneys in New York, their affairs and career ambitions, but make no reference to the pivotal role of the Irish mother in the narrative and in the drama of conflicting values. The central opposition of mother and daughter-in-law, of traditional belief and sceptical individualism, seems to enter the novel at this stage, and the mother represents a severe judgement of the writer, his marriage, and his New York social life. More significantly, perhaps, the sickness that overtook Moore in Ireland may be continuous with his tension in Montreal in the late fifties, which the move to Long Island had seemed temporarily to alleviate. "I am very hopeful that London, peace and quiet and some place to live will cure me of this without serious damage to my work and our life," he writes to Richler.

Mordecai Richler and Diana Athill awaited the arrival of the Moores in London in the first days of August. The family remained in London for eight months, and Moore entered the literary world of the city, contributing a number of essays and reviews to *The Spectator*, and thus counterpointing another literary and cultural milieu to the one he was creating in the novel. Richler even wondered if he himself had been a model for one of Brendan Tierney's colleagues, Max Bronstein, rather than any of Moore's associates in New York. It might also be remarked that Moore had gained aesthetic distance from literary New York because essential dramatic elements draw as much on his professional and social experiences in the magazine world of Montreal in the early and mid-fifties as on more recent events in the American city.

The novel moved forward quickly, and Moore recorded its progress: "First draft over by August 31 1961; Second draft by January 30 1962." Those essential experiences of the culture shock of Moore's own assimilation are embodied in his most ambitious novel to date. In 1967, he told an interviewer, "I've always felt it was my most ambitious book, technically. I mean in style, etc., points of view, construction." Once again, his inspiration and his belief in the book depend on his ability to "become" his central character:

> *An Answer from Limbo* is about three characters, but if Brendan, the most unsympathetic character, had not satisfied me, I would have

dropped the book. I could do the mother with my eyes closed. The wife was a challenge to do, but she could have been a little less well done and the book would still have carried her. But if he wasn't well done, the book would disappear. Brendan was the first person, the dangerous one. So, always, when I approached the scenes with him, I was aware of the dangers. In that book the progression continues as each event happens. There's very little flashback. Each person takes the story up and goes on. That was hard to do; it took a lot of rewriting, moving forward all the time.

As always, Moore was concerned to develop a technique that would engage the reader in the emotional condition of his central character, and this unlikeable protagonist posed problems in a number of ways.

As for Brendan Tierney — people felt a tinge of contempt for him, too. They felt that he was a careerist, an arriviste, which, of course, I intended him to be. One of the reasons, as Thomas Mann has said, that you can't write about genius is because you cannot show artistic genius or depict it. So I dodged this by saying it's not important whether this man is a good writer or a bad writer; the point is, what does he think? . . . I meant him to be corruptible. I've been surprised at the number of good writers who, when they start thinking of a best seller, lose their writing standards.

That loss of writing standards may derive from weakness of character, but in depicting the obsessive ambition that leads Brendan to sacrifice his own moral integrity by abandoning those closest to him — his wife and his mother — Moore writes about a selfishness that mirrors a pervasive moral and metaphysical vacuum in American life. "It is a book about ambition, and it is a book about the conflict between generations in New York. . . . What I'm trying to show in *An Answer from Limbo* is the effect of ambition on one of the characters — the writer — and the effect on his wife of dissatisfaction with modern life," Moore said. The dissatisfaction of Jane Tierney is another form of ambition. He wanted "to juxtapose people born sixty years ago — the protagonist's mother, who was content to live for others — with those born thirty years ago, like his wife, who should have been happy simply to rear her own children, but wasn't." Whatever the individual goal, in the case of husband and wife, a craving for self-affirmation in an ego-driven world is the central impulse, and this is Moore's key to a dark satire of American culture.

Jane Tierney, mother of two young children, asserts her independence by taking a job with a magazine. She quickly drifts into a sexual affair. "All fiction," Moore noted, a little defensively, "is a dramatization or heightening of normal life, and some people might say her action is extreme, but I have known a number of women in New York who in one way or another exemplify some of the traits she possesses." Yet it is not her need for sexual pleasure that interests him. He counters the description of her in a review as a "certifiable witch" by remarking that it is "a hangover from the Victorian era that women don't have sexual desires." Men, he said, "don't like to read about women as they really are" — an idea he returns to in *I Am Mary Dunne* and *The Doctor's Wife*.

Unlike the protagonists of those two novels, however, Jane Tierney's craving for sexual ecstasy leads to a sordid end — although no more sordid than that of her self-absorbed husband when he neglects his mother and leaves her to a lonely death. *Limbo* is a realistic narrative of literary life and of marital dissatisfaction that develops into a moral fable because the dilemmas in which these characters find themselves mirror a society in spiritual and cultural crisis. It is not surprising that a favourite novelist of Moore should be the arch-satirist Evelyn Waugh, Catholic convert, heir of T. S. Eliot in his depiction of the wasteland of modern urban life, the "fear in a handful of dust."

Moore insists that he despises Waugh's values and admires only his technique, yet he, like Waugh, Eliot, or many other heirs of modernism, is searching for a fulcrum for his disaffected vision of a twentieth-century spiritual abyss. Moore's New York, recreated while he was living in London, exemplifies the "unreality" of American life that Roth and others had articulated, but it also bears the imprint of another American, exiled in London, and his image of the "unreal city." Eliot's London is fused with Joyce's Dublin in this and later images of Moore's New York. This is the first novel in which he reveals himself as a fierce satirist of modern American life, the vulnerability of the conscience-bound artist being the litmus test of the forces of unreality in modern culture.

The return to Ireland appears to have inspired new ways of thinking about his childhood home and its beliefs. His remark that "round about that time my mother had died" suggests that the return to Ireland at the time of writing had collapsed the four-year interval and that her death became disturbingly immediate. "She was a more sophisticated woman than Mrs. Tierney," he added,

but in many ways she resembled her. She never came to America to see me. I went to Ireland to see her and took her to France once for a holiday. While I was in France with her, I saw her in an environment I had never seen her in before. I was in my thirties and I just began to realize — as many people do — that parents had many, many qualities that I didn't think they had when I was twenty; and I think the book was about that. I've always felt, too, that for most people any faith is better than no faith. It gives them something to live for and with. Part of the admirable thing about my mother was that while she was sort of depressive, her faith kept her from being self-centred. And Brendan *is* self-centred, Jane *is* self-centred, Mrs. Tierney is not self-centred.

Moore went to some lengths to distance himself from the traditional, pious Catholicism of Mrs. Tierney, "We can't go back to being our parents — we cannot will faith," yet reviewers and critics were almost unanimous in identifying the emotional and moral centre of the novel as the protagonist's mother. Although he said that "her values were wrong," and so seemed to say that both the Irish mother and the New York writers were equally limited, he was forced to agree that Mrs. Tierney's symbolic status in the satirical paradigm was a privileged one: "One of the things I tried to show is that it is much easier to live, as the mother does, with a fixed set of beliefs, even if they are wrong ones, than to make up rules as one goes along. Unfortunately, it is more difficult to live without a faith than with one."

Even if Moore does not take sides, his sympathies in this novel and for the rest of his career begin to clarify. In answer to the question "If Irish Catholicism is destructive, and if America offers only a rootless wasteland, then where is the solution?" he replied: "I really don't know the answer to this one. If I did, I wouldn't be writing novels, I'd be writing treatises. I feel that I am working towards answers for myself."

While the tension created by these contrasting characters and world-views is at the heart of the American and satirical aspects of the novel, there is another, more private, tension also that is, perhaps, of equal interest to Moore and is connected to the set of insoluble psychological and metaphysical issues that preoccupy his later work. He has remarked that the only truly autobiographical note in the book is the description of his mother's burial. "When you're a writer, you no longer see things with the freshness of the normal person. There are always two figures at work inside you, and if you are at all intelligent you realize that you have lost something. But I think there has always been this dichotomy in a real writer. He wants to be terribly human, and he responds emotionally, and at the same time there's this cold observer who cannot cry." That theme — the loss of primal sympathy, the sacrifice of self to the state of being "beyond all self-recognition" — is raised on the opening page of the novel and recurs as a probing motif in the portrait of the artist this novel presents.

The closing scene of the novel at the graveside of Mrs. Tierney has been glossed by Moore in notes for himself: "He [Brendan] sees his success at the end as obtained at the price of a murder. He sees that inadvertently and by refusing to think of her as a person of equal value with Jane and himself, he has been guilty of the almost Auschwitz crime." That crime of indifference, of dehumanization, is a recurring moral criterion in Moore's fiction and the source of his deep commitment to his characters.

At the end of the novel, as Jane and Brendan assess their responsibility for Mrs. Tierney's death, Brendan begins by reflecting with relief, "Indifference, it seems, is not a crime punishable by law," and wants to believe that "It's nobody's fault . . . it was just bad luck." But he ends in anguished self-recognition: "Am I still my mother's son, my wife's husband, the father of my children? Or am I a stranger, strange even to myself?" That recognition of the loss of compassion or of the ability to love is the price he has paid for becoming a writer. Narcissism, that "albatross of self," Moore recognized as the particular moral danger of expatriate writers and of North American society.

In April 1962, the Moores left London for a three-week holiday in Italy before returning to North America to await the publication of the new novel. A Canadian newspaper reporter spoke to him in London at this time. The reporter notes his contradictory affiliations — "I think of myself as a Canadian writer today" and, half an hour later, "I am a European" — and sums up: "He will be classified as an American writer" and an "archetypal writer beyond nationalistic or racial classification," but he is "more at home in Canada than anywhere." Although Moore still owned his house in Montreal, New York once again became home, and he was usually described thereafter as a resident of New York.

Notes written on his return to Amagansett in spring 1962, as well as book reviews written while in London, indicate that a Jamesian counterpointing of Europe and North America helped him to clarify the moral outlook of the novel:

Limbo is the modern condition: a place, neither heaven nor hell, a place of oblivion. . . . Living in America today, is, for a European, living in the future. London, Paris, and Rome seem provincial capitals compared to New York. I have just come back from a year in which I visited all three. . . . American writing today reflects American society:

its absence of ideals, its concern with the private self: it seems to me that this concern with the self has narrowed to the point of narcissism: we no longer understand even the smallest widening of the ripples around the pool in which our own faces are reflected: the old ties of family, friends, small community are breaking and we are doing nothing to prevent their breaking.

In spite of this critical tone, Moore goes on to say that "America, not Russia, is the pattern for the future of the West. For this reason, living in New York is like living in the Imperial Rome of our day, and there is a wild dirty electricity to the city which makes it an ideal place to live." While there is an atmosphere of Cold War debates about such musings, the moral preoccupation with narcissism and with the "unreality" of American culture was a lasting interest. He accepts a responsibility at this time to be a critic of society: "The art [Brendan Tierney] attempts to practice is the novel; a novelist is a moralist and his sense of morality should carry over into his own life otherwise he is a false prophet preaching a message he does not believe in."

*An Answer from Limbo* came out in New York and Toronto in October 1962 and in London the following March. "I thought when I finished it that it would have a big audience," Moore has said, "but it did the same as the others. No change at all." He is speaking here of sales, yet the novel did receive a large number of very favourable reviews. Among the most prominent was one by the influential Granville Hicks in *Saturday Review*, and his comments are not only extraordinarily perceptive and sympathetic but recognize the essence of Moore's talent:

Moore has the great gift of looking at people and places as if no one had ever seen them before. New York is rendered with a kind of pristine sensitivity. Even the literary life of the city, which has so often been written about in a banal fashion, is seen so freshly that the reader can be moved to astonishment and sometimes horror. The characters, including the minor characters, behave with the mysterious combination of predictability and unpredictability that is the essence of life. . . . The novel communicates with perfect lucidity the author's vision of the complexity and pathos of life.

The novelist was proud of his accomplishment in meeting the challenges of dramatizing a central character such as Brendan Tierney, more intellectually and emotionally complex than earlier characters, in a new social and cultural context. His confidence that his talent could grow was confirmed by the experience of writing *Ginger Coffey* and *Limbo*, for his embracing of a North American literary life meant a great deal to him. Some years later, he commented, "I think I am the first Irish-born writer who came to America and has made the transition to writing about American people. . . . I've never been faulted by anyone in that I wrote bad American idiom, or that my Americans don't seem real. Maybe that might be my little niche in history because the Irish writer and the English writer have a curious inability to leave home fictionally." A bitter irony of this time was that he was disqualified from nomination for a National Book Award for the novel because he was not an American citizen.

At the end of 1962, a lucrative commission from Time-Life to write a book on Canada for its "World Library" series brought him back to Canada. The Moores spent Christmas in Montreal, where Brian's brother Seán still lived, now a professor of pathology at McGill University, married with young children, and the occupant of the Moores' house in Westmount. Moore travelled extensively across the country at the end of 1962 and beginning of 1963 before he settled down to write. In his portrait of his adoptive country, he wrote with feelings of attachment about the landscape, about immigrants, and about the possibilities of creating a more open, multicultural society.

While writing *Canada*, Moore heard from Mordecai Richler that he was seriously considering moving back to Canada from London. Moore's response was encouraging: "I think you are wise to move back to Canada. I say this with the experience of the exile who did not move, would never move now but always wonders whether it would have been better if I had. One thing is certain. You do not belong over there, but over here. I wanted to change my nationality and forget it all: you do not. . . . Writing *Canada*: it's turning out very bitter indeed and not because I was bitter when I was there, but the more I read, the less I admire your countrymen. The English Canadian ones anyway." In this month he sold his house to his brother Seán, thus confirming his sense of himself as a writer detached from Canada as from Ireland, and, indeed, also from his life in New York.

## 13
### RADICAL INDIVIDUAL DECISIONS

The failure of his ambitious American novel to make the impact Moore had expected, and his increasing disillusionment with the "parochial" publishing scene in New York, were expressed to Richler in February 1964: "Sour about the book world and the expectation here that a professional novelist must go on churning out book after book." In fact, so gloomy were his thoughts about the fate of the literary novel that he thought "what poetry is today the novel will be tomorrow . . . there's a smaller and smaller audience," and he foretold that film and television would dominate a future that would be a "visual time."

Moore took to heart the disappointment of his American publisher that he did not follow *An Answer from Limbo* with another "American" novel, and the fact that Jack McClelland had voiced his difficulty in publishing and finding an audience for novels, such as *Limbo*, set outside Canada. During the renegotiation of Moore's contract, McClelland had raised the matter of the novelist's ambiguous national affiliation and the perception that his books were not Canadian. In fact, McClelland was personally committed to Moore and wanted to have him as one of his star authors, but Moore was aware from this time on that his books were not commercially successful in Canada and that McClelland's loyalty to him endured in spite of small sales.

The struggle for the novelist with artistic aspirations is to reach a discerning audience and yet preserve his integrity in this commercial and visually driven culture. Moore's longstanding animus against the type of writer who degenerated into a "personality" on television became more intense during the New York years, and he witnessed the "sad performance" of the Irish writer Brendan Behan with some horror. "In the careers of certain writers the gossip columnist is the Angel of Death," he wrote three months after Behan's premature death in 1964. "As the flow of sub-literary 'news items' and anecdotes increases, the writer's work withers and stales until, in grim transference, his life becomes his oeuvre and he his only character. The Angel is now at the head of his bed. His time is up." From his earliest experiences working as a journalist, often writing about celebrities and stars, Moore had been determined to avoid that fate. "Few writers," he commented, "have the courage to disappear from the literary scene in search of [their] own salvation." Over the next year, he would face the "radical individual decisions" he had pondered as early as summer 1962 when he posed this challenge to himself.

The bitterness and disillusionment with publishing reflect the difficulty he was having with his own decision to write a "European" novel. In summer 1963, he had begun a "novella," and in August wrote to Richler that "after a year of commercial work," he yearned to "get a lock on the novella, but it's going to be hard . . . I sometimes get low at the idea that nobody seems to give a damn about novels." In November, he announced that he had started "on a book — a novel," although he was very tentative about its quality, and in February 1964 he told of having completed one hundred pages of "one of those worst selling novels which take so long." Through 1964, he continues to speak of the "rough time" he is having with it, "plodding away intermittently on the novel."

In spite of its title, taken from the American poet Wallace Stevens, *The Emperor of Ice Cream* is a deliberate effort to move away from the moral and satirical perspective on the American Dream of his two recent novels:

> It has been at the back of my mind for many years to try to write a novel about the odd, faintly comic set of attitudes with which we in Ulster met the advent of Hitler. The Italian novelist Curzio Malaparte and others on the German side have written about the odd attitudes which prevailed in Italy and Germany — Günter Grass's novel *The Tin Drum* comes to mind, but, so far as I know, no one on the Allied side has been similarly frank. And we, in Ulster, were in a faintly *opéra bouffe* situation. I thought that now, 25 years later, passions will have cooled enough for someone to tell the truth about those days in 1939 and 1940. . . . The air raids on Belfast were a terrible thing, but in some way, they were the great lesson we, in Ulster, needed. Until they happened the Ulster I knew was racked by dissent and bigotry, consumed with petty passions and old spites. When the Germans hammered us in 1941, they hammered Orange and Catholic alike, Unionist Blimp and Labour firebrand.

Moore was now ready to write the *Bildungsroman* that he had long avoided. *The Emperor of Ice Cream* marked the moment when he took a new look at his Belfast childhood and reassessed the feelings and perceptions of adolescence that had set his life's course:

> The events of those terrible nights made not only my adolescent hero grow up — they made Ulster grow up. Our little wars — our 12th of July processions and our window-breaking, rock-throwing little hatreds — seemed childish and silly. The Nationalist's secret hope that the Germans would win seemed, as it was, a horrible, childish self-deception, as idiotic as that Orange oratory which saw the enemy of Ulster as Rome and the Pope. At the end of my novel Gavin, the hero, forgives his father for his father's foolish bigotry. His father weeps, realising how stupid he has been. I meant it as more than a "happy ending." I meant it was what happened, I hope, in Ulster at that time. We all grew up.

Just as he reassessed the image of the mother in *Limbo*, the time had arrived for a new start with the image of his father, and in the new novel he would be able to adopt a largely comic tone towards his own younger self, towards his father and towards Belfast. The energy in the writing seems to have come from his realization that the growing-up process of the adolescent Gavin Burke mirrors a parallel process of growing-up that his father and others of his generation must also undergo; that the adolescent state was a common condition; and that illusion and fantasy were typical personal and cultural states of those years in Ireland, and, perhaps, also of the North American world in which he now lived.

A decision not to continue with another novel on the large issue of the spiritual and cultural condition of America coincided with his discovery of Jorge Luis Borges and with a reassessment of his sense of himself as a maker of fictions. "I saw how [Borges] created imaginary worlds which seemed totally real. How the fantastic could be made to seem mundane, simply through the skill of his writing. And so in some way I broke free from the realism of my early novels." Although this comment seems to refer more directly to later novels of dream and fantasy, such as *Fergus* and *The Great Victorian Collection*, Moore has identified the moment of his change towards a freer and more experimental approach to writing as this period after *Limbo*.

Moore's optimism that the war had awakened both sides of the sectarian divide in Belfast from their childish self-deceptions proved to be premature as an historical generalization, yet the novel reflects his sense of a larger truth about war. In 1956, when he read Isaac Babel's stories of the

Russian Revolution and Civil War, he commented: "Horrors, but very real, not literary horrors, but true ones for he is telling you his own life." Gavin's experience of the bombardment reproduces Moore's own experience — in this single novel, he has said, he knew at the outset what the ending would be — and he has remarked that the air raids and the volunteer job coffining bodies had a strong effect on him, but "if I'd tried to handle it when I was twenty-four I probably couldn't have written it, I would have been too emotional and too off-balance." His experience of wartime deepened and focused his sense of value in life, and the historical and personal truth he disclosed in this fictional situation actually coincides with a rite of passage which is central to all his novels: from self-delusion to a disconcerting facing-up to reality.

Some years earlier, while making notes for *Ginger Coffey*, he wrote in his Commonplace Book: "The constant companion is death. Money is the thing, the pursuit of which keeps most men worrying on a false level: survival is better than non-survival. Why in wartime men are happy." These remarks suggest that Moore's "worrying" about success "on a false level" during the years in New York, exemplified most directly in *An Answer from Limbo*, led to a reaffirmation of his commitment to "the commonplace" and his radical alienation from the "unreality" of much of the American Dream. His Commonplace Book also makes reference to Yeats's concept of "tragic joy," and on many occasions at this time, he refers to the necessary acceptance of the view that life is tragic — "Yeats said that you can only enjoy life once you realize that it is tragic" — and from this acknowledgement, optimism or joy or love may follow.

*The Emperor of Ice Cream* continues and extends Moore's lasting search for characters whose grasp of the ordinary truths of suffering and endurance undermines self-serving illusions. "The ARP figures are types rather than people," he has said, "they exist to parody the attitudes of the time," and the same may be said of other minor characters, yet Moore's self-discipline in creating this gallery of types, and his general sense of character in fiction, should be noted:

> Villains are what we identify with enormously because we release our aggression on them. I write without villains, which makes my books difficult for a big audience; and even when I have a 'villain,' I always wind up trying to see him in the round because flat characters are always caricatures. In *The Emperor of Ice Cream*, for instance, the original of the character of the ARP chief, the real man, was a villain who will die a sadist. Writing in the American style on that, I would have had a camp

homosexual sadist romp with these people. . . . But I was using the view-point of the seventeen-year-old Gavin . . . so I underplayed it.

The challenge in writing, then, appears once again to have been one of finding the appropriate point of view. That "underplayed" tone allowed fantasy, irony, and parody to colour a seriously realistic treatment of awakening from illusion.

The central drama of the novel is within Gavin's consciousness and in a bitter conflict between him and his father. Gavin Burke's adolescent fantasies of power — sometimes sexual, sometimes iconoclastic — always rest on a knife-edge of indecision and powerlessness, of shame and humiliation. His rational sense of an historical drift towards tyranny, articulated for him by the left-wing thirties poets, is usurped by his impotent fantasy: "War was freedom, freedom from futures." His fantasies and his father's equally self-serving *pronunciamentos*, "echoing the mysterious judgement of all authority," are put to the test when the bombs fall. Both are brought to an admission that a radical change has taken place which they must learn to live with: "The looking-glass room, unchanged since his child-hood, had changed at last. . . . standing in the cowering light of the can-dles, he feared the house. It had died. Its life had fled. The dead, their faces dirty and pale, dried blood on their lips, their bowels loose in the final spasm, sat on his mother's sofas and chairs, moved in the shadows." Wallace Stevens's poem of death refers not to a "literary horror" but to a real horror known intimately in wartime.

Father and son who have been bitter adversaries throughout the novel are reconciled through that shared knowledge of the horror of war, and Moore found it again necessary to defend his ending against charges of sentimentality: "I had built up Mr. Burke, Senior, as a man who admired Hitler. And it was literally true that people of my father's generation imme-diately realized that they were wrong when the war started, and they were big enough to admit it. I probably wasn't a good enough writer to carry off that feeling, but that was an honest ending, and any other way would have been dishonest. It was a sort of quick *volte-face* — that was the point." While this historical truth is Moore's first concern, there is also an issue of literary truth here: "I think that life itself is very close to the sentimental. . . . How much easier for the boy to have done the simple thing like not forgiving the father, or the father coming back and saying nothing quite so direct and leaving it all in a nice vague *New Yorker*ish way; and no one would have complained."

But the question of the "happy ending" and its historical or literary truth is not the whole story of Moore's commitment to the characters and to the world of this novel. While *Emperor* began as an historical novel, albeit with a thematic focus not far removed from Moore's novels of contemporary North America, it was also an autobiographical novel, given shape by the model of the *Bildungsroman*. He was finally able to write a version of the novel of his family and of growing up in Catholic Belfast that had escaped him in the 1950s. His distance from the sexual, religious, and familial conflicts of his eighteen-year-old alter ego, or his twenty-year-old self, as well as his distance from the historical events, seems to have increased during the third phase of his exile, the years in New York, and to have allowed him to envision his own adolescence with balance.

If doubt, the collapse of faith, is at the heart of a modern tragedy in *Judith Hearne*, here it is treated in a more gentle manner, in the endless comic dialogues of the Black Angel and the White Angel. Moore's dramatic device for enlivening the circling inner monologues of the uncertain adolescent is a major element in establishing the tone of the novel: "The White Angel sat on his right shoulder and advised the decent thing. The Black Angel sat on his left shoulder and pleaded the devil's cause . . . the trouble was, the Black Angel seemed more intelligent; more his sort." If this device seems to recall Ginger Coffey's habit of talking to himself and looking at his "imposter" self in mirrors, it also looks forward in a more decisive way to the next novel and the inner monologue which dramatizes the many selves of Mary Dunne.

The angels are more than a technical device, however, for Moore's notes from the 1950s reveal his interest in the idea of the double, an interest perhaps intensified by his reading of Dostoievski: "The alter ego in everyone: the suspicion that inside there is something which is not sweet and innocuous. . . . The layers of politesse hiding the sudden terrible driving force of Christie the sex maniac. . . . Is the hidden evil the real force or is it a siamese twin?" These notes accompany reflections on Millington and Barnett, his Belfast associates in the Drama Guild, and seem, therefore, to originate in Moore's sense of extreme repression in own life during his last years in Belfast. They may also refer to his state in the late 1950s and early 1960s as he disengaged himself mentally from his social milieu and grew estranged from Jackie.

These notes also seem to be related to the bitter monologue of 1959, "Preliminary Pages for a Work of Revenge," and to other monologues of that time. *Notes from Underground*, the Dostoievskian model for "Revenge," also seems to have been the model for an early beginning for *Emperor*: "We underpeople usually congregate on the underside of cities, although we can be found in any community . . . our lives are lived in drama, in passion and, above all, in private. We do not make history, yet we affect it. . . . We are antipathetic to causes and crusades. Our heaven and hell is here and now. Our God is Number One." The characterization of "failure" in this six-page draft is intimately autobiographical, tracing the familial and educational difficulties, the conflict with his father, joining the ARP, and the absurdity of the ARP routines. *Emperor* presents a mature and balanced treatment of issues that were deeply disturbing to Moore during the period that is captured in the novel and at later stages. His dramatization of the radical awakening and maturing of Gavin Burke, and his optimistic assumption that everyone in Belfast "grew up" when confronted with the reality of war, reflect also the new beginning in his own life in 1964.

Looking back on that change in 1967, he remarked, "I am much happier now than I was when I was thirty-five or forty. *Emperor* was written at a crucial time in my life. It was the first book after I changed. I started a new life halfway through the writing of it, I fell in love, remarried and so on. . . . Unlike Devine, Miss Hearne — unlike my heroes — I have never been afraid to risk everything. I have never been afraid to act, to change. People's lives change them." The later years in Montreal and the years in New York and London had gradually brought him to a point at which he was prepared to "risk everything," to take a "radical individual decision."

In 1963–64, the Moores had settled back into their New York routine after the months in London and in Canada. Brian started work on *Emperor.* Jackie was contributing occasional articles to magazines such as *Harper's* and *Holiday*, and appears to have been content with the role of "Mrs. Brian Moore." Her husband's deep restlessness is indicated in his correspondence, where there are frequent references to feeling old and insecure, and to having "an all alone and agonising time" making progress with the novel, "and that, as you know, is ulcer making." They continued to live in a Manhattan apartment, but their first base at Amagansett still drew them. They spent the late summer of 1963 there and, having sold their home in Montreal, made an unsuccessful offer towards the end of 1963 on the house they had been renting. Some months later, they bought a farmhouse in Frenchtown, New Jersey, in conjunction with new friends, Franklin and Jean Russell.

The Russells had moved to Manhattan in April 1963 from Toronto, where Frank Russell, a New Zealander educated in England, had settled as a freelance writer in 1954. In the late 1950s, he had worked as a science writer for Maclean-Hunter publications, but he also contributed travel and natural history pieces to a variety of magazines. One of these articles, "The Secret Life of a Pond," in *Maclean's* magazine, came to the attention of publisher Alfred Knopf, and in this way Russell's highly successful book *Watchers at the Pond* (1961) became the first of many he wrote for children and adults in the burgeoning field of nature writing.

It was at Maclean-Hunter that Frank Russell met Jean Denney, who was working at *Maclean's* magazine as an editorial assistant. Her family was from Newfoundland, and she had grown up in Kentville, Nova Scotia. In addition to her work in publishing, she was also pursuing a career as an actress under the name Jean Lewis. In the early sixties, now married to Russell, she developed a strong interest in art and design, interior decoration and antique furniture, while her husband became more rooted imaginatively in her earlier landscapes in Atlantic Canada.

Brian Moore and Frank Russell met in the spring of 1963, and soon the Moores had introduced the Russells into their New York social circle. During 1964, the friendship between the two couples underwent a dramatic change. In June 1964, Jackie and Michael moved to the house in Amagansett for the summer months, but Brian stayed in Manhattan at the apartment on East 79th Street. This decision conformed to his long-standing habit of wanting to be alone at a critical stage in the writing of a novel. Frank Russell had won a Guggenheim Fellowship and left Manhattan on a research trip to the small islands in the Bay of Fundy and off Newfoundland that he would soon describe in *The Secret Islands*. During this summer, Brian and Jean became lovers, and when Jackie and Michael returned to Manhattan in September, the novelist moved out to an apartment on Gramercy Square.

The change in the Moores' domestic arrangements appears to have been mutually accepted at first. Letters from Jackie at the end of 1964 indicate the depth of her distress at being abandoned by Brian, but an intimate partnership also commenced at this time between her and Frank Russell. The new alliances were declared in the way the two couples recognized as official — in print. Moore dedicated *The Emperor of Ice Cream* "to Jean," and Russell dedicated *The Secret Islands* "to Jacqueline and Michael." Both books appeared in spring 1965. Towards the end of Russell's book, describing the perilous state of a lone fox, who must survive for eight months on food it has collected and stored, he comments: "I could not bear the thought of life surviving against such odds. Once, when betrayed by a great friend and spurned by a wife, I had felt this helplessness at the state of my world. How weak I was! How self-pitying when I knew so well that the unstemmable urge of life must have its way and that I must say yes to it."

The style of Russell's book about the fishermen and wildlife he encountered in 1964 in Atlantic Canada is somewhat mystical, but the philosophical composure expressed here did not last long and the sudden ruptures in both marriages soon led to conflict and bitterness. When news of the Moores' separation reached Montreal, the loyalty of friends was tested and strained, and Brian found himself isolated. Only Richler, still domiciled in London, was able to maintain a semblance of normal contact with both Brian and Jackie. Although relations between Brian and Jackie were not amicable, he believed for a time that her anger and hostility would modify shortly. In fact, he expected Jackie to agree to a divorce as early as 1965, although as time went on, she would become less willing to arrive at a negotiated settlement. Jackie put strict limitations on Moore's opportunities to see Michael and made large financial claims. She and Michael initially continued to live in the apartment on East 79th Street, but in June 1965, they moved to live permanently with Russell in New Jersey.

By that time Brian and Jean had left Manhattan for a temporary stay in California to work on a film with Alfred Hitchcock, but their social isolation encouraged them to stay on, so that almost unawares, California would become the next habitat of the chameleon novelist.

*Entr'acte*

# THE HALL
# OF MIRRORS

In "Imagination and Experience," Brian Moore dwelt on Tolstoy's preoccupations while writing *Anna Karenina* in a way that challenged me as a biographer: could I trace the story of Moore's own transformations of experience into art to which he alluded in that autobiographical essay? I had already written about some themes that unified his body of fiction — the transition to North America, the Victorian inheritance — and so I rushed in. Then I discovered that, in addition to the published sources, I would be able to study private papers too. The novelist had kept and made available to scholars the contents of his desk drawers, as if he welcomed this kind of attention.

While the implicit invitation to investigate how a novelist creates works of fiction drew me deeper into those personal papers, I also came to realize that my freedom was circumscribed. I had not taken into due consideration that in becoming a biographer I would be drawn into reflections on controversial or painful episodes in the personal lives of people still living, and that those people had a right to keep certain episodes private. In becoming a biographer I had to learn to recognize the patterns in a life that offer more significant kinds of truth than those particular details not available to me. The absence of documents or of personal confessions forced me to trust my imagination and to preserve a sense of what was important for the investigation I was undertaking.

Moore's break-up with his first wife, Jackie, was undoubtedly a momentous event that took on multi-layered significance, because it brought into focus larger patterns in the overall shape of Moore's life as a novelist, both before and after the critical months of 1964–65. While Jackie and his life with her in the 1950s was at first the means to free him from the constraints of his Belfast Catholic past, the marriage had gradually become embedded in its own restrictive patterns in ways that were dispiriting. When he fell in love with Jean, another life in the future became not only possible but began to appear in the light of an urgent necessity. Why did he decide to "risk everything" in changing his life so quickly and so dramatically?

Brian Moore spent the first forty and more years of his life as a victim and beneficiary of happenstance, of the particular circumstances of family and place of birth, of the war years, of exile and employment opportunities. Increasingly, especially since the early 1950s, his energies were marshalled to wrestle with those circumstances, to master them and free himself. The goal of that effort of mastery was the writing of novels, and the work of writing these obliquely autobiographical fictions was also an act of mastering all those dark figures that had the power to undermine his confidence and plunge him into failure. Luckily he was blessed with the gift of language and with the narrative and dramatic skills that allowed him to bring to life his cast of characters inside the controlled world of fiction. In his novels he could be the actor, the director, and the scriptwriter; he could become his characters, experience again aspects of his own life and achieve self-mastery.

Moore has said that when he wrote *Judith Hearne* in 1953–54, the book incorporated his own loneliness, yet this statement seems odd in the light of his circumstances at that time: he was recently married, had close friends in Montreal, and became a father midway through the writing. Why did he believe that the primary identification with his character was through loneliness? Moore's guilt about wanting to be a writer (an indulger of fantasies) rather than a doctor (a healer of illness), became a form of self-hatred and ambivalence. His own feelings of estrangement from home and its primary values and roles led him to identify with his first literary character in her lonely passion — the collapse of her social roles and her journey into estrangement.

Judith Hearne was an ordinary woman, and her loss of faith took on the force of reality and truth; the nakedness of her estrangement was undisguised. She could not conceal her desperation with middle-class resources of power, status, money, or education; she was a failure by his father's standards. In 1953, Brian Moore had all those resources to conceal his loneliness, but he had yet to prove that he had the ability to write a literary novel. If the collapse of identity became the touchstone of reality in the world of migrants that Moore became part of, creating a character like Judith Hearne became the means to both affirm that reality and survive its desolation.

In proving to himself and to others that he could write a novel worthy of critical respect, he did not free himself from what he called loneliness. Its recurrence as his theme — and he has said that in writing that first novel he discovered his theme — suggests that the feelings of estrangement and isolation, even from his wife and others most intimately connected to him, were a permanent condition. While writing *Judith Hearne*, he isolated himself from Jackie, who was pregnant; a few months after the birth of Michael, he set off for Spain alone; while writing *Ginger Coffey*, he uprooted the family and moved to Amagansett, and they moved again, to London, when he was writing *Limbo*. While the requirements of a peaceful work-place, free from distractions, may explain these efforts to distance himself from others, the association of a more fundamental state of loneliness and writing is unmistakeable. Was the compulsion to write the cause or the result of such loneliness?

While both *Ginger Coffey* and *Limbo* dramatize a marital crisis, as indeed does *Intent to Kill* a few years earlier, alienation and self-absorption are explained in *Limbo* as the price the artist pays for being an incessant observer. And it is shown to be a high price, not only in self-hatred and a detached, caustic perspective on other people, but in Moore's moral evaluation of his own actions. In contrast to his defence of the "optimism" of the ending of *Emperor*, his comments on the "happy ending" of *Ginger Coffey* suggest that he felt he had compromised a larger truth in the portrayal of the reconciliation of Ginger and Vera. While that fictional marriage was salvaged, the marriage of the Tierneys in *Limbo* remains in crisis.

By the time he wrote *An Answer from Limbo* and *The Emperor of Ice Cream*, he was not only a very successful novelist, but he had also revised the images of his mother and his father, in their limitations and their strengths, so that he could accept them as part of himself. Like Gavin Burke, he had grown up. Yet it is crucially significant that in these novels, as in *Ginger Coffey*, *The Feast of Lupercal* and *Judith Hearne*, there are sexual and marital difficulties which might be seen to precipitate the crisis in each novel. Each novel rehearses the same narrative pattern: the protagonist becomes enmeshed more and more in "commonplace" circumstances of psychological and social, domestic and spiritual conflicts to the point of disorientation, breakdown, and loss of purpose. These are narratives of crisis, of accumulating tension to a rupture point and an ambiguous and ironic release; apart from Gavin Burke, it is not clear that these protagonists have become free or will have the opportunity to start over.

In those other hidden novels of his first decade as a writer, a similar narrative pattern is evident, except that in the thrillers, the entrapment of the isolated protagonist is usually due to criminal circumstances, and the tension builds towards violence and death. The need to indulge in fantasies of freedom, of taking risks, of exotic adventures, and of starting over at the end is integral to those formulaic novels. Yet they are part of Moore's own self as writer, however ashamed of them he became. They represent a male desire to escape from confining circumstances, to make a clean break and to start over. In 1959, he jotted a note to himself: "Possible character. One might be the man who suddenly walked out of his home in middle class suburban New York one day, leaving wife, children, good job — disappeared completely and now lives as a proofreader." Such a pattern of needing to start a new life recurs in the scenes of sexual or marital discord in which many of his characters are caught, literary characters — both male and female — as well as the puppets of his potboilers. And that pattern is one he followed in his own life by abandoning his first marriage and its established contexts and by starting over with a new partner in another new place.

By the time Brian Moore fell in love with Jean and decided to leave Jackie, the first marriages of many of his closest friends had also ended: John Vachon, William Weintraub, and Mordecai Richler had all experienced marital breakdowns. Moore was privy to the build-up of tension in these foundering relationships, even as his own marriage became increasingly unhappy. Ann Vachon's memoir of her father, for instance, reveals that throughout the 1950s, her father's dependence on alcohol became ruinous, while her mother's depressive illness led to hospitalization and suicide. The evidence of novels like *An Answer from Limbo* and *I Am Mary Dunne* is that the social scene of which Moore was a part in Montreal and New York included dark and self-destructive forces; the background to the break with Jackie reflects a feeling that he too was caught by such forces and felt compelled to escape from them.

Throughout the late 1950s and early 1960s, the evidence of intense stress was there in Moore's constant battles with ulcers, in his heavy drinking, in the weariness and exhaustion of his prodigious output of work, in his expressions of anxiety about old age, and in his embracing of a sense of the tragic nature of life. But more than the personal crises of his friends coloured his outlook and affected the climate of his own marriage. It was not only the weight of the past that overwhelmed him and forced him to take this extreme step; it was the weight of the present also. At some fundamental level, Moore wanted to feel free of the roles, behaviour, and beliefs that governed his place in the marriage; his life had taken on the character of a lie. His own sense of integrity and identity was undermined, whether by the personality of Jackie and his relationship with her or by his own constant need to write. At any rate, it seems that there was a steadily growing conflict for many years.

There is also reason to believe that the private and hidden estrangement of Brian from Jackie included a sexual incompatibility, for Moore has spoken on many occasions of the central importance of sex in key decisions of his life. He says that he fell in love with Jean and that he became happy in a way he had not been for ten years. A number of later novels depict sex as both the source of profound and disturbing tension and also as the source of love, the bedrock of security and of self. He writes also of sexual attraction as a kind of madness, akin, in certain aspects, to the narcissism and disorientation of breakdown; yet it is also the source of a clearer moral purpose, an element of "commonplace" experience that liberates characters such as Mary Dunne from the hall of mirrors, from the unreality of excessive self-consciousness and speculation.

While the abrupt abandonment of his wife and son and the early uncertainties of this new life would provide stresses that not every new couple in such circumstances would survive, the life that Jean and he began together in 1964 has now survived for thirty-four years. In 1965, he dedicated *The Emperor of Ice Cream* simply "To Jean" and after twelve such dedications, he varied it in 1995, "To Jean, *encore et toujours*" and in 1997 "To Jean, *comme d'habitude.*" The truth is that these dedications are a record of their life together. Looking back in 1997, he commented on his life with Jean and her devotion to his work: "My wife had jobs before we met. We made a sort of pact when we married, that we would always travel together and stay together. In a way it's like having your own world wherever you move to. So I'm very lucky." The commitment to each other in a lasting and emotionally satisfying marriage allowed him to become a new kind of writer, endlessly inventive, endlessly the chameleon. The novels he wrote were no longer rooted in realism, at least not in the psychological and social realism required by his investigation of his own earlier life.

Since the mid-1960s, Moore has chosen isolation over social involvement. Jean accepted that isolation with him and became his constant companion. His first marriage had been an urban affair, energized by involvement in a lively social and professional scene; Brian and Jean have opted to withdraw almost entirely from that kind of busy social and literary milieu. Not only does Moore disappear into his identity as novelist in the second half of my biography of him, Jean disappears also. Many times he has drawn attention to his daily isolation in front of a typewriter, keeping to a strict daily routine for months on end. He has spoken of the impoverishment of such a monk-like life, but if it is cut off from the constant stimulation of social interaction, it is surely rich in other ways.

This withdrawal in middle age of a man who had grown up in a busy household of a dozen people, who had relished the cameraderie of his wartime years and of the Press Club, who had entered into a lively scene of parties in Montreal and New York, is indeed striking. It is as if he decided that in the end he needed to be with only one person to fulfil his identity and ambitions as a writer. From their comfortable domestic hermitage in Malibu, he could look back over his memories, and over written history, and out across diverse cultural contexts; he could write whatever kind of fiction he chose to write, and his energy could be concentrated as never before on his writing.

As I examined the notes Moore wrote in 1965–66, during the first year of their life together in California, I was struck by a sudden change in his handwriting. For more than fifteen years, the journalist-turned-novelist recorded his thoughts in a quick scrawl written with a fine-nibbed fountain-pen or typed headlong, the text replete with misspellings and crossings out. Suddenly, notes for the novel he is working on take on the character of a monk's script. The novelist becomes a calligrapher, practising his self-conscious and stylized lettering on the backs of plot outlines. By summer 1966, the transformation is complete: he now writes personal letters in a carefully crafted hand and signs with a new signature.

My subject is not only a "chameleon novelist" but also a "chameleon" in life. This irony was revealed to me over and over as I got closer to events, none more so than the way in which his domestic life suddenly erupted in 1964–65. And that irony grew until it became clear to me that I would have to develop two different styles of writing to accommodate the two radically different personae I encountered in the first half and the second half of Moore's life. For as the chameleon changes to better conceal itself in a new environment, so must the observer look with new eyes on his wary subject.

*Part Two*

# "MY WRITING
# IS MY LIFE"

# 14

# HOLLYWOOD AND
# HITCHCOCK

At the beginning of 1965, just as Moore sent off the completed manuscript of *Emperor of Ice Cream*, he was contacted by Alfred Hitchcock. The acclaimed director had an idea for a new film — a Cold War thriller about an American scientist who defects behind the Iron Curtain — and invited the novelist to visit him in Hollywood to discuss the project. Accompanied by Jean, Moore flew to California for a week in February. To Jack McClelland he wrote: "I have to make this trip to the money factory because as you might guess, my expenses this year will be very heavy." While the Hitchcock project is linked in his mind to his divorce settlement with Jackie, to buying his freedom to have a new beginning, he writes to Diana Athill in a different vein: "I *will* write about Wonderland. There's so much to write." From the beginning, then, he saw the chance to go to California as an opportunity to have new material, to discover, perhaps, a new "emotional territory."

The exploratory trip to Hollywood at Hitchcock's invitation was not Moore's first visit to California, for he had gone there for a week in October 1963. He had spent the summer months of that year writing a screenplay of *The Luck of Ginger Coffey* for Irvin Kershner and then flown to San Francisco for a week to consult with producers, who had resources far beyond anything book publishers could invest in his work. Although he had been on the margins of the entertainment world before, during his frustrating efforts to prepare a stageplay of *Judith Hearne* for a Broadway production, and during on-again-off-again plans to make a film of it, his experience on this occasion was more promising. From California, he reported to Richler that "they all love the script now and are very hot on it," and *Ginger Coffey* did turn out to be his first successful collaboration with producers and directors.

Kershner had become interested in Moore's work after the publication of *Judith Hearne*, although it was John Huston who first paid for an option on that novel and retained it for six years — an annual income Moore called the John Huston Fellowship! Moore received many such "fellow-ships" from this point on, although only a handful of the novels were actu-ally made into films. This collaboration on *Ginger Coffey* marks the begin-ning of a pattern in which filmwriting and the sale of film rights became his main financial resource, taking the place of the thrillers a decade earli-er. As always, his aim was to establish his future financial security as firm-ly as possible in order to be free to complete a novel in his habitual open-ended method of trial and error. Following his dissatisfaction with the way *Ginger Coffey* was finished, Moore now had a rule of thumb, that at least two years were needed for the truth of his material to emerge and for the discovery of the technique appropriate to it.

His Commonplace Book records a statement by Auden: "The difference between a pure craft like carpentry and art is that when the carpenter starts work he knows exactly what the finished product will be, whereas the artist never knows just what he is going to make until he makes it. But like the carpenter all he can or should consciously think about is how to make it as well as possible, so that it may become a durable object permanently 'on hand' in the world." Auden's homely distinction may be taken as an indi-cation of Moore's different attitudes towards his work for film or maga-zines, undertaken to pay the bills and his novels, in which his true talent would reveal itself.

On this trip to California he was taken to Malibu, which he described to Richler as "something else," and "if one wanted to go to hell on pot and gin and to stay stoned and suntanned and sort of woozy all through life, then that's the answer." This first glimpse of the "unreal" Californian soci-ety was in some respects not much different from what he had discovered of the New York and Amagansett artistic community, or, indeed, on a somewhat different scale, of affluent Montreal society. Little did Moore know then that Malibu would become his home in a few years, not this celebrated Malibu location of the 1960s, but a quiet place on the ocean, far removed from the entertainment industry and its gaudy subculture.

The film of *Ginger Coffey* was shot on location in Montreal and in the Ottawa studio of Crawley Films in February–April 1964. The producer, Leon Roth, and director Kershner had originally hoped that Richard Harris would play the role of Ginger, but, in the end, it went to Robert Shaw, a less experienced actor, whose wife, Mary Ure, had already been cast for the role of Vera. Moore returned to Montreal to observe the film-ing, and his comments years later reveal how worldly-wise he had become on the production process and how a film and a novel are essentially so dif-ferent in his mind. His dissatisfaction with film stems from the fact that a novel, written alone, "remains the work of the person who invented it." A film, on the other hand, takes on "not a life of its own, but a sort of corporate life infused into it by actors, and a director, by its real setting, weather, money considerations, and, almost always, the desire to make a film which will be very popular."

He speaks with good humour of how, at the last minute, street locations had to be changed, and how, even in February, there was not enough snow, yet he is satisfied that the realistic aspects of the immigrant's life were preserved. He likes the "haunting quality" of the "baroque" film score composed by Bernardo Segall, a South American concert pianist, and is glad that Irish reels were not used. He is less happy with changes made spontaneously to the script by the leading actor, including the omission during the court scene of a key speech for the understanding of Ginger's character. He is least satisfied with the ending of the film: "I wrote an ending which was clear. . . . We shot it in snow. There were problems with traffic. . . . The next day when Kershner went back to reshoot it, there was no snow and still too much traffic and he became disgusted and decided on a filmic ending, the sort of thing beloved by European directors. . . . It looks pretty, it looks almost poetic, but audiences didn't know and still don't know just what's going on." The novelist believes that films must have a good story above all, and that big stars do not automatically make for good characters or provide credible motivation, but his experience with *Ginger Coffey* seems to have been an apprenticeship in the compromises that a writer must make for that other medium.

The film was released in North America in September 1964 and in London the following spring. It did not "make a lot of money, nor did it lose money," but it did launch Moore into the film world. By the time it premiered in Montreal, he was already at work on another script, *The Goat*, which he abandoned, but he did go on to prepare for Kershner two other scripts, *The Slave*, written between March and September 1966, and *Judith Hearne*, written in March–April 1967. Although Moore was paid for these scripts, neither was actually filmed. At no time does Moore appear to have viewed the cinema as an artistic medium, although he did preserve the wish to write for the theatre — not simply dramatizations of his novels, which he later did in the case of *Catholics* — but an original play.

When Hitchcock contacted Moore, he was looking for a screen-writer who had demonstrated a talent for handling a woman's viewpoint. Moore's earliest notes indicate that Hitchcock had become interested in Burgess and Maclean, the British spies who defected to Moscow, but more particularly in the dilemma in which their defection placed their spouses. "What would be the attitude of a young woman, perhaps in love with, or engaged to, a scientist who could be a defector?" The director had approached Vladimir Nabokov and James Goldman before Moore was recommended to him.

By the time the novelist came to Hollywood, Hitchcock had read *The Feast of Lupercal* and, having gone to an English Jesuit school, the director was fascinated and impressed by Moore's recreation of a comparable ambience. Hitchcock's biographer writes that "the cordiality and mutual understanding were instant," and notes that Moore related to the director as someone who belonged to his father's generation: "He never had to explain to me his allusions to Marie Belloc Lowndes or English Catholic schools or various aspects of Edwardian society."

In spite of their affinity, Moore was not sure he wanted to return to the kind of work he had done for Harlequin, Fawcett, and Dell in the 1950s, the Hitchcockian world of suspense in which plausible characterization would be secondary to the director's trademark style. "I found him thoroughly engaging and sensible," Moore reported, "but after we had discussed his idea, I decided that this was not really right for me. In the rather perverse way of such things, of course, that convinced them I must be the best person for the job, and at once they doubled their initial offer and said they would pay me fifty thousand dollars."

The novelist agreed, "very much against my own judgement but willing to do the best I could." From Hitchcock's basic idea, he first sketched some rough possibilities for a scenario. Complications of motive might arise in the twilight zone of overlapping security agencies and in the possibilities of the defector being seen as a double agent. "This type of story is an emotional, psychological one, expressed in terms of action and movement, and, naturally, that would give me the opportunity to indulge in the customary Hitchcock suspense," he wrote to the director.

It may be that Moore was able to find the idea workable because of his years in Warsaw, or because he welcomed the opportunity to collaborate with the celebrated director, but at any rate he prepared a story outline, and a contract was signed in early March for a film to be called *Torn Curtain*. The arrangement was that Moore would move to Hollywood for six months to work on the script. He and Jean moved to Hollywood in March, to "a great house on top of a canyon," and he invited Jack McClelland to visit them in their "very large pad here, lots of bedrooms and a splendiferous view." Supported in this unreal world by Universal Studios, the new couple began what the novelist called their "adventures in Wonderland."

"When I first worked with Hitchcock, I worked with him for only one reason," Moore insisted later. "I was broke and he offered me a large sum of money which I thought would mean writing three more novels, so I jumped at it." Moore had an office at Universal Studios, and, working with his customary professionalism, honed in the writing of the thrillers a decade before, he produced a story synopsis and went on to complete a script in three months. Hitchcock liked to develop the script with the writer, even though he never actually took writing credits, and so, as was his custom, he worked with Moore almost every day.

Moore decided to view Hitchcock's whole canon systematically, so for a part of each day he watched his movies and tried to become familiar with the director's characteristic tricks. "The problem I had with Hitchcock was that he was a living legend. He'd done fifty films and I'd done zero, so I tended to take his word for everything." Of one thing he was sure: even though the director paid obsessive interest to superficial details of setting and plotting, this "covered a profound ignorance of human motivation." With this sense of the limitations of his colleague, he worked with Hitchcock from April until the end of August in the spirit of trying his best to provide what Hitchcock required.

In retrospect, Moore speaks of this opportunity to work with Hitchcock as a valuable experience:

> He taught me things about films which you could actually apply to all fictions. He said the audience has no morality. Hitchcock's example was this. A woman is coming in to rob a bank. She's a villain and she walks along a narrow corridor to go into the bank. She's coming in at night, let's say, secretly, she's going to come in and rob and sneak out again, and she walks along this corridor and she's wearing white gloves. She drops a glove and she walks another ten paces . . . and the whole audience says "pick up the glove; pick up the glove, stupid." And this is true.

The film director's sense of the intense involvement of an audience in the atmosphere created by the film, and of the possibilities for influencing the sympathies of an audience in that state of suspended disbelief, is similar to Moore's own lifelong interest in "tone" or "voice" and the suspense created by narrative momentum.

He speaks of another lesson learned from Hitchcock, the importance of preserving the state of suspended disbelief through a meticulous attention to detail. The importance of research was hardly a lesson that the trained journalist had to learn, yet Moore credits Hitchcock with teaching it.

Moore's interest in narrative movement may also have been sharpened through this collaboration, for he speaks of the care with which flashbacks have to be handled within a novel. "Flashbacks should be small digressions. I have very strong feelings that you should never have a whole chapter in flashback because it can become another book. Either the narrative must keep moving forward and can't be interrupted or else the digression must nearly fit into the narrative. You can't be back-pedaling. If you keep flashing back, then why should you go on? You're damaging the narrative in that sense."

In view of the work he began in September 1965, *A Woman of No Identity*, later *I Am Mary Dunne*, a novel in which memory and flashback are both theme and technique, such comments suggest that his time in "*l'univers Hitchcockian*" was well spent. Yet when he spoke to *Cahiers du cinéma* about the experience, he expressed his scepticism about the adulation with which many French cinema people treated the work of the "great man." As far as Moore was concerned, Hitchcock was a "carpenter," rather than an artist, in the sense that he had a shooting script, planned to the last detail, before he began filming. In creating that script with a screenwriter like Moore, he knew from long experience the effects he wanted to achieve and how best to achieve them.

*Torn Curtain* came at an inauspicious time in Hitchcock's career; his films immediately preceding it, *The Birds* and *Marnie*, had not been commercial successes, and so Universal Studios imposed the popular Julie Andrews on him as the leading actress. In other ways, also, the studio made clear to Hitchcock that it wanted a film that would rival the runaway box-office success of the James Bond films in these years. There was considerable strain and uncertainty surrounding the project from the beginning. Some American critics had expressed irritation that Hitchcock was aiming to be an *auteur* rather the maker of commercial suspenseful films. Brian Moore fell victim in a number of ways to the anxieties that overcame the director during this project.

For most of the summer, the collaboration went well, for at some point Hitchcock "offered me an enormous contract . . . something like $250,000 a year to write four pictures for him, and I said no, I don't want to be a screenwriter. And I also knew that if he fell out with me at the end of the first year I wouldn't have any chance at the $250,000. I'd be fired. It sounded great, but it wasn't worth the paper it was written on." Moore's prescience was wise, for all did not continue to run smoothly.

At the end of August, as the script was completed, Moore's opinion of the product of their collaboration was very low. He told Hitchcock frankly that he thought the characters and much of the narrative unbelievable and that if it were to be made the film would be a failure. He never heard from Hitchcock again; the director immediately hired two new scriptwriters, Keith Waterhouse and Willis Hall. "I realized that taking criticism or confronting disagreement was another problem for Hitchcock. As with all living legends, no one had the courage to tell him that anything was wrong. That was very bad for the poor man. And because of his own personality and background — as the lonely, frightened boy — he had a horror of confrontation with people. He wasn't able to argue something out face to face. So he did things through intermediaries, or he sent someone on a vacation and then replaced him."

This is exactly what happened in Moore's case. "I've finished my Hitchcockian labours," he told McClelland, "but as these are the summery months here we've decided to stay on until possibly Christmas." He and Jean bought a second-hand car and drove to San Francisco. "Jean and I just took a week off and drove up to San Francisco, via Big Sur and the Monterey Coast. Big Sur is the place to make one's worries seem small. It seemed to us the most beautiful coastline we'd ever seen, and one of the most wild," he wrote to McClelland a few weeks later. The couple subsequently returned to Los Angeles and found an apartment on Lookout Mountain Avenue.

He also had medical advice for McClelland: "As an old ulcer man who's been through it for years, including a haemorrhage, I can tell you that diets, regimens, all those things just don't remove it. I've found that it absolutely depends on one's state of mind and is related to stress and strains, and, so, when your doctor counsels a holiday . . . it is the best treatment." These words were as much for himself as for his correspondent. He was managing to keep the tension of working for Universal Studios in perspective. The trip to Big Sur was a confirmation that life in California with Jean suited him, offered a kind of serenity that he had not known in the stressed and ulcer-ridden life he lived in Montreal and New York.

Although he started right away on a new novel, these months were occupied by legal proceedings on a number of levels to protect Moore's credit as the screenwriter on *Torn Curtain*, a battle he eventually won. The other two screenwriters claimed equal credit with Moore, and he appealed through a New York lawyer to the Writers' Guild of America. The case dragged on until December 29 when the Writers' Guild informed him that he should be given exclusive credit. Only a few months earlier, dissatisfied with his work on the script, he had been willing to drop all credit for it and to continue to work with Hitchcock: "As I've told you before I vastly enjoyed working with you and learning from you and am anxious to contribute any time or work necessary to ensure the total success of the film." In fact, he had not heard from Hitchcock, and the shooting of the film had actually begun in November. This Hollywood situation — in which the writer is a pawn in a complex game with many conflicting interests — is captured in *Fergus*, with the character of Boweri as a thinly disguised Hitchcock.

In the case of *Torn Curtain*, the commercial pressures from the studio combined with Hitchcock's technical mastery to produce an old-fashioned, stilted film with wooden characters and predictable plotting. When it was released in July 1966, critics compared it unfavourably with the James Bond thrillers that used stylish and elaborate variations on the old formula. Even by Hitchcock's own earlier standard, it was judged to be a failure.

The novelist had lost interest in the project long before this time; he was now deeply immersed in writing a novel about the world he and Jean had left behind. His return to writing fiction was buoyed up in late 1965 and 1966 by the publication and success of *The Emperor of Ice Cream*. The new novel had been published in North America in September, just as he realized that his work with Hitchcock had been abruptly halted, and, to his surprise, it had been receiving enthusiastic reviews. Early in 1965, he changed publishers, because Seymour Lawrence had left Atlantic/Little, Brown and was planning to set up his own publishing imprint. This did not come to pass, and so the novel went to Viking. Now in October, he was astonished by a "rave" review in the *New York Times*, and he told McClelland that American sales had passed the seven-thousand mark, more than he had achieved with any of the previous novels. In December, it would be named one of the five best novels of 1965 by the *New York Times*. In January 1966, it also received enthusiastic reviews in Britain and Ireland.

In September 1965 Moore remarked to Richler that he was "vegetating and edging around another novel." As if in reaction to the superficiality of Hitchcock's view of human beings and their motivations, he was driven to immerse himself in the stuff of character — an intimate fiction of one day in the life of one woman, told from her point of view. The intensity of his dramatization of Mary Dunne's effort to define the very core of her identity reflects not only his skill in becoming his character but a crucial phase in his own redefinition of himself as a novelist in his new stage of exile.

# 15

## WRITER AS
## EXILE

The "First Mss Pages" — he labelled them thus many years later — of the new novel reveal a sure instinct for the direction it will take:

> It occurs to me there isn't a man alive who has the faintest idea of what a woman is, how she thinks and feels, what *happens* to her in the course of a day. All this talk about black and white and how we can't know how it feels to be black and brought up in Harlem, well, let me tell you, compared to that, to be a woman and brought up anywhere. I mean are we ever going to get through the Iron Curtain of male generalizations about women?

The creator of Judith Hearne had returned to what he knew he could do well. But what earlier he had done by instinct, as it were, through his ability to release a female side in his own character, he now returns to do with a new cultural and political awareness of women's issues remarkably advanced for 1965. This North American voice — assertive, sarcastic, vulnerable, reflective — is far away from the voice he had assumed for Judith Hearne — closer, perhaps, to Jane Tierney in *An Answer from Limbo* than any other character — but, even if it draws on the same Manhattan world dramatized in *Limbo*, it is also a new departure for him, and a very risky one.

The fabric of this woman's character is woven of many strands: of marital discord, divorce, and guilt; of displacement, death, and change; of self-absorption and depression; of remembering and forgetting; of feeling victimized by male chauvinism and sexual exploitation. This material is explored through the intense effort of an intelligent young woman to orient herself in the face of her own fragmented sense of self:

> You can't generalize, you can't generalize at all, you just have to put down what happened to you, Maura Laverty, yesterday in New York, the way you felt, the people you met, the things you did and what it all meant to

you then when you were living it. But memory, even very recent memory, is imperfect, an arranger, a liar and already, trying to write it all down I am being false to the truth of what really happened. But even an imperfect truth is some truth and I should start by being honest about my motives in writing all this down. I want to know who I am.

That effort to capture an "imperfect truth," to hold on to the details of one day and in them to discover the essence of "who I am," remained the central effort of the two years of writing that followed. Maura Laverty became Mary Lavery, the central character of *I Am Mary Dunne*, and "yesterday" became a lifetime through a complex network of flashbacks, echoes, and set pieces in which other characters insist on remembering or recreating versions of her earlier life for her. Yet the richly textured fiction that Moore produced in this, his sixth novel, is driven by the central impulse to establish an authentic truth by autobiographical means. In addition to being a narrative steeped in memories and recollections presented in a first-person point of view, the novel also questions the kinds of subjective truths that form and deform identity.

In one sense the problem of identity is highlighted by amnesia, by the fact that so much of one's past is forgotten or imperfectly recalled. The motif Moore chooses for this is the woman's name: born Mary Dunne, she has been married three times, and on the morning of this day, temporarily can't remember which name is her current one. "Descartes said, I think, therefore I am; and I was trying to say, I remember, therefore I am. And what we remember is really the only part of our lives which we retain. And how she remembers her former husbands is how they exist in this book." Moore is speaking here of what can be recalled and verbalized, what can be written out — and the first draft began in the form of a journal and a deliberate decision to write down what could be recalled, as if to set the record straight for a particular person.

It is difficult not to believe that this fiction reflects the recent experience of Brian Moore and Jean Denney. Many details betray such origins. Born near the Bay of Fundy in Nova Scotia in the early thirties, the protagonist moved to Toronto where she worked at a magazine, attended acting classes, and married a free-lance journalist, educated in private schools, with British experiences in his background. She left him for a successful writer of Irish-British background, living in Manhattan. While many details might be sketched in to demonstrate superficial connections between Mary Dunne and Jean Denney, alias Jean Lewis, alias Jean Russell, and soon to become Jean Moore, it is also clear that an equal number of details reflect Brian Moore's own experiences in Montreal in the 1950s with Jackie and their friends.

The novel seems to grow out of the situation in which the two real lovers found themselves in their Californian limbo, each of their pasts cut off, to be shared only as stories. Moore seized the moment of instability, "as we wait to get on with our lives," to recreate those states of uncertainty and dissatisfaction in Montreal, Toronto, and New York that had brought both of them to desire a new life together. Mary Dunne remarks, "This life I live isn't believable, not even to me," and at the heart of her depressive "dooms" is the conviction: "I am a changeling who has changed too often, and there are moments when I cannot find my way back." Superimposed on the struggle of a young woman to maintain an equilibrium in the face of change are all of the novelist's preoccupations with sexual passion, exile and dissolving identity.

The new life of Brian and Jean continued in a kind of limbo as they waited to formalize their relationship. "Months just slip away, and we have no long range plans," he reported to Richler. "For all that we enjoy the climate and the strange peace of living here . . . If I lived here permanently and with kids I'd be very tempted to live on the ocean where it's like living in an-again-peaceful-Amagansett all year round in June weather." In fact, they did move to the ocean in summer 1966: "We're in a shack on the Pacific now. The sea comes right under the house. I work mornings on the novel and afternoons on alimony drudgery. It's a sort of dream life, sitting at the typewriter and watching the surfers under the window. I wish it would continue."

"Have been back to go a few times," he told Richler, about what he referred to as *A Woman of No Identity*, "but now am hoping to keep it inching forward for the next year or so." The calm contentment of this "dream life" and the absence of the frustration so often registered during the composition of the previous three novels are measures of how happily Jean and he were solidifying their relationship. "I'm more pleased than ever, two years later, that I did what I did," he told Richler. "Anything else would have been really self-destructive on my part." As Moore himself remarked decades later, he and Jean have been inseparable through the years, and the foundations for their domestic life were quickly set. By the end of 1966, he wrote: "We are at the moment angsting over whether or not to rent a house on this coast, lonely, overlooking a beautiful beach, north of here, it's about forty miles from LA and would be a good novel-writing spot." After renting this house for a few seasons, they bought it and made it their permanent home.

"I had hoped it would be in some sense a research into the form of fiction," he wrote to himself in early notes, and not only is this conscious preoccupation with the nature of contemporary fiction central to his work from this point on, but Moore's Commonplace Book reveals a man more preoccupied than before with experimental writing, notably reading Jorge Luis Borges, and with speculative philosophy. These abstract preoccupations led to new insights into the presentation of character and into such matters as perception and reality, but, as always, Moore does not stray far from the novelist's business of inventing a fictional character and a fictional world.

From the beginning, he seems to have thought of the new novel as a portrait of a modern woman, Mary Lavery, looking back over her earlier relationships before she found happiness with her new husband, Terence, and seeking "the found thing, the creation of a self." It was to be "a chronicle of a woman's moods rather than a story with a conventional plot," and those moods, on this day coloured by premenstrual tension, are to be states of panic, of grief and guilt, and of returning depression, as she struggles to understand her fear that she has "no identity."

Moore wanted "the creation of a self" to embody the triumph over depression and panic, and in this way the novel seems to be a further development of the "optimism" in the face of the horror of death in *Emperor*. "My new book was written and is being finished in this new happiness which is my present life," he remarked in 1967 as he worked on the second draft. However content, Moore's was not a state that allowed for happy endings, and from the beginning the nature of Mary's happiness was seen to be ambiguous:

> Is her happiness the other side of the coin: happy with Terence, clinging to Tee because she has seen the other side, the abyss of despond, happiness possible because of the abyss. And yet — happiness of self is the only happiness she can enjoy — yet she knows there is supposed to be a greater happiness, the happiness of giving to others, the losing of the self in others, the Eastern happiness which is loss of self. Yet the self which is lost resents its loss, and fights back.

Such thoughts seem to echo the Yeatsian notion of "tragic joy" and, more generally, the poet's constant "dialogue of self and soul," and it was to Yeats that Moore turned for the epigraph to the novel: "O body swayed to music, O brightening glance, / How can we know the dancer from the dance?" The ambivalence affirmed by the question in the epigraph seems to undermine the dramatic assertiveness of the concluding line, "I am Mary Dunne, I am Mary Dunne." This notion "I remember, therefore I am" is a motif counterpointed from the beginning by the unreliability of memory: "She might begin to tell and then become sidetracked: the theme." In the design of the book, the "sidetrack" is as significant as any other remembered incident: the process of remembering and forgetting, of creating one's own history in the theatre of the mind. If the novel embodies the happiness of his new life, it is in the aesthetic accomplishment of the novel — and perhaps in his own experience of writing it — rather than in the character of Mary Dunne herself.

It is not surprising that the realistic novelist should turn to reflect directly on the process of autobiographical ordering of experience: "When I wrote *I Am Mary Dunne*," Moore wrote in 1969, "I wanted to write about a fairly ordinary person's loss of identity, about the feeling so many of us experience, that feeling that we are no longer able to relate to our own past, that we no longer know the person we were ten years ago. . . . Exploring the role of memory has certainly been one of my main literary preoccupations in the last ten years."

The deliberateness of Mary's effort to remember, and the panic associated with her forgetting her own name, set the novel apart from the celebration of involuntary memory in, for example, Proust. Moore has suggested that his own coma in 1953, following the motor-boat accident, was partly the origin of the novel: "One morning some years ago I woke up in a Canadian hospital and for a panicky moment I could not remember my own name." This connection suggests that although the loss and recovery of identity are dramatized specifically in the life of an educated and emancipated young woman living in Manhattan, there are here, as in *Judith Hearne*, many of Moore's own deepest feelings about these issues:

> I am Mary Dunne because I have taken my own life and transmogrified it into hers. I have taken my years of wandering from country to country, my changes of nationality, my forgettings, rememberings, my feelings of being lost and a stranger and have, I hope, made them hers. For two years I have wakened in the mornings, gone into a room, sat at a typewriter and, like an actor going on stage, like a medium trying to induce a trance, I have tried to think myself into the skin and into the mind of a young, troubled, pretty woman. And, like a medium speaking in the voice of another person, I have written the book in the first person singular, in her voice, the voice of Mary Dunne.

If I have succeeded the book will be Mary Dunne's autobiography, not my novel. The author will be Mary Dunne, not Brian Moore, for the voice which speaks to the reader is her voice, not mine, and if the book is right, as I hope it is, the fact that I, a man, wrote it will be forgotten by my readers. Perhaps this is what all fiction writers do, or hope to do. Take down dictation. Perhaps the talent for writing fiction is a talent for listening to people, a talent for reproducing and ordering the voices of fiction. In my two years writing *I Am Mary Dunne*, I became Mary Dunne. And if I have found her voice, then I have found my own.

Those words were written just before the novel's publication, but their eloquent account of the process of writing exemplifies for Moore belief in the truth of Flaubert's dictum *"Madame Bovary, c'est moi."* In fact, it may have been Flaubert's dictum that gave him the title or, perhaps, his more recent discovery of Borges's parables on the inseparability of the artist from his creation, "Borges and I," and "Everything and Nothing." Moore's Commonplace Book quotes extensively from Borges at this time, and one passage from "A New Refutation of Time" appears more than once:

The poet, like God, is a creator of hallucinations, uncertain, and in deluded search of "that moment when man should know forever who he is," for he must know that there is no forever, and that he does not exist as an identity. And yet, and yet . . . Time is the substance of which I am made. Time is a river which sweeps me along, but I am the river; it is a tiger which mangles me, but I am the tiger; it is a fire which consumes me, but I am the fire. The world, unfortunately, is real; I, unfortunately, am Borges.

The aspiration for the absolute and the recognition of circumstance are exemplified in special ways in Moore's character, and if his notes make reference to Romantic writers and metaphysical speculations on the nature of the self, his work remains anchored in the challenge of making real that other voice in her own world.

Moore set about creating a portrait of a woman so as "to catch in a book the inconsequences, the immediacy of a day in someone's life," and Mary Dunne's day is packed with interwoven incidents and memories, the trivial becoming the profound as she struggles to bring order to a psyche that has become unhinged. Only at mid-point in the novel is it revealed that the model for the trauma of this day was an earlier one in Juarez, Mexico, where she went to get her divorce from her second husband. This delayed revelation is a technique he had used in *Judith Hearne*, where Judith's secret drinking is not revealed until well into the novel. Here he keeps "the Juarez dooms," a key explanation for Mary's hysteria, until the mid-point: "I couldn't remember my name and I got up from the bench and ran past a line of Mexicans who sat and ignored me (I was flies.) . . . I remember thinking for the first time what I have thought many times since. I am no longer Mary Dunne, or Mary Phelan, or Mary Bell, or even Mary Lavery." Diary entries reveal that the feelings and images of this central scene were recorded in Juarez and El Paso when Moore accompanied Jean there for her divorce.

Apart from the "Juarez dooms" associated with temporary namelessness, the reasons why Mary Dunne has slipped into this state of "no identity" are many, as are the means by which she tries to assert herself in a whirlpool of subjective impressions and interpretations. While "the dooms" are biological in origin, the experience of panic and loss reflects not only her premenstrual state but more generally the fact that she is a woman. "In what way do women lose their identities?" Moore asks himself in the planning notes. Apart from the changes of name she has undergone in her marriages, her sexual identity as a woman is also a source of anxiety. In the opening scenes, she is verbally abused by a bystander, "I'd like to fuck you, baby," and her outrage frequently brings her thoughts back to that moment, "he simply wanted a face and a body which happened to be mine," and to her sense that "you can't fight male solidarity."

Her feelings of sexual exploitation in her first two marriages are recurrent — "in modern marriage, the involuntary whoredom of the woman," Moore notes — and, more generally, although she is a talented woman she feels that she is living in a man's world, and that it is easier for men to feel secure in their identity. Mary Dunne seems to have reminded Moore of Judith Hearne — although the later protagonist is much married and much travelled — because both have a primal need to belong, to feel loved or cared for, to be able to trust other people's feelings about them. "In love or not in love: a time of finding oneself in a time when one has been abandoned/rejected. Stocktaking." On the first page, he pencilled a note: "I think, therefore I am: the fear that when she ceases to think clearly or remember well, madness is begun."

The existentialist tone of Camus' *L'Étranger* is also recalled in Moore's notes: "My mother died yest or was it today, it doesn't matter — the Camus thing transposed to her lover — my lover left, yest, or was it today." Loneliness and alienation are acutely felt and are heightened early in the day by a primal fear, the loss of one's mother. About Mary, Moore notes that "even the childbearing experience was denied her." It is evident that a primal sense of death is in the background of the book from the beginning: the dread that her mother may die, back in Nova Scotia, the recent death of Mary's second husband, Hat, and the earlier death, in sexually compromising circumstances, of her father, whose promiscuous tendencies she fears she may have inherited. It may be that Moore's sensitivity to the deaths of his own father and mother — in different ways apparently fixing the writer's outlook — entered into the characterization, although during the writing, Jean's father died in Nova Scotia and, as Moore began the novel, Jackie's brother, Billy, died in a New York hotel of a heart attack.

Moore's notes include references to this early death, and there are details that indicate Mary's fear that her mother may die incorporate his own feelings about his mother's death. But such details are of less importance than the way in which Jean's attachment to her family and to Kentville led the novelist to see Nova Scotia in a special way. It is unclear when the urban protagonist was given a childhood in Nova Scotia, but it may be that the visit of Brian and Jean to Nova Scotia in summer 1967 was the moment when he discovered a new "emotional territory" and superimposed it on the novel. Speaking of his experiments with point of view in the early drafts, he commented, "It's always a search for tone. With *Mary Dunne* I wrote about a third of it in the third person, and realized that was absolutely wrong. It was only when I got to the part about Nova Scotia, and the wedding, that I suddenly realized this would be far better if it were her voice telling the story. Then I went back and rewrote the whole novel."

Nova Scotia as an "emotional territory" became more than a spur to his imagination: after many long summer stays, it would become his second home and he would build his own house there on the Atlantic coast. In June 1967, he wrote to Jack McClelland: "I have felt in the short time that I have been here that this is a sort of Proustian place." Moore's feelings for this sense of the place remained. Nova Scotia and Ireland began to fuse at some level, and in the decades ahead, as he remained apart from the urban literary centres, the Atlantic coastlines of these two places would become an imaginative touchstone associated with the memory of his father's stable sense of self, just as Mary Dunne's mother in her childhood home provides the anguished Mary with a belief in stability and permanence. "When I was with Jean in Nova Scotia," he wrote to McClelland, "I was terribly struck by this vision of Nova Scotia as the unchanged Canada of our ancestors, but an unchanged province which cannot last in this pristine state."

Mary Dunne finds some balm in hearing her mother's voice in Nova

Scotia, "the voice of my childhood," but for the course of the novel, she is not only an individual, uprooted woman, she is also a contemporary person: "The pre-menstrual tension is in a way the symptom of the madness we all feel, the tension of normal life; the tension of every big city — London, New York, any big city — is that there are too many people in it. So if you write about people living in these cities, the city becomes a character in the novel. New York is an aggressive character in the novel." The alienation that she feels so acutely appears to have been with Moore through the Montreal and New York years, and the major portions of the book set in Montreal, or recalled by the two visitors from her past, Janice Sloan and Ernie Truelove, echo many of Moore's own feelings and his reasons for wanting to get out of those cities. It would seem that in his peaceful isolation on the Californian seashore, Moore needed to write Montreal and New York out of his system, as he had done with Belfast in his first novels.

In other ways also, Mary's experience is both more personal and a reflection of a general cultural condition. The question of moral judgement and accountability is a constant issue, focused most on Mary's guilt regarding her abandonment of Hat and his subsequent death. "At lunch Janice starts the train of thought of Hat's downfall; it happened when she walked out? At the end of the day, Hat would have been Hat without her." Yet the issue is not so simply resolved in the broader context of memory and identity: "Are we what people remember us as? . . . If others persist in inventing personae for us then are we responsible for the figments of their imagination?"

A summing up at the end of this page of notes seems to draw on Moore's deeply felt thoughts on identity, originating in adolescence: "Other people conspire to destroy our identity by inventing new identities for us." It would seem that the "grammar of emotions" of the first family and marriage may be what underlies this feared conspiracy "to destroy our identity," although in the novel itself, it is both her marriage to Terence and her memory of her mother that strengthen Mary's sense of self. Her challenge is to overcome the fictional identities which others impose on her, as well as her own panic-stricken self-dramatizations.

A final strand Moore wished to weave into his exploration of the personal and cultural contexts of identity appears to be a spiritual one: "Her fear (*accidie*) no less because it is without motivation." Elsewhere, he refers to "a part of the theme": "Religion is part of the identity loss — it symbolises a loss of a self who had certainties: we all live in this post Christian era." It is easy to read into this "accidie" Moore's constant preoccupation from *Judith Hearne* on with the crisis of faith of the Catholic and the spiritual emptiness of modern life; undoubtedly this is an aspect of Mary's characterization, but his notes also signal an intention to stress what Mary has gained by leaving aside her childhood Catholicism: "The ex-Calvinist–Catholic: at what point in one's life does one stop punishing oneself by believing in the value of work-as-work — the belief that life *should be* basically boring, dreary, 'a-getting and a-spending we lay waste our days' and move towards the position that we *deserve* that our work and our lives be enjoyable? (Mary has reached that point)."

The autobiographical resonances of this spiritual and psychological struggle hardly need underlining in a life so singlemindedly devoted to his work as a writer. It would seem that his vision of Mary Dunne's life is of one that incorporates and transcends his own "ex-Calvinist–Catholic" self through the sheer power of his creative effort in becoming her "voice."

The dramatic compression of a life into one day appealed to Moore because, after *Limbo*, he had begun to think of the novella as a more appropriate contemporary form of fiction: "Ideally, I'd like it if people could sit down and read one of my novels in one evening, giving it their full attention, undistracted by television, movies, conversations with other people. There are so many distractions today which militate against reading." Such a practical approach may have come to him because of the success of short novels he admired, such as Philip Roth's *Goodbye, Columbus* or, especially with the unity of the day in mind, Saul Bellow's *Seize the Day*, but the heightened hallucinatory quality of both *Mary Dunne* and *Fergus* derive from literary models that take the reader into more phantasmagoric recreations of consciousness than either of these American novels.

Moore himself was aware of other antecedents. As so often, he returned to *Ulysses*, in the case of this novel to Molly Bloom's monologue. His notes indicate that he also studied Svevo's *Confessions of Zeno* and, again indicating how far beyond the Anglo-American traditions he was ranging at this time, Giuseppe Berto's *Incubus*: "That's the book I've enjoyed most in the last few years. It's written in a strange style — a sort of galloping monologue like a psychoanalysis where he tells all." Apart from Joyce, the English-language novelist he seems to have been drawn to most in relation to displacement, expatriation, and identity is Malcolm Lowry, and at the time of writing *Mary Dunne*, he praises as "a first-rate book" *Under the Volcano*, Lowry's novel of a day in Mexico as experienced by a drunken British ex-consul.

At this time he was also reading Beckett, "the most interesting of the experimental writers," and the idea of the nameless character, obsessively trying to capture the true version of his life-story and failing, may have been suggested by his fellow Irishman. A further model that may have encouraged Moore's examination of the lasting imprint of the Catholic upbringing especially, and of the tragic weight of one's past actions, not simply in this novel but from *An Answer from Limbo* on to *Fergus*, is Eugene O'Neill's *Long Day's Journey into Night*, which had impressed him when he saw it in New York in 1957.

Whatever Moore's influences were, in the end the texture of Mary Dunne's life and her contemporary North American voice were qualities of the book only he could create. And he did so, as usual, by trial and error:

> I started my current book in the third person, and then I went back to the first person, and by that time I had done a lot of work. Then I decided that the interesting way to do it was to put it all in the historical present, and so I rewrote nearly two-thirds of the book in that way. And then I read it all over again and I decided that first-person, non-historical present was the most interesting way and gave me the most interesting feeling, because it all takes place in one day with movements into the past. So I had to go back and do the whole thing over again. Now I've got two-thirds of the book written, but the end section does not suit me. It doesn't suit me, interestingly enough, because the character I introduce at the end [Ernie Truelove], who has not been met up to then, is too grotesque. The first time round, I tended to emphasize his grotesque qualities, and now I'm trying to change him completely around.

As Mary's recollections brought more and more characters from her past into the narrative, the challenge for Moore was to suggest the confusion and lack of clarity of Mary's perceptions on this day and, simultaneously, to preserve the realism of those characters in their own world. A device he used to overcome this difficulty was the set piece, and Mary's stream of consciousness is interrupted regularly by dramatized episodes that can almost stand alone as short stories. The first marriage to Jimmy and the second to Hat are recalled in a set of scenes with overlaid meditations from a present perspective, but more important are episodes such as the visit of Mr. Peepers to view Mary's apartment — a scene Moore allowed *Tamarack Review* to publish as "The Apartment Hunter" while the novel was still in progress.

The evening visit of Ernie Truelove is another such piece, but the one that especially pleased Moore was the lunch date with Janice Sloane:

> It's what writers call a set piece in the novel. It's a thing which you could understand on its own, an incident which is almost like a short story, could almost stand on its own. I wanted to show the peculiar relationship

that also exists between well-educated, fairly well-to-do women today who do meet over lunch, discuss things extremely frankly, and there are all kinds of hidden barbs behind it. Also what I wanted to do in that is say something about psychoanalysis. I discovered when I lived in New York that a lot of people have been psychoanalyzed and the analysis had not taken. They had reached the point in the analysis where they had transferred, let's say, their guilt about their behaviour to their parents. But then they had moved into the second stage where they merely blamed their parents for everything. Then they reached the third stage where they absolved their parents. So Janice Sloane is a perfect example of the kind of person who has been unsuccessfully analyzed. She blames everybody else for everything, and that makes her a comic character in a sense. . . . Graham Greene wrote me a nice letter about the book, picked on that one incident, and said that in a sense was his favourite incident in the book, because he recognized it was technically interesting to do and get away with it.

The writing of the novel progressed constantly, in spite of the strain of the two years during which all efforts to have Jackie agree to a divorce failed. It continued to move slowly from his announcement of its beginnings in September 1965 until he told Richler in March 1967, "I have finished a first draft of my novel and will now have to put it aside and return to scriptland (doing the *Judith Hearne* thing with Kershner)." He worked on the filmscript of his first novel for about three months — a film project that received much publicity, with the popular Deborah Kerr apparently committed to the lead role, but which in the end was abandoned.

Towards the end of June 1967, Brian and Jean had to vacate the house in Malibu for the summer months. They spent almost four months in Nova Scotia, England, and Ireland. When Jackie finally agreed on the terms of the divorce, they returned to New York where they married in October "in a very civil ceremony in New York City Hall." Seán and Cynthia Moore came down from Montreal and were the only witnesses. The novelist also visited Michael at his residential private school in Philadelphia. "He has decided to come out and stay with me this Xmas, which, as you can guess, pleases me a lot," he wrote to Richler.

Moore announced the completion of *I Am Mary Dunne* at the beginning of November. He and Jean settled back into the house at Malibu, and with the first responses from Viking very positive, Moore declared himself "relieved and relaxed" and "the pressure of the novel off at last."

# 16

# CALIFORNIA DREAMIN'

Following their marriage, Brian and Jean returned to their quiet retreat overlooking Zuma Beach, north of Los Angeles. Forced by the terms of their rental agreement to vacate it for the summer months, they spent June through September 1968 travelling to New York, Montreal, Nova Scotia, Ireland, London, and France — an itinerary they would follow on many occasions in future years, even after they became owners of the house.

Since the early 1950s, Moore had found a change of residence a spur to creativity — to getting a novel started, or to discovering an ending. Now Jean travelled with him, and the exchange of their isolated, domestic routine for comfortable hotels, stylish restaurants, and art galleries became an enjoyable annual ritual. They were not travellers who sought exotic or new places; over the decades they would return over and over to the same cities and landscapes.

Around this time Moore began to show a marked new interest in European painting — not simply in particular paintings or artists but in the "timeless" dimension of art objects and in the enigmatic character of impersonal artefacts. The move to California and to his new life with Jean gave him the calm and the leisure to read and reflect as never before, and his notes and jottings from these years mark a radical contrast in the breadth of his cultural references from the earlier diaries. His belief in the museum of the mind stocked with the masterworks of the visual arts and the "supreme fictions" of literature deepened as the "unreal cities" of the east and of Europe were displaced by the ahistorical culture of California.

At the end of 1967, Moore began to make notes and drafts for a novel with the working title *Le Musée Imaginaire*, a phrase he took from his reading of the art history of André Malraux. His interest in the French novelist and cultural historian probably went back two decades, but his attention was refocused by the publication of the autobiography of Malraux, significantly called *Anti-mémoires*. Moore's notebooks show that he copied down some of Malraux's own thoughts, and from an article by Maurice Blanchot he took a statement of Malraux's idea:

> *Le musée imaginaire* symbolizes first of all this fact: that we know all the art forms of all civilizations that devoted themselves to art. . . . We know that all of ancient art was different from what it seems to us to have been. The bleached statues deceive us, but if we restore their paint-ed surfaces, it is then that they appear false to us (and they *are* false for this restoration denies the power and truth of time which has effaced the colours). . . . Furthermore the very means of our knowledge trans-form almost at will that which they help us to know. Through repro-duction, art works lose their proportions — the miniature becomes a full-size painting, the painting separated from itself, fragmented, becomes another painting. Fictive arts? But art, it would seem, is this very fiction. Art is religion, says Hegel. . . . The disappearance of prayer resulted in the appearance of monuments and art works, made of paint-ing an art available to our eyes.

Such meditations in 1967 were only indirectly a preparation for the next novel, but they do have a significant bearing on *The Great Victorian Collection*, at least on the part of it written five years later. *Fergus*, the novel begun in late 1967, is a return to aspects of *An Answer from Limbo*, and even to some of the preoccupations of the 1950s. "The character of Preliminary Pages: always waits redoing," he told himself: "The man which you and you and you and I and I and I have made of me." In 1965, at the beginning of *Mary Dunne*, he had noted, "The novel as memoir: reminiscences of parents," and so it appears that these two novels have a common source in the desire to lay the ghosts of the past — Irish and Canadian — at the beginning of the new life in California.

Apart from those notes of 1965 that suggest a common origin for the next two novels, the earliest notes for *Fergus*, as well as some early draft openings, show that a primary motivation was to explore the unreal state in which he existed in 1965–66 when he first arrived in California. "[Fergus] starts his diary in some way to record the increasing abstractness of his life here: there is also, (growing more certain) the suspicion in his mind that he cannot return — his dream of a less unreal life in, say, Europe, is only a dream. . . . At least if life is unreal for him here, it is unreal equally for many of the other disconnected and aimless strangers he sees in the streets." The words echo the earlier preoccupation of *Ginger Coffey*, the "misfit" finding his natural element on the "underside" of cities, yet the "unreality" is no longer occasioned only by emigration and displacement but also by the estrangement of deeper and more permanent forms of spiritual exile.

Cut off from his earlier domestic milieu, from friends in New York and Montreal, and first closeted with Hitchcock in the movie-making milieu of Hollywood and then living anonymously in Los Angeles, waiting from month to month for Jackie to agree to a divorce, Moore had felt profoundly alienated. In many details, the narrator seems to be close to Moore's own experience:

> I don't know why, but when I sat down with the idea of writing about what is happening to me, the first thing I thought was to say something about my clothes. . . . I believe my present wardrobe is a comment on what has happened to me in California. I have been here two years. I no longer think about the books, records, clothes, furniture and other possessions I left behind in my apartment in New York. . . . I have trouble remembering the faces of people I knew in other cities and other countries. I have no photographs here to remind me. That is why I took photographs of my son when he came out to visit me. But the camera did not work. There were no exposures on the reel.

The voice of this early draft reflects disorientation and loss due to both personal and cultural instability.

Moore considered writing an article on Los Angeles, and his earliest reflections highlight an aspect of the setting of *Fergus* and, indeed, of *The Great Victorian Collection*, his Californian novel of the 1970s:

> The buildings and landscapes of the films of our childhood. In the present we return to a past in which we never lived, a fantasy landscape of our own past. The locations were chosen to simulate other places — Cannes — Paris etc. — and then at some point one suspects Bev Hills etc. began building stores etc. in imitation not of the real thing but of the imitation — and so in some Gidean measure Los Angeles is become the city playing a city that never was except that unknown to Los Angeles it is playing itself.

That postmodern "fantasy landscape" suggests that perhaps Moore's critical observations — a decade before Umberto Eco's North American travels led him to think of "hyperreality" — are grounded in his reading of Borges.

Fergus recalls a scene soon after he had arrived: "Los Angeles was an interesting location for an anti-novel because it was post-capitalist and post-possession." "It's as though everything here is designed to deny one's existence," he comments and proceeds to speak in a state of raw shock of the alienated existence of people living in efficiency apartments. The heart of this reading of Californian culture lies, however, in the satirical scenes with Boweri and Redshields, the film producers, and more generally in the influence that the movie industry has had on the appearance of LA and on its cultural life. On this day of hallucinations, Fergus reflects, "There was seemingly no difference in the reality of Boweri, who could be here in this place at this time, and those others, who could not." In explaining his association of fantasy with California, Moore has quoted Gertrude Stein's remark about Oakland: "There is no there there."

Preparation for writing the new novel would progress slowly during 1968, as Moore had a heavy schedule of scriptwriting. In addition to his work on *Judith Hearne* he prepared a filmscript of *Mary Dunne*, and a script based on Bernard Malamud's story "Black Is My Favorite Colour." None of these projects actually came to the screen, but, for the fourth year in a row Moore earned a substantial income from this work.

This novel of one day in the life of Fergus Fadden — Irish-born novelist, estranged from his wife and child, and recently become a resident of California to write a filmscript — is a purgation of fears and fantasies embedded in the character during childhood and adolescence. Threaded through the novel and establishing its essential structure is a series of encounters between Fergus and his parents. The personal histories of the novelist and his parents correspond in extensive detail with the biographical contours of James Moore and Eileen McFadden and their son Brian. Other family members, neighbours, friends, and priests also appear during the course of a day of hallucinations. The emotions surrounding these meetings range from dread and guilt to nostalgia, curiosity, and a desire to achieve clarity, understanding, and tranquillity. *Fergus* is at once an autobiographical novel and, perhaps more importantly, an exploration of how memory and the passage of time contribute to the ordering process of fictional creation:

My parents, now dead, continue to live in my mind but as my warped and childish misapprehensions of those people who *were* my parents. The parents who exist in my mind are not my real father and mother, but, again, my projections of those real people. Yet because time modifies and often clarifies our judgements, perhaps my "real" parents continue to struggle within my consciousness to present their true selves to me and thus remove from the scales of my memory, those masks and deformities with which I have disfigured the reality of my true parents.

Perhaps they continue to live in my mind, their image, over the years, becoming more true; perhaps, some day, they will emerge in my memory as they "really" were, their actions judged dispassionately and sympathetically by the adult person I will be then, an adult capable of understanding their adult behaviour, and not, by me, the forever child, ever misjudging and blaming them.

But, conversely, because children feel weak and need reassurance, they tend to project onto their parents their hopes and fantasies of being intelligent, powerful, wise, honest and good. So, in continuing to exist in my memory, my parents run the risk, equally great, of their eventual degradation by that one-day adult who will no longer see them through the adoring eyes of their child.

This scenario of fictions of identity rooted in the shifting mutual projections of desire is familiar from the sexual relationships and friendships dramatized in *Mary Dunne*. Speaking of that novel, he has said, "I was trying to bring up all these things that worry us, how guilty are we, or how responsible are we for other people's lives, for the lives of the people we are mixed up with." Here Moore is placing the ambiguous and conflicting needs of parent and child at the centre of Fergus's consciousness, but this phantasmagoric drama is extended to include many other figures from his childhood and distant past. All contribute to a climate of uncertainty and misrepresentation, of self-scrutiny and fluid identity.

In November 1968, "after one month concentrated writing on it," Moore wrote a note that marks an important breakthrough in the discovery of a structure for this inchoate series of hallucinatory encounters: "It is a trial: he is being judged: the *musée* figures tell him, perhaps half way through the book, and from then on, for a period, Fergus sees everyone through their eyes. Finally he sees that he must judge them to save himself and he judges them / they judge him / he judges them / in this is the resolution / a forgiveness?" Although this structure is not adhered to schematically, this novel of one day in a man's psychic life does move from morning, weaving visitations from the past with encounters in the present, towards a first trial in the late afternoon; then, after an evening interlude, in which the present — personified in Dani, Fergus's young girlfriend, and her mother — becomes more real, the hallucinatory narrative gathers momentum again towards a much longer trial scene, a midnight "kangaroo court" on the beach.

Moore knew that his experiment, blending the ghosts of the Irish past with the Californian present of his protagonist, would be difficult. "The great problem in the book was to make the — I hate to use the words 'ghost figures' — make the ghost figures as real as the other people, to describe their clothes intimately, to describe their manners intimately, to make you feel that they were just as much in the room as the other people, the real ordinary people you meet every day. And, secondly, to make two totally different worlds, contemporary life in southern California and life in Ireland, middle-class Ireland of say twenty five years ago, totally believable, so that you believed as much in the dead father being in the room as you did in the repairman being in the room at the same moment. That was technically difficult. But technically — you can tell when you're writing a thing whether it's succeeding or not. . . . in *Fergus* for some extraordinary reason, it began to succeed almost from the beginning moment I wrote it." As usual, the voice is the binding medium for a range of tones and styles that play about a basically realistic narrative: serious and tragic, satiric and comic, colloquial and literary, allusive and symbolic.

If *Fergus* is a novel haunted by personal ghosts, it is also haunted by literary ghosts. While there are passing allusions to Joyce and embedded allusions to details of *Ulysses*, the sense in which it is Joycean is, perhaps, most obvious if Fergus is compared with Gabriel Conroy in *The Dead*. Gabriel struggles with the mysterious weight of the shades and that twilight world inhabited by "the living and the dead": "His own identity was fading out into a grey impalpable world: the solid world itself which these dead had one time reared and lived in was dissolving and dwindling." After all, Joyce's beginnings in Flaubertian realism were gradually overtaken by other realities, of night and dream, and of language itself and its constructed poetic meanings. If *Mary Dunne* was indebted to Molly Bloom's soliloquy, *Fergus* is indebted to the "Nighttown" episode in *Ulysses* not only for its hallucinatory technique and its sexual frankness but for the "nightmare of history" experienced as a personal burden. And if the theme of son searching for father is worked out through the characters of Stephen and Bloom, that relationship is also the central one in *Fergus*.

In naming his protagonist Fergus Fadden, Moore associates his mother's family name with the Yeats of an early poem on a Celtic mythological figure, "Who will go drive with Fergus now?" The return to Irish material in this novel signals also a return to the literature and the cultural mores associated from childhood with his mother's "Celtic" and other-worldly image and the mythologically oriented literature of the Irish Literary Revival of Yeats and of his uncle Eoin MacNeill.

In summer 1968, after visiting Doe Castle in County Donegal, the place of his childhood visits to his mother's family, Moore made a note that was incorporated into the novel: "The sun shone as rain fell. Remembering that as a child, in the grass and weed inner courtyard, the chirp of birds — the imminent rain — often felt afraid." This memory of fear in such a setting is highlighted by an historical note on the castle, and when it is recalled by Fergus in the novel, he wonders if the "Hansel and Gretel playhouse" in his garden is, like the castle, "haunted ground" and remembers standing in "the death-haunted yard" in which "men had been flung to their deaths in the bloody days of MacSweeney NadTuath." Fergus now fears for his own mortal life, an apprehension guiltily associated with Catholicism, Irish nationalism, and sexual fantasies.

An encounter with his sister Maeve, imagined as she was at age sixteen, links the novel's concerns with childhood memories and the unreal world in which Fergus now lives. "As a Catholic," she tells Fergus, "you were brought up to believe in a life after death. But you can't believe in it. So you invent a substitute. You start worrying about your reputation outliving you. Your work becomes your chance to cheat the grave." "Nonsense" is the reply, but she persists: "How can you be sure? Your trouble is, you can't be sure of anything. You have no laws, no rules, no spiritual life at all. You have to make up your own rules of conduct." When Fergus responds, "Are you sure there's a life after death? Is any believer really sure?", Maeve's reply is a Yeatsian one: "Can you tell me right this minute if there is a life here on earth? Can you tell me if I'm your dream or if you are my dream?" She departs, leaving him without answers to his questions, but on the beach she joins a Yeatsian fisherman who throughout the afternoon becomes a touchstone of reality for Fergus. The sea and the fisherman now become symbolic in a type of fiction that no longer limits its domain to the commonsense meanings of realism.

While the matter is serious, the treatment remains comic — most comic of all, perhaps, that at the moment of sexual union with the object of his adolescent fantasies, the woman, Mrs Findlater, tells him that her husband believed "you took it, I mean your writing ability, from your father's side of the family," but she disagrees: "Let me tell you that no one has a way of telling a story the way Julia Fadden has. . . . The Kearneys, your mother's family, they were all great storytellers." From this point on in Moore's career, further associations with his mother's cultural inheritance and image, apart from her Catholicism, seem to have heightened his interest in Yeats and in the West of Ireland as a new "emotional territory" from which part of his talent and otherworldly interests originate. *Fergus* is a tribute to Yeats's poetic dialogues, and to his sense of the creative mind as a theatre in which different aspects of the self, real people, and hallucinatory presences participate in a séance-like drama.

In a more direct and practical way, a recent literary discovery may have encouraged the novelist to take the major risk of asking the reader to accept the dramatic "reality" of characters who are passing through the memory of the protagonist. It is unclear when Moore became aware of the work of Brian Friel, perhaps in the early 1960s when many of his stories appeared in the *New Yorker* and in a 1962 collection. Moore had already left New York when *Philadelphia, Here I Come!* had its triumphant nine-month run on Broadway. The text was published in 1966, and it is impossible that Moore did not become aware of it, for Friel's play — set in the Donegal region of Eileen McFadden's childhood — is directly relevant to Moore's own preoccupations.

Friel uses two actors on stage to represent the private and public Gar O'Donnell; in dramatizing the inner struggle of the young emigrant, Friel has the invisible, private Gar move about next to the real characters, and this device is a source of considerable comedy and poignancy. This daring dramatic innovation may have encouraged Moore in the risks he was taking in *Fergus*. By the time the novel was finished in 1970, he and Friel had become friends, probably from an initial meeting in Ireland in the summer of 1969, and this friendship would lead to Moore's welcome into the company of contemporary Irish writers through the 1970s.

The ending of *Fergus* remained open until very late in the novel's second draft, and Moore considered various options. As late as 9 September 1969, he was still uncertain, as notes written in London indicate. At this stage he is refining the details of the second trial scene, and most of these details do appear in the final version of the novel, but the outcome of this suggested climactic scene is still unclear.

> Appeals to father to help him, but father retreats in gibberish — breakdown, afraid, weeping on sands — some cathartic moment needed — (like *I Am Mary Dunne* ending). Maybe the name of the girl — but it was a trick of his memory, she was not his girl, not his guilt, a trick of memory, but memory has righted itself now — we forget nothing, that is our penalty — oblivion our blessing — he goes up to the house in the dawn. He enters, there will be no more ghosts, never, not ever. He goes towards the room where Dani sleeps.

Earlier notes had raised other possibilities: "The trial: reprieved by memory? Was the encounter, death? At death they say one's past life is reviewed in a flash." Such a thought may reflect Moore's new interest in the work of Flann O'Brien and, especially *The Third Policeman*, in which the protagonist, already dead, is recollecting events in life through a dreamlike condition. But a further note shows that he connected this moment-of-death experience with Dr. Fadden as medical doctor: "Patients, terminal, sometimes say they think on their lives at such times."

It is this line of thinking that led to the appropriate "cathartic moment" needed by the novel. Fergus suffers a minor heart attack and is comforted by his father, who shows himself to Fergus in the persona of doctor for the first time. When his body experiences the attack, "pain so intense that he lost his vision, standing, swaying, blind, as the pain fell on him like a wave," his father comforts him and reassures him with "an old medical joke" that "this world is a matter of life and death." He takes leave of his parents, "releasing them" from their lifelong conflicts, and his father "saw the good-bye wave, and, grateful, raised his old white hat in salute." That moment is surely a significant one in Moore's thirty-year dialogue with his own father. The medical doctor's joke becomes the basis of the grace note with which the novel ends: "In the east, dawn came up. Breakers slammed on the morning shore, monotonous as a heartbeat. He walked towards the house."

That ending has a special significance in the novelist's own life. Both his father and mother had died of heart attacks, and so it was with some anxiety that he discovered in 1967, during a routine medical examination, that he had an irregular heartbeat. Looking for reassurance, he sent the ECG to his brother Seán, who consulted a cardiologist. Although the verdict was that this inherited trait was inconsequential, the shock of its discovery became the occasion for a radical reassessment of his lifestyle. For decades, he had been a heavy smoker, but he now quit. Always a lover of good food and drink, and as a result much overweight, he began an exercise and diet programme. A daily régime of jogging on the beach became the norm, and his jovial, well-rounded contours gradually yielded to a slight and almost skeletal figure. And so this final image of the heartbeat, monotonous as a wave on the seashore, has a reassuring resonance for the novelist. This genetic link to the father, as it were, reconciles the two roles of the doctor-father and the image includes also one of the novelist's favourite memories of his father, on the beach at Portstewart in summer.

During the years of the novel's composition, the domestic life of Brian and Jean gradually assumed a routine that suited each of them. Moore refers frequently to the happiness of his new life and to his luck in having a wife content to share and support the monastic régime of the novelist at work. Jean did not pursue an independent career; instead, she drew on her talents for interior decoration, gardening, and cooking to create and renew their domestic oasis overlooking the Pacific.

Although the novelist has spoken of his satisfaction in escaping from the social life of the New York literary and cultural scene, he gradually found new friends with literary interests. The Californian novelists Joan Didion and John Gregory Dunne — originally an easterner of Irish background — became close friends, so that in the next decades they would holiday together at Christmas-time on a number of occasions. Other new friends connected Moore more directly to Irish literary interests and to an international lifestyle resembling his own. Living in Los Angeles was Julia O'Faoláin, daughter of the prominent Irish short-story writer and cultural critic Seán O'Faoláin, herself at the beginning of her career as a novelist. Married to Lauro Martines, a professor of Italian History at UCLA, O'Faoláin divided her time between L.A. and London, where she kept an apartment. In the decades ahead, the friendship of the two couples would continue on both sides of the Atlantic.

Yet, if the novelist had left the Californian limbo of the mid-sixties behind, and had made a home there, he was also rerooting in Ireland and in Nova Scotia — the two places becoming increasingly linked in his imagination. While the visit to Connemara with Jackie in 1961 had become a nightmare, the Atlantic coast of the West of Ireland was a place he frequented more and more with Jean. Two events of the summers of 1968 and 1969, one in Nova Scotia and the other in Connemara, would combine to provide him with the inspiration for *Catholics* in 1971.

*Fergus* was completed in mid-January 1970 and published in North America in September. Days after he had completed the manuscript, he was already at work on another novel. In January 1970, he remembered a dream he had had some time earlier in a motel in Carmel-by-the-Sea, en route from San Francisco to Malibu. The dream had been of a miraculous event which, on awakening, the dreamer discovered had actually happened. This dream took place while he was still working on *Fergus*, and he has remarked that it was probably inspired by the Borgesian nature of that fiction. He recalled the dream and began to think of it in terms of a story. Two overlapping versions grew during the first six months of 1970, each of which would eventually develop into a novel, *The Great Victorian Collection*, completed, after interruptions, in summer 1974, and *Cold Heaven*, not completed until the summer of 1982.

The story that evolved out of that California dream began to grow and it occupied him fully into the summer. Two pages of notes written in May 1970 mark the moment when the energy that had fueled the new work seemed to wane: "Periods in the so-called 'creative' life: between books, ideas etc. The abortive ideas: all seem very fresh at the outset but dreamlike: outré. The Canadian Railroad story which *is* the great Victorian Collection in another form: held in the mind of an idiot, an empire; *Railroad. Victorian* is held in the memory (learning) of a scholar; a collection of realities." The nature of this dream-inspiration — this "collection of realities" being an analogy for his own accumulating fictions — is not only a metaphysical conundrum that the novel will explore but a psychological one also, of immediate concern to the working novelist.

In his notebook Moore practises his recently adopted uncial script and admonishes himself to "cultivate good rhythm [in his handwriting] and you will write well." This private pleasure of "good rhythm" seems to be a metaphor for art itself, for what transforms merely reportorial "story" into personal literary truth. Art is placed at risk in the case of the Victorian Collection by the impulse of the journalist Waterman to make his own name by breaking the news of the miracle dream. More generally, the impulse to adapt art to a social function with a political or commercial mandate is Moore's real concern. The activism of the 1960s in the United States, in civil rights and anti-Vietnam-war demonstrations, and the general Marxist climate of cultural criticism touched Moore, who grew to feel that his freedom to be an artist was threatened not only by the commercial constraints of the publishing business but also by politically charged public discourse on the social utility of art. It is a paradox not lost on Moore that at the beginning of his life he had felt that his freedom was smothered by the right-wing political discourses of Catholicism and nationalism.

It is not, then, surprising that the final note on these pages is "Idea for a story on a monastery in Ireland after ecumenical revolution," for the novella *Catholics* dramatizes a world of the future in which not art but traditional religious belief (and increasingly they become synonymous) is subject to the reductive functional imperative. The ex-Catholic Irishman and declared agnostic, in his hermitage in Malibu, had begun to reflect again on the meaning of art and of religious belief in contemporary society — even before he was drawn into contemporary events by the upsurge of political violence in Ireland that began in 1969.

Work on the earliest version of *The Great Victorian Collection* came to an end in summer 1970, although notes made in Paris in September seem to indicate that he intended to continue the artist-novel on his return to Malibu. The reception of *Fergus* in New York threw him off course and called into question his intention to continue working in the magic realism vein. The verdict in the *New York Times*, written by Julian Moynahan, was negative, as were almost all other reviews. Moynahan wrote: "For me the weakness of the book emerges in Fergus's virtually total inability to defend himself, to mount any sort of counter-attack. . . . as a novel it has the wrong sort of indeterminacy and spookiness. The creatures of a writer's imagination are entitled to solicit him as they choose, not, however, at the expense of concreteness and a clear viewpoint in the novel that results." These words led to Moore's experiencing a temporary crisis of confidence, questioning as they did the central thrust of his sensibility as he worked on fictions of the interplay among heightened subjective states — memories, dreams, apprehensions of miraculous events — and the "unreality" of Californian society.

His notebook records how he took Moynahan's words to heart: "Was Fergus's weakness that he did not fight? This was also a criticism of Brendan in *Limbo* and of Ginger and Devine. Mayhewson must defend his Collection." These remarks foreshadow the fact that, although Moore abandoned *The Great Victorian Collection* for more than a year, when he did return to it a new theme and a central motivation of the protagonist became the dreamer's responsibility for guarding and protecting his Collection, and for fighting back against those who misinterpret and question it.

In early October, Moore allowed himself to be persuaded by Jack McClelland to go to Montreal and observe at first hand the crisis brought on by the political kidnappings by extreme nationalist members of the Front de Libération du Québec of a provincial cabinet minister and the British High Commissioner. After *Fergus*, the novelist had expressed interest in working on a reality-based novel, and the political events in Montreal drew him back to the city with that possibility in mind. Brian and Jean stayed in Montreal for three months, watching as events unfolded, and after returning to Malibu, he wrote *The Revolution Script* in the first few months of 1971.

The escalating and intractable violence in Northern Ireland was the real background to his writing about the crisis in Quebec: "In a peculiar sense I knew when I started this book that I had the expertise, if you like, and I had the story. . . . There's a great parallel with Ireland and with the kind of people I knew there, ex-Catholic and *lumpen* intellectuals, which is really what [the Québécois revolutionaries] were." Interviewers were surprised that he should choose to write of the revolutionary nationalists of Quebec rather than of Ireland — which had world-wide press coverage at this same time — but the sense of history assuming the infernal logic that he had known intimately as a child colours the writing of both *The Revolution Script* and *Catholics*.

# 17

# REVOLUTIONARY
# SCRIPTS

If *The Emperor of Ice Cream* had seemed to offer Moore's final rendering of the epoch of his growing up in Belfast, he was clearly shocked and inspired by the ways in which Ireland and especially Belfast were now becoming a centre of his imaginative life once more. This reassertion of old themes took place in a number of ways, and his gloomy and pessimistic interpretations of contemporary history, especially developments in the Catholic Church, make most sense in relation to what he discovered in Ireland on his annual summer visits in the late 1960s.

The summers of 1969 and 1970 were particularly disturbing. He observed on visits and through close contact with his sister Una and her family in Lurgan the terrifying descent of Northern Ireland from an American-style campaign for civil rights into the bloody sectarian strife known as "the Troubles." He speaks regularly of feeling depressed when he remains any length of time in Belfast, not simply because of the violence itself but also because he has a prophetic sense that it is engrained in the society and cannot be avoided. "It occurs to me that there is something sick about Belfast. Perhaps it has always had this sickness. Perhaps it is incurable. . . . The same old riots we had in my childhood. Mobs of rampaging Protestant *lumpenproletariat* trying to terrorize their equally ignorant Catholic *lumpenproletariat* neighbours. . . . Ordinary people set against ordinary people because there is something old and rotten still alive here." Such thoughts made their way into an article that appeared in *Atlantic Monthly* in August 1970 with the title "Bloody Ulster: An Irishman's Lament" and in the Belfast periodical *Threshold* under the title "Now and Then."

In this essay, Moore includes a brief historical analysis of the conservative hegemony of the Unionist establishment and the political exploitation that has maintained a festering power-relationship based on fear, "and yet, this time, there *is* a difference. These troubles . . . were inspired by an outside force. . . . Television, the agitprop of modern revolt." He goes on to trace the influential example of the civil rights marchers in the United States and of the student revolutionaries, known to the world at large through the emblematic television images. The new Troubles are focused in mass demonstrations and marches before they become bloody. "The standard-bearers of these new banners dutifully incline them in the direction of the television camera: the devout making obeisance toward their altar. And rightly so. Television begat them. Only television can win for them."

There is a despairing passion in recalling the menace he had known in the twenties and thirties, riots much more bloody than anything seen by "the electronic eye" to date, yet he believes that "it must escalate. Blood must run in the streets" before the British government and public accept their responsibility for changing the political status quo. He recalls the earlier role of the English soldier: "He fired down this street to save us Irish from ourselves the night I was born," and, accepting that "the wheel has come full circle," he believes that the English soldier must enforce the peace once again. He dramatizes himself at the beginning of the piece as an outsider, seeing images of Belfast on the television news in California, but by the end he speaks of "us Irish" and what "we" must do.

Apart from the raw feelings rooted in childhood memories, what remains when he comes to write his novel of the October 1970 FLQ crisis is that "Bloody Ulster" of the present is like Quebec during its brief "revolution": both events are orchestrated by television. Modern-day revolutions are effective to the extent that they gain and hold the attention of the television journalists and camera operators, and so, as the title of the novel suggests, all those involved — the establishment politicians as much as the young revolutionaries — follow a script.

> I was so curious about what was happening in Canada that I said, All right, I'll go there. . . . I was sure I would never do the book. But then I began seeing the things I did see happening in the media, and the media were so powerful, and I decided that this event was really something very much of our time. . . . It's fascinating, more than frightening, to think that six or seven young people can create a revolutionary situation today with the help of the media, with the *unwilling* help of the media, and the innocent help of the media. The government can be forced into an equally ridiculous counter drama, which happened here.

For most of a decade, Moore had articulated his fear of the growing power of television in North America and had shown interest in the ideas of Marshall McLuhan. The FLQ revolutionaries modelled themselves on what they had seen in a film, *The Battle of Algiers*, but from conversations with their peers, Moore realized that they were not only Québécois nationalists but left-wing revolutionaries in a sixties media-driven style. While there were two distinct "cells" involved in the two kidnappings — of James Cross, the British Trade Commissioner, and of Pierre Laporte, a minister in the provincial government — Moore chose to dramatize the events of the six weeks by focusing on the kidnappers of Cross. Their adversary was the charismatic and media-savvy prime minister Pierre Elliott Trudeau. The Quebec-born Trudeau had come to power in 1968 through a personality-driven campaign that fanned the flames of his unique popularity, resulting in a phenomenon dubbed "Trudeaumania." Trudeau becomes a character in Moore's novel, the politician-as-actor — no more real or influential on the television screen than his invisible adversaries, whose press releases and manifestos issued from hiding controlled the news reporting of the crisis.

The opening sentences of the note that serves as preface to *The Revolution Script* establish the tone and purpose of the book:

> When these extraordinary events occurred, hostages, ministers of state, police chiefs, lawyers, and news commentators crowded the screens and pages of the communications media. But the leading actors — four young men and a girl who set these events in motion by kidnapping James Cross — remained faceless. Even in the last act of this drama, the most publicized event of its kind in history, they still seemed shadows, figments of our imagination, fleeing into exile and silence. This book uses the techniques of fiction to bring these young revolutionaries on stage.

In Moore's hands, the young revolutionaries become more immediate in the narrative than Trudeau, and some readers were surprised by the degree of the author's sympathetic understanding of their motivations and beliefs. Moore's explanation for this has little to do with sympathy for Quebec's separation from Canada — something he has frequently argued against — or, indeed, for sixties radicalism; instead, it reveals him, as he conceives of the novel, harking back to his younger self, the young socialist of the thirties and early forties before he left Belfast. "People always assume that one's highly conservative, especially if one is Irish and an ex-Catholic, but I haven't been. When I was young, I was extremely left wing, but it didn't enter into any of the other books. It wasn't relevant to the subject."

But in spite of this claim and its undoubted relevance to his choice of a narrative approach to events in Quebec, his more authentic imaginative engagement with fiction as a genre led him to have immediate misgivings about this project. In fact, as in the case of the thrillers of the 1950s, he has banished *The Revolution Script* from his list of novels. His reflections on the use of politics in fiction and on the kinds of limitations imposed on the novelist by public events help to clarify his working methods at this time and the kinds of risks he took later when he consciously worked with political issues and recognizable public events in eastern Europe, Northern Ireland, Haiti, and France.

> The other fictions I've written have been based upon a much more uncertain method of work and a much deeper amount of thought. . . . I knew nothing of how it was going to turn out, or what was going to happen. . . . That's one of the reasons I don't think this sort of book is art. The documentary novel, or the new journalism, this is its terrible limitation. It is not free, like fiction. . . . The kidnappers were my only "fictional" characters. They were marvellous; they'd disappeared into history, and they weren't going to talk back. So this is an ideal situation actually, and I seized it with a certain amount of ruthlessness. . . . I try to be bigger than any of my own quirks. Let's say I am an anti-Nazi: I still wouldn't want to put a lot of cracks about Hitler's sex life into a book. I would try to be compassionate, to understand the enemy's point of view, because it seems to me that's the difference between caricature and character in a novel. . . . Great fiction is when a character is unexpected. . . . And in most fictional situations, the description of politics is like pornography: it's so powerful and real that it kills the fiction.

Such thoughts tell a great deal about Moore's working methods as a novelist. His claim that he always strives to create characters rather than caricatures is not true. As recently as *Fergus*, for instance, he had presented the Hollywood producers Redshields and Boweri as caricatures, or in *The Emperor of Ice Cream*, Gavin Burke's colleagues at the ARP. It might be argued that his reason for creating those caricatures is to suggest that they are no more substantial as individuals than their attitudes or adopted roles — that they are "humours," as Moore has said, for the purpose of counterpointing the real and "unexpected" characters, the protagonists of each novel. Moore's point here is that his fictional creations are more real than what the media present as reality: "Fact has become so fictitious and so horrendous and so managed, and we're so bored with the overkill which fact presents, that we may, and we do, seek something in fiction which we don't get in fact."

Moore's experience writing this novel seems to have reaffirmed his determination to write fiction which was not compromised by overt political commitment or the closed plotlines of public events. He insists that what he knows in his own "core of dullness" is that ordinary life is lived at a remove from the images and attitudes affirmed by reporting in the mass media. "We, as writers, are losing sight of that real world in which our parents and relatives still live. In which people in, say, Nova Scotia, or New Brunswick, or here in Toronto still live. Even ghetto people still live in a real, ordinary, dull world even though some of them pretend it's all Black Panther confrontations and heavy stuff, man. It's not true. Most people still live in the old-fashioned world of the nineteenth-century novels."

The extent of the violence and the mass involvement in the FLQ "revolution" was minor compared with the Troubles of Northern Ireland, yet what Moore found interesting in it, apart from his latent sympathy for the anti-establishment Québécois, was the way in which history evolves as a set of theatrical spectacles. "What really captivates me is the fact that we've entered a curiously theatrical era in politics. Trudeau succeeded in coming to power because he's a magnificent actor on television and a handful of the FLQ succeeded in making a revolution because of the existence of the media." The Church and its ceremonies have been replaced by the mass media, especially television, as a medium for transmitting symbolic images that move people to action because they offer a sense of communal faith and commitment.

Moore's antagonism towards Pierre Trudeau is rooted in his life-long suspicion of personality cults and charismatic leaders. The authoritarian power of priests and fascist dictators that shaped the worlds of his youth left a lasting imprint. *The Revolution Script* channels the subversive feelings of his adolescence into the depiction of the Québécois revolutionaries, but it also expresses his fears of a spiritually bereft society and culture in thrall to the totalitarian power of television images. It is this paradoxical situation in contemporary culture — that political power or religious faith may be created or destroyed by the pervasive and intrusive images of television — that gained new resonance in Belfast and Quebec and that became a focal point in *Catholics* and again in *The Great Victorian Collection*.

While his visits to Ireland in the late 1960s brought up close once more a violent and depressing Ireland from which he had long wished to remain apart, there were other Irelands to which he drew closer — an intimacy inspiring for *Catholics* and for his later work. In August 1969, he was interviewed by Michael Paul Gallagher, a young Jesuit academic. The banned novelist, who had been seen to have abused the Catholic Church and its schools, was treated with respect and appreciation by this young priest. Times had changed in Ireland. More significantly, this interview led to a friendship of many years with Gallagher, and the sequence of priest-protagonists that Moore depicted seems to have begun at this time with the idea of writing *Catholics*. In a letter of 1977, Moore refers to Gallagher's "once capacity as spiritual adviser on *Catholics*." Although the novelist had him check facts about institutional matters within the Church, it was Gallagher's imaginative sympathy for his work that allowed Moore to sense a more general spiritual affinity. The articles and reviews of Moore's work written by Gallagher and their meetings on Moore's visits to Ireland seem to have reassured the novelist that he could move beyond the angry and satirical portraits of priests in the novels up to *Fergus*. Beginning with the abbot in *Catholics*, he explored the nuances of faith and doubt through a large cast of priest-protagonists over the next twenty-five years.

The imaginative sympathy that drew Irish and Catholic readers to his novels was especially gratifying when he found his work appreciated by Irish writers of the first rank such as Seamus Heaney and Brian Friel. Following his meeting with Friel in the summer of 1969, a regular correspondence over the next dozen years indicates that a mutual appreciation allowed Moore to feel part of the burgeoning Northern Irish literary movement with the poet and the playwright at its centre. Heaney visited Moore in Malibu in early 1971, when he was a guest lecturer at UCLA, a visit commemorated ten years later in the poem "Remembering Malibu." At the time of writing the poem in October 1980, Heaney wrote to Moore, "I think the movement of the thing came out with some kind of truth for me, which is possibly untrue for you. Anyway. Indeed, the thing should probably be called 'Catholics'." Not only does Heaney's poem draw on images of the bleak Kerry coastline from Moore's novella, but he seems to intuit the spiritual and metaphysical concerns of Moore's imagination.

His friendship with Brian Friel drew him close to the Irish literary community in a way he had not experienced before. At a time when North American readers seemed out of sympathy with his work, he gladly turned to England and Ireland. For more than a decade, Friel offered support for Moore's novels, beginning in early 1971: "*Fergus* got an excellent press here. The most general comment seemed to be that it's your best book so far. This may be true, but I think I liked *Mary Dunne* at least equally well. Both are very ambitious and both daring. And my feeling is that *Mary D.* is more difficult and more courageous and so (to this male writer) more interesting. But *Fergus* is so damn honest and so truthful that maybe it's a photo-finish. Anyhow congratulations and good luck."

In 1972, Friel would agree to write a new screenplay of *Judith Hearne* for a proposed film of the novel, a project which began with the idea of having Katharine Hepburn play the lead and dragged on for many years without success. In turn, Moore wrote of his admiration for Friel's plays: "I know this sounds un-Ulster and extreme, but as it is much easier to say it to you in print than to your face, I am first among your many admirers." Friel urged him to return to live in Ireland so that he could witness the Troubles at close hand, and offered him his cottage in Donegal, but it seems that, in the end, it was the North American dimension to Moore that really interested Friel. The author of *Philadelphia, Here I Come!* — always more interested in the Irish-American rather than the Anglo-Irish cultural axis — soon had the same New York agent as Moore, and much of their mutual support was expressed through a sharing of gossip regarding the American theatre and film scene.

The recognition of him in Ireland as "a writer's writer" is part of a re-rooting of Moore's imagination following the years of upheaval and uncertainty of the mid sixties. This process also included extended stays in the West of Ireland, the landscape of the Atlantic seaboard having a deep spiritual resonance for him. It was there he found the abandoned monastery that gave him the setting for *Catholics*. Yet the rerooting has even more to do with his marriage to Jean and to her familial home on the Atlantic coast of Nova Scotia.

In writing *Catholics*, Moore returns to the conflict between the traditional Irish and contemporary American lifestyles that he had examined in *An Answer from Limbo* and *Fergus*, but with a new simplicity and certainty of style that come out of Moore's confident sense of belonging in an Irish literary tradition. This belonging is embodied in the novella's allusions to Synge, Yeats and Beckett. The spiritual image of that sense of tradition is the bleak seashore, first used in *Fergus*, then in *Catholics* and later novels, and recognized as a key to Moore's imagination by Seamus Heaney.

A poem on exile dated 1971 and among his working notes for *Catholics* sums up the resonances of the Irish and Catholic contexts of his new fiction:

We grow up dreaming of escape
Now we are outside
Escaping
Always escaping
Circumnavigators — sailing round and round
Always coming back.
When did my world become an island?

When my island was no longer the world.
But the world is round.
Sail far enough and you return
To the island.

*Catholics* was written in the summer months of 1971, although the idea of examining the post-Vatican II Church had struck him even earlier than May 1970, when he jotted a note to himself. In the summer of 1967 or 1968, on the annual visit to Jean's family home in Kentville, Nova Scotia, the Moores had been walking one Sunday morning when they overheard a church service in progress. The evangelical style of the vernacular singing led Moore to think it was a Baptist church, but Jean pointed out that it was, in fact, the post-Second Vatican Council (1962–65) Catholic service. It came as a shock to the novelist that the Latin mass of his childhood and the Church liturgy he had been taught was universal and unchanging had changed so radically.

The drama of *Catholics* is a simple one set at the end of the millennium. It is framed by the tactical duel between the Abbot of Muck and James Kinsella, a young American priest who visits the abbot with the purpose of forcing him to cease fostering the long-abandoned cult of the Latin liturgy. By the end of the century, this isolated part of the Atlantic coastline has become a place of pilgrimage: "It was a phenomenon, even in the history of pilgrimage. There were no miracles, there was no hysteria, there was not even a special fervour. The mood was nostalgic. . . . The old way. . . . Sick as we all are nowadays for a past we never knew." The abbot and his monks live on an island off the coast and remain indifferent to the changes in the wider world, whereas Kinsella has been educated in liberation theology and ecumenism by his mentor, Father Hartmann: "The Church, Hartmann taught, despite its history and its dependence on myth and miracle, exists today as the quintessential structure through which social revolution can be brought to certain areas of the globe."

Within this dramatic frame of opposing views of the meaning and purpose of the Church, the abbot is revealed as a prisoner of the power structure he supports. His own faith has been eroded, and he questions the authenticity of his feelings about prayer and miracles, the pivots of whatever meaning his religion has. The temporary loss of his faith on a visit to Lourdes years before plunged him into a depression, and the return to that state of "null" is his greatest fear in life. While he is characterized with great skill as a witty and charming man, and the novella blends satirical and lyrical passages with passages of powerful dialogue, the personal ironies that deepen the abbot's character situate him closer to Beckett's world of displaced and isolated individuals than to the traditional Irish community as recorded in Synge's *The Aran Islands*.

When Moore had written thirty-five pages of the new novel, he wrote to Michael Paul Gallagher, "I find myself sympathetic to both sides of this argument (the Ecumenical and the Traditional) and so perhaps the story will work out." As the story of the abbot came to occupy centre stage, it would emerge that Moore is, perhaps, more antipathetic to both sides than sympathetic to either; it is the sense of loss and the fear that accompanies that loss that truly evoke Moore's sympathy. He is not indifferent to what is lost; although he is a declared agnostic and progressive, a latent aspect of his sensibility is post-Catholic, and he is closer to the abbot because of that sensibility.

The earliest working notes outline the essential idea of the novella: "A visitor from the archbishopric (renamed) comes to the monks with new orders: God in the old sense is dead and they must disband. . . . Old Abbot: was God actually alive then? And if not sure, then how can any of them be sure that as the archbishopric's spokesman now states: He is now dead. In the end all there is is the chapel and prayer: prayer is God. Let us pray says the Abbot." The finished novella does end at this point, and a letter to Jack McClelland clarifies his intention:

> . . . he realizes that in this instance, where the faith of his community of monks is threatened, he must do something exceptional to strengthen their resolves and calm their terrible fear. . . . He must really try to pray, even if, as he knows, it will bring on in him yet another terrible clinical depression. . . . He winds back their faith, but himself is plunged, as he feared, into a depression from which he may never emerge. . . . at his own expense, he saves the faith of the others.

It is finally the abbot's personal dilemma — not too far removed from the situation of Judith Hearne in her loss of faith — that takes precedence over the political and institutional matters that are Kinsella's concern. Yet what is remarkable in Moore's sympathetic identification with the abbot's dilemma is that faith is no longer eroded by the blasphemous anti-clericalism of Bernard Rice, as in Moore's first novel, but by the institutional Church itself. This raises questions about Moore's own attitude towards the forms of belief within the Church and the association of his own work as a novelist with those beliefs.

Since my adolescence I have never been a practicing Catholic and I do not go to church. Someone once asked Joyce, "When did you leave the Church?" and he said, "That's for the Church to say." There's some truth in it because while I left the Church, I've always had a very strong interest in Catholicism. I've felt as a writer that man's search for a faith, whether it is within the Catholic Church or a belief in God or a belief in something other than merely the materialistic world, is a major theme. For one kind of novelist it's the big and ultimate theme. If you're an English novelist you write novels of manners, novels of society, novels of class. If you look at Ireland and Irish literature, there are very few Irish novels because society and class doesn't operate the same way in Ireland. And so I think that this Irish tendency is to pick on the meaning of life. The Gael is interested in the meaning of life and he's usually pessimistic about it.

Such comments suggest that Moore's identification of himself here as a "Gael" disguises a claim to a spiritual depth and awareness which have been lost by English fiction and may even have been lost by the Catholic Church also. Moore blames Pope John XXIII: "He was a kindly man, however, he took an enormous gamble and failed. And history will judge him on his failure. History will very much account Pope John's papacy with the beginning of the irrevocable decline of the Catholic Church. . . . The Catholic Church always had this great strength, whether you liked it or not, it didn't change. It didn't run with the current tide. Now that's what it is doing." The irony that the novelist should defend the position of the traditional Church in terms that his own father would have used is certainly surprising, and, indeed, in *Catholics* there is a ghostly presence of the father in the abbot's visit to Lourdes, where Dr. Moore's faith was strengthened by the confirmation of miraculous events.

Moore's comments after he had completed the novel suggest that the events in Ireland and, perhaps, in the 1960s generally, had stirred an apocalyptic pessimism in this "Gael":

I'm not a Catholic. But this is an important subject, of interest to us all. For if the Catholic Church goes, you remove a great sense of purpose from a huge segment of the Christian faith. Then what will ultimately happen to the Christian faith itself? That is the ultimate question. What have we got to put in its place? If we breed two generations of the young who do not hold Judeo-Christian values, what's going to happen to us? I find myself amazed to be saying these things, but we could have a new amorality, the like of which we never realized possible.

There appears to be a gloomy paradigm of history here, public events and ideas moving in large apocalyptic patterns within which individuals are impotent. The Irish colonial and civil wars, within the larger frame of the European wars of the thirties and forties, seem to have left the once progressive Moore with imaginative models of conflict and of the curves of historical change that colour our lives, yet the essential experience of the individual is private and apart from the public drama.

The two fictions of this year, 1971, reveal new directions in Moore's pre-occupations and literary styles. He increasingly focuses on western spirituality and conscience, and on the television age, and he makes use of parable and allegory as fictional models. While *The Revolution Script* and *Catholics* allow a reconciliation between Moore the literary novelist and Moore the reporter of current events, they also probe the power and limits of art and the mass media, subjects already present in the drafts of *The Great Victorian Collection* and earlier. They do so in relation to wider cultural and historical changes familiar to everyone. This contemporaneity of non-fictional material may be seen as a step forward from the historical novel *The Emperor of Ice Cream* towards that set of political and religious thrillers that came to dominate his career from the mid-eighties and that explore contemporary public events. Those later novels, in particular *The Colour of Blood*, *Lies of Silence*, *No Other Life*, and *The Statement*, would mark a return to the earliest stages of Moore's writing career when he wrote commercial thrillers, yet they have a more serious origin in the implicit decision to discover a new and more public style of narrative to offset the intense and introspective literary fictions he had been writing under the influence of Borges.

An implicit program for much of his fiction in later years may be detected in a comment he writes down for his working notes on *The Great Victorian Collection*. American literary critic Irving Howe glosses an essay by the historian Isaiah Berlin as follows: "What Berlin does is to ask himself is whether the rigid totalitarianism of a few decades ago — and we might raise the same question about the fluid anarcho-authoritarianism of today — is a phase in a prolonged crisis of Western civilization, one root of which is the decay of Christianity. For the hunger after quasi-religious experience seems insatiable in our, and perhaps any other, time." That "hunger after quasi-religious experience" is something that links *Cold Heaven*, *The Great Victorian Collection*, *The Mangan Inheritance*, and *The Temptation of Eileen Hughes*. In some of these novels and others, the miraculous event is associated with sexual experience, so that religious and sexual experiences come to be seen as vital. It is the absence of such vitality and the awareness of its absence that are at the core of a crisis in Western civilization.

*The Revolution Script* was begun on 10 January 1971 and was completed in three months, with a short break at the end of February when Moore was a guest at an academic conference in Virginia, and he and Jean travelled on to New York and Montreal. As soon as the novel was completed, Moore set about preparing a filmscript and completed a second draft by July. The plan he had agreed on with Jack McClelland was that the book would appear in Canada on 5 October 1971, the anniversary of the first kidnapping. Moore met the publishing deadline, and the work appeared a month later in New York. The book won wide attention. The London *Sunday Times* ran three extended excerpts when it appeared in England in January 1972.

Throughout much of 1972, the possibility of raising the money for filming was actively pursued by Potterton Studios in Montreal and Wolper Productions in Los Angeles, and Moore worked with the Canadian director Donald Brittain on the project. In the end the film was not made. The film that *was* made was *Catholics*. John Huston had expressed interest in it before publication and Moore prepared a screenplay early in 1972. In the end, Huston's project also foundered but the book was made into a television film directed by Jack Gold and starring Trevor Howard as the abbot. The filming took place on location in Ireland, on an island off the coast of Connemara in October 1972, just as the novella was published in Canada and the United Kingdom. First publication in the United States was in the *New American Review* in September, and it was issued in hardcover in April 1973. Both the novella and the film were highly praised: *Catholics* won the prestigious British literary prize, the W. H. Smith Award in December 1973, and after its presentation on CBS "Playhouse 90," the film was acclaimed and went on to win a Peabody Award in 1974. Eventually, in 1977, it was released for showing in cinemas, and the novella continued to preoccupy Moore as it was adapted into a stage play in the early 1980s.

# 18

# AMERICAN
# APOCALYPSE

The American coolness towards *Fergus* in the fall of 1970 had shocked Moore, coming so soon after the appreciative reception of *I Am Mary Dunne*, and that shock seems to have made him wary of returning to the miracle fictions of early 1970. Friel and he shared their feelings about the wounding fickleness of critics and their power to make or break a play or novel with one review. The reception of the novel was very positive in England and Ireland, as Moore had predicted earlier to his English agent, and in April 1971, Friel wrote "to congratulate you on *Fergus* which I liked enormously." Two months later, Friel wrote encouragement once again because "you sounded depressed about *Fergus*."

Moore confided in Friel his fear that *Catholics* would not be published; "I enjoyed writing it," he tells him, but seems to feel that he was losing his sense of rapport with an audience, his own satisfaction with the work no longer being a reliable guide to the response of critics. He had trusted Viking editor Aaron Asher's support for *Fergus*, but he now came to believe that his earliest sympathetic audience — in England — was probably going to be his permanent audience, willing to accept him in his various experimental moods. He had to face the fact that the American readership he had worked to win was less secure. This recognition that, paradoxically, his Californian novels would find their largest audience in England, combined with Friel's encouragement, which seemed to guarantee him an Irish readership, emboldened him to return to the "miracle" material at the end of 1971.

The critical reception of *Fergus* also forced Moore to reflect on the way *Judith Hearne* was "an albatross" that had limited the ability of American critics to accept his new styles of writing. "*The Great Victorian Collection* is a paradigm of the life of the artist — that was a book I did write with that in mind. I wrote *Judith Hearne* which was, while not enormously successful in sales, enormously successful critically, and was like an albatross around my neck for many, many years. I was only known to people as the person who had written *Judith Hearne*. And so *The Great Victorian Collection* came out of reading Borges and speculating on that." When he resumed work on the abandoned novel, Moore decided that it was his own chameleon character as a writer, rather than his talent as a realist as exemplified in his early novels, that allowed him to be creative and to apply his talent. He knew he could not repeat himself, even if he had wanted to do so. As he remarked to Jack McClelland, "Sometimes I don't choose the books I write: they choose me. *The Great Victorian Collection* is such a book." And so he returned with renewed conviction to the idea that continued to obsess him.

The challenge of breaking out of the realistic mode *Fergus* initiated was reaffirmed by the dream of January 1970 as a fate that he must follow; and he did follow it, starting again in late 1971, after he finished *Catholics*. Finding fictional modes that would mirror his perception of the unreal world of California and incorporate the lessons of Borges and of Yeats would continue to occupy him more or less consistently until *Cold Heaven* in 1983. In retrospect, it is evident that Moore had to accept his literary destiny and take the major risks with genre that mark this experimental phase.

Moore's dream became Mayhewson's dream of a Victorian Collection that materialized and had to be protected from the curious and exploitative visitors to the motel in Carmel where the miracle occurred. Mayhewson, later called Mahon, and eventually Maloney in the published novel, is trapped by persons and forces at whose mercy he places himself — news media, Management Inc., experts in Victoriana and in parapsychology. All exploit him for their own gain, and, at first, he is so captivated by the fame they offer him that he co-operates in the exploitation. From the beginning, it is evident that the dream is an allegory of the artist in America.

Moore's Commonplace Book includes a note on the composition of the novel from the beginning. "A dream I had in Carmel. January 1970: remembered in story form: The dream is laid out and totally visualized by one man: police come to protect it. Must immediately train a successor to this knowledge, so that when the original dreamer dies, the transference can be made. July 1970: that was the dream form, but in the first draft 100 pages somehow the question of a successor did not come up."

This early draft of the novel came quickly, and in a letter to Aaron Asher on 1 June 1970, he remarks: "I seem very pleased with myself these days for I have just done about 100 pages of a short novel in unbelievably fast time. It is very odd (and I hope original) idea and I am very much enjoying writing it, which is a good sign." Soon after this he and

Jean set off for a few months in Europe, where he notes "Aug 1970 Now start 2nd part." His mind was still preoccupied with it in Paris in September, as his notes indicate:

Again: Make it a Paradigm of writing:
He discusses whether or not he was ever ambitious to be famous.
Isn't everybody today?
There must be the question of wishing this fate on himself.
Those who surround fame.

A pedant, but somehow with that other ordinary life.

Give to the writing even in the beginning a mixture of Ernie's pedantry and a writer's earnestness.

Questions to ask of this narrative
Is it gripping? Suspense
Or funny? Droll
Or affecting?
Would a reader have any identification w/ Mayhewson?

The world of *Mary Dunne*, recalled here by the reference to Ernie Truelove, overlaps with this early conception of Mayhewson, especially in the issue of narrative perspective and the ambivalent presentation of the protagonist. These notes focus, however, on an issue that seems to explain why Moore abandoned the work and gladly turned to Montreal and the reality of the FLQ crisis. This issue is Moore's own ambivalence about being a writer, about ambition, fame, the writer's earnestness and pedantry, all of this being brought into focus at the end of September in Paris.

The idea of the artist as one whose sense of identity is amorphous, whose sense of self flows between the work of art and the social self, had occupied Moore as he wrote *I Am Mary Dunne* and is central to *The Great Victorian Collection*. "I wanted to write a sort of *Portrait of the Artist*, a parable of the life of anyone who becomes an imaginative writer or painter. But if I let the allegory show openly, then readers will completely turn off the book. It would be a mistake to tell the reader, or signal to the reviewer that it is a parable and so I have to risk bafflement, I suppose."

*The Great Victorian Collection* did turn out to be a mysterious and baffling book, although its origins and development followed the characteristic preoccupations and questions that Moore had probed earlier. He might equally well have associated the idea of the poet as dreamer with Yeats, who was a major presence in the writing of *Fergus* and remained so during the writing of *The Great Victorian Collection* and *The Mangan Inheritance*. More generally, the dream seems to have its origin in the idea of the power of the Romantic imagination, summed up in one of its most celebrated expressions by Keats, "The Imagination may be compared to Adam's dream — he awoke and found it truth." At any rate, the idea of the dreamer who seems possessed by a magical power reflected Moore's feelings about California as a place and also his gloomy thoughts about the fate of the artist and his art in America.

One of his earliest notes indicates Moore's strategy for making the miraculous event credible: "To go back in some measure to the origins of the novel. Defoe: the attempt to induce belief in the unbelievable by footnotes (seeming confirmations, etc.)." The invocation of the first journalist-turned-novelist, whose major works were written two hundred and fifty years earlier, might be apt, but Moore's insistence that Borges was the main influence on his conception of the novel is explained in a later remark: "I saw how he created imaginary worlds which seemed totally real. How the fantastic could be made to seem mundane, simply through the skill of his writing." In this sense, the new supernatural novel would push further the risks he had taken in *Fergus* by blending a documentary style of investigative report with a basic narrative realism.

In November 1971, after writing *The Revolution Script* and *Catholics*, his anxiety about the idea of the ordinary person who becomes extraordinary is not expressed as a technical challenge but as a doubt about his own isolation in Malibu and whether he had become too removed from the ordinary preoccupations of ordinary people. This worry may explain why the antiquities his protagonist dreams of turn out to be no more ancient than the Victorian period in England. His experiments with the fantastic and the allegorical, his explorations of dreams and exotic paranormal states, could be conducted only by anchoring them to a firm ground, a sense of the real world of his Victorian father, preserved for him in the classic realistic novels by Tolstoy, Dostoievski, and Flaubert. That dull, ordinary world captured in literary realism had become a vision of the authentic life at the moment when his Californian fictional world was becoming increasingly subjective and dream-like. His early novels, in which he had portrayed that ordinary world, were Moore's own Victorian collection, yet set against it from the beginning was the private world of fantasy, and the new novel would dwell on the exploitation of that fantasy by American media, commerce, and academia.

Moore's Commonplace Book includes a typed quotation that suggests he had done some reading on this issue. Jacques Rivière had written in the *Nouvelle revue française* fifty years before:

> In the novelist a kind of stupidity is an integral part of his creative power. If he tries to explain what he has done, he sets forth childish reasons that will make a man with a critical mind laugh when he hears them. . . . Another aspect of the creator's ignorance is his docility with regard to objections; however stupid they may be, he is immediately persuaded that he was wrong . . . he remains overwhelmed by his work; he does not go beyond it in any direction; he had managed to get through it. That is all we can say; but there is nothing left to allow him to be its master, to dominate it, to defend it against others.

The words seem apt for the state Moore was in after the disappointing reception of *Fergus*, which became a central part of the developing character of his protagonist in *The Great Victorian Collection*.

At a certain moment, Mayhewson realizes that his ordinary, earlier life has been lost. His wife, his mother, his colleagues at McGill University, and his friends in Montreal no longer recognize him as his earlier self or wish to maintain their earlier relationships with him. He cannot return to Montreal, nor is he capable of recovering his freedom in California:

> Sitting on the grey sands of Carmel staring at the relentless ocean, he thinks fondly of that former life. "The journey not the arrival matters," as the poet justly said and a lost nostalgia haunts Mayhewson when he recalls those former days when, young, known only to his few friends and family, he was a person to whom anything or nothing might happen. . . . his fame was the beginning of extraordinary status and, thus, the beginning of his loss of self. . . . Perhaps that is why this memoir is written in the third person, I am become another. And that former me is dead.

This key to the parable of the artist, probably written in 1972, has central autobiographical significance for Moore. It is the dilemma he found himself in, perhaps as early as the late fifties when the success he had craved began to disrupt his life. He first began to assess in fiction the price he had paid in *An Answer from Limbo*, which closes with the following self-scrutiny by the writer Brendan Tierney: ". . . I asked myself if my beliefs are sounder than my mother's? Will my writing change anything in my world?

To talk of that is to believe in miracles. . . . Am I still my mother's son, my wife's husband, the father of my children? Or am I a stranger, strange even to myself? . . . I have altered beyond all self-recognition. I have lost and sacrificed myself."

Moore's dilemma is that of the artist committed to his talent and its development according to its own grain, yet living and publishing in worlds that shape both the public identity of the artist and the significance of his work according to critical and commercial fashions. All of Moore's fictions that explore the transformation of the "ordinary" person into an "extraordinary" one are allegories of Moore's own concern about lost integrity. When Maloney's mother visits him in California, she "stared up at him as though he were some impenetrable stranger whose language she did not speak." The artist/magician becomes an adept of a secret power, and yet he is an anxious creator, forever alienated and doubting that he will recover the power.

This anxiety is part of the allegory that Moore hid in the novel at least as early as the 1972 version, when Maloney was known as Michael Francis Mahon:

Paradigm:
Writes first novel: known as his work. Success: Can he dream another dream?
Disappointing dream:
Can't fulfil early promise. Perhaps dream a further Collection?

A successor: otherwise if no school of his work the work will not survive. the Disciple comes:
He dreams each night the television dream: one day, no dream is there any more.
The agent: selling the dream:
en vogue then, not now.
Perhaps the disciple will start A Great Victorian Village, which will attract many more customers than the original.
It could end with Mahon's death.
The death of the creator, the period of decline, the lack of a successor, and yet the Successor is the great Victorian Village.
The Village, abandoned almost. Silent. The guards grow old.

The distillation of Moore's sense of the challenge and risks of his own career grew as he worked on the novel, so that he identified intimately and also distanced himself from the protagonist's character and situation. Whatever the satirical details of the narrative and its gloomy resolution in the dreamer's gradual self-destruction, Moore's own sense of the irrevocable fate of being a writer is central. A later comment illuminates Moore's compulsion not to repeat his earlier successes:

*The Great Victorian Collection* was something I was led into, because I have never wanted to repeat myself. I had begun this exploration of the past coming up to deal with the present in *Fergus* and I felt that I had to continue with it. *The Great Victorian Collection* seemed to be the metaphor I wanted. I love that idea of the past on our door-step, unchangeable, irrevocable, the feeling that we can't walk away from it. Of course, at the same time the book is a paradigm of artistic creation. In a way, I have my own "Collection" to escape from; if I had not changed and written these new novels I would be very much like the hero in *The Great Victorian Collection*, caught, trapped, forced to dream the same dream, to repeat versions of *Judith Hearne*, to write those Belfast novels over and over again. I have deliberately avoided this and that is why *The Great Victorian Collection* is for me a more imaginative novel than my others, because in it I feel that I have managed to dramatize this avoidance in an oblique way.

Midway through the writing of the novel, he took a step that marks a recognition of his status as a literary novelist and of his place in a community of west-coast writers. In September 1973, he became an Adjunct Professor at the University of California at Los Angeles. He began to teach a class in creative writing, which required him to be on campus one day a week. A year later he was appointed Regents Professor at the university, a post previously occupied by W. H. Auden, as he noted with some pride at the time, and he would be followed in the position by Joan Didion. In addition to the stable income this affiliation with UCLA provided, the opportunity to be in touch with young people broadened Moore's experience in a way he welcomed.

Brian Friel teased him about his new position: "Delighted to learn that Academe continues to taste like honey. We'll overloook the shabby detail that you've gone over to Them. As long as you are handsomely paid and the pool is convenient. As the Co. Clare Parish Priest said of Edna O'Brien: 'She sold her soul for a pound of hairy bacon!'" In fact, of course, Moore did worry in private and aloud about "selling out" or losing his "soul" — to journalism, to theatre and film producers, to the publishing/

television world of literary "personalities," and to professional interpreters and teachers in academe who have the power to decide which authors and books become present-day classics. *The Great Victorian Collection* is a direct presentation of all the ways in which he might sell his soul, or have it stolen.

Moore's ambivalence towards academe became apparent in the 1960s in frequent dismissive comments on "academic" novelists like John Barth and on novels he opined were written to be taught. In general, he disliked the systematization of literary criticism and took little interest in academic modes of discourse. Although peripherally aware of different ways in which literature is read and analyzed — Freudian, structuralist, and so on — and of theories such as the *nouveau roman* of Robbe-Grillet and Sarraute, he refers to theoretical formulations with scepticism and, at times, derision. In fact, he had developed a considerable degree of speculative interest in philosophical writing, and his comments sometimes suggest that the autodidact who had failed to matriculate has an axe to grind. A certain anxiety of this kind is betrayed by early comments in the 1950s, yet by the late 1960s, as academic interest in his own work began to develop, he became more at ease in fielding questions from scholars and even grew to accept that some of his most perceptive readers were university teachers.

Late in 1973, DeWitt Henry, editor of the new literary journal *Ploughshares*, wrote to Moore. He was writing a long appreciative assessment of Moore's work and sent him the article with a request for clarifications. A letter to Henry at the end of November provides a clear glimpse of Moore's thinking about his reputation as a novelist just as he was coming to the end of *The Great Victorian Collection*. He speaks of his "'neglect' since I moved away from New York," noting that none of his books were in print in the United States: "Of course I would like to see my books back in print in the US. I have had better luck in England and in Canada which, I suppose, helps me to maintain the illusion that I am not 'neglected.'" While this concern with neglect seems to have been prompted by Henry's regret and frustration that the books were not available, it obviously touches on Moore's own disappointment about his failure to achieve an American niche. His letter ends on another note: "It is the feeling of experimentation and doing something new which keeps me at work and makes me happy, whether or not I have a large audience. In a very real sense my writing is my life and I am I think both lucky and happy to have had the success I've had to date."

This letter clarifies further the attitude that it is, to a degree, Moore's lack of American success that has enabled him to continue writing, and this idea is pertinent to the form and content of *The Great Victorian Collection*:

> I have always been a loner in my writing and an outsider in whatever country I chose to settle. I often think that this has helped me to continue to write and to move on to new directions in my work. Had I had the popular success some people have had at the beginning of my career I might have felt a let down as the years passed. I have always had to contend with people's particular feeling for *Judith Hearne*, a feeling they do not have for my other books. But the thing that has kept me writing is the fact that I don't write the same book twice and while my new directions may sometimes lead to a failure with readers — as in *Fergus* — it isn't by calculation or even choice that I take the direction I do. It is almost as though it becomes what I have to experiment with next. My new book, which I am just finishing, may well be my most far out and unsuccessful experiment — and I am not even sure that I will publish it.

In fact, he had just made tentative contact with Aaron Asher, who had moved to Holt, Rinehart, and the editor's first reaction initiated a few months of further work on the novel. Letters to Asher indicate the many changes that were made before Moore showed it to his agent, Perry Knowlton, or to his other publishers. On 26 January 1974, he wrote to Asher:

> I sent *The Great Victorian Collection* back to the typist yesterday. I have been working on it steadily and, indeed, constantly since about December 10. It is now some fifty pages longer. In addition, I have tried to remove anything at all which will prematurely telegraph any allegorical overtones. I have changed the name of the main character, have tried to make him more of a "person," involving him in the Collection, and so on. Also, importantly, I think, there is a stronger sexual overtone to the book now. The scenes with Mary Ann, with the exception of the original Victorian one, all have been changed to tie in with his "Victorian" obsession. There is also much more description of the Collection, including stuff about its secret parts which it did not have before. . . . This is a book which must be as perfect as one can make it in order to overcome its difficult premise and to produce that "suspension of disbelief" which will keep the reader moving ahead.

He continued to be anxious about the book, as another letter to Asher indicates:

Again I've not sent the book out to Tom Maschler or Perry or Jack McClelland until we've discussed it again. There may still be improvements which I can make. Don't hesitate to mention any that occur to you. The main point that I'm not clear on even now is whether the Collection is still too easily accepted by the public. Although, as you see, I've tried to show that it was not accepted as a dream come true at any time, by anything but a minority of the people who saw it or read of it. Still, again I've done so much revising and been so close to it, that it's hard for me to see it in perspective.

Late in February, as he reached a point of satisfaction with the novel, an unexpected change in Asher's own situation threw his already anxious feelings about publication into confusion. Although a vice-president of Holt, Rinehart, Asher had a disagreement with the new president, which led to his abrupt departure from the company. Moore had moved from Viking with Asher and now his loyalty to his editor put the plans for publication into limbo. Although he had been reworking the novel with advice from Asher, no formal contract had been signed, and Moore preferred to await a new step in Asher's career. Maschler in London and McClelland in Toronto accepted the novel for publication when they saw it in March 1974, but publication in Britain and Canada was held up until the American situation clarified. In late February, Moore and his agent agreed that they should postpone the publication date until spring 1975.

Friel and Moore continued to be mutually supportive through these years in a constant campaign to preserve their integrity as artists and to find a sympathetic audience for their work. In September 1974, Friel wrote: "You sound a bit depressed about the *G. V. Collection*. Slightly defiant, too. I think you usually find that something you're very uncertain about turns out well. Did you discard the idea of publishing it under another name? As long as there's a drop of creativity in you — and have enough to pay the bills — I'm sure you should do your own work."

A month later, Friel again wrote in a similar tone of concern: "I am genuinely concerned about your reaction to other people's reaction to *Collection*. (I have had this experience so often. One fluctuates between despair and arrogance.) Nor have I any advice except to let the thing take its course and get on with the new job — which is nice and pat and not at all helpful. But it is a small consolation that Moore's world is defined by the corpus of his work and not by one volume. Right?" But it appears that Moore could never rest on his laurels as Friel advised, and he remained anxious to begin a new novel in hopes that it would satisfy him more than any in the past. In fact, *The Great Victorian Collection* is an allegory of his anxiety that he would never escape from the reputation he had won with *Judith Hearne*; as a working novelist, he always looked ahead to what he could do with the genres of fiction that he had not done already.

# 19

## SEX AND
## DESTINY

In November 1973, Moore wrote to DeWitt Henry that completing *The Great Victorian Collection* "was something I had to do before starting on my next book, a larger more *Limbo*-like novel which will have, I hope, the sort of 'felt' and 'imagined' quality which you like." At this stage he still had a few months of writing to do on *The Great Victorian Collection*, to be followed by more than a year of anxiety before the publication of this successor to *Fergus*. This remark suggests that *An Answer from Limbo* had provided him with a standard of accomplishment he wished to recover and expresses his continuing fear that this experimental phase was a dead end for his American career. Henry's letter had noted that most of Moore's books were unavailable in the United States, whereas this earlier novel had just come out in paperback in England, and Brian Friel wrote: "Saw in the paper the other day that *Limbo* (paper) was top of the best-sellers here. Bravo!"

Disappointment over the critical and commercial failure of *Fergus* together with the anticipation of failure with *The Great Victorian Collection* combined to create an anxiety about his American reputation so great that Moore even contemplated using a pseudonym for the new novel. His plan to write another "*Limbo*-like novel" reflected, then, a desire to return to a less fantastic and risky style and to win back the American audience he feared he had lost forever with *Fergus*.

In July 1974, as soon as the final corrections had been made on the manuscript of *The Great Victorian Collection*, he moved very quickly to begin a new novel. It was called *Mrs. R* and *Confessions* during the successive drafts that would occupy him fully for eighteen months; the new novel would eventually be published in September 1976 as *The Doctor's Wife*. This book is very different in style and preoccupation from *Limbo*, and the certainty with which he began the writing suggests that it imposed itself on his imagination with some urgency. The idea of a "*Limbo*-like" novel did stay with him, however, for it is obvious that the opening section of

*The Mangan Inheritance,* written in 1976–77 is a reprise of the material and style of the earlier novel.

*The Doctor's Wife* is a portrait of a woman which, in many ways, recalls both *Judith Hearne* of the mid-fifties and *I Am Mary Dunne* of the mid-sixties. While Sheila Redden is the wife of a Belfast doctor — and the deadening claustrophobia of that setting is evoked in even darker shades with the pervasive violence of the Troubles — she has some of Mary Dunne's sophistication and is transformed by a sexual adventure in the exotic settings of Paris and the Côte d'Azur. Moore called on his old strength for female characterization, a strength that had won him wide acclaim, and this novel was to regain some of that earlier attention.

It may be that what postponed the writing of the *"Limbo*-like novel" was Moore's recognition that the miraculous fictions — *Fergus* and *The Great Victorian Collection* — had led him away from the "commonplace" experience he saw as the moral anchor of his work. Those portraits of the artist drew on one kind of miracle that Moore knew intimately — his own creative inspiration — yet more ordinary experiences could also be seen in a miraculous light, in particular, falling in love. Moore has spoken of the central importance of sexual experience in his own transformations and in the impulsive initiation of his new life in California; this is the "miracle" he now explores.

A recurring motif in Moore's Belfast novels is of entrapment by the past and the secret desire to be free to choose a new life. This is as true of Judith Hearne as it is of Gavin Burke or, indeed, of Fergus Fadden. In all cases, it is not simply that the social and religious climate imposes claustrophobic and paralyzing limitations on the protagonists, but that in their frustration, all the characters are driven towards fantasies of power and sexual pleasure, and to the edge of emotional breakdown. In spite of the atmosphere of death and destruction given to the setting by the current Troubles — and Sheila Redden has nightmares of bloody incidents she has witnessed on the streets of Belfast — the depressive atmosphere and her character go back in curious ways to Moore's own life there in the 1940s.

In his Commonplace Book are notes for a novel he did not write in the late 1950s, but those notes are remarkably close to what he began to write about in 1974. "Everyman has a dream of escaping from life's cares and worries — to leave everything and go — The sign on Shaftesbury Square — "Fly to Canada" — go — arrive here with wife and children left behind him. Anonymity — the greatest desire — To escape he goes to a new country where passports don't count." The reference to the sign "Fly to Canada" is, of course, a recollection of Moore's abrupt decision in early 1948 to go to a new country, to leave his past behind.

Moore has said that *The Doctor's Wife* recalls his own love affair with Margaret Swanson, although he is to be identified with Sheila Redden in her transforming experience through her sexual awakening, rather than with her young American partner, Tom Lowery. In contrast to Sheila Redden, who does not follow Lowery to North America, Moore has given this failed relationship as his reason for emigrating to Canada in search of Margaret Swanson. The reference to suicide in these notes and in other notes of the 1950s, citing Camus' writings — as Sheila does, when she contemplates killing herself — suggests that Moore's depressed state when he returned to Belfast at the end of 1947 underlies the character of his female protagonist.

Moore's characterization of Redden conforms in outline to a traditional and archetypal situation in realistic fiction — the models that Moore often refers to being *Madame Bovary* and *Anna Karenina* — while at the same time he gives it a contemporary point of view. The woman who decides to make a radical new start is not punished for her adulterous affair, as her nineteenth-century prototypes were, yet in her isolation and anonymity she pays a price for her decision. Moore's deep commitment to realism denies his fictional heroine a romantic outcome, and his ambivalence about his affair with Margaret Swanson and its consequences may also be detected here in the tone and point-of-view of the novel.

The search for the novel's centre of consciousness was an arduous one, as the many drafts reveal, but as he explained when the book was published, this was always for him the essential element of discovery in the creation of fiction:

> I rewrite a lot. I rewrite beginnings up to fifty times. I believe that the reader is seduced in the first ten or fifteen pages. The decisions are made then: whether to trust the writer or not; or to be enchanted by the style or not to be enchanted. The critic disappears in fifteen pages, or the critic remains to the end of the book. It's like plunging into the sea; you plunge into the sea of this writer's work, and you swim in that sea; and then you have to come out of that sea, getting out is terribly important, too. If you stub your toe coming out, or if you're half drowned, that's not going to be good. So beginnings of books are everything. And that's why I believe that beginnings should be seamless.

The novel begins after the central events have taken place and Sheila has disappeared, when her brother comes to Paris "as though he were not living his own life but acting in some film, a detective hunting for a missing person or, more likely, a criminal seeking to make amends to his victim." This opening engages the reader's interest with its sly recall of Moore's career as a writer of thrillers, but this soon gives way to the direct, chronological presentation of the few weeks during which Sheila Redden was transformed. Moore's notes indicate that from the beginning his sympathy lies not with her doctor brother or her doctor husband, nor, for that matter, with her lover, but with Sheila herself and with her efforts to accept responsibility for her actions:

a chance at a new life; dream of this chance.
when it happened, the dream that she could start all over again.
Then the worry about right and wrong: making life over for her happiness, not his. Coupled with fear that she might be manic depressive, because they said she might be.
A married woman starting to run away, the hardest runaway feat of all.
wake; not sleep; Dream of T. : Think of him : Stranger on the street might be T.: Tired: weep easily:
Now a contest: was she in love or was she in fugue? The memorial to her love is to be her sanity:
A convalescence — or a struggle to prove her sanity against what they said of her.

This is precisely the territory that Moore had explored in North American circumstances in *Mary Dunne*, but he appears to have wanted the challenge of juxtaposing the more sharply defined worlds of Belfast and France. In *The Doctor's Wife* it wouldn't have been as interesting, he has said, to have a Californian woman go to Paris

because there is really no past to escape in California; it wouldn't have had that ring I wanted in the book. I wanted, as I've done before, to contrast the American and Northern Irish character and the crucial thing is that you have to be very strong in your feeling for both these life-styles. For example, I couldn't do a middle-class English woman, because I don't have her speech rhythms, I couldn't hear her voice; but I know that I can still create Irish characters because it's in my bones and I know that my ear won't mishear them.

In spite of this intimacy with Sheila Redden's background, dilemmas and choices, and his antipathy towards the doctors in her life, Moore presents her with considerable dispassion. She is referred to throughout as "Mrs.

Redden," and while much of the narrative is in Moore's favourite point of view — third person keyed to the inner voice of the protagonist — there are also scenes from the perspective of other characters, and her motivations and the reasons for her decision to end the affair remain unarticulated and enigmatic. Moore's creation of this woman with sympathy and dispassion is an effect he evidently worked hard to achieve, a measure for him of truth to life and of the refusal to sentimentalize his characters.

While his aim at the outset is to suspend the reader's disbelief, to "plunge the reader into the sea," and "beginnings are everything," endings always are a source of great anxiety until the appropriate way out is discovered. In this case, he wanted to preserve the idea of open-endedness, of the possibility of change, although his comments over-generalize the importance of this kind of ending in his other novels:

> The character of Sheila Redden at the end of the book has completely cut all ties with her former life and may never be heard of again; but at least she has faced up to her existential dilemma. And there is the possibility that something else could happen in her life. There's a possibility with Judith Hearne that something else could happen in her life. I like to leave books with open ends, as they are in life: when you haven't heard from a person for years and you suddenly say, "Whatever became of so-and-so?" That gives the book the feeling of life; part of the strength of a novel is to leave the character in a position where people can discuss them as they might a real person.

Apart from the many versions of the opening pages, the novel was written in three drafts between mid August 1974 and the end of January 1976. The winter of 1974–75 turned out to be a time of considerable anxiety about matters other than his reputation and the impending publication of *The Great Victorian Collection*. In February 1975, he reported to Diana Athill that he "had a bad bout with bleeding ulcers," an ominous recurrence of a medical condition that, since the 1950s, he associated, according to the conventional wisdom of the time, with excessive stress.

During that winter, he was also drawn into a battle to remain in possession of the cliff-top house that he and Jean had made their home — a battle that would continue for many years. The view of the ocean, the beach, the hilltop garden, the house itself had become the hermitage of Moore's long, "dull," routine of composition since 1966, but now the State of California, which already owned the forests across Pacific Coast Highway behind the house, decided to expropriate the Moores and their isolated neighbours. The Moores fought the expropriation notice; in March 1975, Brian wrote to Friel, "They threaten to condemn in June, but we squat on like tenants awaiting the bailiffs."

Their battle continued for a few years — in 1976, they were "the last holdouts" — until they were eventually allowed to stay, although by then they were even more isolated than before, for their neighbours had moved away. One of those neighbours along the highway at Trancas was Joan Didion, and through the 1970s she and her husband, writer John Gregory Dunne, had become friends of the Moores. Didion has written an essay on the seven years that they spent there. "Quiet Days in Malibu" describes this "most idiosyncratic of beach communities, twenty-seven miles of coastline with no hotel, no passable restaurant, nothing to attract the traveler's dollar. . . . Malibu tends to astonish and disappoint those who have never before seen it, and yet its very name remains, in the imagination of people all over the world, a kind of shorthand for the easy life."

Coinciding with the threat of an impending move occasioned by the expropriation, Moore sold his papers to the University of Calgary in 1975. The papers deposited at Calgary include material from his earliest efforts at story-writing in 1948–49 and from every year of his writing life from then on. Moore's retrospective survey of the evolution of his career, which he undertook with considerable interest, as is evident in his methodical organization of material and accompanying annotations, stirred many old thoughts and attitudes. The autobiographical aspects of *The Doctor's Wife* and of *The Mangan Inheritance* reflect this reassessment of earlier experiences and selves.

The papers were right up to date and included the drafts of *The Great Victorian Collection*. That novel, which had caused him so much anxiety, eventually appeared in the United States and Canada in June 1975, and in England four months later. By then his anxiety about the book had changed to confidence. In November he wrote to Tom Maschler at Cape: "I feel happy about this book, after publication, which is something I rarely feel. It's also a favourite of mine, and I do have hopes that it will, like the Collection, outlive its creator and over the years take on a life of its own." From 1971, this novel had this special association in his mind: "I have a very Catholic attitude toward that. I want more, much more, to be read ten or fifty years after I'm dead than to have a large audience now."

His anxiety about its reception in the United States proved to be well founded. The *New York Times*, the *New Yorker*, and the *New York Review of Books* damned it with faint praise, all three reviewers saying the book deserved to be read, but that Moore failed to develop properly the potential of the initial idea. Elsewhere the novel became a critical success immediately, winning Moore his second Governor General's Award in Canada and the prestigious James Tait Black Award in England, and preparing the way for his first Booker nomination the following year.

Early in 1976, the award of the Governor General's prize for fiction to Moore's novel sparked a controversy in Toronto newspaper columns. *Globe and Mail* book reviewer William French argued that Moore should not be considered a Canadian novelist since the criteria of birth or residence did not apply. Moore had regularly made a point of the fact that although he lived in the United States, he had kept his Canadian citizenship, but the designation "bird of passage," used of Moore some years before, seems to have stuck. Robert Fulford defended Moore's entitlement to the prize and argued against the narrow definition of residence and continuing involvement in Canadian literary culture as criteria.

This controversy publicly marks the decline of Moore's status in the eyes of the Canadian cultural nationalists who codified critical discourse in the 1970s. A new generation of novelists and critics, notably Margaret Laurence and Margaret Atwood, had come to prominence in the sixties and seventies, and their work displaced Moore's. The increasing influence of this generation and its major impact on the teaching of Canadian literature in universities and colleges, as well as on the formation of the canon of writers whose work was taught and written about, ensured that Moore's work was largely ignored in the following decades. McClelland and Stewart continued to publish his novels, and each new book received generous reviews, but as a figure on the Canadian literary landscape, Moore's diminishing stature may be traced throughout the 1970s.

As usual, Moore heard from Graham Greene. Greene's response to this new work by his "favourite living novelist" — "[Moore] treats the novel as a tamer treats a wild beast" — was to be quoted often in future years, eventually to Moore's chagrin. The original comment saluted Moore's courage in taking such a great risk in *The Great Victorian Collection*, a kind of novel that Greene could never write, but it was later misrepresented to mean that Moore was a Greene-like novelist.

The enthusiastic comments of the poet Derek Mahon, a sympathetic reviewer in London weeklies of a number of Moore's earlier novels, led to direct contact between them. Moore responded to a review-essay: "I was delighted with it and I use the word 'delight' advisedly. It's the first piece ever done on my writing which has noticed the 'writing,' and which picks interesting quotations. Also the stuff about the 'fictions' is very perceptive and right. It's one of the few pieces about my work that I read with interest as though it were about some other writer." This was to be the beginning of an important and enduring new friendship. Mahon was from Protestant Belfast, but Moore would write that he was the Irish writer to whom he felt closest in sensibility. He would praise him as Seamus Heaney's "most talented Ulster contemporary."

The third draft of *The Doctor's Wife* was written as the critical reception of *The Great Victorian Collection* was gradually revealed. Moore worked on a screenplay of *Great Victorian* during the summer of 1976 while awaiting publication of the next novel. At that in-between time, he also wrote his first short story in fifteen years, for a collection entitled *Irish Ghost Stories*. "The Sight" is a surprising and revealing coda to the Californian miracle narrative. It tells of a worldly and wealthy New York lawyer who is suddenly faced with his own mortality when his doctor reveals some doubt about the effectiveness of the removal of a benign growth from his back. In a comic style, the narrative traces the lawyer's efforts to disguise and repress his fear and the further implications of his anxiety. The story's dénouement hinges on the fact that his housekeeper, a maternal and earthy old Irishwoman, has inherited the ability to foretell imminent death from the facial appearance of the victim. The story ends in comedy as the desperate protagonist is even more bewildered by her enigmatic responses to his demand that she tell him what she sees in his expression.

This slight and clever entertainment suggests that the idea of the Californian miracle may have been related to the idea of prophecy and fortune-telling, abilities that are associated by Moore with the peasant lore of his mother's Donegal home. The peasant character of the housekeeper associates her with powers such as faith-healing that were commonly practised in rural Ireland. By coincidence, at this time, Brian Friel was working on *Faith Healer*, a play with many points of similarity to *The Great Victorian Collection* — something recognized by Friel when Moore read his play later: "I was delighted with your response. . . . Because, as you know, one finally holds the press/reviewers/critics in disdain; and the reaction of one's fellow artists is the important response. And it occurred to me that there are many similarities — in attitude, in objectivity and by God in overall gloom — between *F.H.* and *The Great Victorian Collection.*"

During the Moores' summer visit to Ireland in 1976, RTE, the Irish television station, made a documentary on the "return home" of the Belfast-born writer. Soon after he returned to California, near the end of October, he and Jean were photographed for a feature in *People* magazine. A biographical sketch of Moore's career accompanies the photographs taken in the Moores' living room "filled with antiques from Nova Scotia." It is

Moore's closest brush with celebrity status, with becoming the kind of writer he had often professed his fear of — a "personality" known through media exposure to many people who have never read his books.

The media's appetite for such exposure had been created over the summer when Moore's agent Perry Knowlton managed to put together an unprecedented financial package for his latest work. *People* reported that *The Doctor's Wife* "is already in its second printing — with 22,000 copies out before publication. Paperback rights have brought an advance of $100,000, movie rights fetched another $200,000." The magazine was referring to the novel's earnings in the United States alone; newspaper reports in Canada went so far as to claim that overall the novel had earned Moore close to $500,000, a figure the author said was far from accurate.

Whatever the precise final sum, the novel made him a rich man on the basis of its potential to become a bestseller, an expectation that was not in fact fulfilled. Moore was described on numerous occasions in 1976 and 1977 as the successful Californian novelist driving a dark-brown Mercedes convertible. A decade earlier, when he arrived in California, he had not yet learned to drive and had never owned a car. The Mercedes became the symbol of his new success, and Brian Friel's characteristically witty comment put the situation in sharp perspective when he wrote in early 1977: "Give my warmest love to the Elegant Jean. I can't see you in that Mercedes Sports (you're a Raleigh and trousers-in-socks man at heart) but Jean is born for it."

*The Doctor's Wife* was a Literary Guild selection, but the American reception was mixed and, once again, much less favourable than reviews in England, where it was nominated for the Booker Prize. Some years later, Anthony Burgess included it among the "ninety-nine best novels in English since 1939," a surprising choice from among Moore's fifteen novels, yet a measure of the high esteem in which many readers hold the novel. While Moore's comments at the time of the novel's publication reflect his feeling of satisfaction with the sympathetic neutrality of his dramatization, he commented later that it was "a real downer." In retrospect, he realized that the novel was not as uplifting as he felt it was when he was writing it. Although it was a moneyspinner for Moore, *The Doctor's Wife* confirmed his gradual apprehension that he could never write a bestseller because his characters were too disturbingly real, and his books closer to a tragic perspective than most readers would wish for. "One of the reasons why my books have not become bestsellers is that while people like to read them, they don't give out much solace."

In spite of his declared intention to celebrate the possibility of change and those characters prepared to take risks to create new lives, Moore found he had written a novel not too unlike *Judith Hearne*. Before the book's appearance, Brian Friel had written to him about his own difficulties with the screenplay of *Judith Hearne* that he had been reworking for a number of years, each time failing to satisfy the film producers. Friel's words provide a bitter and humorous summary of Moore's dilemma from his first novel to this latest one:

> You know, of course, that what has screwed up the whole thing ever since John Huston was a nipper is *your* lousy ending to the book. What is needed is a Beautiful Upsurge — Judith as international president of AA, or plunging back into the arms of mother church and becoming a stigmatist, or eloping with the Professor's wife. But you funked that kind of truth and settled for the Gaelic glooms. . . . I'm sick of them all [film producers]. They don't believe in anything. They know the value of nothing. They are all sustained by the energies of their own pretenses.

Friel counterpoints what he and Moore have in common: the "Gaelic glooms" of their sensibility versus the world of commercially driven producers and publishers on whom they are dependent.

While 1976 marked the year Moore's earnings established a lasting financial security, it is also remarkable for a significant change in his personal life. After a lengthy battle with cancer, Jackie succumbed to her illness, and her death helped make possible a renewed relationship with Michael. Although in the first year or two of the separation Michael had come to California for vacations, Jackie's attitude gradually hardened, and by the time of the divorce settlement in 1967 she had made it impossible for Michael to stay with his father. From 1967 on, Moore paid for Michael's education at his "posh" boarding school in Pennsylvania, but he has said that he did not see his son during his adolescent years. In the mid-seventies, Michael was a student at Boston College, and father and son — now aged twenty-two — met in Boston, perhaps on Moore's way to Europe in September and again on his way back at the end of October. At any rate, by November, he had already visited Boston twice, with, as Michael wrote, "a parent's knack for catching me at the most inopportune times" on both occasions.

Michael's letter to his father includes what is certainly the most unusual review *The Doctor's Wife* received. "A bit strange at first (naughty bits by one's father) but after that barrier, I found a really good book. It was a difficult thing to do well, but I think you succeeded." He regales his father with stories of his fellow orderlies at the hospital where he is working, of their ragging him about his father's pornographic novel and about discovering it in the erotic section of a Harvard Square bookstore. In fact, Moore would later regret that he had written such sexually explicit scenes, because "it might seem pornographic to people, and I didn't do it for pornographic reasons."

While there is a measure of tension and self-consciousness in the son's letters to his father, there is also evident relief and pleasure in the renewed relationship. Michael and his girlfriend, Karen, visited Malibu for Christmas, and their happy time there gave Michael the idea of moving to the west coast. Eventually, a few years later, he and Karen married and settled permanently in San Francisco.

In the midst of the publicity surrounding the appearance of *The Doctor's Wife*, Moore was already working on a new novel, the "*Limbo*-like novel" he had spoken of in late 1973. Now, in 1976, he returned in imagination to the time and setting of *Limbo*, to New York City and to two characters whose marriage has just ended. In the earliest notes the woman is known as Beatrice Abbott, and the sketch includes the key elements of her character in the finished novel:

> Why does she leave him? So many "darlings" and hugs and kisses and exaggerated protests of affection in her world that it was hard to know if its denizens really liked anyone. . . . Ultimately, she is better as an actress; she says: "but everybody acts: I do professionally: I'm not inventing my character, I don't have one: I'm the characters I act: the rest of the time I'm the non-person phoning and waiting to be asked to be a character. . . . The real performance is in how you can bend this persona — say Joan of Arc, to meld with — not you as you are — but with this blend of you and her to create what is (perhaps unconsciously) that perfectly whole persona which will satisfactorily replace that one you lost and end your guilt about Black/White."

This sketch recalls the character and situation of *I Am Mary Dunne*, but it is evident that the new novel is not going to be an intensive study of a woman of this New York milieu, but of the man she has abandoned. Further notes, made while Moore was travelling in Europe in September and October, suggest that *The New Life* was going to be a reprise of an abandoned male character such as Fergus who uproots himself and, as Sheila Redden does in *The Doctor's Wife*, searches for a new life in European tourist spots. Here, as in the recent novel, Moore goes back to a defining moment in his own life, the breakup of his first marriage and the transformation that came after it.

Back in California, at the end of November, he noted:

> Even after 3 or 4 months holiday from writing novels and even after what should be ample time to think and plan, it seems there's no other way for me with this particular book but to start writing, knowing almost nothing about where I'm going or what I'm trying to say. I only have Mangan, alone, in his posh apt., wife having left him for another man, finding out that not only has he no friends in the marriage but that in some way she has stolen his image (like primitives' fear of photography) and he must find it again.
>
> Then unexpectedly, she dies in crash w/ new lover, leaving Mangan as sole heir.

Already the name Mangan appears, and soon, it seems, the linking to James Clarence Mangan, the early nineteenth-century Irish poet much appreciated by the young James Joyce, emerges as an embryonic plot line:

> Is her money to compensate him for stealing his soul, or should he reject it as he rejects her furniture which will now be returned to him as his property?
>
> Somehow he will try to link self with James Clarence Mangan, the Irish poet who's believed to be his ancestor:
>
> Or/and — find that person who has changed/ The person who unsatisfied with the facts has begun to live out a lie — becoming an imaginary character.

But the working out of that link appears to have been postponed while Moore elaborated the character in his New York setting.

The link to James Clarence Mangan at this stage appears to be through the idea of precocity and early death, an idea perhaps suggested by Saul Bellow's huge succcess with *Humboldt's Gift*, based on his friendship with Delmore Schwartz, which had appeared in 1975 and had been on the *New York Times* bestseller list for six months. The autobiographical connection to Moore's own situation in New York around 1960–61, the gifted young novelist on the threshold of fame, is evident. His notes include the question "Do not all of us sense this void of non achievement and is everything achieved/ o'ergloomed by that fear of future failure?" His alter-ego Brendan Tierney in *Limbo* sensed this "void" as had Moore himself.

During the writing of *Limbo*, he had considered Bellow the best contemporary American novelist, and his interest in his work had continued, although he had not liked *Herzog*. Now, in 1976, he noted this comment by Delmore Schwartz as a kind of inspirational motto for his new work: "The nature of fiction makes it possible to enter a complete world of reality as if one lived in it oneself. The reader inhabits the interior of another being in a way no other art makes possible." Moore's aim at this stage is to create that "world of reality" in New York, which is felt to be a world of unreality by his protagonist.

The characterization of Jamie Mangan seems to be developing too in the direction of the anguished efforts of Mary Dunne and Fergus Fadden to catch hold of a stable sense of self. As before, Moore's imagination is drawn to metaphysical and psychological resonances of key symbols, such as the daguerrotype:

> To isolate and define moments of experience in which the presumed identity of self, of here and now can be fathomed and recognised as a tragic illusion.
>
> Leon Bloy: "There is no human being on earth who is capable of defining who he is. No one knows what he has come into this world to do, to what his acts, feelings, ideas, correspond, or what his real name is, his imperishable name in the registry of light."

That "tragic illusion" of selfhood is a recurring preoccupation of all these portraits of the artist, and yet the capturing of the essence of selfhood is the very goal and purpose of Moore's fiction. The novel grew into a search for a paternal ancestor, and for the Irish Victorian inheritance of the protagonist, but it is centrally concerned with the father-son bond, and so James Moore's hobby of photography during Brian's childhood seems to have supplied the novelist with a personal symbol of the mystery of his own Victorian identity.

It is unclear how far the writing of the new novel had progressed by the summer of 1977. In April, an adaptation of *The Emperor of Ice Cream* was staged at the Abbey Theatre in Dublin. Moore was delighted to hear of its success, and of the decision to run it again in August. He planned to be in Dublin then and had already decided that he needed to do extensive research there on the life of James Clarence Mangan. At a performance of *Emperor*, he collapsed with a very severe attack of bleeding ulcers and was rushed to Jervis Street Hospital. He was persuaded to undergo surgery immediately, and spent a number of weeks in hospital recuperating. In

September he gave an interview in which he paid tribute to the doctor who he felt had saved his life, yet all was not well. Although by November he was strong enough to travel back to Malibu, his recovery was not complete. He underwent further examinations and more surgery was decided on. He needed time to build up his strength and so did not enter hospital in Los Angeles until April 1978. This time the operation was successful and his slow recuperation continued throughout all of that year.

During this period, although he was unable to read, Moore found that he could concentrate enough to write; that, in fact, writing was the one thing that freed him from his severe pain and distress. And so *The Mangan Inheritance* was developed and written in the shadow of another near-death experience and in the aftermath of a debilitating illness and slow recovery. It was completed by the fall of 1978.

The historical material on James Clarence Mangan and the decadent Romanticism of his Victorian milieu is joined to other Irish material:

Remembered a true story I had heard in my childhood, a frightening story of incest and mutilation.

Emigrants, ruined towers, a true story of incest, and my own life in America, . . . . ~~my own annual return in search of a past~~.

The Mangan Inheritance, the story of a Canadian, a failed poet of Irish origin who believes himself to be related to James Clarence Mangan.

That "true story" — either a story heard in childhood or, in another version, reported in the *News of the World* — of an Irish policeman whose penis was cut off in revenge by the sister of a girl he had seduced, reflects a brutal and unromantic aspect of life in Ireland. It is certainly an inversion of the tourists' view of scenic landscapes and unspoiled peasants, or of the "poetic" view of, say, Yeats's "Celtic Twilight" period, or of nineteenth-century antiquarians. The journey to Ireland of Jamie, the failed contemporary poet, is imagined by him as a search for roots, as a rhapsodic regeneration of self, and he feels drawn back magnetically by the spirit of his ancestor.

The story of squalor, incest, and mental breakdown in *The Mangan Inheritance* is written in a gothic mode. The murky adventures in which Jamie becomes embroiled, including a semi-incestuous affair with a young cousin, are presented in a rambling, nineteenth-century, melodramatic fashion — which seems appropriate for the fevered and incoherent character who experiences them. The satirical treatment of the egocentricity and self-indulgence of the naïve North American becomes the basis of a study of the Victorian literary inheritance that the Canadian-born Jamie wishes to appropriate. Moore entertains himself and the reader with elaborate literary allusions and pastiche that become a deconstruction of Romantic literary traditions and of the cultural forms they validate.

The novel is an inversion of the "finding one's roots" novels then in vogue and of the romantic fictions of identity and authenticity on which such works are based.

What happened to me with *The Mangan Inheritance* was that living in Canada I began to see Ireland and the West of Ireland that I had been visiting as a romantic place in people's minds. And the actual place and the actual physical life of the people there might not be exactly what Irish Americans thought it was. I said, I'll try to write it, start the book as a novel of manners in the Canadian way, they're Canadians living in the present day world, the wife dies, he's in our world in a way, and then he goes over to Ireland with a romantic notion of what he's going to find. He finds the dark side of Ireland, the black side, the fact that there are sexual horrors and all kinds of terrible things and at the same time that he is part of it, his heritage is part of it. Now that destroyed the book for many readers, interestingly enough for reviewers, because they could not accept that a novel which started as a novel of manners became a gothic novel. They saw it as a gothic novel, but you never expected him to fall into the second half of the novel; whatever you thought was going to happen in Ireland, you never expected this to happen to him.

When the novel was published, Moore had to make efforts to justify this radical separation in style between the New York episodes and the episodes set in Ireland. While the experimental extravagance of the second part of the novel — including a long send-up of the Yeatsian poet in his Norman tower, the "last Romantic" presented as the archetypal narcissist — is a deflation of Jamie Mangan's obsession with self, it also reflects contrary aspects of Moore himself and his ambivalence about both Ireland and romanticism. *The Mangan Inheritance* undermines the idealized Irish-American view of the West of Ireland, yet Moore shares the idea that it is a place where miracles can happen. While Moore's sensibility is deeply antipathetic to official romanticisms, he has his own belief in other forms. This treatment of the West of Ireland is ambiguous; in addition to the miraculous aspect, he also characterizes the Donegal of his childhood as a place in which sexual inhibition was unknown, in contrast to the middle-class urban world of his family. Yet the treatment of the sexual life of generations of Mangans re-evaluates this lack of inhibition as male exploitation of women; the moral centre of this novel is, as in *An Answer from Limbo*, the suffering mother-figure, Eileen.

But these contradictions are characteristic, and Moore has given thought to the implications of his own attraction to both realism and romance. Like himself, his characters live in doubt and vacillation rather than certainty, and he finds doubt a more attractive human quality than belief, whatever that belief may be. Doubt exposes layers of fear and yearning — sexual and spiritual — that more truly interest him. The literary analogues of moral certainty versus subjectivity and dreams are Victorian realism versus romanticism, and, in the end, these conflicting forces correspond to the characters of his father and his own youthful self. The sexual and spiritual destinies of Sheila Redden, Belfast woman, and Jamie Mangan, Montrealer, mirror the ever-present contradiction in which Moore's sensibility is rooted. His protagonists are Romantics in anguish, with whom he identifies as an artist, and yet his fictional medium is anchored in the "commonplace" truths of ordinary daily life.

While Moore was working on *Mangan* and slowly recovering from his surgery, he was brought face to face with another commonplace truth; his response to it clarifies a set of moral principles that guides much of his later fiction. Josh Greenfeld, a constant friend from his early days in Amagansett, had also moved to Los Angeles; one day he visited Moore accompanied by his mentally handicapped son, Noah. Although Moore had seen the boy infrequently over the years, he was shocked to discover that at age eleven, Noah was "a mad child, now becoming a mad man." He wondered how Greenfeld had managed to devote himself to caring for his son: "I did not know and was afraid to ask." The answer was given shortly after the visit when Greenfeld published a journal of the daily life of his family entitled *A Place for Noah*. "It is a record of failure and a testament to endurance. It is, above all, a true story about love. I was moved by it, I learned from it, and was humbled by it," Moore wrote in a review of the book, and these simple words of commendation will reappear in following years as in his fiction he tries to define a kind of secular sainthood.

Greenfeld's revelation of his character as father of a severely disabled son is told, Moore says, without "illusion." The account is unsentimental and "surprisingly, a joyful one," because the author is revealed as "a kindly, unmalicious man, alive to the gallows humour of his situation." In this tribute to his friend as father in the most extreme situation a parent might face, Moore ends with a passage from Montaigne that casts a long and ironic shadow over his own life-long preoccupation with his father's disapproval of him: "I never knew a father, how crooked and deformed soever his sonne were, that would either altogether cast him off, or not acknowledge him for his owne: and yet (unless he be merely besotted or blinded in his affection) it may not be said, but he plainly perceiveth his defects, and hath a feeling of his imperfections. But so it is, he is his owne."

# 20

# THE NOVEL
# OF SUSPENSE

The frailty of our hold on reality and on our sense of identity is a constant preoccupation of Moore's characters from Judith Hearne to Jamie Mangan. Moore's next two novels, *The Temptation of Eileen Hughes* and *Cold Heaven*, explore somewhat bizarre aspects of this preoccupation, including obsessions, visions, and paranormal medical conditions, and yet the novels clearly grow out of earlier work. In important ways they are codas to that work, for the long perspective reveals that they mark a transitional phase from the writing of the 1970s into the 1980s.

From 1978, after *The Mangan Inheritance*, to 1982, when *Cold Heaven* was completed, Moore entered a period of stocktaking which extended into a reassessment of the previous decade and of the major orientations of his career. The reorientation towards political and historical fictions that became evident in the mid-eighties, is almost certainly due to a feeling that he had come to the end of his store of autobiographical material — not simply the social and psychological material of relationships, but also the aesthetic and philosophical issues related to the character of the artist.

That feeling of exhaustion or ending may also have arisen from a heightened sense that he was living on borrowed time, that the long illness of 1977–78 was a watershed. "I was very close to death for quite a long time. That focused my attention very closely on the years that I have left." A year after his recovery, he commented: "I think it's had a big effect on me, but I don't know what that effect is yet. I'm going to become one of those boring old men who jog. I've gone through a parody of what it must be like to be about ninety-two and not very well. It was like being a novelist — I was thrown into a role except that this time it wasn't fantasy." And as if to counter that role in life, Moore became even more committed to keeping fit through daily sessions of swimming and jogging. He lost more weight and even began to look physically frail.

The severity and duration of that illness intensified thoughts of mortality and aging that had been associated for decades with his repeated hospitalization for surgery for ulcers, with the familial predisposition for heart attacks, and with near-death experiences, such as the speed-boat accident in 1953. The tension and urgency that had always characterized his work — as if through it he were saving his soul, redeeming his failure — now took new literary forms, at first what he called "metaphysical thrillers."

This shift towards new stylistic and generic emphases, as well as a gradual turning away from the "literary territory" of earlier decades, also meant a move away from a preoccupation with character and towards narrative as a primary end: "I have a certain skill in narrative and in keeping you reading the story. I think that's the important thing in writing novels: to remember that no matter how high your ambition is, the reader deserves to be held." At the end of this transitional period, he spoke of his "very healthy, unacademic respect for the power of storytelling:" "Once you decide on the form, you must work within the genre. The very fact that you conceal information from the reader, the fact that the thing must move, means that you can't develop character. You must sacrifice character for plot."

One particular storyteller became a renewed source of inspiration. Graham Greene had been one of the first English writers to praise Moore's novels, and Greene's enduring appreciation was conveyed to him publicly or privately as each new novel appeared. More significant for Moore's writing was his life-long admiration of Greene's technical ability. He spoke frequently of Greene's skill as a scene-setter, as a story-teller who created a fictional atmosphere in which the reader quickly becomes absorbed. "If you take an older writer like Evelyn Waugh, he can take two men in a room and you can *see* exactly what they are doing, but in very understated prose. Similarly, Greene is one of the great scene-setters of all time. Their techniques are very cinematic. We tend to take cinematic as a pejorative word in writing, but I'm not using it that way at all."

A decision to immerse himself in Greene's later work — fiction, essays, and autobiographies — may have been prompted by Moore's sense of advancing years following his illness, for in a brief tribute he wrote, he remarks: "To read down this list [of Greene's books] is to recall a lifetime of pleasure in reading his work. It is also an antidote to that *accidie* which sometimes makes us falter in our writing careers."

At this time, in 1978, Greene published *The Human Factor*, inspired by his friendship with Kim Philby, the double agent and defector to Moscow in the 1960s, and it became an immense success, especially in the United States. Moore's letter to him is a measure of the intensity of the identification and inspiration:

I was so anxious (as usual) to read your new book that I managed to get hold of an advance copy. It's midnight here and I've just finished it. I feel very shy about writing to you and usually that shyness wins but this is such a marvellous book that it's conquered my inhibitions. I was completely *there* with the characters, who all behave with that touch of unpredictability which is the mark of a great novelist. The book is completely contemporary and in this age of deception and confused loyalties it's the real gold as against the ormolu of Le Carré and others who've tried to deal with this milieu. And, of course, it's much more than that. It's one of your highest peaks and like all of your work it will last. Again my thanks for the great joy of reading it.

These words, written by Moore in his fifty-eighth year, were received by the seventy-four-year-old Greene in Antibes, who wrote back:

It's still three hours before midnight here and I received your letter this afternoon. I don't have to tell you what it meant to me because you know how much I admire your books, and praise from a writer one admires is the only praise worth while. I woke this morning with depression, with a sense of being finished. I longed for something good to arrive, something unexpected — and then in the afternoon your letter came. . . . You've made my day.

In 1979, after completing *The Mangan Inheritance*, Moore had many different ideas of what he wanted to do in fiction, but he thought first of following up his old interest in writing for the theatre. His frustration in attempting to adapt *Judith Hearne* had led him to doubt his ability. In the early 1970s, Mary O'Malley at the Belfast Lyric Theatre had approached him about adapting one of his novels, but he had not pursued it. *Emperor* was adapted and staged at the Abbey, but Moore had no hand in this work. It is likely that it was his friendship with Brian Friel throughout this decade and his admiration of Friel's plays that prompted him to try his hand now.

Much of the winter and spring of 1978–79 were taken up with the writing of two playscripts, an original play, *The Closing Ritual*, and an adaptation of *Catholics*. The original play, a black comedy on the theme of death, somewhat in the style of *Waiting for Godot*, was completed by April. Moore's agent expressed no interest in the play, but Friel offered to look at it and to forward it to the Abbey Theatre. Nothing came of this, but Friel did write in August 1979:

244 / Brian Moore

I think it has neither the compression nor the urgency of dramatic language and because it hasn't one gets a sense that it's "seemingly rambling;" it's the difference, I think, between the novelist's and the dramatist's technique — one seduces the reader on primarily by descriptive process, the other by a continuing and unbroken series of tiny emotional lifts where the logic of the emotions takes precedence over the logic of the intellect (that's why it's a trade filled with quacks!) Whatever about that, that's why I had a persistent sense that "The Closing Ritual" could easily be compressed into a one-act play. And I think that would be worth trying.

In the end, Moore abandoned *The Closing Ritual*. He had more success in finding producers willing to consider *Catholics*, and over the next two years it would have an intermittent life. Its first production was in Seattle in June 1980, for a three-week run. It was not a critical success — Friel teased him about bankrupting theatres — and he was dissatisfied with it. He did not let the idea go, however, and although he had completed one novel and was at work on another, he did return to the play. In 1981 he revised it and considered renaming it *Miracles* — a significant change, for he was between drafts of *Cold Heaven*, another "miracle" fiction set in California. The new adaptation remained *Catholics* and was staged in its revised form in Edmonton, Alberta, for a three-week run in the fall of 1981 and in Stamford, Connecticut, two months later.

The success won by the televison adaptation of the novella in 1973 was not repeated in these different versions for the stage, but Moore's extended engagement with *Catholics* had far-reaching effects. The priest-protagonist, the Abbot of Muck, is clearly the antecedent of the priest-protagonists of *Black Robe*, *The Colour of Blood*, and *No Other Life*, written between 1983 and 1993. Moore's renewed focus on *Catholics* would bring him back in due course to a consideration of religious and political material and to a more overt preoccupation with dilemmas of conscience. While his efforts to develop as a dramatist were not successful, they may have been necessary steps in his evolution towards the shorter, leaner "cinematic" fictions of the next decade.

After Moore had pursued these ventures into writing for the theatre in late 1978 and 1979, waiting for *The Mangan Inheritance* to be published, he prepared a documentary for BBC television, significantly entitled "A View from Across the Water." The film was one of a series entitled *Writers and Places*, and Moore chose to take the viewer not to Montreal, New York City, California or to any other of his "emotional territories," but to

Connemara, on the west coast of Ireland. He speaks of his great desire to leave Ireland in the early 1940s and of his surprise when his imagination brought him back in his first fictions a decade later. "But if I left Ireland because I feared it would not change, now I am drawn to return because it has not changed. I come back here every year. Not to the North and its hatreds, but, here, to the West of Ireland. . . . The faces, the people, the faith: perhaps it hasn't really changed since my father's day." He speaks of the inspiration he found here for *Catholics* a decade before and, more recently, for *The Mangan Inheritance*. The feeling of permanence associated again with his father has become a spiritual and imaginative anchor for his work.

The work of these years, then, also reflects this continuing preoccupation with his Irish sensibility and his attachment to place. And yet he finds himself divided. "Reality, real life is the flesh and blood of many novels I have written. Here in the West of Ireland I am in touch with ordinary lives. In touch yet not in touch. For I am a stranger among the local people; after all, I have it easy compared to the harsh realities of their lives. I know that I am an exile and that my condition is irreversible. From now on in Ireland I will always be on the outside, looking in. I will see these people not as they really are but as I imagine them to be." In the end, Moore finds himself rooted imaginatively in this place and yet an outsider, not simply by virtue of being an emigrant but by the fact of being a writer and an observer.

In these same months Moore had similar thoughts about his attachment to Canada. "I'm irritated when I'm not treated as a Canadian," he commented in October 1979. "Canadians tend to ignore the fact that I use Canada and Canadian characters in many of my novels. I'm dependent on Canada for at least half of my literary terrain. I feel at home here, in the social sense. My brother is Canadian; so are my wife, nephews and nieces. Most of my oldest friends are here." He responded to a question about returning to live in Canada by saying it was likely "when the State of California eventually expropriates my property" — something that did not come to pass. Nevertheless, a decade later he would build a Canadian home on the Atlantic coast of Nova Scotia.

*The Mangan Inheritance* was published in September 1979 and in Toronto and London in the following months. Its reception was mixed, but Moore commented that its reception in Ireland and England was generally more positive. It confirmed his feeling that his loyal audience was there and that, irrespective of the experiments with genre and style that he undertook from novel to novel, he could count on those readers, something he could not do in North America.

In late 1979, he began to go back to earlier work associated in his mind with Ireland. *The Girl Who Was God* — which he began at this time and would complete in the summer of 1980 as *The Temptation of Eileen Hughes* — was for a time overlapping in his mind with a novel about a community of mystical nuns. "I have at the back of my mind the idea of writing something, perhaps a little book like *Catholics*," he wrote to his sister Eilís on 1 November 1979, "or perhaps something different, on the situation of nuns in the present day. . . . I am trying to get some picture of the day of a modern nun like yourself. . . . This idea I have is to write a story only about nuns and only about spiritual faith as it must be manifested in a nun truly holy, who has really, in the words of the Jesuit mystics 'emptied her soul, the better to receive God into it.'"

At the end of the month, as a correspondence with Eilís and another nun at her convent in Manchester began, he remarked, "At the moment I'm trying to write another book but it may not work out," this book being about a couple holidaying in London. At first, they are Canadians from Nova Scotia, but soon he settles on Eileen Hughes and the McAuleys from Northern Ireland. He moves quickly into that fiction and away for now from the fiction about nuns, yet the theme of mysticism remains. In fact, this novel was written in a concentrated burst of activity resembling the writing of *Catholics*; the first draft was completed by May 1980, the second draft by July, with further revisions in August. At the time of writing the first draft, he mentioned that it was set partly in Northern Ireland, "realistic in technique and deals with protagonists rather like those in my early novels." In fact, the novel is more like *The Doctor's Wife* than *Judith Hearne*, but, in spite of its cosmopolitan London setting, all its characters, apart from a young American male, are Irish, and it is emotionally rooted in Ireland.

The Northern Ireland of *The Temptation of Eileen Hughes* is a place characterized by war and wealth and by the "international" angst and alienation of Moore's North American novels; as in *The Doctor's Wife*, a sexually dissatisfied woman travels abroad to anonymous adventures. Here there are two female protagonists, the sexually promiscuous Mona McAuley and the innocent young Eileen, who ends up being initiated into marijuana and sex by a casual American stud. Rather than enter Mona's world, Eileen returns to the ordinary world of her invalided mother. She is tempted by the adventure and glamour represented by European cities, yet the other temptation — of Bernard's platonic and possessive love, expressed in his wish to give her everything she desires — leads her to a sharp recognition of the "madness" in which she is trapped. The counterpointing of two worlds recalls *An Answer from Limbo* in addition to *The Doctor's Wife*, and it is hardly accidental that Eileen's mother's background includes many details drawn from Moore's own mother, Eileen McFadden. The point of view in much of the novel is Eileen's, and so the decadent sophistication is seen through the eyes of a character coming from a small town where "suffering is exact."

For Bernard McAuley, estranged from his wife, Eileen has become the temptation, but he describes his feeling as courtly love rather than desire. "Desire isn't love. . . . You can satisfy desire without making it a big part of your life. It's only when you desire some person in particular that you become dependent, as though that person's body is a drug. . . . But love isn't like that. When you fall in love with someone, really fall in love, it's a sort of miracle, it's almost religious. The person you love is perfect. As God is perfect." Bernard had wanted to keep this feeling a secret, but on the London holiday he is tempted to tell Eileen, and she rejects his wish to possess her as a religious icon or an aesthetic artefact. As he descends into a drunken and ultimately suicidal despair, he remarks, "'I was thinking of something I read once. Love is a religion whose God is fallible.' He raised his wineglass and turned to her. 'To my fallible God.'" At this moment, it becomes evident that Bernard, a failed artist and mystical saint, is another version of Jamie Mangan who had drunk an obsessed toast to his ancestor-as-deity: "To my resurrection and my life."

*The Girl Who Was God* refers to Eileen Hughes, who is not a nun, or even an especially religious person. The divine quality referred to in the early working title of the new novel is, simply, the quality of omnipotence accorded to the beloved by an obsessed lover. Moore recorded many ideas from Ortega Y Gasset's book *On Love*, among them: "As the mystic tends to use erotic expressions of his love for God so (vice versa) does the lover tend to use religious expressions of his love for the beloved." The change in the title to one that echoes Flaubert's *The Temptation of Saint Antony* may reflect a degree of ambivalence in Moore's own attitude towards Bernard.

His notes reveal that he has been thinking of Sartre's biography of Flaubert, and he writes out Sartre's statement: "Genius is not a gift but a way out that one invents in desperate cases." While Bernard becomes a victim of his despair and alienation, he represents a character who wishes to be a saint in a corrupt and materialistic world. Early in the novel, Mona reflects "it was as though he felt he was an imposter in his own life," and he speaks of the need to fill the "empty spaces" of his life, surely an allusion to the "lonely voice" of Pascal's *pensée*: "The silence of the empty spaces terrifies me." There is much evidence to suggest that the true artist or the mystic believer remained an ideal role for "desperate cases" — and in a part of him, Moore felt himself to be one.

Whatever the private preoccupations that drew Moore's attention to the ordinary Eileen, and then had him weave around her his usual thematic obsessions, he was attempting something technically adventurous in this new novel. The compression of the action into two days, with an introductory day and a few brief scenes on later days, is an experiment in a kind of psychological thriller he had not undertaken before. *An Answer from Limbo*, *I Am Mary Dunne*, and other novels had used compressed time schemes, in which a marital drama is depicted in a time of crisis and impending disaster, but the timing of events in *The Temptation of Eileen Hughes* builds suspense in a new way. The power of narrative momentum to carry the reader forward, as the characters are carried forward, recalls Moore's earliest successful fictions, the thrillers of the 1950s; after three decades of writing novels of character, there is now a perceptible shift towards dialogue and description that intensifies the narrative momentum.

Each of the three characters in London are on the edge of a revelation or discovery of secrets that put their psychic stability at risk, and appear to be drawn deeper and deeper into a kind of madness. In this thriller, it is not guilt-laden memories as in *Mary Dunne*, or hallucinations as in *Fergus* that engage the reader's interest in the psychological integrity of the protagonists. The source of suspense is of a more primal and enigmatic quality; the actions of Bernard and Mona are determined by sexual and spiritual obsessions that appear to the reader to be beyond analysis. The technique of limited point-of-view and the compressed time-frame ensure that the unfolding of the thriller-like plotting has an irrational and menacing undertow. Suspense is also created and sustained by the use of what Moore calls the "fugue" state, the device of concealing from the reader the states of mind of characters at critical moments by depicting action through the limited awareness of onlookers.

"In *The Temptation of Eileen Hughes*," Moore has said, "I tried to return to the ordinary world. I wish I could go on writing about the really dull ordinary world in which most people live — because that is where all the action is." The loss of that "dull ordinary world" is Moore's moral subject in this and the next novel, *Cold Heaven*, and yet, as usual, he is drawn to writing fictions of the destabilizing process represented by travel and displacement. The writer as exile continues to ponder the way in which his original Irish sensibility has been transformed and continues to weigh his losses and his gains.

During the 1970s, Moore had become increasingly familiar with the work of key Irish writers, such as Friel, Heaney, Mahon, and, in fiction,

John McGahern. His correspondence with Brian Friel reveals the many personal contacts he had made within the community of Irish writers and the degree to which he felt drawn to their work. He wrote an appreciative review of John McGahern's stories in *Getting Through*: "He is an original voice, a writer who works within carefully controlled limits. In these stories, as in all of his best work, he examines the epiphanies in ordinary Irish lives. . . . an almost Beckettian landscape of small pinched lives, of regret for what might have been, of failed chances and momentary joys." Yet in linking McGahern to Beckett and Joyce, he also begins to define the limitations of McGahern's work in autobiographical terms:

> For those writers born and brought up within its shores, Ireland is a harsh literary jailer. It is a terrain whose power to capture and dominate the imagination makes its writers forever prisoner — forcing them, no matter how far they wander in search of escape, to return again and again in their work to the small island which remains their true world. . . . none more so than the great exiles, Joyce and Beckett, whose fictions constantly resod the native turf. John McGahern, one of the finest talents of his generation, is to my mind a perfect exemplar: sure-footed, elegiac, graceful when he moves in the confines of the land of his birth, his people speaking in accents of truth as they do in this splendid collection of stories. But with non-Irish characters his touch is less sure. . . . The leap across the water has not yet been accomplished.

Moore is implicitly defining those qualities of empathy with character and place which the imagination needs for nourishment. For two decades, Moore had prided himself on his ability to capture people and places beyond Ireland's shore, especially in North America. He believed that he had escaped that Irish prison, without suffering a diminishment of imaginative power or artistic achievement. There is a note of pride in these general comments, which suggests that he feels he has enlarged his inherited Irish sensibility without betraying it, as he suggests writers like Wilde, Shaw, Congreve, Goldsmith, and Sheridan did, "released on their own recognizance that they would write and talk and live as Englishmen, banishing their homeland from their pages." In general, Friel's friendship and his work intensified Moore's self-consciousness regarding this key issue of the colonial relationship with England, but, in the end, Moore remained the chameleon, capable of assimilating himself temporarily to whatever literary tradition or style facilitated the working out of the particular technical and thematic challenge of each novel.

In a major review-essay on Seamus Heaney entitled "English Fame and Irish Writers," written in late 1980 and carefully pondered for some months, he developed some of his ideas on Ireland as "literary jailer" and the dilemma of the exiled writer. Moore examined his own situation as a writer with life-long affiliations with England. He insisted that English critics do not pigeonhole work by Irish writers, and yet he seems to believe that there is an imaginative and literary sensibility that is uniquely Irish. What he values in Heaney surely reflects the standard by which he would wish his own work to be judged.

> There is an exhilarating lucky-dip element in his diggings, for his poetry begins in the sort of observation that brings a shock of recognition, in a glimmer of feeling which surfaces with a touch of mystery, rather than in opinions *à parti pris*. He believes that "poetry of any power is always deeper than its declared meaning. The secret between the words, the binding element, is often a psychic force that is elusive, archaic and only half-apprehended by maker and audience."

Although Moore does not write poetry, he is interested in creating a fiction that incorporates "a shock of recognition" and "a touch of mystery," and, like Heaney, he is interested in that "binding element" in words, the "psychic force that is elusive." Moore stumbled over that force when he created *Judith Hearne*; from this point on, he recognized that the force lay, for novelists, in the power of narrative suspense.

> I like in novels to set the clock ticking. I like the novel to take place within a certain time. I have to explain to the reader what made this particular moment different. That to me is the natural moment of fiction, the natural moment of crisis. I do this in order to inject an element of suspense. I've come to have a greater interest in the element of suspense as I grow older. For instance, I will now look at Conrad's *The Secret Agent* in a way I would not when I was young. I look at the suspense in Graham Greene or Borges in a way which didn't interest me when I was younger.

Rather than the American tradition of thrillers and detective fiction, Moore sees his natural ancestors in the suspense genre as these English writers who have adapted Flaubertian and Victorian conventions to create a twentieth-century cinematic style.

"I think readers judge any narrative in the first few pages," Moore said at this time. "If they accept a writer's style and the truth of the way he writes, then they'll leap into the sea of narrative and swim. At the ending of a book, the reader must jump out of the sea and feel he's been rescued." The novelist had been preoccupied with the crucial impact of opening scenes since *Judith Hearne*, becoming especially attentive in novels like *Fergus* and *The Great Victorian Collection*, in which riskier kinds of "truth" had to be accepted by the reader.

The metaphors of swimming and rescue suggest anxiety about narrative rhythm over the length of the novel. In this same interview, he spoke of the "point of fear" experienced by the writer in midstream, when he worries that he has lost that narrative rhythm. What is curious about the metaphor of the reader having to "feel he has been rescued" is that it echoes Moore's own situation in the middle of writing *Judith Hearne*, when he temporarily lost his ability to write after the boating accident. That experience had returned to his mind at the end of 1980, when he used it for the opening scene of the next psychological thriller, *Cold Heaven*. "I couldn't speak and my motor actions were wrong; when I wrote, I wrote gibberish. I was sick for about three days, like Lazarus, a walking dead person, and it left quite an impression on me. I had to wait many months to find out if it had affected me permanently. I never thought I would use it in a novel, but when I started to write this one . . . it came to me when I thought, 'what is a miracle?' Lazarus or Christ rising from the dead. Well, I thought, I had a Lazarus-like condition."

This recognition seems to have come after he had settled on a religious theme for the novel and had developed his interest in his sister's community. His interest in the creative act as a miracle, his memory of his father's belief in miracles at the shrine of Lourdes — although a medical practitioner — and the apparently miraculous tumult in the Californian cliff-face in *Cold Heaven*: all these elements of supernatural agency made manifest seem to have coalesced with his own Lazarus-like awakening, not only in 1953 but much more recently, in 1977–78. The tone of urgency here gives a personal resonance to the new interest in writing novels of suspense, and that was the genre he chose for his tale of religious possession and medical mysticism.

My new book, *Cold Heaven*, is a curious book in that for the first hundred pages you believe you are reading a thriller because you don't know what's happening to the character. It moves very quickly, but on a rather mundane level, the way thrillers do, and then you discover halfway through the book, that this isn't an ordinary thriller — it is a metaphysical thriller, about something more mysterious than that contained in an ordinary thriller. I don't think I could have written a book that way ten years ago. This is a culmination of my experiments along the same lines in *The Temptation of Eileen Hughes* and *The Mangan Inheritance*. *Cold Heaven* goes one step further. So, willy-nilly, I'm going through a cycle of books in the suspense genre. It is important to realize that what I'm trying to do is not write books that are detective stories, but rather are novels of suspense in the detective mode. The power of withholding information from the reader, but not dishonestly, the power of narrative, of unfolding a story by turning pages, builds narrative suspense, which is interesting for your writing, because it forces you to write more leanly — in a direct, clear, clean way.

When Moore returned in the spring of 1981 to the novel of a miraculous happening in California that he had worked on intermittently between 1970 and 1972, he already seemed to know that he wanted to fuse it with the idea of the fiction about nuns that he had mentioned to his sister Eilís in November 1979. His research notes for the book, which he initially entitled *The Call*, include much material on nuns, mystical experience, convent life, vocation, and miracles as well as on the contemporary search for spiritually transformative experiences of a "New Age" type. His sister, as well as his Jesuit friend Michael Paul Gallagher, corresponded with him regarding such matters. He appears to have visited the Basilica of Mission San Carlos Borromeo del Rio Carmelo as a setting for his community of nuns with a Spanish Catholic tradition. But, between 1979 and 1981, probably after his visit to his sister's convent in Manchester in mid-1980, he had come to a conclusion about the original project: "I went to visit them and was very impressed with the sanctity in some of the older nuns — a feeling the mystics had, they had no sense of self, *solus ad solem* in God. I corresponded with them about what they really felt, but I didn't have the intellectual capability, or perhaps the religious capability, to write about them."

Yet while the community of nuns, the Sisters of Mary Immaculate, is seen in the novel from the outside, and through the somewhat fevered mind of the protagonist, Moore's own hand can be felt in the moral and metaphysical status given to them. "As she looked at them it was as though, in their medieval clothing, working under this harsh high sun, they were a representation of reality rather than reality itself, peasants at harvest in a Breughel painting rather than real nuns at work in a convent garden." In a Californian thriller in which gulls and butterflies and climatic changes may be the hieroglyphics of supernatural messages, these nuns become a touchstone of something permanent. In draft after draft, the new novel begins, "In America nothing lasts," and amongst Moore's notes on the mysticism of St. John of the Cross and others is a note on Wallace Stevens: "Relevance of Stevens/Novalis/The Supreme Fiction is to believe knowing it to be a fiction." In this note, the origins of both *The Great Victorian Collection* and *Cold Heaven* may be seen, and the association of religious mysticism with a belief in the "eternity" of poetry.

It may also be that the image of the mystical and the miraculous that Moore associates with the Spanish nuns may be the inverse of the "Juarez dooms" that Mary Dunne had experienced, or of the state of "Null" that the Abbot of Muck had experienced at Lourdes. The notion of the miraculous, Moore insists, is of interest, regardless of one's secular or religious beliefs: "We inherited the miraculous tradition from the Jews and without a miracle there would be no Christian religion." He felt the need to defend his choice of idiosyncratic subject matter, and yet he believed that his novel had a modern-day bearing: "I think what I'm trying to say in *Cold Heaven* is that there is a great hunger for mystical experiences, for sainthood, in all of us today, although we don't recognize it as that."

Marie Davenport is such a representative modern character. The novel opens with a boating accident in the Baie des Anglais on the Côte d'Azur in which her husband, a doctor, is apparently killed. It seems that he "recovers" from death, although he is now suffering from a mysterious comatose condition. A year earlier, Marie had witnessed a supernatural event on the cliffs near Carmel, in California. Her "call" appears to be a call away from the affair she is having and the separation she is planning and a signal to direct her attention to the struggle her husband is waging against his paranormal medical condition. Her responsibility for his survival seems to be connected to her responsibility for disclosing to religious authorities the supernatural sign she has been given and has tried to suppress. She feels that she has lost her freedom and integrity to supernatural forces whose intentions she resists. Moore's notes suggest that his title, borrowed from "The Cold Heaven" by Yeats, is an allusion to Yeatsian ideas of the other world and destiny and, perhaps, to "the Lord of the Terrible Aspect" which Yeats took from Dante and commented on in prose writings at the time he wrote the poem.

The suspense that Moore will exploit in this religious and scientific thriller is the idea of the psychological and irrational maze into which Marie Davenport descends when she can no longer trust her rational assumptions about the phenomenal world and the forces that control it.

The suspense focuses on her efforts to preserve her own sanity after she becomes a "diviner" of signs. She loses her free will and her ability to communicate with anyone:

> Would people believe it? She supposed they would. It would be the sort of story that would get in the newspapers, but it would be the sort of story the newspapers understood. Unlike the other, the unreal true story, which no one would understand. If she told that, people would say she was mad. She would just have to wait for the next move. In the meantime she would tell the made-up story and people would believe it. The true story was impossible. Besides if she told the true story, she would be letting them win. And I will not let them win. Not now.

Marie struggles throughout the novel to free herself from the psychological and metaphysical maze. Moore creates his character with a strong sympathy for her dilemma and without a predetermined outcome. "I knew this was a tough book, and I kept asking myself, 'how am I going to end it?' Finally I decided I would end it by being true to my own beliefs, which are humanistic. A deep belief I have is that ordinary people live ordinary lives, and that even if extraordinary things happen to them they have to go on with living." In the concluding scene, when Sister Anna from the convent has a similar experience of seeing the cliff-face open in a cruciform shape, Marie feels not vindicated but free:

> "It's Sister Anna's vision now. . . . Don't you see what happened? I refused it, and now it has gone on to Sister Anna. She's a nun. She's the right person. There was some mistake." She thought of that life, that ordinary, muddled life of falling in love and leaving her husband and starting over again: that known and imperfect existence that she had fought to regain against ineluctable forces, inexplicable odds. . . . She had been returned to ordinary life, to its burdens, its consequences.

The novel was completed in draft by June 1981. It was called *The Marian Legend* at this point. The process of revision and rewriting began in the summer 1981 and continued until a final draft was completed by May 1982. It was not published for more than a year; in the United States in June 1983, in Canada in July, and in Britain in October. Reviews were mixed, but Moore seems to have relished the opportunity interviewers gave him to explain not only his attitude towards religion but, more tellingly, his evolving attitude towards narrative and towards his audience.

My style has been evolving towards a more plain style. Reviewers have said that when I use a simile or metaphor it stands out. It is not simply piling on description. When I do finally say something about a character, it hits, it has a very big power. I think that is something which is the result of this very visual age we live in. People can't read in the way they used to because their mind's eye is making cinematic cuts. We see prose passages now as films because children are brought up looking at film all the time. I've always thought that the modern reader makes jump-cuts just like directors in films. I think we could move fiction into the realm of short-takes, a way which has not really been attempted. Someday someone will come up with a type of fiction which approximates the cinematic, and that will have a very interesting effect.

As the 1970s came to a close Moore again reflected on the work of his "hallowed mentor" Graham Greene, whose great skill at dramatizing a character and making his world visible while remaining morally neutral and invisible led Moore in the new directions of the next years. In 1982, he wrote a review of Greene's latest book, *Monsignor Quixote*, praising this "novel of his old age" in which the beginnings of *The Colour of Blood* may be seen: "We enter his looking-glass world, that foreign yet familiar universe where left and right are often transposed, a world in which, like God the Father, he reigns supreme." Earlier, Moore had commented on parallels between *The End of the Affair* and *The Temptation of Eileen Hughes*. There are indeed many parallels and echoes, some of which Moore was conscious of, some of which grew out of the "Greeneland" he had entered and remained in love with. Finally, it is Greene's mastery of the novel of suspense which enthralled Moore and which led him to think of the novel in terms of an English tradition that included Robert Louis Stevenson and Joseph Conrad as well as Greene. In the years ahead, Greene's accomplishment in this tradition would be internalized by Moore as the "witness, judge, mentor" of the new direction his own work would take.

# 21

# HEARTS OF DARKNESS

In 1982, Moore returned to Canada for an extended stay. He spent September to December as writer-in-residence at the University of Toronto. Exactly thirty-four years earlier, he had spent three months in the city in a futile search for work, but now he returned as an honoured guest, with few responsibilities other than to be available to students. The advice he gave them was characteristically down to earth: "You can't teach people to write, but you can teach them that writing is rewriting." He took part in a number of public functions and voiced his appreciation of the hospitality offered to the writer by the university, "the only community which is able to receive him — the only community in which he can feel partly at home."

In his farewell speech, he elaborated on his view of the essential homelessness of the writer: "It's an uncertain life and he soon learns there's no help to be had from his fellow novelists. For the literary world is a pitiless universe of judgements and jealousies." This loneliness of the writer he calls the natural state of one committed to a solitary task, and most anxiety-provoking is the uncertainty that surrounds the reception of a new manuscript by publishers and reviewers. "Each time he publishes a book, he is a student facing an examination — will he pass, or will he fail? And the worst of it is, the final grade will not be given until after his death." The sense of community offered by the academy appears to be a case of *faute de mieux*, but in spite of such disillusioned insights from the successful author, he appreciates "the all-important boon" bestowed on him by the university: the time to write.

While the work of the years since his illness and *The Mangan Inheritance* garnered praise in many quarters, this decidedly unglamorous sketch of the life of a novelist suggests that Moore felt that his career was in decline. Yet in retrospect it is evident that the months in Toronto mark the beginning of a renewal and, in surprising ways, his return to Canada seems to have brought him back in imagination to his arrival there in 1948, and to the hardships of survival in the Canadian winter. Coinciding with this was the rediscovery of historical and political events as material for fiction, especially events of his own lifetime.

After completing the final draft of *Cold Heaven* on 29 May, he turned his attention to a script for a five-hour television drama based on Simone de Beauvoir's *The Blood of Others*, which he was asked to adapt by the Canadian film producers John Kemeny and Denis Héroux, the film to be directed by Claude Chabrol. Moore enjoyed the experience of working with the celebrated French director and welcomed the freedom the wartime setting of the novel gave him: "It is easier than working with your own, because you have already seen your novel as a novel. Someone else's work you can approach just as a story — this one is a love story, a period story about Vichy and the Jews."

The novel is set in Paris between 1936 and 1941. The aspects of that milieu that interested de Beauvoir — commitment and impotence, collaboration and deception, resistance, suffering and death — interested Moore also, although he did not like her treatment of them and was glad to be able to introduce new characters and situations. Working with an historical setting in this detailed way and yet having the liberty to invent his own characters was his first experience of a kind of creation that would extend through the political and historical fictions that grew out of this year's work.

De Beauvoir's novel is a study of the transformation of the personal and political commitments of a group of young people by the onset of war. Moore's notes on characters follow roughly the novel's depiction of them. Hélène Bertrand, twenty-one in the opening scene, "very good-looking, passionate in her feelings, hedonistic because she feels that she only lives once, obsessed with the fleetingness of her life, has despised politics and slogans ever since her early years with the disillusion of her parents' story." The love story is that of Hélène and Jean Blomart. He "is handsome and although he wears a working man's garb, carries himself with the air and assurance of a man born into the haute bourgeoisie. Son of a rich publisher, he has broken with his parents for ideological reasons. . . . he is not a communist, but a trade unionist believing in limited ends. Blomart is also silently obsessed by a feeling that he is an interloper in the class he has chosen. . . . He is capable of falling in love but is not capable, at first, of acting out the drama of a great love. His change in the episodes must be shown to be the change which makes him capable of reciprocating, at last, too late, the depth of the feelings Hélène has for him."

Around this uncertain couple are a handful of friends, but Moore added to the novel the drama and intrigue of a political thriller. He achieves this by introducing Madame Gigi Grandjouan, "late thirties, vivacious, dresses à la Coco Chanel, chainsmokes, snobbish manner but charming: she is a dress designer, Left Bank type, an exploiter of her helpers who praises and flatters them but does not pay them. She eventually becomes a collaborator with the Germans, living in the Ritz with a German officer. She is a fixer, a user of influence."

This is Moore at his oldest tricks, learned in the first years in Montreal writing thrillers, and not practised in filmscripts since his work with Hitchcock almost twenty years before. The drive of narrative that he had experimented with in the suspense fiction he had been writing is now applied to historical material. Researching and writing, and doing successive rewrites and cuts for Kemeny and Chabrol appears to have been a surprisingly satisfying experience. In January 1983, he wrote from California to Tom Maschler: "I am at present a great hero here and in France for I managed to make something out of a novel which is basically undramatic (and not very good). . . . So it's been a profitable and interesting time I've had in the seven months since finishing *Cold Heaven*." *The Blood of Others* was shown on Antenne-2 in France and on HBO in the U.S. in 1983, and Chabrol later edited it to feature length for release in cinemas.

This period in 1982–83 coincided with the decision to try a new genre in fiction, a historical novel, to be set in French North America at the time of the arrival of the earliest Jesuit missionaries in the 1630s. The work in cinema was congenial and from it Moore learned that he could write a historical fiction which did not need to be, as he had feared, weighed down with explanation and with the detailed recreation of period. He discovered that a historical drama could be brief if the historical paradigm was envisioned in purely dramatic terms.

An interview he gave in Toronto suggests that he may have wanted to find an indirect way of dealing in fiction with political issues:

My novels have not dealt with the great political issues. I have always feared overtly political novels, because I was a journalist and I know how quickly they can become tracts. For instance, no good writer has written about the situation in Northern Ireland. Seamus Heaney hasn't written about it, Brian Friel has just touched on it. Most of us feel that it is too political; a novelist just can't keep up with the events of the day. If you're writing about Israel, then this week it's Beirut. By next week, you're out of date. I have been more interested in the continuing drama of people's lives, the fact that we all go through a cycle in life of depression and joy, marrying and dying. Most of us are not concerned with the big events happening around us; our concerns are narcissistic, if you like.

While Moore's declaration of his interest in the commonplace has been a standard answer for decades, his elaboration here seems to refer to an earlier stage, the time of writing *The Revolution Script*, and this is so also in its references to Heaney and Friel.

He knew that Heaney had struggled for a decade to solve this very problem of how to focus on the Troubles and had alluded in dozens of poems to specific events in the news as well as entitling one of his books *North*. One of Moore's notes for the character Jean Blomart reads: "Guilt at what effect he has on people although he does nothing to bring on their woes. The curse of being a separate being. Guilty if I spoke, guilty if I remained silent." Heaney had adapted a vernacular expression to shed light on his aesthetic dilemma, "whatever you say, say nothing," and yet for a decade and as a constant preoccupation, Heaney had been finding means to preserve his artistic conscience and also acknowledge the political and military realities of his community.

The founding of the Field Day theatre company in 1980 for the production of *Translations* in Derry marked a step by Friel and the actor Stephen Rea towards a more active involvement in political and cultural discourse in Northern Ireland. In fact, *Translations*, set in Donegal in 1833, is the exemplary text with an historical setting which resonates with echoes of current preoccupations, and, as Moore knew, it had won for Friel's work an international reputation. The central dilemma this play explores — the mutually exclusive discourses of the native Irish and the colonizing English, and the personal tragedies that derive from incomprehension — is very similar to Moore's confrontation of native and missionary in *Black Robe*, the historical novel he began to think about in Toronto. It is hard to believe that Moore did not absorb Friel's vision in *Translations* while reflecting on the personal and cultural tragedies of New France and of Northern Ireland.

Yet if Moore wanted to capture the truth of a seventeenth-century Canadian world and the opposing world views which came into conflict, he was primarily interested in writing a tale in a traditional style. In 1982, in Toronto, before he began his earliest drafts of the novel, he declared: "I'm very aware of the power of narrative, like the nineteenth-century novelists were; I'm aware that Poe started the detective story and that the power of narrative started in the mind of Conrad. I use these things constantly because I started as an experimental writer." And after he had finished the novel, he returned to that idea:

> I've moved on and time has moved on, and as I've become older I've become more interested in different forms of writing. I've discovered that the narrative forms — the thriller and the journey form — are tremendously powerful. They're the gut of fiction, but they're being left to second-rate writers because first-rate writers are bringing the author into the novel and all these *nouveau roman* things.

*Black Robe* is an effort to rediscover "that drive, that power, that commitment to holding the reader's attention which you find in Tolstoy and the other great Russians." His return in the early 1980s to a primary preoccupation with that power of narrative was an effort to renew his inspiration in old age, to fight off the feeling that he had nothing more to do. "The only thing that gets me through those days is attempting something I've never attempted before. *Black Robe* is a different book from anything I've done." His effort marks a reorientation of his sense of fiction from what he has always called the "novel" to the "tale" — "I have written some experimental fiction and I have liked doing it, but I still think that ultimately it's a mistake to go away from the tale. Thomas Mann said that every tale must tell itself. I know exactly what he means."

Unlike *Cold Heaven*, or other novels that resisted his best efforts to force the pace of composition, *Black Robe* — like *Catholics*, the novel it most resembles — came easily and was written quickly. "I've used Canadian characters in some of my novels but this was a totally different experience. I didn't pick Canada in this instance, I think Canada picked me." Moore's manuscripts and notes show that he wrote drafts and fragments of many scenes in early 1983 after returning to Malibu, but his chronology for the writing of the novel says that "writing of the novel took 1 year June '83/July '84 with one month to write filmscript of *Brainwash*." That script, prepared for John Kemeny, was based on a thriller by John Wainwright; it was never actually made into a film. Before he settled down to intensive writing, Moore also travelled to Scotland as the recipient of the Neil Gunn International Fellowship of the Scottish Arts Council.

The first draft of the novel was two-thirds complete in January 1984. At that stage it was entitled *Jesuits*, but as this draft was revised, the title became *Cain's Land*, from the reported words of Jacques Cartier when he first came in sight of Canada in 1534: "This must be the land God gave to Cain." In March 1984, Moore returned to Canada to visit various sites and museums of Iroquois, Algonkin, and Huron culture, in particular Midland, Ontario, where the original Jesuit mission of Sainte Marie Among the Hurons has been reconstructed, complete with Huron long-houses and village. The novel had assumed the narrative form of a journey by his protagonist, Father Laforgue, and this was his destination when he set off from Quebec with his Algonkin companions to travel up the Ottawa River.

Moore's research of the period combined with his buried feelings about the alienating aspects of the Canadian landscape and climate. "I could never have written *Black Robe* if I hadn't been in Canada, if I hadn't spent a winter, if I hadn't wondered as we all do how did those first people ever survive the winters here." Moore's first year in Canada, his experience in northern Ontario, left a strong impression deeper than this simple issue of physical survival. He speaks of the magnificence of the landscape, "the extraordinary scenery, the extraordinary emptiness of it, and frightening scenery. . . . everything human is dwarfed here." Realizing that one could go out into the wilderness forests of northern Ontario and be lost within a matter of minutes left him with a sense of a primordial Canada that was spiritually alien. "I don't think Canadian writers have explored enough the frighteningness of the change of seasons; Winter is so absolute and shuts you in and closes you off."

These were some of the feeling he tried to get into the novel, and he appears to have found it easy to recapture that early phase of his life in Canada: "I would go into my room and my mind would go back to the Montreal winter I remember and the cold and the St. Lawrence river. When I thought of the river I could see it, because I'd gone up and down it so many times." His experience on that waterway into the heart of the North American continent became a metaphor for the perilous journey into the native lands by the young missionary.

I went into the wilderness of this book I suppose, compared to my other books, because I'd never written a book like this before. I didn't want to write an historical novel because I don't particularly like historical nov-els. . . . I wanted to write this as a tale. I thought of it in terms of authors I admire, like Conrad. I thought of *Heart of Darkness*, a tale, a journey into an unknown destination, to an unknown ending.

The experiments with landscapes, with the unique feelings that Moore associated with the West of Ireland or the Californian coast, is now extend-ed to include this Canadian spiritual landscape. But if those places stirred in him premonitions of the miraculous, of significance, here the alien landscape is one in which individual lives and human cultures are inconsequential. Natives and Europeans live in fear of the inhuman forces which determine their very survival. Moore's tale became an experiment in bringing the character of the committed priest Jean Laforgue to the limits of his beliefs and of his ability to endure.

The Canadian forests became a metaphor for the wilderness of the individual psyche under extreme duress and of conflicting interpretations of supernatural signs. "This young priest and the boy who go on the journey enter a terrifying wilderness but at the same time they enter a wilderness of their own spirit." Moore's own journey into this historical material took on surprising directions. "A lot of my books deal with religion, but I approached this book in a different way. I felt what would happen to me if I'd been foolish enough to become a Jesuit and believe in all these things and suddenly landed up in this wilderness, Canada, with people who refuted all my arguments, that seemed highly intelligent and yet people I was terrified of living with."

Moore's discoveries about his protagonist and about his own deep sympathy for his dilemmas came gradually over the course of writing.

> When I wrote my first draft of it, I made him into more of a holy fool and an idiot than he actually turned out to be. But it's interesting that the truth of this story dictated what the character did, which in a way it's never done with another novel. When I wrote it and had him as a holy fool and totally inept and couldn't paddle, I simply realised the Indians would have left him behind. He had to be more of a decisive person because he would never have been able to make that journey. And the few of these priests who did make the journey had to discipline themselves and to be physically very tough and mentally very tough. He's deaf, he suffers illnesses, he suffers from various things. While he becomes physically stronger as the book goes on, he's mentally more doubting; self-doubt enters his mind. I kept in mind that he was a man from another time. People believed in the devil as well as God and that belief was something I didn't want to scant. I didn't want to make him into a modern character in seventeenth century dress.

In short, the challenge of creating Laforgue as an authentic seventeenth-century character forced Moore to revise his early assumptions. At first, his sympathies lay with the native people whose culture and way of life were endangered by the proselytizing Jesuits, but as he was forced to try to understand how Laforgue might have behaved, his respect for the Jesuit grew. Gradually, the priest became a character trapped in circumstances, somewhat like the abbot in *Catholics*. "I'm attracted by that sort of figure. I'm attracted by people who can no longer believe in something they did believe in but nevertheless go on for some humanistic reason. Well, it's the lack of belief in some things I said which has haunted me all my life, the fact that I am so selfish, that we are all so selfish and that we look at these people and wonder what is it that makes them different from us."

Those revisions to his conception of the missionary led, in turn, to changes in his depiction of conflict and plotting and in his presentation of the native people. "I tried to show in the book that the Indians feared, despised and were alarmed by the Jesuits in very much the way that the Jesuits feared and were alarmed by the Indians. . . . So everything that strikes us as a sort of primitive superstition was repeated in their view of us. And for that reason I thought that if I didn't show the violence and I didn't show the polygamous behaviour and so on, it wouldn't be right." Just as he wanted to portray the Jesuit as authentically and realistically as possible, neither romanticizing nor lampooning his convictions, an even-handed treatment of the natives as they actually were became necessary.

He felt somewhat on the defensive, wanting to guard himself against romanticizing native culture in a sentimental way and, also, against indulging in sensationalism by using an excess of violence and coarse language.

> Maybe there was an indulgence in it; you know the author never knows if he's indulging himself. But I was so struck by it that I didn't want to scant it; I worried a bit about showing the ritual cannibalism — feeding children — which occurs in the book. But when I went on reading and saw the Iroquois, for instance, would attack enemies and go in and literally tear babies from their mother's breasts and dash their heads out against a wall so that the Algonkin women would say "these men are not men but wolves." In fact, I used that phrase in the book, the mind and the cruelty was something that we find very hard to understand.

On the other hand, Moore wanted the native people to be attractive. "The interesting thing is that the Indians had very few ugly people. The Jesuits themselves mentioned that." In sum, he wanted to preserve the mystery and the reality of the native people and to depict them as they would have appeared to the Europeans at that time.

I did think of *Heart of Darkness.* . . . the Huron characters and the Algonkin characters are very important in this story and so for that reason I thought it was different from a Conrad story. It's a different time, the natives are the natives; the natives are among the strongest characters in the book, they're not Nigger Jim or anyone like that.

An unease about the genre of historical writing is revealed by the fact that Moore took the unusual step of appending an "Author's Note" to preface his novel. Here he provides an account of the novel's genesis, and, not surprisingly, he reveals that the original idea began in his reading of Greene. "A few years ago, in Graham Greene's *Collected Essays*, I came upon his discussion of *The Jesuits in North America*, the celebrated work by the American historian Francis Parkman (1823–1893)." Greene's opening sentence identifies Parkman as "a creative artist" who showed exemplary dedication in working all his life to realize the substance of his original vision. The historian is described not as an academic in a study but as a missionary and an explorer, who set out at the age of eighteen to travel across the Indian lands, as well as to the European centres, and to live the drama he would write about.

"Since the seventeenth century no historian had so lived and suffered for his art," Greene writes. "The work planned at eighteen, begun at twenty-eight, was only finished at fifty-nine, in the year before his death, by working against time and his own health. This was a poet's vocation, followed with a desperate intensity careless of consequences." Apart from this dedication, Greene praises Parkman's skill at creating "the great drive of his narrative" and instances the "value of bald narrative" which the sketch of one priest, Noel Chabanel, exemplified. The priest's vow in the seventeenth century mirrored the vow that Parkman himself had made and that had governed his life.

There is one final aspect Greene identifies as being close to the heart of Parkman's talent, the poetic imagination that allowed him to recreate the Indian sense of immortality and the other world, "in the general belief . . . there was but one land of shades for all alike. . . . for all things, animate and inanimate, were alike immortal, and all passed together to the gloomy country of the dead." The rhythms of this passage by Parkman seem to anticipate one of the most celebrated paragraphs in Irish literature, the conclusion of Joyce's "The Dead," a text surely implanted in Moore's imagination and also a resonance in the story he began to write of the conflicting interpretations of the place of the living in relation to the dead.

"I began to read Parkman's great work," Moore says, "and discovered that his main source was the *Relations*, the voluminous letters that the Jesuits sent back to their superiors in France. From Parkman I moved on to the *Relations* themselves, and in their deeply moving reports discovered an unknown and unpredictable world." His reading went beyond the *Relations* to include the work of anthropologists and historians "who have established many facts about Indian behavior not known to the early Jesuits," and from that reading, "I was made doubly aware of the strange and gripping tragedy that occurred when the Indian belief in a world of night and in the power of dreams clashed with the Jesuits' preachments of Christianity and a paradise after death. This novel is an attempt to show that each of these beliefs inspired in the other fear, hostility, and despair."

Moore's comment on the self-abnegation of this missionary zeal carried to the point of martyrdom reveals his central interest in this material and in the creation of his protagonist, Father Laforgue. "*A solemn vow*. A voice speaks to us directly from the seventeenth century, the voice of a conscience that, I fear, we no longer possess." It is, then, the notion of a "solemn vow," the capacity for such total belief in divine purpose as Moore had known in the person of his father and in his sister Eilís's vocation to enter the convent, that leads him to enquire further; and it may be that he is less interested in the historical and multicultural theme than he is in the "tragedy" which accounts for the erosion of the capacity for such faith. "One of the things that was frightening when I finished this book, I felt this book is quite different from anything I've written and it wasn't written by me, it was written by someone else in the past and I had a feeling of great emptiness when I'd finished it."

This resonance accounts for the nostalgia and sadness in his sentence on the dedication of the Jesuit priest. In Catholic Belfast, Moore had grown up in a world in which absolute faith was still possible; and surely it is a small step from this enclosed faith to accept that the Protestant zeal to preserve the "liberty" won in the seventeenth century by William of Orange is an equal and opposite faith — a puritan theology which had become a politics also; hence the dramatic juxtaposition of Jesuits and natives conceals an allegory of the Catholic-Protestant deadlock in Northern Ireland.

The whole thing could be a paradigm for what's happened here. Originally I'd have said that wasn't true, but maybe subconsciously I was thinking of it. The only conscious thing I had in mind when writing it was the belief of one religion that the other religion was totally wrong. The only thing they have in common is the view that the other side must be the Devil. If you don't believe in the Devil, you can't hate your enemy, and that may be one of the most sinister things about Belfast today.

And so in that historical situation there are resonances on many levels that drew Moore into the material and made the journey of Father Laforgue to his outpost a mythic search into another "heart of darkness."

While the modern myth derived from and exemplified in Conrad's novella was certainly in Moore's mind as he wrote, the "instinctive storyteller" Graham Greene, in *Monsignor Quixote*, had reminded him of another myth, of the idealistic medieval hero journeying into the real world of confusion and compromise. "Where other celebrated novelists habitually consolidate their fame by writing careful variations on their few and favorite themes, Greene remains reckless, a searcher, a risk-taker, unclassifiable, even by himself. For now, looking back, can we — can he — really make distinctions between his 'entertainments' and his novels? All of his works are countries of his mind." Moore's comments on Greene's accomplishment in this book focus on his protagonist. "Greene, in this novel of his old age, has created for us, memorably, a man who is truly humble, truly good, a man filled with the delightfully silly simplicity of the truly spiritual person — in short, that most difficult of all characters for a novelist to attempt — the character of a saint."

The Jesuit priest in *Black Robe* did not develop in this direction, but such a saintly character was a figure of continuing interest to Moore. "We've got to find some spiritual reason for living. . . . We've got to destroy this terrible absorption with self, with our egos, our individual lives. We've got to realize that true happiness is in being able to give yourself to the good of other people, in that sense to lose yourself completely. . . . The truly saintly people do not have these beatific visions; they simply go on struggling, filled with doubt." This paradoxical conundrum of Quixote, of the personal faith of the saintly person being deepened by doubt, mirrors the broader cultural perspectives he will investigate in the next novel, *The Colour of Blood*, and later in *No Other Life*.

Moore's interest in Greene's work is also now an interest in his character as a novelist. At this time he read Greene's autobiographies, *A Sort of Life* and *Ways of Escape*, and in both he praised "the brilliant discussions of craft which remain in our memories when the books are closed." But a recurring theme in Greene's novels is now seen to reflect his own character as the self-absorbed and isolated novelist: "Writing is a form of therapy; sometimes I wonder how all those who do not write, compose or paint can manage to escape the madness, the melancholia, the panic fear inherent in the human situation." Greene later speaks of the "melancholia which falls inexorably on the novelist when he has lived for too many months on end in his private world," so that it is unclear if "melancholia" is cause or result of the isolation and deep concentration which novelists must undergo. But if Greene's Monsignor Quixote discovers "how a sense of doubt can bring men together, perhaps more than a sharing of faith," that comic vision is largely absent from Moore's grim tale.

Throughout the summer and fall of 1985, a Canadian film crew followed Moore as he made his annual journey from Malibu to Europe, to Montreal, and back to California. A profile of the author of *Ginger Coffey* and *Black Robe* was being made for the National Film Board. Moore speaks without regret of his decision to leave Ireland, of how he had been "living a lie," and it is clear that both the city of Belfast itself and revived family memories contribute to the depression he experiences when he revisits his first home. He is glad to leave once more, and seems certain that he will never again write of the place. "I've thought many times of writing another book about the North, about Ireland, but I realize now that I'm not the person to write this book. My period is over. It'll be some young writer who lives here now, who's experienced all the things that are happening here now who will write the good novel about the North of Ireland today. I'm a person who has tilled that field personally. I have to move on." Yet in the not-so-distant future, he will write a novel set in Belfast, the thriller *Lies of Silence*, and the novel which he will begin later in 1985, *The Colour of Blood*, will have allegorical resonances of Belfast, a place of absolute and unchanging convictions.

Surprising echoes of that Belfast world and of his earliest models of worthwhile accomplishment in life appear elsewhere in this film profile, during the interview taped in blinding sunshine amongst the flowerbeds of his Malibu home. The narrator announces at the outset that Moore "says he is at home everywhere, and nowhere. . . . But the one place he is truly at home is at his typewriter." Moore comments on the experience of sitting each morning at his typewriter: "Writing for me is the moment when I'm happiest. . . . I go into the room and I go into another world. Sometimes that world won't wake up for me. . . . You have to be able to concentrate. There's a trick to writing I find, which is extreme concentration for short periods of time but it must be extreme in that short period of time. It's as if you're always in an intensive care ward where the patients may die. You've got to be a nurse and keep constant attention to them." The analogy is fascinating. The writer is not parent to his invented characters, or a God-like creator, but a life-preserver, like his doctor-father and his nurse-mother. The act of writing has become a matter of psychic life or death, his ability to concentrate the equivalent of intensive care! He is happy at his typewriter because away from it is the despairing panic of life-threatening illness or depression and *accidie*.

That creative concentration, which is the vital self of the novelist, is possible, he says, because he contrives to challenge himself "by doing something new." *Black Robe* had been a new challenge and was being received with acclaim in that summer and fall of 1985. Critics in Canada, the United States, Britain, and Ireland had found him writing at the top of his form. When he arrived in London, however, in September, he discovered that the novel had not been shortlisted for the Booker Prize, as his publisher Tom Maschler, at Jonathan Cape, had expected. This annual prize for fiction in the English language outside the United States has become the pinnacle of publishing success, and the media interest and sales generated by it are considerable. First nominated for *The Doctor's Wife*, Moore, his publisher and many British critics believed that he deserved a nomination, if not the prize, for *Black Robe*.

During this summer of 1985, Moore had been at work on a screenplay of the novel, and plans were already under way to have it made as a Franco-Canadian production with Gérard Depardieu as Father Laforgue. There was much enthusiastic talk of a major movie, but, in the short term, this flurry of activity did not lead anywhere. Eventually all these stirrings of fall 1985 did bring delayed rewards. In June 1986, he was given the Royal Society of Literature Award. A second Booker Prize shortlisting came his way a year later, and another three years after that; but it took even longer, six years, for the film of *Black Robe* to appear. In the meantime, Moore returned to Malibu in November to begin a new novel.

The writing of *The Colour of Blood* would occupy him throughout 1986, and was a new technical challenge. Although the study of a priest/cardinal trapped in the public compromises of institutional and national politics resembles in many ways the novel he had just finished, and, indeed, *Catholics* of fifteen years earlier, the new novel is also an attempt to get close to current political events and to develop an even more taut thriller style than he had used in *Cold Heaven*. The challenge of this novel was to write a brief, engrossing, political fable. Having found a way of fusing his interest in a character in crisis with an historical context which lent itself to fable and allegory, Moore now turned from New France to the twentieth century and to the inheritance of political violence, coercion, and barbarism he had known in the thirties and forties, especially in Poland.

The idea for the new novel came during a visit to Northern Ireland when he was stopped at an army checkpoint. "It reminded me strongly of my days in Poland, and I thought it would be interesting to write about an imaginary country that wasn't Ireland and wasn't Poland." In fact, the events are set in an unnamed eastern European country which is identifiable from many internal details as Poland, especially the dilemma in which the Church found itself as both supporter of Solidarity and go-between with the Communist state in an effort to avoid Soviet invasion and large-scale violence.

Northern Ireland in its state of contained civil war, with soldiers, tanks, checkpoints, and sections of Belfast in ruins, could easily have reminded Moore of Warsaw in the post-war years, and the atmosphere of conspiracy and menace in the two places certainly coalesced in his creation of this fictional country. A change in outlook that he underwent at that time also seems to be at the heart of his inspiration.

When I was sixteen or seventeen I was very left-wing. I never joined the Communist Party but I was a left-wing Marxist sort of person and totally uninterested in religion, the opiate of the people, *I thought*. But I discovered that I was very interested in religion. While living in a communist country, I became disillusioned with what was happening. I discovered that whatever it was that made me go toward the revolutionary solution, it was the same idealistic impulse that would have made me religious if I'd gone the other way, and I was quick enough to recognize that in myself as a writer.

The "idealistic impulse" he had investigated in the character of Father Laforgue in *Black Robe* was expressed in the priest's missionary zeal, and that unquestioned faith was tested. Here in *The Colour of Blood*, the Catholic faith of Cardinal Bem is also tested. Moore's choice of an Eastern Bloc country and his recollection that his own socialist faith was tested in Poland suggests that his interest is in the moment when absolute convictions, like his inherited Catholicism or his chosen belief in Marxism, are put to the test. Yet his comment on the "idealistic impulse . . . in myself as a writer" may well be the deeper faith that lies at the heart of the novel and is also put to the test.

That Moore should decide to set a novel about the examination of artistic conscience in an eastern European country is not surprising. Throughout the 1970s, poets and novelists of Poland and Czechoslovakia had become well known. One of them, Czeslaw Milosz, winner of the

Nobel Prize in 1980, was a California resident and fellow teacher at UCLA. Praising Seamus Heaney for his many "excellencies," one of them being "his refusal to employ his *batterie de poésie* for statements rather than states of feeling," Moore quotes Heaney writing about the persecuted Russian poet Osip Mandelstam: "We live here in critical times ourselves when the idea of poetry as an art is in danger of being overshadowed by a quest for poetry as a diagram for political attitudes." The army checkpoint is a symbol, as it is in Heaney's poetry, for an examination of the conscience of the artist in a time of politically inspired violence.

In *The Colour of Blood*, the Secret Police who shadow Cardinal Bem, and whose behaviour and motivations are directed by the inscrutable pragmatism of ministers of the State, are mirrored by uncompromising traditionalists within the Church. The lines of command, joining bishops and Catholic terrorists, are equally inscrutable, for the Church has internal conflicts regarding what is justifiable co-operation with the state and what is collaboration. These conflicts provide the plot with the labyrinthine deceptions and erosions of trust in which the protagonist is trapped. The cardinal is isolated and alone with his conscience while on the run from enemies on both sides.

But if Bem's goal as a public figure is clear — to prevent violent confrontation between members of the Church and the forces of the State — even at the risk of sacrificing his own life, the sequence of actions and reactions that make up the tense plot also define the conscience of the cardinal in his private and spiritual realm. Moore is interested in constructing a narrative vehicle that will bring current political compromises into an allegorical framework, but he is equally interested in how the spiritual life of Cardinal Bem is affected by his public role. "I wanted to take the reader along on the journey with the cardinal, to experience each revelation as he experienced it." The novelist refers to his technique as "spare" and "particularly visual," and in describing the novel as a book of "suspense," he goes on to insist that "if you want a thriller, characters can't spend too much time thinking about what they're doing." The inner life is reflected obliquely, then, and yet it is this inner life that turns the thriller into a fable of conscience.

"I wanted to write about a good person," Moore has said, "a religious, dedicated, honest person." It seems that the novelist's preparation for depicting such a saintly character led him to read further to understand the nature of religious conviction. He read the memoirs of Cardinal Bea, Pope John XXIII's spiritual mentor: "What surprised me was how insecure, how uncertain he was." And so Cardinal Bem tries to withdraw from the pressure of events and enter a mental space in which "the silence of God" will not be absolute, that God's will may become known to him and that he may continue to believe that he is acting in accordance with God's will. In the opening scene of the novel, before the assassination attempt that sets the chase in motion, he tries to enter this spiritual zone by reading the words of Saint Bernard of Clairvaux: "Do you not think that a man born with reason yet not living according to his reason is, in a certain way, no better than the beasts themselves? For the beast who does not rule himself by reason has an excuse, since his gift is denied him by nature. But man has no excuse."

Moore uses the words of the saint to establish the tone of Bem's religious belief, yet these words also initiate a humanistic allegory on the fate of reason in a world dominated by violence and bloodshed. In the sermon Bem preaches on the occasion of the bicentenary of the Rywald martyrs, the occasion when he joins them as a modern martyr; he speaks of "the tyranny of an age when religious beliefs have become inextricably entwined with political hatreds, when, day after day, in countries all around us, innocent people die from bombings, from terrorist attacks, from political and religious reprisals and revenge."

The opportunity to give this sermon is an emblem of the freedom Bem must win for his own words. The action of the thriller hinges on this, for he must outwit and survive the different forces which would censor him or silence him permanently. That freedom to speak, and to use his position to influence the behaviour of his flock, is a primary value in the world of Bem, yet it is ultimately extinguished, for he is assassinated. Bem is a martyr to his cause: "Remember that, no matter which government rules us, we remain a free people, free in our minds, free in an unfree state. That is the greater heroism." His words suggest that, apart from the obligation to use his authority as a cardinal and leader of the church to speak out, it is the spiritual freedom of introspection and prayer that he really values. Private faith and the judgement of God are more important than the nature of the temporal power or "the world of his duties." While he is prepared to compromise with ideologically opposed institutions, his conscience is anchored in an ideal of simplicity and clarity.

The assassination attempt that failed to kill the cardinal in the opening scene did kill his driver, Joseph, who sacrificed his own life in an effort to cut off the assassin's car. Throughout the four days of the subsequent chase, Joseph's devotion to duty represents to Bem the truer sainthood of innocence and selflessness. His name suggests his role, and in the sermon, Joseph's martyrdom is evoked as a moral standard: "I beg you to think of the deaths of others. Remember, the terrorist and the tyrant have that in common. They do not think of those deaths." The ultimate freedom is simply to live, and the novel's title seems to affirm that blood is the essential element of humanity, whatever the ideological or theological colouring of the person's actions or thoughts. The title comes from "Black Is My Favorite Colour," a story of racial conflict written by Bernard Malamud and adapted by Moore for the screen twenty years earlier.

As Joseph was a victim of expediency, so also is Cardinal Bem himself, and the reader is left to wonder about the belief of the cardinal. At the moment he faces the assassin's gun, in the final paragraph of the novel, he experiences doubt: "The silence of God: would it change at the moment of his death?" If we are to believe Moore's own words on the saintliness of his protagonist, that doubt, that uncertainty about the afterlife, seems to make him even more a saint in Moore's eyes than his stated beliefs. It is the hidden drama of the inner life, of doubt underlying faith, and of the complex pressures to which conscience is subjected, that engages Moore's interest in his character.

Moore did not go to Poland to research the settings of the novel. In fact, there is evidence in the novel that he relied for some details on Graham Greene's account of a visit to Warsaw in the mid-fifties as a guest of the Pax movement. Greene provides an analysis of the complex and delicate balance of Church and State in the post-war years and also comments on the "faithfully reconstructed" buildings of the Old Town, the rebuilding already in progress, a symbol of the Poles' will to survive.

But if Greene's account of communist and Catholic Warsaw in *Ways of Escape* reawakened Moore's memories and contributed such details, it is more important for having strengthened his sense of purpose in writing a political and religious thriller and in imagining the character of Cardinal Bem. Greene comments, "the world is still the world our fathers knew," which is precisely Moore's sense of what remains permanently of interest to him in Ireland in spite of many changes and the violence of the Troubles. Cardinal Bem may have aspects of Moore's own moderate father and of Eóin MacNeill's idealism in a time before disillusionment.

The novel was published in London, New York, and Toronto in September 1987 and reviewers were divided, some enthusiastically positive, others regretting a decline in Moore's talent. "This is the work of a masterly writer now at the height of his powers," Neal Ascherson wrote in the *New York Review of Books* and went on to single out for praise what Moore himself would see as a primary criterion of success: "A great many ideas are carried by the characters of *The Colour of Blood*. Not for a moment, however, do they cease to be unpredictable, genuine human beings. . . . It may be that Moore would not wish to be called a 'Catholic novelist.' But he shares with some other novelists who are Catholic (and some of the great Russians) the capacity to make characters who remain entirely convincing whatever burden of 'significance' they carry." Years later the words Moore recalled from the reviews of *The Colour of Blood* were those of the novelist and critic Thomas Flanagan: "Moore's real subject, in this as in many of his novels, is the fragility of the self."

Although this novel was shortlisted for the Booker Prize, it did not win. However, a few months later it was awarded "Britain's newest and richest fiction prize," the *Sunday Express* "Book of the Year," and in Ireland, Moore shared the Hughes Prize for Fiction. At this time *The Temptation of Eileen Hughes* was adapted for television and was shown on the BBC in early 1988. Throughout the 1980s, Moore's work continued to attract more and more attention in Britain and Ireland; he was especially touched by the Honorary Doctorate given to him by Queen's University, Belfast, in July 1987. The citation recalled that his father had been a member of the Senate of the university in the novelist's childhood and youth, but did not allude to Moore's failure to matriculate; instead it praised him as "a modern master of the art of fiction, one who has brought great distinction to his native city of Belfast and enriched all our sensibilities through the imaginative generosity of his creative vision."

# 22

# THE TRUTH
# OF EVENTS

"I'm extremely conscious that most novelists don't do their best work past sixty and often seem to run out of material. What keeps me going as a writer is the belief that I can write new kinds of books," Moore remarked in 1995. He had begun to be concerned about old age as early as forty, and twenty years later he frequently referred to the challenge of surviving as a writer past the age of sixty. As he moved well beyond that limit, and the illness and recovery of the late 1970s faded, he seemed to become happier. "People used to tell me when I was younger I was always saying I was old and now they tell me I've stopped saying that. I think I've had a good life and would just like to go out happily." He continued to say that he was happy only at his typewriter and happiest in the middle of a new novel, solving technical problems of the narrative as they arose and before he became anxious about the ending. And he continued to express his appreciation for the good luck of having Jean share his life of alternating periods of travel with monk-like withdrawal to the isolated house on the Pacific coast and, increasingly, to the isolated Atlantic coast of Nova Scotia.

The fictions of his old age were indeed "new kinds of books" as he moved far away from the "narcissistic" concerns of before: "At some point your own life and the lives of your friends, their adulteries and their different things. . . . you don't have anything more to say about that." What he still had much to say about were the public themes that he had deliberately kept out of his novels or admitted obliquely. From his youthful socialist commitment and his observation of the "silent collaboration" enforced in Belfast by the Catholic Church, by Irish nationalism and British unionism, to the rise of fascism, the war years, and the Communist take-over of Poland, to the lifestyle revolution of the 1960s, the advent of the television age, and the transformations within the Catholic Church, Moore had always been an alert and engaged observer. The next set of novels were a distillation of a lifetime of meditation on such constant and recurring issues as the exercise of moral conscience in compromising historical circumstances.

After the success of *The Colour of Blood* in 1987, it — and its antecedent *Catholics* — became the model of the brief, impersonal, political fables that he would go on to write in the 1990s. He returned, surprisingly, to do what he said he would never do: set a novel in contemporary Belfast of the Troubles; and then he moved to Haiti of the Duvalier dictatorships and of Aristide before writing of contemporary and of Vichy France. Remarks he made in the aftermath of *Black Robe* and *The Colour of Blood* indicate that as a storyteller, a teller of tales, he wrote the historical novels not to explain or simplify events but to provoke reflection. These late fictions are the work of a professional storyteller, proud of his ability to select the telling metaphor and to pare down a narrative to its essential elements:

> The best symbolism must be unconscious. . . . If you describe something well and accurately, its meaning will be universal. That's what novel writing is all about. . . . The interesting thing is that Americans do their best work with shorter fiction. Saul Bellow is definitely at his best with shorter fiction. It's true of other writers as well. My favourite Tolstoy work is *The Death of Ivan Ilych*; my favourite Dostoevski is *Notes from the Underground*. They're short works in which you find the essence of the writer.

He no longer focused on autobiographical material but seemed to be aware that this work continued to be a kind of personal "exorcism" and a distillation of his fundamental vision.

In *Lies of Silence*, the contemporary novel set in Belfast, he came closer than ever before to using his fiction to make a political statement. Moore goes beyond the making of a statement, however, for, in fact, this novel belongs in the sequence beginning with *The Colour of Blood*, in which the theme of the statement, the freedom to speak out with conviction on controversial political matters, is central. Moore examines the costs of exercising moral conscience in remaining silent and in the public expression of religious and political beliefs.

Only in a magazine article, "Bloody Ulster," on the outbreak of the Troubles, did he express directly his anger and despair about the bigotry and hatred enveloping Belfast. The Northern Irish background of *The Doctor's Wife* and *Eileen Hughes* served only as distant backdrop to the Parisian and London settings. "I feel that fiction can't compete with the daily news," he said in 1982.

In 1980, speaking of Seamus Heaney, he had said that a writer must not be interested in "statement" but in "states of feeling." Yet *Lies of Silence* seems to indicate that he had come to regret his overly oblique treatments of the moral, political, and human cost of the bigotry of Belfast. His anger and frustration at the fact that the destruction of individual and familial lives could be ignored in decade after decade of the "terminal illness of bigotry and injustice" led him to use the thriller genre to reach a wide audience. "I wanted to write a book that people who weren't interested in Northern Ireland would read, because most of the books being written about Northern Ireland are now being written by specialists, because most of the world is tired of it."

*Lies of Silence* arose out of an incident that took place in Belfast when he was there in July 1987 to receive his honorary doctorate. "I was in the Wellington Park Hotel, near Queen's University, and we had a bomb scare in the middle of the night. We were all put out in the street, and I saw these French tourists there. I was listening to them, and they hadn't the slightest idea what was happening. So I thought about what happened and wondered about what it would have been like if they were killed and they didn't know who killed them."

This incident appears to have epitomized the fact that innocent and uninvolved civilians were often pawns in the strategies of intimidation and terror of paramilitary groups:

> The second thing that occurred to me was the whole question of hostages and seeing that the IRA or the UDA go into people's houses: they hold them overnight; they use their cars; they use them for various purposes, but you never hear one interview with, or one word of, the hostages and that's the silence I was interested in.

It is the dilemma of such ordinary people and their absence from the moral calculus of the Troubles that aroused Moore's anger.

The "lies" of the title refers to specific instances of public indoctrination: "lies told over the years to poor Protestant working people about the Catholics, lies told to poor Catholic working people about the Protestants, lies from parliaments and pulpits, lies at rallies and funeral orations, and, above all, the lies of silence from those in Westminster who did not want to face the injustices of Ulster's status quo." Those lies are the background to the plot woven of "proxopera" — as Ulster novelist Benedict Kiely had named the practice of hostage-taking and the coercion of civilians into delivering car-bombs — and the situation of the potential informer on the run.

The moral dilemma faced by the hostages Michael and Moira Dillon — to "escape" into silence and safety or to speak out and risk assassination — engages the novelist directly. At first, Moore appears to have thought of a thriller with Michael Dillon at the centre: "I felt as an expatriate that I wasn't the person to write the big Northern Ireland novel, so I made the hero someone like me, who doesn't want to be in Northern Ireland, who left it, and just has no desire to go back there, hates the place, and then I'll be able to identify with him, and so that's how it came about." But Dillon's dilemma is complicated by his desire to separate from his wife, and by Moore's counterpointing of Moira's own working out of the issue of silence and conscience.

As in almost all Moore's novels, he builds the tension of the situation by focusing closely on the experience of the protagonist in a state of crisis: "I like to go in with them into that crisis and write the novel about that crisis, without knowing myself how they are going to solve it. Quite often they don't solve it, and I leave them bleakly at the end of the crisis, which is often how things actually happen in real life." *Lies of Silence* turned out to have an ending very similar to *The Colour of Blood*, although this came about, Moore says, without premeditation: "I didn't know he was going to die when I started to write the novel. But it came to me that it was inevitable he was going to die, because once you start dealing with terrorists and start vacillating, you're almost dead already, because they have reason to distrust you, and when they distrust you they want to kill you."

Moore's attitude towards the continuing violence in Northern Ireland is palpable throughout *Lies of Silence*. It is voiced by many characters directly, and the simple plot of the hostage-taking, the bombing, and the evolving dilemma of Dillon as a man who can help the police identify the IRA members who kidnapped him, all reaffirm it. As Moira Dillon puts it, addressing her captors, "You're not fighting for anybody's freedom. Not mine, not the people of Northern Ireland's, not anybody's. The only thing you're doing is making people hate each other worse than ever." For her, the puzzle is that by the inactivity, the silence, of the great majority of ordinary people like herself, "we have let you get this far."

At first, Moira is portrayed as somewhat helpless and dependent, deeply insecure about her personal and sexual appeal, but she emerges in the crisis to be the more courageous of the pair. She confronts the adolescent gunmen who take her hostage, challenging them verbally and making an escape attempt. Michael conceals his roles as carrier of the bomb that exploded at his hotel and as informant in alerting the police — in the process risking the life of his estranged wife — but Moira decides to speak out. Even though his action has saved the lives of many people, he "was not brave or defiant as he would have wished to be, he was afraid." In contrast, Moira decides she does not want to be spirited away from Belfast for her security; "You can't avoid responsibility by pretending things aren't there," she tells him, "if people like us let the IRA push us around, how do you think we're ever going to change things." Her courage is foolhardy, as her mother tells her, "Another martyr for the cause? You'd stay here and get yourself killed to make a political point against the IRA. . . . It's all madness."

The arguments go back and forth without clear resolution, because, although Michael does not speak out to the media as Moira does, and instead leaves for London to start a new life with his girlfriend, he is called on by the police to speak out in another way: to identify his youthful hostage-taker in a line-up. Moira now changes her mind about the high cost of her own gesture and counsels him not to be a police informer, at the risk of becoming a martyr too and of endangering his girlfriend's life also.

The Dillons' freedom to act with self-respect is variously tested, but in the end, they become victims of the circumstances in which their lives have been entangled:

> There had been no war in his life. He would never be called up as a soldier and put to the test of bravery in battle. He would never be asked to perform an act of heroism as a member of a resistance group. He had, instead, been put to the test by accident, a test he had every right to refuse. And yet . . . the moment he told [the police] he was afraid, he would lose for ever something precious, something he had always taken for granted, some secret sense of his own worth.

There is no absolute resolution of the moral and personal issues raised, but these words reveal a private ending to the statement that Moore wishes his suspenseful moral thriller to make about Northern Ireland.

The reference to the Second World War and the Resistance recalls the standard by which Moore measures heroic action and endurance. "Bloody Ulster" must not be compared to the just war of resisting Hitler's tyranny. Moira's caustic statement to her adolescent kidnappers, "you're not fighting for anybody's freedom," introduces a set of allusions to the theatricality of heroism perpetrated by the media in its presentation of the IRA as "freedom fighters." It is not only adolescent males who are seduced by such role-playing, for it is also suggested that even Moira's gesture of speaking out on television has an element of this also, as her potential employer warns: "It's all very well to play Joan of Arc, but I don't want to be sitting here waiting for some gunman to walk in the door of this place and blow us all to smithereens." Michael is particularly aware of the role the media had played in creating the "madness." Watching the televison image of his bombed hotel, he feels a momentary excitement: "He had been plucked from the invisibility of ordinary life." He perceives that the face of Reverend Pottinger, the Ian Paisley figure, "looked more real on television than when he had seen it this morning." Dillon's escape to London will provide him with the chance, he hopes, "to slip back into the safe anonymous river of ordinary life."

The statement Moore wants to make about the truth of events in the public realm is unmistakable, yet, as in *The Colour of Blood*, the individual consciousness of the protagonist is permeated by doubt, and that doubt goes deeper than that called for by the thriller genre itself. His characters lack the certainty and clarity of deeply held beliefs in circumstances where the powers which govern life and death are motivated by the clear logic of prejudice and terror. Nuances of feeling and uncertainty of belief are the more human truth of ordinary lives as Moore has always conceived of them, and it is for this reason that his protagonists are heroic in their crises and ultimate martyrdom.

The late 1980s were years of considerable public success as Moore was increasingly admired for his talent as a writer's writer, especially in Britain and Ireland. He was the recipient of awards and honours, and was frequently in the news as three of his novels were made into films. First, Nicholas Roeg bought the rights to *Cold Heaven* and plans for making a film, without involvement by Moore as scriptwriter, came and went, until, eventually, the film did appear in mid-1992 and failed to make an impact with audiences. Then there were frequent reports that *Black Robe* would be shot by the Quebec director Yves Simoneau, but this project was postponed, and the film was not made until 1990, when it was directed by Bruce Beresford. In the meantime, after thirty years of false starts, *The Lonely Passion of Judith Hearne* was filmed in Dublin in the summer of 1987 and released at the end of that year. The film was made by a British director, Jack Clayton, and starred the British actors Maggie Smith and Bob Hoskins. None of the earlier screenplays was used; the credit now went to Peter Nelson.

Moore was not happy with the outcome. "They made the ending much more hopeful than it should have been. Setting it in Dublin was a big mistake because everyone in Ireland said this was a book about Belfast." The film version seemed to him to be a betrayal of his most intimate inspiration, yet Hoskins and Smith were widely praised, as were many of the supporting actors, for the authenticity of the representation of character. Many critics disliked the bleakness of the film, and one critic who admired it made the shrewd comment that "the cinema, in the end, may be better suited to conjuring fear than loneliness."

*Lies of Silence* was published in spring 1990 and, not surprisingly, was reviewed, especially in Ireland, in the way that Moore had always feared a political novel would be reviewed: according to the political bias of the reviewer. It was greatly disliked by those who disagreed with the book's angry and overt statement about the "madness" and the "terminal illness" of Northern Ireland. Seamus Deane expressed his shock that Moore, whom he placed among the best living novelists, "was willing to risk improbability for the sake of a propagandistic point." Another reviewer praised the novel, finding it "as effective an indictment of Northern Ireland's horror as is likely to be found in modern fiction." Others, more distant from Irish affairs, praised Moore's craft as a writer of thrillers or faulted it for falling below his own standard of characterization.

*Lies of Silence* was nominated for the Booker Prize, but the prize went to A. S. Byatt's *Possession*. John McGahern's *Amongst Women*, a poetic family novel which explores the sources of violence in repression and authoritarianism, was also shortlisted and was favoured by the jury ahead of Moore's novel. The book-buying public had no difficulty making up its mind. This novel sold more copies than any of Moore's others, especially in Britain, where forty thousand sold, and it quickly went into paperback.

After changes of directors and actors and frequent rescheduling, Moore's own script of *Black Robe* became the basis for Bruce Beresford's film, shot in the summer and autumn of 1990 along a tributary of the St Lawrence, in the Saguenay region of Quebec. Beresford had recently won an Oscar for *Driving Miss Daisy* and the Quebec actor Lothaire Bluteau, who had played the lead in the Cannes award-winning film of 1989, *Jésus de Montréal*, was chosen for the lead. The film also came to the screen just after the blockbuster *Dances with Wolves*, the first film to present native Americans speaking their own language on screen, with subtitles. *Black Robe* also used this technique to heighten the authenticity of its depiction of racial difference and conflict. For all these reasons, it was expected that the film would generate big box-office returns, but, in spite of many reviews that expressed admiration for its visual qualities, the film was only a modest success. The aspect that was most often faulted was the lack of depth in characterization, the very aspect of film-making that always made Moore a reluctant screenwriter.

Moore liked Beresford's work and their collaboration inspired two ideas that led him in the direction of his later fiction. His attention focused on wartime France again, and perhaps it was his proximity to the Australian director that led him to see in the celebrated film *Gallipoli* a model for a movie about the disastrous raid on the German-held port of Dieppe.

*Mordecai Richler, at Dorval Airport, mid-fifties. Brian and "Mort" became close friends in 1953.*

Courtesy *The Gazette* (Montreal)

BRIAN MOORE

JUDITH HEARNE

'The book is a triumph'
ANTHONY RHODES: SUNDAY TIMES

'Extraordinarily gifted'
JOHN RAYMOND: NEW STATESMAN

*Second impression*

*Cover of the first edition of* Judith Hearne, *published by Andre Deutsch in May 1955; a second impression of this edition was rushed into print a month later with extracts from the first reviews on the dust-cover.*

Courtesy Andre Deutsch

*Diana Athill, editor of* Judith Hearne *at Andre Deutsch, a friend and supporter from 1954, when she accepted his first novel.*

Courtesy Reprint Society

*Cover of the first of two thrillers published by Dell in the "First Edition" series.* Intent to Kill *is set in the Montreal Neurological Institute where Brian recovered from brain damage suffered in a boating accident in July 1953.*

Courtesy Dell Publishing

## INTENT TO KILL

The glaring lights above the operating table had been burning for most of the day. A man's brain lay exposed, and silent, white figures examined it and worked over it with urgent skill and care.

The patient lay quietly, fully conscious. As the electric stimulator touched certain areas of his brain, he told of his reactions — his arm moved, his leg moved, but no sound of the agonizing pain escaped him.

The surgeon poised, then lowered the scalpel to the damaged area. A barely heard moan, and the patient was unconscious.

And in a hotel room near the hospital, three hired killers waited grimly to do their job in case the operation succeeded.

*Christmas party, 1957: Jackie Moore, Berenice Weintraub, and Gloria Cherney.*

— Courtesy Alex and Gloria Cherney

*Christmas 1957, Bill Weintraub and Brian impersonating the American critics George Jean Nathan and H.L. Mencken.* — Courtesy William Weintraub

*Brian, in mid-fifties.*                                    — Courtesy Alex and Gloria Cherney

*Michael Moore at
Amagansett Beach,
summer 1959.*

Courtesy
Alex and Gloria Cherney

*Portrait of Brian with his dog, Bonnie, by Sam Tata.*
Courtesy Sam Tata

*498 Lansdowne Avenue, Westmount. Bought in October 1955, this house in Montreal's most affluent suburb was Moore's first permanent home since the Blitz destroyed his childhood home in 1941. Moore sold the Westmount house to his brother Seán in 1963.*
Courtesy Conor Sampson

Periods in the so-called "creative" life: between books, ideas etc,
the abortive ideas : all seem very fresh at the outset but
dream like : outré : The Canadian Railroad story:
which _is_ : the Great Victorian Collection , in another form,
held in the mind of an idiot, an empire; Railroad
Victoriana is : held in the memory (learning) of a scholar ; a
collection of realities :


Write a line of of each letter group:
as f f f f m f f f g l m  n a n d u  n u n n u
and you will write well.
lullwrite good rhythm as found in n small n the keys & it
good rhythm and fine handwriting go hand in hand.
May I 1970.    Idea for story on monastery in Ireland.
after ecumenical revolution.

*A page from Brian's Commonplace Book, 1970. The first hint of two later novels,*
Catholics *and* The Great Victorian Collection, *may be found among these notes,*
*where he also seems to be practising the uncial script he adopted as his new handwriting*
*from the mid-sixties.*

*Brian, surrounded by his brothers and sisters (except for Marie-Therese), outside the post-Blitz home of the Moore family on Cliftonville Road, late sixties.*
Courtesy Seán Moore

*Brian on the right, with his younger brother, Seán; Jean Moore is second from left and next to her is Cynthia Moore, Seán's wife; in the kitchen of Seán's house in Montreal, 1970-71.* — Courtesy E.C. Balch

*Brian, following the conferring of an honorary doctorate, D.Litt,
at Queen's University, Belfast, July 1987.*
— Courtesy *Irish University Review*, Spring 1988

Beresford and he agreed to work on a film that would be ready by the fiftieth anniversary of the raid by Canadian soldiers in 1942. This film was never made, but it is evidence of Moore's continuing preoccupation with the war years: the idea came to him midway between his adaptation of de Beauvoir's *The Blood of Others* and *The Statement*, the novel he would publish in 1995 about the collaboration of Vichy France in the Holocaust.

Moore's visit to the location of *Black Robe* was partly a nostalgic journey to the waterway he had frequently travelled while on the shipping beat for the *Gazette* forty years before. The chosen location was inland, close to the town of La Baie, about five hundred kilometres northeast of Montreal. This is a part of what is referred to as *le Québec profond*, an isolated and long-settled land, entirely French-speaking and having little contact with the rest of Canada. In the 1970s and 1980s it had expressed the most solid support of any region for the separation of Quebec from Canada.

This strongly nationalistic and Catholic community stirred in Moore's imagination the idea of inventing a character who had grown up in this place. He imagined this character as a priest who had left it to become a missionary. This priest would become the protagonist-narrator of *No Other Life*, the novel he would work on over the next year and a half. Moore has said that the church steeple in La Baie became vital to his conception of the inner life of Father Paul Michel. "I don't think I'd have been able to write this book if I hadn't kept in touch with Canada. Even though *No Other Life* takes place on a Caribbean island, the narrator provides the novel with a very Canadian sensibility." While the austere and isolated location of *Black Robe* may have given him a local origin for his missionary priest, that novel may also have recalled to Moore the idea of displacement in a racially different "heart of darkness." This time the moral wilderness would be a revolutionary Caribbean island.

This memoir of a retired teacher looking back over his career as a missionary priest is combined with a political narrative of Ganae, an island with strong geographical and historical associations with Haiti. Moore purposely did not visit Haiti. "I didn't want it to resemble Haiti too closely. Besides, I live in a kind of Caribbean atmosphere." Nor did he read widely. "People say, do you leave out a lot of factual detail? No. I don't put it in in the first place. There's too much information in most novels. Novelists showing off." Moore's narrative is not, then, in competition with either the documentary reports of journalists covering the events involving the figure of President Aristide or the longer perspectives of historians.

Nor is it in competition with another well-known novel of Haiti, Graham Greene's *The Comedians*. "This book is the first time there would have been a connection," Moore commented. "When I started to write this novel, that suddenly flashed in my mind. Oh, my God, I'm going to get that Greene thing again, so I went and got it off the shelf and of course it was different." The novelist had grown irritated by now with the constant comparisons with Greene. Nevertheless, it would seem that the conception of Father Michel may owe something to the world-weariness of *A Burnt-out Case*, with its protagonist a world-famous architect travelling to an African leper colony run by Catholic priests, in an effort to escape from his successful self. It begins "The cabin-passenger wrote in his diary a parody of Descartes: 'I feel discomfort, therefore I am alive,' then sat pen in hand with no more to record. The captain in a white soutane stood by the open windows of the saloon reading his breviary." *No Other Life* is more than another version of *Heart of Darkness* told in a Greene idiom, but the opening introduces the same note of self-assessment *in extremis*: "My life here has ended. My day is done. . . . I think of these things because I am looking at the empty pages of my life."

There is, of course, an echo here too of the opening page of *I Am Mary Dunne* with its parody of Descartes, for at this stage of Moore's career the urban wilderness of North America and the theological and political wildernesses of his latest novels had become one: at the heart of all these fictions, underlying the fast-paced and engrossing narrative structure, is the urgent and anxious voice of one with a frail and tentative grasp on life itself. On the publication of *No Other Life*, the aging novelist seemed to sum up a sense of life not essentially different from Greene's: "Our lives are so flimsy and ephemeral — we're like actors in some little play." Greene's epigraph to *A Burnt-out Case* had come from Dante: "I did not die, yet nothing of life remained."

While there are aspects of *No Other Life* that mark it as the work of an older man, it is also a surprising throwback to the beginning of Moore's career, to 1953, for it was then that Moore actually visited Haiti with Jackie. He recalls that his "young liberal ideas" were undermined by the corruption and poverty, by the colour and caste snobbery, and by the cynicism of America's interest. "This is a place nobody cares about," he discovered, one of the "little places," perhaps like Northern Ireland before the world's media were drawn to it by the first television images of violence. The shock he experienced in Haiti was partly captured in "Off the Track," a story written for broadcast on the CBC in 1960, an early version of his "heart of darkness" fables of later years.

Father Aristide, the radical priest elected to power in 1991, focused in Moore's imagination a set of issues that had occupied him for a long time but had not found fictional form. First there is the paradox of the priest-politician: "I would be very happy if I could write a book about a committed reformer of his country for political reasons," he said in 1985, before he began *The Colour of Blood*, "but power does corrupt, and it's very hard to find such a person who wouldn't be corrupted. Whereas the religious person has no power." That was one of the paradoxes he explored in the character of Cardinal Bem. Now, he says of *No Other Life*, "My book is based on Haiti, on Fr. Aristide, but I was always interested in messianic leaders and here was a Catholic priest becoming leader of a country when no Catholic priest is allowed to hold any position in politics. Interestingly enough they didn't dismiss him, and the reason I think is they would have risked losing the faithful in that country." Although the practice of *realpolitik* within the Church is part of his interest here, as in *The Colour of Blood* and, later, in *The Statement*, his primary interest is in the idea of the messianic leader.

I've always been interested in the idea that someone could influence other people's lives to the point that when they spoke or exhorted them to do things they would do them. So much of the trouble in the world has come from that, from Jesus on. They all seem to be Jesus figures, whether they're Lenin or the Ayatollah, and they all seem to have that charismatic thing of being able when they speak to move other people. For the rest of us, we can only ask are they saintly or are they not.

Concern with the role of charismatic figures in twentieth-century history has always occupied Moore, from Mussolini, Franco, and Hitler to de Valera in Ireland and Trudeau in Canada, but this is the first time he faces the question of a messianic figure genuinely motivated by compassion for the poor.

The novel's Father Cantave, known to the people as "Jeannot," is shown to have the rhetorical skill to move his followers through incantatory speeches, but as violence increases and he is forced to defend his interests, the justice he is led to dispense is less than saintly. "The book is about preachers who become Jesus figures. Whether they become saints or rabble rousers — that's the question." As Father Michel observes his protégé and spiritual "son," he finds himself recalling a remark of Diderot which he heard on more than one occasion during Jeannot's rule: "Between fanaticism and barbarism there's only one step."

The political, theological, and moral maze in which Father Michel finds himself is reflected in the novel's epigraph, taken from Borges: "God moves the player, he, in turn, the piece. But what god beyond God begins the round of dust and time and dream and agonies?" It is a surprise to find Moore returning to his inspirational mentor of twenty or more years earlier, especially in this context, but the vision of Borges may be appropriate if we recall the "Irish" fable in *Labyrinths*, "The Theme of the Traitor and the Hero." Moore's most recent Irish fiction had been a tale in which, as in *No Other Life*, the awareness of "history" as a maze of overlapping and competing fictions, as a battleground for the supremacy of particular interpretations and myths, was clear. Borges's distillation of the colonial histories of Ireland into inspiring dramas of betrayal and martyrdom, into the mythologizing impulse to identify a leader as at once "traitor" and "hero," is surely a source for Moore's treatment of Jeannot.

Father Michel is not an historian, then, but a teller of a story, a true story. "I think it is that — the knowledge that the truth of these events may never be known — that makes me want to leave this record." And so he becomes an autobiographer even as he becomes the biographer of the revolutionary priest. He sets out to tell the truth of his own perception as he tells the truth of what happens to Jeannot. Father Michel has a secret that he wants placed on record: he knows the later fate of Jeannot when he disappeared from public view after the coup d'état which deposed him. Jeannot had reappeared in public but, in parallel with events in "The Theme of the Traitor and the Hero," he stage-managed his own disappearance. He disappeared into the realm of legend, perhaps more powerful and influential as a vanished hero than as a political activist.

The memoir's tone of melancholy and loss, and the missionary's conclusion that he should never have brought Jeannot away from his village and "adopted" him, are counterpointed by the erosion at the end of his life of his religious faith. In this aspect of the novel, Michel's similarity to Moore becomes even more evident. In the middle of *No Other Life*, after many years' absence, Father Michel returns to La Baie to visit his dying mother. He is met by his brother Henri, a doctor who has remained there, "he, the older brother, responsible, provider for his mother, his wife and his children; I, the impractical younger brother." Returning home triggers many doubts about the course of his life: "My life's choice came back to haunt me. What if I had stayed in Ville de La Baie and become a doctor like my father and my brother?" It would seem that this remote Quebec village is superimposed on the novelist's own Belfast, this visit of Father Michel a transcription of Moore's own visit to his dying mother in October 1957. The sensibility of Father Michel is less Canadian than Irish, the memoirs of this aging priest being an allegorical version of the novelist's own probing of the shape his own life has taken.

The priest-narrator is portrayed as a man who has lost faith in everything in the public realm except, perhaps, his own written record of "the truth of events." Through writing the narrative of these events, he wishes to redeem the "empty pages" of his life. The burden of being the creator of a "surrogate life" and of "a legend" is the allegory that unites Moore and the "empty pages" of Father Michel's life. "Writing is like making yourself deformed, for you're deliberately cutting yourself off from other people, deliberately choosing this thing which is a solitary occupation." The monk-like régime that Moore had chosen in California, the intense dedication to articulating an elusive and uncertain truth, was the final stage in living out the logic of his life's choice. Having lost his belief in the pieties of his first family and community and chosen a left-wing political belief, and having lost his belief in that, a fanatical commitment to discovering the truth of self and of events became his creed. Yet, like Father Michel, much as his lifetime's activity has been dedicated to his creed, Brian Moore has doubts and even guilts that resurface. "Writing novels is a way to dodge thinking about that. Sometimes I think that's all it is."

Yet that world-weariness he has been able to transfer to his invented character, and the satisfactions of being a novelist still return. "There is an excitement to me in writing a novel when it's working that I don't get with anything else. There's a despair when it's not working out, when you're not going to finish it. For instance, with this book I was worried about the ending, and then it just came into my head at the very last moment and the feeling of pleasure was incredible." He found the ending, Jeannot's Borgesian escape into mythology, in the summer of 1992 in Nova Scotia, and that allowed him to complete the novel by fall.

*No Other Life* was published in London in February 1993, an early publication date because it was felt at Bloomsbury that after three Booker shortlistings, this novel had to be a winner. A longer lapse of time between publication date and the selection of the shortlist was considered to be a necessary step, and so Moore travelled to London in February and went on a promotional tour that took him to many British cities. In one interview he found it necessary to defend himself against an implicit charge that he was deliberately writing, in the later phase of his work, according to a Booker-winning formula. He dismissed the charge although granting that he wanted to write "accessible novels" that will receive good reviews and have healthy sales.

In the end, *No Other Life* was not even nominated for the Booker Prize, although it was prominently reviewed and warmly received, especially by fellow novelists. John Banville, himself nominated, spoke of it as "a peculiarly powerful work of art." Banville regrets that Moore "cleaves unashamedly to the adventure novel," but says that he "has an extraordinary way of darkening and deepening his fictions by the most economical of means. . . . the theme of religious failure, of despair and eschatological terror, which Moore insinuates so delicately into his fast-paced narrative, confers the ineluctable, subversive aura of a nightmare."

Later in the year, another Irish novelist wrote at length on *No Other Life* in the *New York Review of Books*. William Trevor's essay was a tribute to Moore's art and surprised the novelist with its sympathy for his later work. "The action of this novel seems almost to write itself, but this impression is a deceptive one. Smoothly, quietly, everything is managed and the puppet-master's strings aren't visible for an instant. . . . *No Other Life* is a beguiling, marvellously readable account of a good priest's vocation. As all successful novels do, it reverberates and haunts, its intensity lingering long after the book has come to an end. Brian Moore has written nothing as subtle, or as perfectly sustained."

In these years, Moore commonly quoted a line from a poem by Yeats: "The best lack all conviction and the worst are full of passionate intensity." He had grown to like more and more the prophetic poems of Yeats, for the poet seemed to capture not only the apocalyptic violence of Ireland in civil war but to anticipate the global violence of the century and the perversion of moral principles by mass movements and messianic leaders. From his youth, Moore had been alert to intimidation and "silent collaboration," and in the aftermath of the war, many friendships had sensitized him to the test case of such silencing: the extermination of the Jews by the Nazis and their collaborators in many European countries.

His final novel in this sequence of political thrillers investigates the role of leaders of the Catholic Church in southern France in concealing for forty years a member of the *milice* who had personally shot Jews in a round-up and had co-operated in sending Jews from France to extermination camps. *The Statement* follows closely the case of Paul Touvier whose trial for crimes against humanity took place in France in early 1994 after decades of legal, political, and theological sophistry.

Set in 1989 at a moment when the net is tightening irrevocably on the protagonist, Pierre Brossard, *The Statement*'s short chapters, alternately focusing on those who are hunting and on the hunted, also allow for flashbacks to earlier stages of Brossard's evasions. The novel is a meditation on the historical processes governing the post-war decades by which vicious acts were concealed by the forces of compromise and reconciliation.

Brossard skilfully exploited those forces, especially certain contemplative clerics and conservative factions within the Church.

The political events that inspired the novel are simple in outline and complex in their implications, and the suspense builds on many fronts. The protagonist is being hunted by two assassins even as he is sought by a gendarme acting on behalf of a judge appointed to investigate him for crimes against humanity, and by a team of historians appointed by the Church hierarchy to establish the facts. One of Moore's characters remarks, "The study of history is not so different from the practice of law. The primary aim of both is to discover the truth of events." As if to highlight the difficulty of that task, the statement pinned to the body of the assassinated Brossard is a deliberate deception; the novelist calls on his fiction-making powers to explore the darker side of belief and commitment, of public and private lies, which colours "the truth of events." In this sense, he is rewriting *Lies of Silence*.

Moore reveals his fascination with the conditions that make war crimes or crimes against humanity difficult to pursue. As in the lead-up to the Second World War, post-war conciliation is revealed to be neither a neutral nor a disinterested process. Midway through the novel, Brossard reflects: "In those years everyone wanted to be forgiven. The clergy, the politicians in the National Assembly, people in shops and factories and on the farms, every sensible person said that what happened in the war years was best forgotten, that the war trials were revenge not justice. He was a victim of the times, wasn't that the truth?"

In spite of Brossard's guilty memories of the hatred that led him to kill Jews, he claims the pardon of the confessional as a higher justice and a higher measure of accountability. His case evokes the sympathy of many Catholics who chose to ignore the killings in the light of another reading of events, and Brossard is able to persuade himself of the primacy of this traditional vision: "It was in monasteries that he felt most at home. There, hospitality to strangers was the rule, passed down through centuries of the Faith, a reminder of a time when the Church was a power, independent of any authority, free to grant asylum to any fugitive it chose to aid. Behind the monastery walls, the world did not exist." And so the vicious Brossard has saved his own skin by hiding in the folds of those who are won over by thoughts of "the true France, *la France profonde*, of values, beliefs and customs fast disappearing in this end-of-century turmoil."

Moore adeptly etches in the many strands of Catholic belief and practice in the closed religious houses of Provence, whose clerics, in essence, pardon Vichy and Nazi Germany because of their opposition to atheistic communism and to modernism. Opposed to this world-view is that of the progressive Judge Levi, who, in spite of decades of frustration caused by bureaucratic and judicidal diversions, is pursuing the case of Brossard's crimes against humanity. "I suspect that we will find out that over the years Presidents, Prime-ministers, Cardinals, judges and prefects of police have all been part of this conspiracy. And unless the whole truth is brought out into the open it will forever be a stain on the conscience of the country."

Moore is faithful to recorded history in the documentary elements of the case and in the correspondence of his characters to many actual people, to their roles and stated beliefs. In addition to being in France as the legal process unfolded against Paul Touvier, he carried out research which included the reports of commissions of enquiry. But Moore departs from what actually happened to Paul Touvier after he was captured in 1989. It is as if "the truth of events" that Moore wishes to uncover is not, in the end, the truth of history or of the justice system. In fact, those historians, churchmen, and justice officials who wish to discover the truth are confounded by another force — those individuals who do not wish their own past behaviour to be examined; Moore's thriller is in the end not a documentary novel but a dark fable on the persistence of lies and deception and on how the nostalgic and conservative Catholicism at the heart of French society made possible collaboration and the subsequent cover-up.

Moore has said that if he had been born in France, his father would have been a supporter of Pétain and the Vichy regime. In this sense, the inspiration for this novel goes back to Moore's efforts to understand his father's conservative Catholic belief and his initial support for Franco, Mussolini, and even for a time Hitler, not simply to understand but to free himself again from the shame he felt at Catholic Ireland's silence and collaboration by virtue of its neutrality. "Neutrality is shameful. It is sickening to think of people standing back, thinking they're great because they stayed out of it."

It seems that just as he once had felt compelled to write his adolescent pain in Belfast out of his system, *The Statement* is a way of ridding himself of the shame of his father's attitudes and beliefs, which he found repeated in France. Again he wanted to make a statement on an issue that had haunted him, and he wanted to use the thriller form to provoke readers to become aware of it: "The young may be bored by the Second World War but it happened, and appalling crimes were committed." The novel he wrote is a statement once again on the ordinary and innocent victims of those whose beliefs are simple and clear. The truth of events is in the end that individuals were slaughtered, but the enveloping debate is a maze of sophistry Moore wants to penetrate in his own fashion. "I never thought that novels changed the world. I still don't believe that. But I just thought that this was a story which really should come out."

In October 1995, when *The Statement* was published, Moore visited Belfast, toured once more many of the places of his childhood and youth, and noted how many landmarks were no longer there. For the first time in almost sixty years, he walked covertly through St. Malachy's; "I'll never forget it. If you were late, only seconds late, there'd be a priest standing here with a cane. As an adult I'd wake up in sweats, having dreamt about running up here against the clock and never getting there on time." The tension, the guilt, the sense of failure — "My generation felt that you only had one chance" — were exorcized, Moore says, by writing out those experiences in *The Feast of Lupercal*. Yet in the books of his old age, his characters seem to be "running against the clock" and all of them seem to be unable to avoid punishment; tension and dread have become the constants of his narratives.

He walked towards the ruins of his first home, the house on Clifton Street where he was born. It had been demolished only a month earlier:

> I think as a writer it is very symbolic. Your past is erased. Now it's as if it's completely died. I was here a few years ago to film a documentary and I stood in front of the shell and I could remember my father's brass plate at the door, the patients to-ing and fro-ing. Now what is it? It's a paradigm of man's existence on earth. The earth remains and man does not.

Earlier in the summer of 1995, his house on the Atlantic shore of Nova Scotia had been finally completed: "It's beautiful. It looks out on a bay that looks just like Donegal. It's very wild there and empty. I love it for its emptiness. It's like Ireland probably once was. Now that I'm so old it seems crazy to build another house, I know. Especially there. But I'm very happy I did it all the same."

*Envoi*

# THE CLOSING
# RITUAL

———————

Prompted by Brian Moore's essay "Imagination and Experience," I embarked on the writing of this portrait, which has become, rather than a complete biography, a double image of the creator of fictions. As I arrive at the end, the focus of that image has been disturbed and adjusted once more by the publication of yet another novel, *The Magician's Wife* in 1997. In spite of this adjustment, I know enough now to recognize the patterns in Moore's life that are constant. Most of all, the novelist wishes to remain chameleon-like — hidden from himself and from others. This writing life must remain fluid and open to improvisation. And so *The Magician's Wife*, like all the other novels, surprises with its inventiveness. Moore deliberately resists a pre-determined blueprint in the discovery of his way into each new novel. Even the mastery of technique is itself a danger that must be resisted if each novel is to be a new probing of the meaning of his experience.

Initially in Moore's writing career the repetition of a known fictional formula was the key to financial security, but by the mid-fifties when he wrote *Judith Hearne* he came to recognize the *élan vital* he craves as a writer; without the technical challenge of doing something new, he is not able to "keep the story alive and suspend the reader's disbelief" — the compact he enters into in writing each novel. In addition to keeping the writing alive for his readers and for himself, he embraced experiment and change because the "surrogate life," the life of the imagination, became his real life.

By midlife, he had come to know enough of the patterns of his own earlier experience to feel the compulsion to make a break from Jackie and his established domestic and literary contexts. The boy who had wondered in Alexandra Park about the identity of the "unknown creator" of the puppet-show had grown up into a puppet-master himself. His shame at becoming a puppet-master in his earliest formula fictions led to his eventual suppression of those fictions, about which he now prefers nothing be written. The worldly journalist gradually began to withdraw into his self-created image as artist. He wanted to "become his characters" and remain an invisible presence; and yet, by the time he wrote *An Answer from Limbo*, he had begun to feel that the identity of the novelist was again too knowable a role and altogether too like the predictable characters he knew in the literary scene in New York.

In a decade, he had proved to himself everything he needed to prove about his ability to write dramatic realism. He had constructed credible fictional representations of three cities and three different societies — Belfast, Montreal and New York. He had invented a range of characters, all of whom had drawn high critical praise. He had been recognized as a master of narrative technique. His power and stature as a novelist had been widely honoured, yet, for observers looking back over the subsequent three decades, it appears that the successful realistic urban novelist needed to enlarge his identity to include the romantic poet of miraculous places.

Moore's withdrawal to the sea coast has Wordsworthian echoes: "The world is too much with us; late and soon / Getting and spending, we lay waste our powers." Alienation from the impermanence of city life and from the self-conscious performance of expected roles led Moore towards his monk-like retreat in his California hermitage. His spiritual quest through memory and history, his moral preference for the truth and integrity of ordinary lives, and his anxious need to constantly renew and demonstrate his imaginative power are attitudes of the Wordsworthian poet and his Romantic confrères.

The first novel of his new life in California, *I Am Mary Dunne*, is a defiant and courageous assertion of the chameleon nature of the novelist's identity and of the risks that must be undertaken to prevent the imagination from calcifying. And yet the moral and psychic dangers in this way of life are only barely averted in that novel. Mary Dunne, and Fergus Fadden in the next California novel, are enclosed in their own minds, haunted by their own speculative memories and elusive sense of changing selves. The isolated protagonist in *The Great Victorian Collection*, imprisoned in a motel room by his Collection, loses all touch with the "commonplace" as he slides into madness and suicide. Moore's own isolation gave him more and more control over his social life and his work, yet it also removed him from the risky and painful encounters of everyday life central to common human experience.

*The Magician's Wife* is a remarkable recapitulation of many of the preoccupations that arose out of the dilemma in which the novelist found himself. Apart from its outer coverings of political parable, this time focused on colonialism, and of an historical novel set in Moore's favourite period, the mid-nineteenth century, it incorporates a personal statement on the ambiguous blessing of talent and the dubious gain of spending a lifetime cultivating it.

This novel of two journeys undertaken by magician Henri Lambert and his wife Emmeline in 1856, the first to the French court as the guests of the Emperor, and the second later in the year to Algiers and out into the Sahara Desert, is once more a novel of displacement, role-playing, and the craving for belief. Emmeline is the centre of consciousness in the narrative, which carries her into a moral and emotional limbo between two worlds; Henri is a supremely successful performer, a conjuror who uses scientific principles to beguile his naïve audiences, yet as a husband, he is absent —

egocentric, obsessive, and sexually impotent. These travellers grow increasingly estranged as Emmeline observes her husband's cynical collusion in the sham social rituals of the court and in the imperial policy of colonizing North Africa and converting the Arab tribes to French culture. While Henri sells out for the glory of France and for his own glory, Emmeline's estrangement from her own provincial world and its beliefs leads her to feel more "at home" in the desert.

Brian Moore is, of course, both Emmeline and Henri. The exiled and lonely consciousness of Emmeline is due not only to the geographical displacement or to the different racial and religious identity that she discovers among the Muslims in Algeria, but to her alienation from the deliberate and over-civilized social forms of French culture. The conventions, fashions, and roles that are required of those who aspire to a higher social status impose an inauthentic identity, one Henri finds easy to embrace for his personal identity has been subsumed into the public role of magician. Yet this playing of public roles eventually disgusts Emmeline, who ultimately refuses to collaborate with Henri in a scheme to subjugate the Algerians. While the woman's painfully won freedom rewards her with a sense of moral and emotional authenticity, her husband's desperate need to be in control, not only of the finer details of his performance but of the clockwork environment he creates in his home, ends finally in the loss of his power. His desire to obliterate the feelings of vulnerability which arise from chance events, such as illness and death, has made him a monomaniac who has lost all roots in the "commonplace" facts of life.

The character of Henri has been glimpsed earlier in Brendan Tierney in *Limbo*, in Maloney in *The Great Victorian Collection*, and in the Mangans in *The Mangan Inheritance*. In other guises, Emmeline has appeared earlier in *The Doctor's Wife*, and of course, she is also a cousin to Mary Dunne and Judith Hearne. These estranged characters are Moore's archetypal figures, and they represent the core dilemma of the novelist himself — a dilemma that he cannot and will not resolve, and yet is able to draw on as the hidden allegory at the heart of his work. The nineteenth-century inheritance of Moore incorporates, then, not only the moral coherence of his father's world, and the narrative line of dramatic realism, but also the self-consciousness of the alienated Romantic poet.

After the success of *Judith Hearne*, Moore had to go on writing; to stop would have been to risk becoming an utter failure like his character. Yet to rely only on words, which evoke states of feeling in one's readers, is to risk also the breakdown suffered by the Abbot of Muck in *Catholics* when he prays without believing. Brian Moore's discovery in writing *Judith Hearne* was that his own loneliness was inseparable from the activity of writing; that writing separates him and alienates him from other people. Yet write he must: his obsession is his belief, his one true faith. Luckily for his readers, he had the talent and the self-discipline to make the most of that obsession.

Moore has credited his discovery of Borges with the change of direction in his career in the early 1960s. Some readers believe that his breaking free from the realism of the early novels led him astray, and that nothing he wrote afterwards was as good as *Judith Hearne*, but he had already come to think of that first novel as a millstone. He had to break free to renew himself and to incorporate into his work a Yeatsian dimension as he had earlier incorporated Joyce.

Moore's accomplishment has been to register the impact of the forces of change in North America on many dimensions of the exiled self, from the social and psychological to the spiritual and metaphysical to the moral and historical. The sign of his ability to absorb and reflect such transformations is to be found not in the circumstances of his measured life but in the risks he took with the genres of fiction. This decision to adopt no particular style or genre as characteristically his own allowed him to search through all the possible resources of novel-writing and to blend many perspectives — from interior monologue to political parables, novels of suspense to satire and history, documentary to fantasy.

Rather than be guided by the limiting affiliations of national literatures or traditions — Irish, Canadian, or American — his fiction grew into an eclectic blend of all aspects of his own earlier experience. As a writer as exile, he meditated again and again on his experiences in all those places that he called his "emotional territories," and with time he found that he did not have to be limited by historical period or place. Living quietly in California, he became an international writer, and it is as such that his achievement will be evaluated: he is an Irish and a Canadian and an American novelist, but it is his ability to travel in imagination between these places and beyond them that is his talent and distinction. If in the first half of his life he exposed himself to recurring rituals of displacement, initiation, and bonding to new terrains, the second half quarries that "lived" life in a spirit of detachment and retreat.

One of the many surprises I experienced as I worked was the discovery of *The Closing Ritual*, a two-act play written as Moore was recovering from his illness of 1977–78. Set in the Père Lachaise cemetery in Paris, this variation on the deep-seated preoccupation of the doctor and nurse's son with death and the ultimate survival of his work is a black comedy reminiscent of *Waiting for Godot*.

In a park-like space in the cemetery, four daily habitués of the park come and go. A fifth character, Stranger, is a source of grim comedy about cemeteries; he is knowledgeable about their grotesque history in earlier centuries, and his recalling that "those who forget history are condemned to repeat it," implies that the history that everyone forgets is that everyone is mortal.

The Stranger is gradually revealed to be a doctor. Yet he is a doctor with a difference, and the practice of medicine, the profession that had guiltily haunted Moore throughout his working life, is portrayed in a most curious light. Rather than wish to keep people alive and healthy, he wishes to ease them into a peaceful death. When the young writer Daniel has a heart attack, the doctor cares for him by helping him to die. He persuades Daniel that this is a natural end, the outcome he has always wanted. Death, like alcohol, is imagined as a kind of anaesthetic. But Daniel is not convinced and struggles to the end against the dark arguments of his grotesque guardian.

In spite of much black comedy, it is obvious why this grim play did not make it to the Broadway stage. It is a play of Moore's recovery from a severe illness, yet it is also a meditation on a long-standing theme. The wild invention here, the enduring faith in the continuing performance of the artist, is a model of an attitude to life itself first touched on in *Judith Hearne*. "Everybody thought Faulkner was corny when he said in his Nobel Prize speech, 'I write about man's capacity to endure,' but I thought that was quite a moving thing to say," Moore has stated. The endurance of the artist himself is not an inconsiderable achievement for it is an affirmation of the spirit of survival in the face of difficulty and mortality.

In *The Closing Ritual*, the Professor guides visitors to the graves of people who had been models for Proust's characters in *À la recherche du temps perdu*. His declaration of the theme of the novel seems to be closer to the theme of the Professor's own life than to Proust's work. His image of the subservience of human desires to the inexorable passage of time reflects an aspect of Proust, and an aspect of Beckett, and, perhaps, even of Moore himself, yet all three writers are much larger in their vision of life and death than is the Professor.

Brian Moore's work is not to be evaluated by the measure of Proust or Samuel Beckett, although he felt a kinship to both of them. Like them, his work includes a life-long preoccupation with the paradoxes of the storytelling self, yet he is less an avant-garde modernist or post-modernist than he is a Victorian novelist recording an anguished response to what he imagines as the moral and spiritual estrangement of the century. The ideal images of "complete integrity and truthfulness" that he associated with his

Uncle John and his own father, eventually, are the fulcrum for the images of loneliness, dissociation, and estrangement evoked by the novels.

While individual novels in the long career of novel-writing touch on issues close to the news, and are easy to recognize as dilemmas of our time, it is the whole corpus of his work that constitutes Moore's world. The restless, probing, dissatisfied imagination that underlies the poised and finished narratives is at the heart of that world. The dissatisfaction, the inability to defer or to cease writing fictions, registers the quality of Moore's life, that dubious pilgrimage in search of immortality. In *The Closing Ritual*, the Stranger mocks Daniel's thought that there is such a thing as immortality. He urges him to accept that he has already passed the turning point in his life, that he has missed the tide that "leads on to fortune."

The shape of Brian Moore's life is clear; there is no tide that comes and passes by: it is forever brimming and withdrawing and returning once more. He chose to be by the ocean, from Portstewart to Connemara, from Amagansett to Malibu, and then to Nova Scotia. In novel after novel he came to breast that tide, forever alert to the possibilities of the new wave that may carry him on to fortune.

# NOTES

In these notes, I have quoted from the following editions of novels by Brian Moore; titles are abbreviated as indicated.

*Judith Hearne.* London: Deutsch, 1955. (JH)

*The Feast of Lupercal.* Boston: Little, Brown, 1957. (FL)

*The Luck of Ginger Coffey.* Toronto: New Canadian Library, 1972. (LGC)

*An Answer from Limbo.* New York: Dell, 1963. (AFL)

*The Emperor of Ice Cream.* Toronto: McClelland and Stewart, 1965. (EIC)

*I Am Mary Dunne.* New York: Viking, 1968. (MD)

*Fergus.* London: Penguin, 1977. (F)

*The Revolution Script.* New York: Pocket Books, 1972, rpt. 1973. (RS)

*Catholics.* New York: Pocket Books, 1973. (C)

*The Great Victorian Collection.* New York: Ballantine, 1976. (GVC)

*The Doctor's Wife.* Toronto: McClelland and Stewart, 1976. (DW)

*The Mangan Inheritance.* Toronto: Penguin, 1980. (MI)

*The Temptation of Eileen Hughes.* New York: Avon, 1982. (TEH)

*Cold Heaven.* New York: Holt, Rinehart and Winston, 1983. (CH)

*Black Robe.* Toronto: Penguin, 1987. (BR)

*The Colour of Blood.* Toronto: McClelland and Stewart, 1987. (CB)

*Lies of Silence.* London: Arrow, 1991. (LS)

*No Other Life.* Toronto: Vintage, 1994. (NOL)

*The Statement.* Toronto: Knopf, 1995. (S)

I have also used abbreviations as follows:

BM   Brian Moore
GG   Graham Greene
MR   Mordecai Richler
JMcC Jack McClelland
WW   William Weintraub
BF   Brian Friel
DS   Denis Sampson

References to drafts, notes, typescripts, etc. in the Brian Moore papers in the Special Collections Division, University of Calgary Library, will be identified according to *The Brian Moore Papers, First Accession and Second Accession: An Inventory of the Archive at the University of Calgary Libraries*, compiled by Marlys Chevrefils, Jean F. Tenner, and Apollonia Steele (Calgary: University of Calgary Press, 1987) as simply "Calgary 0.0.0." Similarly, references to letters in the McClelland and Stewart papers, William Ready Division of Archives and Research Collections, McMaster University Library, are indicated simply as, for instance, "McMaster Box 44." Letters to John Vachon have been provided by Ann Vachon.

I have relied on many interviews with Brian Moore, and after the initial identification and date of publication, references will be cited as "to (interviewer)" unless otherwise indicated.

Also, I cite the full publishing information for books and articles, etc., in the first reference. Later references will be cited by title and page number only. I have dispensed with p. and pp. for page references.

## The Opening Scene

"Imagination and Experience," in Clare Boylan, editor, *The Agony and the Ego: The Art and Strategy of Fiction Writing Explored*. London: Penguin, 1993, 47–54.

"There is no point," quoted by BM in a tribute to GG, "Witness, Judge, Mentor," *Adam International Review* 446–48 (1984), 16–17.

"treats the novel as a tamer," GG, letter to Aaron Asher, quoted by BM in letter to JMcC, 25 March 1975. McMaster Box 90.

"The reader instantly forgets," unpublished interview with DS, October 1994.

"Once upon a time," review of Marie-Claire Blais, *St. Lawrence Blues*, *National Observer*, 2 November 1974.

"beyond all self-recognition," AFL 288.

## 1. The Victorian Inheritance

"English soldiers," "Beginnings," *Today*, 11 October 1980, 3.

"'moderate in politics' (nationalist) and 'extreme in religion' (Catholic)" "BM: Biographical Note" (prepared for Andre Deutsch in 1954).

Calgary 31.1.1.

"For the novelist, the door closes," "BM: The Tragic Vein of the Ordinary" (Conversation with Donald Cameron, 16 November 1971). Donald Cameron, editor, *Conversations with Canadian Novelists 2.* Toronto: Macmillan, 1973, 69.

"Our life," "Beginnings," 3.

"Once it was one of six houses," "The Writer as Exile," a talk delivered at York University, 3 November 1976. *Canadian Journal of Irish Studies*, 2:2 (1976), 12.

"Anyone who had that kind," Ray Comiskey, "Moore's Almanac." *Irish Times*, 1 November 1983.

"I was brought up," "girls hired by my mother," and "those were the days," "Beginnings," 3.

"In a curious way, they are more honest," BM in conversation with Rosemary Hartill. Rosemary Hartill, *Writers Revealed: Eight Contemporary Novelists Talk about Faith, Religion and God*. New York: Peter Bedrick, 1989, 137.

"have the power of incorporating," Conor Cruise O'Brien, *Maria Cross: Imaginative Patterns in a Group of Catholic Writers*. London: Burns and Oates, 1954, rpt. 1963, 87.

"the O'Rawes," Michael Tierney, *Eoin MacNeill: Scholar and Man of Action, 1867–1945*. Oxford: Clarendon Press, 1981, 43.

On grandfather's conversion: "He changed his religion for reasons I can't understand, because he must have lost most of his practice," to Hartill, 134.

"flowery style," to DS.

"gained numerous scholastic distinctions," *Irish News*, 3 March 1942.

"a real countrywoman," and "I have these two Irish strains," "Beginnings," 3.

"she had a sense of humour," to DS; see Marie Crowe, "Moore Gets Better," *Social and Personal*, November 1983.

For Eoin MacNeill, see Tierney, *Eoin MacNeill*; see also F. X. Martin and F. J. Byrne, editors, *The Scholar Revolutionary: Eoin MacNeill,*

*1867–1945*. Shannon: Irish University Press, 1973.

"If I left Ireland," and "It is, perhaps, this feeling," "A View from Across the Water," written and narrated by BM for BBC television, filmed in September/October 1979, broadcast 4 March 1980. Typescript, Calgary 32.

Mother as social inferior: see interview with Hallvard Dahlie, 12 June 1967, *Tamarack Review*, 46, Winter 1968, 8.

"My mother seemed to be more in sync with me," to DS.

"perhaps there's something feminine in my character," "the fact of the history of a life," and "one of the things I tried to show," to Rochelle Girson, "Profile of Brian Moore," *Saturday Review*, 13 October 1962, 20.

"Women live in a personal world," to Hartill, 137.

"Anger and bitterness," "Imagination and Experience," 53.

"Parents form the grammar," *The Lonely Passion of BM*, a profile by the National Film Board of Canada, filmed in late 1985, released in 1986. BM also used the expression "grammar of emotions" earlier in *Fergus*.

## 2. Vocations and Roles

"I think he meant," "The Writer as Exile," 12.

"I'm sorry that I can't," "BM in Conversation with Tom Adair," *Linen Hall Review* 2:4, Winter 1985, 4.

"REMEMBER 1690," "Bloody Ulster: An Irishman's Lament." *Atlantic Monthly*, September 1970, 59–60.

"My father, in an infrequent traverse," "Bloody Ulster," 59.

"My father was an omnivorous reader," Richard B. Sale, "An Interview with BM," 13 July 1967. *Studies in the Novel* (Spring 1969), 68.

"unseen human being," review of *St. Lawrence Blues*.

"surrogate life," "Imagination and Experience," 54.

On the importance of the sea: "I live on the sea now, I think, because every summer, my father always took a house for a month at some Irish seaside place," to Hartill, 135.

"Donegal is an extremely wild and rocky-looking place," "Beginnings," 3.

"the most unassuming of men," "cold and realistic," and "a stage upon which they might," review of Michael Tierney, *Eoin MacNeill. Times Literary Supplement,* 31 July 1981, 869.

"I started going to Confession," to Adair, 1985, 4.

"In the beginning was the word," "A Vocation," *Tamarack Review,* 1 (1956), 18.

"I wrote that little story," to Adair, 1985, 4.

"There was Sin," "A Vocation," 19.

"the headmaster called me in," to Sale, 68.

"I discovered," to Sale, 68.

"I had nightmares," John Wilson Foster, "Q & A with BM." *Irish Literary Supplement,* Fall 1985, 45.

"I used to say that my secondary school," to Hartill, 131–32.

"As a child," "Preliminary Pages For a Work of Revenge," *The Dolmen Miscellany of Irish Writing,* editors Thomas Kinsella and John Montague. Dublin: Dolmen, 1962. rpt in BM, *Two Stories.* Northridge, California: Santa Susana Press, 1978, 13–15. An abbreviated version of this episode also appears in AFL, 6–7, as a recollection of Brendan Tierney.

"A six-year-old boy says," "The Expatriate Writer," *Antigonish Review,* 17, Spring 1974, 27–28. This passage appeared previously in AFL, 26, in a recollection of his childhood by Brendan Tierney.

"I would always read," to Sale, 68–69.

"You must trust the children," Hermione Lee, "Profile of BM," *Independent on Sunday,* 14 February 1993, 24.

"father went to the school," and "in some ineluctable way," review of *Eoin MacNeill.*

"While I disliked Catholicism," to Dahlie, 20–21.

## 3. A Youth of the Thirties

"Sweating green walls," FL, 162.

"a failure in life," EIC, 119.

"I was very good at some subjects," to Dahlie, 8.

"I was good at most subjects," to Adair, 1985, 4–5.

Spanish Civil War: "I grew up at the time of the Spanish Civil War. I was about seventeen at the time, and I thought my father was wrong, very much as Gavin thought his father was wrong," to Dahlie, 9–10.

"The left-wing thing was in the air," to Adair, 1985, 5.

"The Irish question," to Dahlie, 9–10.

"My early friends were," to Foster, 44.

Theatre in Belfast: see Sam Hanna Bell, *The Theatre in Ulster: A Survey of the dramatic movement in Ulster from 1902 to the present day*. Dublin: Gill and Macmillan, 1972.

"At seventeen I met a much older man," to Sale, 69.

"What happened was," BM in conversation with John Graham, 1970. John Graham, *The Writer's Voice: Conversations with Contemporary Writers*. New York: Morrow, 1973, 57–58.

"strange how quickly," EIC, 19.

"Can ye stick it?" "The People of Belfast," *Holiday*, February 1964, 58–59.

"because the Ulsterman," to DS.

"I will arise and go now," to DS.

"In 1939 when I was eighteen," "Old Father, Old Artificer," *Irish University Review*, 12:1 (1982), 13–14.

"the story of one's early life," to Sale, 71.

"I'm absolutely convinced," *Lonely Passion of BM*.

## 4. Leaving Home

"Nothing would change," and following quotations in three paragraphs EIC, 135–36; 6; 119; 117, and 191–92.

For the events of April/May 1941, see *Bombs on Belfast: The Blitz 1941*, a "camera record" first published by the *Belfast Telegraph*, 1941, rpt. Belfast: Pretani Press, 1984. Introduction by Christopher D. McGimpsey.

"I found myself being punched," to Graham, 53.

"The city mortuary," *Bombs on Belfast*, xii.

"his heroic work," *Irish News* (Belfast), 3 March 1942. Tribute written by a colleague, Dr. F. McSorley.

"My father, who was pro-German," to Graham, 55.

"My father died when I was eighteen," *Lonely Passion of BM*.

On James Moore: obituary notices and tributes. *Irish News*, 2, 3, and 4 March 1942.

"He believed totally," to Dahlie, 7.

"Somehow that feeling," to Foster, 45.

"How does a person," "The Expatriate Writer," 28.

"I sat among the real emigrants," "The Expatriate Writer," 28–29.

### 5. War and Wanderlust

"I was terribly excited," to Dahlie, 11.

"In Europe I had been a spectator," "The Expatriate Writer," 30.

"disjointed, strange life," to Dahlie, 11.

"I was suddenly projected," and "gave me a sort of confidence," Hubert de Santana, "Who is BM?" *Books in Canada*, October 1977, 5.

"Daddy would have supported Pétain, "de Valera," "The Allies," and "the hero become the stooge," "BM talks to Eileen Battersby," *Irish Times*, 12 October 1995, 13.

"emotional territory" to Adair, 1985, 6.

"I have a French cast of mind," to Dahlie, 28.

"lost generation," "The Crazy Boatloads," review of Malcolm Cowley, *Exile's Return. The Spectator*, 29 September 1961, 430.

"Sometimes I'd feel unhappy," "The Writer as Exile," 8.

"When the war ended," to Dahlie, 11.

"Over six million had died," *UNRRA: The History of the United Nations Relief and Rehabilitation Administration*, 3 vols. New York: Columbia University Press, 1950, Vol. 1, 201.

"Unlike cities in Western Europe" and quotations in following paragraphs *Poland 1946: The Photographs and Letters of John Vachon*. Edited by Ann Vachon. Introduced by BM. Washington, D.C.: Smithsonian, xiii–xvii.

"The two articles," the first article, on the disappearance of Stanislaw Mickolajczyk, is dated Warsaw, Nov 1st [1947], and the second, on the role of the Catholic Church, Nov 14 [1947]. Typescripts in Calgary: 31.46.2. and 31.46.2.

travelling around Europe, to Adair, 1985, 5.

"I believe in a real world," to Sale, 76.

"I had lived abroad," "The Writer as Exile," 10.

### 6. Settling in Montreal

"We were among the first post-war emigrants," "The Writer as Exile," 9.

"When I came to Canada," to DS.

"Canada. Cruel landscape," MI, 16.

"A baby spot," "A Fresh Look at Montreal," *Holiday*, September 1959, 50–51.

"The Montréal of many pleasures," see WW, *City Unique: Montreal Days and Nights in the 1940s and '50s*. Toronto: McClelland and Stewart, 1996.

"He was enterprising," tribute to BM by WW, Harbourfront International Festival of Authors. Toronto, October 13, 1994.

"a crash course on North American life," Adrian Waller, "BM Comes Home," *Gazette*, 9 January 1971.

"In the 1950s, . . ." unpublished interview with Charles Foran, Spring 1993.

"You won't get your name," quoted in Sandra Djwa, *The Politics of the Imagination: A Life of F.R. Scott*. Toronto: McClelland and Stewart, 1987, 222.

"I am passing a reposing day," Letter to WW, undated (Spring 1951?), quoted in tribute at Harbourfront, 1994.

"his ship to come in," LGC, 3.

"The discipline of newspaper work," Brian Cahill, "How Novelist Moore Didn't Start," *Gazette*, 30 August 1955.

"His supporters bribed," to Foran, to Spring 1993.

the de Bernonville case: see WW, *City Unique*, 258–61.

Paris was the post-war city, see MR, "A Sense of the Ridiculous: Paris, 1951 and After." *New American Review*, 4, August 1968, 114–34.

"a wonderfully rambunctious," WW to DS.

"whole damn priesthood," AFL, 125.

"In 1955, he reported," biographical note prepared for Atlantic/Little, Brown. Calgary 31.1.1.

"When will we swap," letter to MR, 21 July 1954. Calgary 36.9.19.

"This is in fact the only place," interview with Brenda Zosky. *Gazette*, 14 September 1983.

"Immigrants are people," "What Do They Think of Canada?" *Weekend*, 16 May 1953, 9.

## 7. Formulas and Fantasies

"This is not because," and "Canada is a good place," to Cahill.

"The best-seller is the day-dream," Robert Fulford Interviews BM. *Tamarack Review*, 23, Spring 1962, 7.

"The novel tells a story," "Imagination and Experience," 54.

"When I wrote those stories," to Dahlie, 12–13.

"I hated detective stories," Tom Christie, "Q&A with BM," *Los Angeles Reader*, 2 September 1983.

"You Never Give Me Flowers," *Weekend*, 29 September 1951, 20.

"Richler remembers," conversation with DS.

"Imitate Hemmy," letter to MR, undated (September 1954?). Calgary 36.9.19.

"It just seems to me," letter to MR, undated (20 May 1955?). Calgary 36.9.19.

"ruthlessness, sheer goddamned ruthlessness," AFL, 44.

"In that first novel I discovered a subject," "The Writer as Exile," 10.

"I was hit by a motor-boat," and "I said, I don't have an eternal ticket," *Lonely Passion of BM*.

## 8. The Writing of *Judith Hearne*

"In my twenties," "Old Father, Old Artificer," 14.

"I made a very grave mistake," to Adair, 1985, 5.

"I had to exorcise Hemingway," "Old Father, Old Artificer," 15.

"I found myself writing," "The Expatriate Writer," 30.

these "*croyants*," letter to Seymour Lawrence, 21 September 1956. Calgary 31.1.4: "The system of education described in *Lupercal* is still the way most Irish Catholics are untaught in everything save cowardice, conformity and cruelty. This is, I feel, Ireland today — a place which has nothing in common with the stories of Frank O'Connor . . . and other old brogue writers, who, as *croyants*, always did subordinate their art to the demands of their faith."

"a new generation," letter to MR, 28 January 1959. Calgary 36.9.19: "All we need now is to get Mavis on the list with us and we three will be in tandem everyplace." Since all three had been published in London by Andre Deutsch, this is presumably a reference to finding the same Canadian or American publisher.

"On one occasion," 24 January 1955. Calgary 36.9.19: in these years, and with other correspondents besides Richler, he indulged his liking for role-playing by addressing his correspondent and signing himself with the names of many other writers.

"Mavisian." Calgary 31.48.10.

"a matter of style," to Fulford, 9.

"when . . . I quit my job," and "I wanted to write," "Old Father, Old Artificer," 15.

"I was trying to write short stories," to Adair, 1985, 5.

"I began to write about Belfast," "The Writer as Exile," 10.

"When he embarks," and "He walks," "Witness, Judge, Mentor," 16–17.

"To my surprise I discovered," Robert Sullivan, "BM: A Clinging Climate," *London Magazine*, December 1976/January 1977, 65–66.

"If, in a book like *Judith Hearne*," to Sullivan, 68.

"She was trapped," to Dahlie, 18.

"without knowing it," and "It touched," "Brian Moore: In Celebration of the Commonplace" in Bruce Meyer and Brian O'Riordan, *In Their Own Words: Interviews with Fourteen Canadian Novelists*. Toronto: Anansi, 1984, 183.

"It helped enormously," Richard T. Bray, "A Conversation with BM," *The Critic*, xxxv:1, Fall 1976, 46.

"I realized when I was writing it," to Bray, 48.

"That phrase popped into my head," to Bray, 46.

"Shoes shined," JH, 35.

"Fifteen dollars and three cents," LGC, 3.

"I was obsessed," to DS.

"It would be marvellous," to Dahlie, 16.

"round robin of interior monologues," "Old Father, Old Artificer," 15.

"I was lucky," to Cameron, 82.

"I studied *Buddenbrooks*." Calgary 31.7.2.

"Judith Hearne believes," to Cameron, 66.

"One of my beliefs in writing that book," to Bray, 43.

"The aunt's picture," to Bray, 47.

"I never know what the ending is," to Cameron, 75.

"Ordinariness is one of my main concerns," to Cameron, 79.

## 9. Success

"after some little delay," to Fulford, 5.

"*Miss Hearne* is perhaps a joyless book," Letter to Andre Deutsch, 18 June 1954. Calgary 31.1.1.

"quite buoyed up," to Fulford, 5.

"At times it seems to me," MR, *New American Review*, 122–23.

"an almost classic example," Oliver Edwards, *Times*, 19 May 1955, 13.

"I would have liked," letter from Eileen Moore, 2 June 1955. Calgary 31.1.3.

"I felt that in *Judith Hearne*," to Adair, 1985, 6.

"an absolutely invented character," to Dahlie, 17.

"moment of love," this was the title given to paperback reprints of the novel in England.

"I saw then and I see their dilemmas now," to Sullivan, 66.

"The interesting thing about Devine," to Dahlie, 17.

"I tried to use him to show," to Dahlie, 18.

"When I began to write," and "In the end," "Thoughts on finishing first draft of DEVINE." Calgary 31.6.1.

"In *Lupercal*, I saw some of the mistakes," to Dahlie, 16.

"I felt it was a less artificial plot," to Dahlie, 16–17.

"I've been accused," to Sale, 80.

"the ghost of Joyce," "Old Father, Old Artificer," 15.

"fizzle — he couldn't change," to Bray, 44.

"the hero gets on a boat," to Sale, 72.

"You really are my best critic," letter to Diana Athill, 10 February 1957. Calgary 31.1.4.

"Saint Michan's is an imaginary college." Calgary 31.12.3.

"This boy is merely biting," to Dahlie, 9.

"I had nightmares," *Lonely Passion of BM*.

## 10. Uprooting

"I have just finished," GG, letter to Seymour Lawrence, quoted by Lawrence in letter to BM, 13 June 1957. Calgary 31.1.5.

"The attention," the mutual admiration of GG and BM for each other's work led to a meeting in April 1956, when GG was passing through

Montreal. They may have met on one other occasion in Montreal in October 1957. See BM's letter to MR 16 September 1957. Calgary 36.9.20.

"What do you really think," letter to MR, undated (July 1956?). Calgary 36.9.19.

"ten-year test," this criterion, often recalled by BM, was first formulated by Cyril Connolly in *Enemies of Promise*. BM's interest in Connolly's work is further indicated by the following: "Autumn is here and now is the time for all good men to read *The Unquiet Grave* by Cyril Connolly. I reread it the other day for the third time. This is a book that suits me very much." Letter to John Vachon, 8 September (1955?).

"*La Nausée, L'Etranger* only touch the first belief," "Development of this," and "the *croyant*'s wish," Commonplace Book. Calgary 31.6.1.

"I fled Him, down the nights and down the days," Francis Thompson, "The Hound of Heaven," ll. 1–4. *The Norton Anthology of English Literature*. New York: W.W.Norton, 1986. Fifth Edition, Vol. 2, 1710.

"The foregoing," and "The small things," Commonplace Book. Calgary 31.6.1.

"Wouldn't it be terrible," Séan Moore to DS.

"Why had she cared more for them," "Grieve for the Dear Departed," *Atlantic Monthly*, August 1959, 46.

"Do you remember," NOL, 73.

"I remembered," AFL, 284–85.

"My old mother used to say," "Uncle T.," *Gentlemen's Quarterly*, November 1960, rpt. *Two Stories*.

"Mr. Weintraub and I," letter to MR, 16 September 1958. Calgary 36.9.19.

"Much worse," letter to MR, undated (September 1958?). Calgary 36.9.19.

"The doctor says," letter to MR, 1 October 1959. Calgary 36.9.19.

"this bloody novel," letter to MR, 28 January 1959. Calgary 36.9.19.

"At the end of the book," letter to MR, 9 February 1959. Calgary 36.9.19.

## 11. A Canadian Novelist in New York

"In my third novel," "Imagination and Experience," p. 53.

"The Irish drifter of no past," and "Hero arrives at camp." Calgary 31.12.1.

"A middle-aged man," etc. Calgary 31.12.1 and Calgary 31.14.1.

"A part of him is an amalgam," to Fulford, 17.

"The covering up of weakness." Calgary 31.12.1.

"Evelyn Waugh," Goodridge MacDonald, "BM at Work on Another Novel," *Gazette*, 31 March 1962.

"there were a lot of writers," Henry Fenwick, "The Luck of BM," *Radio Times*, 1 March 1980.

"Life in New York is great," letter from Jacqueline Moore to MR, 1 February 1960. Calgary 36.9.20.

"I suppose I am attracted," "both provincial societies," and "This book was a first-person novel," to Fulford, 9–10.

"galley slaves," LGC, 72.

"a horse coloured Canada," LGC, 11.

"Money is the Canadian way," LGC, 70.

"the filmed America no longer seemed true," LGC, 171.

"I've always been afraid," to Sale, 73.

"I don't think anybody's a dolt," to Fulford, 15.

"Yes, if we're talking," to Dahlie, 19.

"He is unrealistic," to Sale, 74.

"all in a sense losers," to Sale, 75.

"I did want to break," to Fulford, 14.

"I felt the ending," and "I wanted the ending," to Fulford, 18.

"the new generation," Robert Weaver, editor, *Ten for Wednesday Night*. Toronto: McClelland and Stewart, 1961, xvii.

"Ginger Coffey is out of Leopold Bloom," Jack Ludwig, "A Mirror of Moore," *Canadian Literature*, 7, Winter 1961, 21.

## 12. An American Novelist in London

"Some of the best young writers," to Fulford, 14.

"Philip Roth is my neighbour," letter to MR, 16 September 1959. Calgary 36.9.19.

"The American writer," Philip Roth, "Writing American Fiction," *Reading Myself and Others*. New York: Penguin, 1985, 120–21.

"fascinating and controversial essays," "McCarthy shrewdly," and "Our world has become so irreal," review of Mary McCarthy's *On the Contrary, Spectator*, 27 July 1962, 119.

"My fiction begins to move," to Cameron, 67.

"I have never been a member," to Dahlie, 24.

"I think with Flaubert," letter to MR, 9 February 1959. Calgary 36.9.19.

"I lived in Greenwich Village," to Dahlie, 19–20.

"When I went to live," to Cameron, 67.

"When does youth end?" Calgary 31.17.2.

"That's a problem," to Sullivan, 67.

"We have to get out of Bleak House," and "I am very hopeful," letter to MR, 30 June 1960. Calgary 36.9.19.

"First draft over," note by BM. Calgary 31.17.2.

"I've always felt it was," to Dahlie, 27.

"AFL is about three characters," to Sale, 79–80.

"As for Brendan Tierney," to Sale, 75.

"It is a book about ambition," "to juxtapose people," and "All fiction is a dramatization," to Girson, 20.

"certifiable witch," interview with Dusty Vineberg, *Montreal Star*, 30 November 1962.

"She was a more sophisticated woman," and "We can't go back to being our parents — we cannot will faith," to Dahlie, 20–21.

"One of the things I tried," to Girson, 20.

"If Irish Catholicism is destructive," to Dahlie, 21.

"When you're a writer," to Girson, 20.

"He [Brendan] sees his success." Calgary 31.17.2.

"Indifference, it seems," AFL, 282–85.

"I think of myself as a Canadian," to MacDonald.

"Limbo is the modern condition," "America, not Russia," and "The art [Brendan Tierney] attempts to practice." Calgary 31.17.2

"I thought when I finished," to Dahlie, 27.

"Moore has the great gift," Granville Hicks, "Asphalt is a Bitter Soil." *Saturday Review*, 13 October 1962, 47.

"I think I am the first Irish-born writer," to Graham, 73.

"I think you are wise," letter to MR, 8 February 1963. Calgary 36.9.19.

## 13. Radical Individual Decisions

"Sour about the book world," letter to MR, 10 February 1964. Calgary 36.9.19.

"what poetry is today," to Dahlie, 26.

"In the careers of certain writers," "The Quare Fellow Scapa-flowed." Review of Brendan Behan, *The Scarperer, Book Week: New York Herald Tribune*, 21 June 1964, 3.

"Few writers have the courage," and "radical individual decisions," review of *On the Contrary*, 119.

"after a year of commercial work," letter to MR, 12 August 1963. Calgary 36.9.19.

"on a book — a novel," letter to MR, 6 November 1963. Calgary 36.9.19.

"one of those worst selling novels," letter to MR, 10 February 1964. Calgary 36.9.19.

"plodding away intermittently," letter to MR, 27 July 1964. Calgary 36.9.19.

"It has been at the back of my mind," and "The events of those terrible nights," letter to Rory Fitzpatrick, 23 January 1966. Calgary 31.2.3.

"I saw how [Borges] created," "Imagination and Experience," 53.

"Horrors but very real," Commonplace Book. Note written in February 1956, on reading Isaac Babel's *Collected Stories*. Calgary 31.6.1.

"if I'd tried to handle it," to Graham, 53.

"The constant companion is death," Commonplace Book. Calgary 36.6.1.

"Yeats said that you can only enjoy life," to Dahlie, 29.

"villains are what we identify with enormously," to Sale, 76.

"War was freedom," EIC, 7.

"echoing the mysterious judgement," EIC, 119.

"The looking-glass room," EIC, 248.

"I had built up Mr. Burke," to Dahlie, 29.

"I think that life itself," to Sale, 80.

"The White Angel sat," EIC, 10.

"The alter ego in everyone," "Notes for an Unwritten Novel Circa 1959," Commonplace Book. Calgary 31.6.1. "Christie" refers to a criminal case reported in the news media.

"We underpeople usually congregate." Calgary 31.19.3.

"I am much happier now," to Dahlie, 29.

"an all alone and agonising time," letter to MR, undated (Spring 1964?). Calgary 36.9.19.

"The Russells," see JMcC/Russell correspondence in McMaster Box 54, and a small number of letters in the MR and BM papers at Calgary, although researchers are not allowed access to all letters.

"I could not bear the thought of life," Franklin Russell, *The Secret Islands*. Toronto: McClelland and Stewart, 1965, 233.

### Entr'acte: The Hall of Mirrors

"I had already written," see DS, "'Home, A Moscow of the Mind': BM's Transition to North America," *Colby Quarterly*, XXXI:1, March 1995, 46–54; "BM's Autobiographical Allegories of the Artist in Exile," in Robin Burns and Michael Kenneally, editors, *The Irish Abroad in Fact and Imagination*. Amsterdam: Rodopi, 1998; "BM and the Truth of Events," *Irish Literary Supplement*, Spring 1997, 11–12.

"Possible character," Commonplace Book. Calgary 31.6.1.

"Ann Vachon's memoir," "Afterword," *Poland 1946: The Photographs and Letters of John Vachon*, 157–71.

"My wife had jobs," Frank Shouldice, "Lonely Passion of BM," *Irish Independent*, 20 September 1997, 11.

## 14. Hollywood and Hitchcock

"I have to make this trip," letter to JMcC, 7 March 1965. McMaster Box 44.

"I *will* write about Wonderland," letter to Diana Athill, 1 April 1965. McMaster Box 44.

"They all love the script now," letter to MR, 11 October 1963. Calgary 36.9.19.

"The difference between," quoted by BM in Commonplace Book. Calgary 31.6.1.

"something else," letter to MR, 11 October 1963. Calgary 36.9.19.

"remains the work of the person," "I wrote an ending which was clear," and "make a lot of money." Calgary 49.24.14.

"What would be the attitude of a young woman," BM, "Untitled Original Espionage Story Subject by Alfred J. Hitchcock." Calgary 31.4.1.

"the cordiality and mutual understanding," Donald Spoto, *The Dark Side of Genius: The Life of Alfred Hitchcock*. Boston: Little, Brown, 1983, 487.

"he never had to explain to me," "I found him thoroughly engaging and sensible," and "very much against my own judgement," BM to Donald Spoto, 20 February 1982, quoted in *The Life of Alfred Hitchcock*, 487.

"This type of story," BM, "Untitled Original Espionage Story." Calgary 31.4.1.

"a great house on top of a canyon," letter to JMcC, 22 March 1965. McMaster Box 44.

"When I first worked with Hitchcock," *Lonely Passion of BM*.

"The problem I had with Hitchcock," to Meyer and O'Riordan, 180.

"He taught me things about films," *Lonely Passion of BM*.

"the importance of research," Marke Andrews, "BM: Ireland's Runaway Rebel Son," *Vancouver Sun*, 9 June 1990, D17.

"Flashbacks should be small digressions," to Meyer and O'Riordan, 179.

"*l'univers Hitchcockian*," "*Hitchcock vu par son scénariste*," *Cahiers du cinéma*, 175, February 1966, 14.

"offered me an enormous contract," *Lonely Passion of BM*.

"I realized that taking criticism or confronting disagreement," quoted in *The Life of Alfred Hitchcock*, 489.

"I've finished my Hitchcockian labours," letter to JMcC, 18 September 1965. McMaster Box 44.

"Jean and I just took a week off," and "As an old ulcer man," letter to JMcC, 30 September 1965. McMaster Box 44.

"As I've told you before," letter to Hitchcock, 2 September 1965. Calgary 31.4.1.

"vegetating and edging around," letter to MR, 1 September 1965. Calgary 36.9.19.

## 15. Writer as Exile

"It occurs to me," and "You can't generalize." Calgary 31.21.3.

"Descartes said 'I think, therefore I am,'" to Graham, 62.

"as we wait to get on with our lives," letter to MR, 23 June 1966. Calgary 36.9.19.

"This life I live isn't believable," MD, 95.

"I am a changeling who has changed too often," MD, 115.

"Months just slip away," postcard to MR, January 1966. Calgary 36.9.19.

"For all that, we enjoy," letter to MR, 28 February 1966. Calgary 36.9.19.

"We're in a shack," letter to MR, 10 August 1966. Calgary 36.9.19.

"Have been back to go," letter to MR, 23 June 1966. Calgary 36.9.19.

"I'm more pleased than ever," letter to MR, 23 June 1966. Calgary 36.9.19.

"we are at the moment angsting," letter to MR, September 1966. Calgary 36.9.19.

"I had hoped it would be in some sense a research," "A Woman of No Identity." Calgary 31.21.3.

"the found thing, the creation of a self," and "a chronicle of a woman's moods." Calgary 32.21.1.

"my new book was written," to Dahlie, 29.

"Is her happiness the other side of the coin," Note on "A Woman of No Identity." Calgary 31.21.3.

epigraph to the novel, W. B. Yeats, "Among School Children," *Collected Poems*. London: Macmillan, 1950, 245.

"She might begin to tell," Notes for "A Woman of No Identity." Calgary 31.21.1.

"When I wrote," "Brian Moore talks to Michael Paul Gallagher," *Hibernia*, 10 October 1969, 18.

"One morning some years ago," and "I am Mary Dunne," Typescript "BM Tells About *I Am Mary Dunne*," prepared for *Literary Guild Magazine*. Calgary 31.2.5.

"The poet, like God, is a creator of hallucinations," Borges, quoted in Commonplace Book. Calgary 31.6.1.

"to catch in a book the inconsequences," Notes for "A Woman of No Identity." Calgary 31.21.3.

"I couldn't remember my name," MD, 114.

"In what way do women lose their identities," notes for "A Woman of No Identity." Calgary 31.21.3.

"I'd like to fuck you, baby," MD, 13.

"in modern marriage," "In love or not in love," and "I think, therefore I am: the fear," notes for "A Woman of No Identity." Calgary 31.21.3.

"My mother died yest or was it today" Camus, quoted in notes for "A Woman of No Identity." Calgary 31.21.3.

"even the childbearing experience was denied her," notes for "A Woman of No Identity." Calgary 31.21.3.

"It's always a search for tone," to Cameron.

"I have felt in the short time," letter to JMcC, June 1967, McMaster, Box 44.

"When I was with Jean in Nova Scotia," letter to JMcC, 8 November 1967. Calgary 31.2.5.

"the pre-menstrual tension," to Graham, 59.

"At lunch Janice starts," "Are we what people remember," "other people conspire," "her fear (*accidie*) no less," and "religion is part of the identity loss," notes for "A Woman of No Identity." Calgary 31.21.3.

"the ex-Calvinist-Catholic." Calgary 31.21.1.

"Ideally, I'd like it," to Dahlie, 23.

"That's the book I've enjoyed," and "a first-rate book," to Dahlie, 23.

"the most interesting," to Sale, 77.

"I started my current book," to Dahlie, 25.

"It's what writers call," to Graham, 63.

"I have finished a first draft," letter to MR, 7 March 1967. Calgary 36.9.19.

"He has decided to come out," letter to MR, 8 November 1967. Calgary 36.9.19.

"relieved and relaxed," letter to MR, 8 November 1967. Calgary 36.9.19.

## 16. California Dreamin'

"*Le musée imaginaire* symbolizes," notes from an article on Malraux by Maurice Blanchot. Calgary 31.24.1.

"The character of Preliminary Pages." Calgary 31.24.2.

"The novel as memoir: reminiscences of parents." Calgary 31.21.1.

"He starts his diary in some way to record." Calgary 31.24.2.

"I don't know why, but when I sat down." Calgary 31.24.4.

"The buildings and landscapes," "Notes for an article about Los Angeles." Calgary 31.24.1.

"Los Angeles was an interesting location," F, 102.

"It's as though everything here," F, 103.

"there was seemingly no difference," F, 56.

"There is no there there," Gertrude Stein, quoted by BM to Foster, 45.

"My parents, now dead," "*Musée*: Parents." Calgary 31.24.2.

"I was trying to bring up," to Graham, 62.

"It is a trial: he is being judged," "November 1968: Note on Chapters I and II of Fergus novel." Calgary 31.24.3.

"The great problem," to Graham, 68.

"The sun shone as rain fell." Calgary 31.24.1.

"Hansel and Gretel playhouse," F, 93–94.

"As a Catholic," F, 46–47.

"You took it, I mean your writing ability," F, 68.

"Appeals to father to help him." Calgary 31.24.3.

"The trial: reprieved by memory," and "Patients, terminal, sometimes say." Calgary 31.24.2.

"pain so intense that he lost his vision," F, 167.

"In the east, dawn came up," F, 171.

"Periods in the so called 'creative' life," "Cultivate good rhythm," and "Idea for a story on a monastery." Calgary 31.31.2.

"For me the weakness," Julian Moynahan, review of *Fergus*, *New York Times Book Review*, 27 September 1970, 4.

"Was Fergus weakness." Calgary 31.31.1.

"In a peculiar sense," to Cameron, 72.

### 17. Revolutionary Scripts

"It occurs to me that there is something sick," "and yet, this time," "The standard-bearers," "it must escalate," and "he fired down the street," "Bloody Ulster: An Irishman's Lament," 62.

"I was so curious," to Cameron, 70–71.

"When these extraordinary events," Prefatory Note, RS, iii.

"People always assume," to Cameron, 73.

"The other fictions I've written," to Cameron, 72–74.

"Fact has become so fictitious," to Cameron, 84.

"We, as writers, are losing sight," to Cameron, 75.

"What really captivates me," interview, *Globe and Mail*, early 1972.

"once capacity as spiritual adviser," letter to Michael Paul Gallagher, 30 June 1977. Calgary 49.4.1.

"I think the movement of the thing," letter from Seamus Heaney, 30 October 1980. Calgary 49.4.22.

"*Fergus* got an excellent press here," letter from BF, 14 April 1971. Calgary 31.4.11.

"I know this sounds un-Ulster," letter to BF, 18 June 1971. Calgary 31.4.11.

"We grow up dreaming." Calgary 31.29.3.

"It was a phenomenon," C, 13–18.

"The Church, Hartmann taught," C, 25–26.

"I find myself sympathetic," letter to Michael Paul Gallagher, 10 July 1971. Calgary 31.29.1.

"A visitor," Commonplace Book. Calgary 31.6.1.

"he realizes," letter to JMcC, 18 March 1972. Calgary 31.3.4.

"Since my adolescence I have never been," to Bray, 44.

"He was a kindly man," interview with Kenneth Bagnell, *Globe and Mail*, 11 October 1972.

"I'm not a Catholic," to Bagnell.

"What Berlin does not ask himself." Calgary 31.29.3.

## 18. American Apocalypse

"to congratulate you on F," letter from BF, 14 April 1971. Calgary 31.4.11.

"you sounded depressed," letter from BF, 10 June 1971. Calgary 31.4.11.

"I enjoyed writing it," letter to BF, 10 October 1971. Calgary 31.1.2.

"GVC is a paradigm," to Foster, 45.

"Sometimes I don't choose," letter to JMcC, 10 March 1974. Calgary 31.3.7.

"A dream I had," Commonplace Book. Calgary 31.6.1.

"I seem very pleased," letter to Aaron Asher, 1 June 1970. Calgary 31.2.7.

"Aug 1970 Now start 2nd part," Commonplace Book. Calgary 31.6.1.

"Again: make it a Paradigm of writing." Calgary 31.31.1.

"I wanted to write," letter to JMcC, 10 March 1974. Calgary 49.3.55.

"to go back." Calgary 31.31.2.

"I saw how he created," "Imagination and Experience," 53.

"In the novelist a kind of stupidity," Jacques Rivière, "The Adventure Novel," *Nouvelle revue française*, 1920, quoted in Commonplace Book. Calgary 31.6.1

"Sitting on the grey sands of Carmel." Calgary 31.31.5.

"I asked myself if my beliefs are sounder," AFL, 284.

"stared up at him," GVC, 72.

"Paradigm." Calgary 31.31.2.

"GVC was something," to Sullivan, 69.

"Delighted to learn," letter from BF, 26 December 1973. Calgary 49.3.81.

"Of course I would like," "It is the feeling," and "I have always been a loner," letter to DeWitt Henry, 25 November 1973. Calgary 31.4.7.

"I sent GVC back," letter to Aaron Asher, 26 January 1974. Calgary 31.3.7.

"Again I've not sent the book out," undated letter to Asher (February 1974?). Calgary 31.3.7.

"You sound a bit depressed," letter from BF, 25 August 1974. Calgary 49.3.81.

"I am genuinely concerned," letter from BF, 16 September 1974. Calgary 49.3.81.

## 19. Sex and Destiny

"was something I had to do," letter to DeWitt Henry, 25 November 1973. Calgary 31.4.7.

"Saw in the paper," letter from BF, 26 December 1973. Calgary 49.3.81.

"Everyman has a dream," Commonplace Book. Calgary 31.6.1.

Moore has said, see "A Compulsive Novelist: Terence de Vere White met BM," *The Irish Times*, 7 September 1977.

"I rewrite a lot," to de Santana, 6.

"as though he were not living," DW, 5.

"a chance at a new life." Calgary 31.37.1.

"because there is really no past," to Sullivan, 71.

"plunge the reader into the sea," to de Santana, 6.

"The character of Sheila Redden," to de Santana, 6.

"had a bad bout," letter to Diana Athill, 11 February 1975. Calgary 31.1.2.

"dull," to Cameron, 76.

"they threaten to condemn," letter to BF, 28 March 1975. Calgary 49.3.81.

"the last holdouts," letter to Derek Mahon, 17 January 1976. Calgary 49.4.51.

"this most idiosyncratic," Joan Didion, "Quiet Days in Malibu," *The White Album*. New York: Simon and Schuster, 209.

"I feel happy," letter to Tom Maschler, 20 November 1975. Calgary 31.3.8.

"I have a very Catholic attitude," to Cameron, 80.

"bird of passage," George Woodcock, *Odysseus Ever Returning: Essays on Canadian Writers and Writing*. Toronto: McClelland and Stewart, 1970.

"favourite living novelist," and "[Moore] treats the novel," GG to Aaron Asher, quoted by BM in letter to JMcC, 25 March 1975. McMaster Box 90.

"I was delighted with it," letter to Derek Mahon, 17 January 1976. Calgary 49.4.51.

"most talented Ulster contemporary," "English Fame and Irish Writers," *London Review of Books*, 20 November 1980, 6.

"I was delighted with your response," letter from BF, 26 May 1979. Calgary 49.3.81.

"filled with antiques," *People*, 26 October 1976, 62.

"Give my warmest love," letter from BF, 31 March 1977. Calgary 49.3.81

"One of the reasons," to DS.

"You know, of course," letter from BF, 29 June 1976. Calgary 49.3.81.

did not see his son during his adolescent years, to DS.

"a parent's knack," letter from Michael Moore, 1 November 1976. Calgary 49.4.68.

"A bit strange at first," letter from Michael Moore. 1 November 1976. Calgary 49.4.68.

"it might seem pornographic," to DS.

"Why does she leave him," "Even after 3 or 4 months," "Is her money," "Do not all of us sense," and "The nature of fiction" (Delmore Schwartz). Calgary 49.6.7.

"To isolate and define." Calgary 49.6.7.

"Remembered a true story." Calgary 49.24.16.

"What happened to me," to DS.

"a mad child," "I did not know," "It is a record," and "I never knew a father" (Montaigne), review of Josh Greenfeld, *A Place for Noah*, *Washington Post*, 16 April 1978.

**20. The Novel of Suspense**

"I discovered during that period," to Meyer and O'Riordan, 175.

"I think it's had a big effect," interview with Wendy Quarry, *Gazette*, 13 October 1979.

"metaphysical thrillers," "Imagination and Experience," 53.

"I have a certain skill," to Quarry.

"Once you decide on the form," interview with Charles Foran, *Varsity* (University of Toronto), October 1982.

"If you take an older writer," to Meyer and O'Riordan, 174.

"To read down this list," "Witness, Judge, Mentor," 17.

"I was so anxious (as usual)," undated letter to GG (January 1978?). Calgary 49.4.10.

"It's still three hours," letter from GG, 30 January 1978. Calgary 49.4.10.

"I think it has neither," letter from BF, 13 August 1980. Calgary 49.2.56.

"But if I left Ireland," and "Reality, real life," "A View from Across the Water."

"I'm irritated when I'm not treated," to Quarry.

"Canadians tend to ignore," interview with Ken Adachi, *Toronto Star*, 11 October 1980, F12.

"when the State of California," to Adachi.

"I have at the back of my mind," letter to Eilís Moore, 1 November 1979. Calgary 49.14.1.

"at the moment," letter to Eilís Moore, 23 November 1979. Calgary 49.14.1.

"realistic in technique" letter to Hallvard Dahlie, 28 March 1980. Calgary 49.3.55.

"suffering is exact," Philip Larkin. BM referred to the association of Larkin's and his work as "brilliant" — "I am an admirer of his poetry." Letter to Kerry McSweeney, 14 June 1981. Calgary 49.4.64.

"Desire isn't love," TEH, 76.

"I was thinking," TEH, 75.

"To my resurrection," MI, 53.

"As the mystic tends," Ortega y Gasset, *On Love*, quoted in notes. Calgary 49.10.1.

"Genius is not a gift," J. P. Sartre, quoted in notes. Calgary 49.10.1.

"it was as though he felt," TEH, 12.

"empty spaces," TEH, 50. Pascal's *pensée*, "The eternal silence of the infinite spaces terrifies me," was quoted as the epigraph to Frank O'Connor's study of the short story, *The Lonely Voice*.

"In TEH, I tried to return," Adele Freedman, "BM Sees Himself as a Literary Nomad," *Globe and Mail*, 1 July 1981.

"He is an original voice," "For those writers born," and "released on their own recognizance," review of John McGahern, *Getting Through, Detroit News*, 3 August 1980.

"There is an exhilarating lucky-dip," "English Fame and Irish Writers," 5.

"I like in novels to set," to Meyer and O'Riordan, 173.

"I think readers judge," to Freedman.

"I couldn't speak," to Comiskey.

"My new book," to Meyer and O'Riordan, 173

"I went to visit them," to Comiskey.

"As she looked at them," CH, 66.

"In America nothing lasts," see successive drafts from 1970, 1972, and 1981, in the sequence Calgary 49.14.5 to Calgary 49.14.12.

"Relevance of Stevens/Novalis." Calgary 49.14.1.

"We inherited the miraculous tradition," *Gazette*, 3 November 1983.

"I think what I'm trying to say," to Christie.

"The Cold Heaven," W. B. Yeats, *Collected Poems*, 140; see also "Anima Hominis," *Per Amica Silentia Luna*.

"Would people believe it," CH, 93.

"I knew this was a tough book," Garry Abrams, "Novelist Breaks Fictional Formulas," *Los Angeles Times*, 14 September 1983.

"It's Sister Anna's vision now," CH, 262–65.

"My style has been evolving," to Meyer and O'Riordan, 174.

"We enter his looking-glass world," (unpublished?) review of *Monsignor Quixote*. Calgary 49.24.11.

## 21. Hearts of Darkness

"You can't teach people," Marion McCormack, "BM Worries About Getting Published," *Gazette*, 11 October 1980.

"the only community," "It's an uncertain life," and "Each time he publishes a book," typescript of speech delivered at University of Toronto, undated (December 1982?). Calgary 49.24.15.

"It is easier than working," to Meyer and O'Riordan, 182.

"very good-looking, passionate," "is handsome," and "late thirties." Calgary 49.21.2.

"I am at present a great hero," letter to Tom Maschler, 31 January 1983. Calgary 49.2.19.

"My novels have not dealt," to Foran, 1982.

"guilt at what effect he has." Calgary 49.21.3.

"whatever you say," Seamus Heaney, "Whatever you say, say nothing," *North*. London: Faber and Faber, 1975, 57–60.

"I'm very aware," interview with Sian Warwick, *The New Edition* (University of Toronto), 2 November 1982, 4.

"I've moved on," "that drive, that power," and "The only thing," Robert Stewart, "The Literary Odyssey of BM," *Gazette*, 6 April 1985.

"I have written some experimental fiction," Joel Yanovsky, "The Literary Passions of BM," *Books in Canada*, August-September 1990, 24.

"I've used Canadian characters," television interview with Hermione Lee, *Book Four*, Channel Four, 1984.

"writing of the novel took 1 year." Calgary 49.19.7.

"This must be the land God gave to Cain." Calgary 49.19.1.

"I could never have written BR," "the extraordinary scenery," and "I don't think Canadian writers," to DS.

"I would go into my room," to Stewart.

"I went into the wilderness," and all quotations in next six paragraphs, to Lee, 1984.

"A few years ago," BR, VII.

"Since the seventeenth century," GG, "Francis Parkman," *Collected Essays*. New York: Viking, 330–31.

"in the general belief," quoted by GG, "Francis Parkman," 335.

"I began to read Parkman's great work," "I was made doubly aware," and "A *solemn vow*. A voice speaks," BR, viii–ix.

"One of the things that was frightening," to Lee, 1984.

"The whole thing could be a paradigm," to Adair, 1985, 6.

"Where other celebrated novelists," and "Greene, in this novel of his old age," review of *Monsignor Quixote*.

"We've got to find some spiritual reason," to Garry Abrams.

"the brilliant discussions of craft," "Witness, Judge, Mentor," 16.

"Writing is a form of therapy," GG, *Ways of Escape*. London: Penguin, 1981, 211.

"melancholia which falls inexorably," *Ways of Escape*, 45.

"how a sense of doubt," quoted by BM in review of *Monsignor Quixote*.

"living a lie," *Lonely Passion of BM*. All quotations in this and following paragraph from this film profile.

"It reminded me strongly of my days in Poland," Liam McAuley, "BM: An Exile's Late Arrival," *Irish Times*, 26 September 1987.

"When I was sixteen or seventeen," to Christie.

"his refusal to employ," "English Fame and Irish Writers," 5.

"We live here in critical times," quoted in "English Fame and Irish Writers," 5.

"I wanted to take," Liam Lacey, "Less is Moore for Brian," *Globe and Mail*, 20 October 1987, D5.

"I wanted to write," to Lacey, 1987.

"What surprised me," to McAuley.

"Do you not think," CB, 2.

"the tyranny of an age," "Remember that," and "I beg you to think," CB, 180.

"The silence of God," CB, 181.

"the world is still the world," GG, *Ways of Escape*, 171.

"This is the work of a masterly writer," Neal Ascherson, *New York Review of Books*, 17 December 1987, 44.

"Moore's real subject," Thomas Flanagan, "Dangerous Amusements," *The Nation*, 3 October 1987, 345.

"a modern master of the art of fiction," citation by John Cronin for Conferring of Honorary Doctorate, Queen's University, *Irish University Review*, Spring 1988, 11.

## 22. The Truth of Events

"I'm extremely conscious," interview with Liam Lacey, *Globe and Mail*, 14 November 1995.

"People use to tell me," Martin Doyle, "The Only Life of Brian," *Irish Post*, 20 December 1993, 13.

"At some point your own life," to Doyle.

"silent collaboration," interview with Joseph O'Connor, *Sunday Tribune*, 1 October 1995, 8.

"The best symbolism," to Lacey, 1987.

"exorcism," — "Everything I've written has in some way been an exorcism for me," to Abrams.

"I feel that fiction can't compete," to Warwick.

"I wanted to write a book," "I was in the Wellington Park Hotel," and "The second thing," interview with Eamonn Wall, unpublished, 1990.

"lies," LS, 70.

"proxopera," see Benedict Kiely, *Proxopera: A Tale of Modern Ireland*. Boston: Godine, 1986.

"I felt as an expatriate," "I like to go in," and "I didn't know," to Wall.

"You're not fighting," and "we have let you get," LS, 61–62.

"was not brave," LS, 128.

"You can't avoid responsibility," LS, 133.

"Another martyr for the cause," LS, 136.

"There had been no war," LS, 124–50.

"it's all very well," LS, 161–62.

"he had been plucked," LS, 129.

"looked more real on television," LS, 130.

"to slip back," LS, 219.

"They made the ending," to Andrews.

"the cinema, in the end," John Pym, review of *The Lonely Passion of Judith Hearne, Monthly Film Bulletin*, May 1988, 142.

"was willing to risk," Seamus Deane, review in *Times Literary Supplement*, 20 April 1990.

"as effective an indictment," Michael Coren, review in *Quill and Quire*, April 1990, 28.

"I don't think I'd have been able," unpublished interview with Charles Foran, 1990.

"I didn't want it to resemble," Beverley Slopen, "BM Probes Lives of Saints," *Toronto Star*, 6 February 1993.

"People say, do you leave out," Hermione Lee, "Nomadic Life of Brian," *Independent on Sunday*, 14 February 1993, 25.

"This book is the first time," to Doyle.

"The cabin-passenger wrote," GG, *A Burnt-out Case*. London: Penguin, 1963, 9.

"My life here," NOL, 1–3.

"Our lives are so flimsy," to Lee, 1993.

"I did not die," *A Burnt-out Case*, epigraph.

"young liberal ideas," and "This is a place," to Lee, 1993.

"I would be very happy" to Stewart.

"My book is based on Haiti," and "I've always been interested," to Doyle.

"The book is about preachers," to Slopen.

"Between fanaticism and barbarism," NOL, 141.

"God moves the player," Borges, quoted as epigraph to NOL.

"I think it is that," NOL, 3.

"he, the older brother," NOL, 70.

"my life's choice came back," NOL, 69.

"Writing is like," "Writing novels is a way," and "There is an excitement," to Doyle.

"a peculiarly powerful," John Banville, review in *Times Literary Supplement*, 19 February 1993, 22.

"The action of this novel," William Trevor, review in *New York Review of Books*, 21 October 1993, 6.

"The best lack all conviction," W. B. Yeats, "The Second Coming," *Collected Poems*, 211.

"S follows closely," see *Memory, the Holocaust, and French Justice: The Bousquet and Touvier Affairs*, editor, Richard J. Golsan. Hanover, N.H. and London: Dartmouth College/University Press of New England, 1996.

"The study of history," S, 68.

"In those years everyone," S, 106.

"It was in monasteries," S, 8.

"the true France," S, 43.

"I suspect that we will find," S, 39.

"Neutrality is shameful," "Eileen Battersby talks to BM," *Irish Times*, 12 October 1995, 13.

"The young may be bored," to Battersby.

"I never thought," to O'Connor.

"I'll never forget it," Tom Adair, "Life of Brian Recalled," *Scotland on Sunday*, 8 October 1995.

"I think as a writer," to Adair, 1995.

"It's beautiful," to O'Connor.

## The Closing Ritual

"keep the story alive," "Imagination and Experience," 49–50.

MW For further discussion of MW, see my review in *The Recorder: The Journal of the American Irish Historical Society*, 11:1, Spring 1998.

"Everybody thought Faulkner," to Sale, 79.

# ACKNOWLEDGEMENTS

I would not have begun this book without my initial contacts with Brian Moore, who responded with interest to a publishing proposal I made to him regarding his interviews and non-fiction. It was with such a project in mind that I met him and taped some conversation. Very soon, in attempting to find a publisher, I was encouraged to enlarge the text by providing biographical contexts. And so it was that my original idea was quickly transformed: the voice of Brian Moore commenting on his own life and work became part of the texture of this biography, which presents my interpretation of how he became and renewed himself as a novelist.

I made a decision at the beginning that I would not ask for his co-operation beyond the permissions that were necessary for accessing and reproducing materials in the archives and in published form. That decision reflects my recognition of his discomfort with a biographical approach to his life and work, although — as is the case of many other writers — he did not seem to act in any way that indicated disapproval of what I was doing. My respect for his achievement energized my efforts to understand the ways in which his inspiration grew out of his own experience; I had no wish to penetrate areas of his life that would cause unnecessary distress, and so I also decided to observe an appropriate reticence in deciding which individuals to approach for help and in the questions I would ask them.

It is in this light that I acknowledge Brian Moore's co-operation and help. Although he has not seen the text I have completed, he has generously granted me permission to quote from published and unpublished sources as indicated in the notes. In other cases he has withheld permission, and as a result, the treatment of certain issues is, to a degree, less vivid or textured than I originally intended. Overall, the substance and style of this work is as I would have wished it to be, and I thank Brian Moore for his willingness to support this endeavour to the considerable degree that he has.

This work would neither have started nor have reached completion without the encouragement of friends and family members, as well as the help and co-operation of many individuals and institutions. My indebtedness in most cases goes far beyond what may be indicated by this formal gesture. Neither would it have been completed and published without the support of the taxpayers of Canada and the courage of Don Sedgwick and Jo O'Donoghue, who accepted the manuscript on behalf of my publishers in Canada and Ireland.

In the early stages of my research I was the recipient of a Research Grant and Time Stipend from the Social Sciences and Humanities Research Council of Canada; I also received a *bourse de soutiens* from the Ministère de l'éducation du Québec; these grants enabled me to take leave from my teaching at Vanier College, and in addition to thanking these agencies and the referees who recommended my research project, I would like to thank David Johnson, Academic Dean, in particular, for facilitating this leave. This book and other scholarly work associated with it would not have been possible without this gift of time.

I am indebted to the work of earlier scholars, especially in the bibliographical area; in particular, I want to thank Richard Studing and Brian McIlroy for "A Brian Moore Bibliography" (1951–73), *Eire-Ireland* 10:3 (Fall 1975), and "A Brian Moore Bibliography 1974–1987," *Irish University Review*, 18:1 (Spring 1988), respectively. I could not have completed this project in the time at my disposal without their work and also the work of Marlys Chevrefils, Jean F. Tenner, and Apollonia Steele in preparing *The Brian Moore Papers, First and Second Accession: An Inventory of the Archive at the University of Calgary Libraries* (University of Calgary Press, 1987). I am indebted also to these dedicated librarians for their help during my time at Calgary and before and since that visit.

I acknowledge the critical and bibliographical work of those who have written studies of Brian Moore's fiction: Hallvard Dahlie, *Brian Moore* (Toronto: Copp Clark, 1969) and *Brian Moore* (Boston: Twayne, 1981); Jeanne Flood, *Brian Moore* (Lewisburg: Bucknell University Press, 1974); Jo O'Donoghue, *Brian Moore: A Critical Study* (Dublin: Gill and Macmillan, 1990; Montreal: McGill-Queen's, 1991). Since this is not a critical work, I have not been conscious of engaging directly with their interpretations of the novels, but it is possible that I have unintentionally incorporated some of their ideas. The work of Robert Sullivan — *A Matter of Faith: The Fiction of Brian Moore* (Westport, Conn.: Greenwood, 1996) — came to my attention after this work was largely completed; my response to his book is in a review article, "Brian Moore: The Truth of Events," *Irish Literary Supplement*, Spring 1997.

I have availed myself of the facilities and of the courtesy of librarians at the following libraries: Special Collections Division, University of Calgary Library, Calgary, Alberta; Social Sciences and Humanities Library and Rare Books Collection, McGill University, Montreal; William Ready Division of Archives and Research Collections, McMaster University Library, Hamilton, Ontario; John P. Robarts Library, University of Toronto, Toronto; Bibliothèque Nationale du Québec, Montreal; National Film Board of Canada Library, Montreal; the *Gazette* Library, Montreal; Vanier College Library, Montreal; Ontario Film Reference Library, Toronto; Public Records Office, Belfast; Linenhall Library, Belfast; Central Metropolitan Library, Belfast; Metropolitan Toronto Reference Library; University of Mississippi Library, Jackson, Miss.; National Archives of Canada, Ottawa; National Library of Canada, Ottawa.

I have drawn on interviews, profiles, reviews, and other material first published in the following newspapers, periodicals, and journals: *Adam International Review, Antigonish Review, Atlantic Monthly, Books in Canada, Cahiers du cinéma, Calgary Herald, Canadian Journal of Irish Studies, Canadian Literature, Critic, Detroit News, Globe and Mail, Harper's, Hibernia, Holiday, Independent on Sunday, Irish Independent, Irish Literary Supplement, Irish News* (Belfast), *Irish Post, Irish Press, Irish Times, Irish University Review, Linen Hall Review, London Magazine, London Review of Books, Los Angeles Reader, Los Angeles Times, Maclean's, Monthly Film Bulletin, Montreal Gazette, Montreal Star, Nation, New American Review, New Edition, New York Herald Tribune, New York Review of Books, New York Times Book Review, People, Quill and Quire, Saturday Night, Saturday Review, Scotland on Sunday, Spectator, Studies in the Novel, Sunday Tribune, Tamarack Review, The Times* (London), *The Times Literary Supplement, Today, Toronto Star, Vancouver Sun, Varsity,* and *Weekend.*

Individuals who have contributed by supplying reminiscences, printed material, photographs, or other help include Mark Abley, Tom Adair, Maurie Alioff, Aaron Asher, E. C. Balch, Alex Cherney, Gloria Cherney, Hallvard Dahlie, Charles Foran, Robert Fulford, John Killen, Terence Killeen, Adrian King-Edwards, David Kotin, Hermione Lee, Jack McClelland, Cynthia Moore, Brian Moore (nephew), Ann Murphy, Jo O'Donoghue, Mordecai Richler, Dorothy Ruddick, Conor Sampson, Maureen Sampson, David Southmayd, Carl Spadoni, Apollonia Steele, Jean Tenner, Ann Vachon, Brian Walker, Eamonn Wall, William and Magda Weintraub, and Grace Wherry. I thank all of these individuals whose commitment of time and effort encouraged me greatly and affirmed my belief in the project. I would like to add that the enthusiastic responses to Brian Moore's novels of many of my students over many years at Vanier College renewed my belief that this body of fiction deserves the kind of honour which this biography is intended to give it.

I acknowledge Seán Moore, the novelist's brother, for very special help with research and photographs. I thank George O'Brien for his friendship as well as constant encouragement and counsel throughout. My agent, Jonathan Williams, joined wholeheartedly in furthering this project, and I thank him for tactful, skilled, and very supportive editorial work, and much more. In the later stages, I was blessed with Anne Holloway, an editor whose keen interest added much to the grace and clarity of the writing. The enthusiasm and work of these individuals and all others who discussed aspects of the project with me have been very valuable; I alone am responsible for any mistakes that may be found here.

Finally, and most importantly, I thank Gay Sampson for her patience and love over more than twenty-five years — without the acceptance and freedom she has given to me, this kind of work would be impossible.

## PERMISSIONS

For permission to quote from copyrighted material, I would like to thank the following individuals: Brian Moore; Seamus Heaney; Brian Friel; Ann Vachon; Sandra Djwa.

Extracts from published novels have been included with the permission of the following copyright holders:

*Judith Hearne*: Andre Deutsch, Ltd., London; Little, Brown, & Co., Boston; and Curtis Brown Ltd., N.Y.

*The Feast of Lupercal*: Andre Deutsch, Ltd., London; Curtis Brown, Ltd., N.Y. © 1957.

*The Luck of Ginger Coffey*: Andre Deutsch, Ltd., London; Penguin Books of Canada; and Curtis Brown, Ltd., N.Y.

*An Answer from Limbo*: Andre Deutsch, Ltd., London; and Curtis Brown, Ltd., N.Y. © 1962.

*The Emperor of Ice Cream*: Andre Deutsch, Ltd., London; and Curtis Brown, Ltd., N.Y.

*I Am Mary Dunne*: Jonathan Cape, Ltd., London; and Curtis Brown, Ltd., N.Y.

*Fergus*: Jonathan Cape, Ltd., London; Curtis Brown, Ltd., N.Y.

*The Revolution Script*: Curtis Brown, Ltd., N.Y.

*Catholics*: Jonathan Cape, Ltd., London; Curtis Brown, Ltd., N.Y.

*The Great Victorian Collection*: Jonathan Cape, Ltd., London; Curtis Brown, Ltd., N.Y.

*The Doctor's Wife*: Jonathan Cape, Ltd., London; Curtis Brown, Ltd., N.Y.

*The Mangan Inheritance*: Jonathan Cape, Ltd., London; McClelland & Stewart, Inc. *The Canadian Publishers*; Curtis Brown, Ltd., N.Y.

*The Temptation of Eileen Hughes*: Jonathan Cape, Ltd., London; Farrar Straus & Giroux © 1981; McClelland & Stewart, Inc. *The Canadian Publishers*.

*Cold Heaven*: Jonathan Cape, Ltd., London; Dutton (Penguin Putnam Inc.) © 1983; McClelland & Stewart, Inc. *The Canadian Publishers.*
*Black Robe*: Jonathan Cape, Ltd., London; McClelland & Stewart, Inc. *The Canadian Publishers*; Curtis Brown, Ltd., N.Y.
*The Colour of Blood*: Jonathan Cape, Ltd., London; McClelland & Stewart, Inc. *The Canadian Publishers*; Curtis Brown, Ltd., N.Y.
*Lies of Silence*: Bloomsbury, Ltd., London; Doubleday (Bantam Doubleday Dell Inc.); Penguin Books of Canada.
*No Other Life*: Bloomsbury, Ltd., London; Doubleday (Bantam Doubleday Dell Inc.); Knopf Canada © 1993.
*The Statement*: Bloomsbury, Ltd., London; Dutton (Penguin Putnam Inc.) © 1995; Knopf Canada © 1995.

Extracts from letters by Graham Greene by permission of his literary executors, Verdant © 1998.

Photographs have been kindly provided by the following individuals: Seán Moore; Alex and Gloria Cherney; William Weintraub; Sam Tata; Ann Vachon; E. C. Balch; Conor Sampson; and by the following: *Irish University Review*; Brian Walker and Hugh Dixon, *No Mean City: Belfast 1880–1914, in the photographs of Robert French* (Belfast: The Friar's Bush Press, 1983); the *Gazette*; the *Globe and Mail*; Chatto and Windus; Bantam Doubleday Dell; Andre Deutsch.

# INDEX